Introduction to Middle School

Sara Davis Powell

College of Charleston

PEARSON
Merrill
Prentice Hall

Upper Saddle River, New Jersey
Columbus, Ohio

Library of Congress Cataloging in Publication Data

Powell, Sara Davis.
   Introduction to middle school / Sara Davis Powell.
     p. cm.
   Includes bibliographical references and index.
   ISBN 0-13-060090-3
   1. Middle school education—United States. I. Title

LB1623.5.P69 2005
373.236—dc22
                                  2004002983

Vice President and Executive Publisher: Jeffery W. Johnston
Executive Editor: Debra A. Stollenwerk
Editorial Assistant: Mary Morrill
Production Editor: Kris Robinson-Roach
Production Coordination: Carlisle Publishers Services
Design Coordinator: Diane C. Lorenzo
Cover Designer: Bryan Huber
Cover image: Getty Images
Production Manager: Pamela D. Bennett
Director of Marketing: Ann Castel Davis
Marketing Manager: Darcy Betts Prybella
Marketing Coordinator: Tyra Poole

This book was set in Times New Roman by Carlisle Communications, Ltd. It was printed and bound by R.R. Donnelley & Sons Company. The cover was printed by Coral Graphic Services, Inc.

Photo Credits: Headshot photos of students courtesy of Alston Middle School, Laing Middle School, Thomas Cario Middle School, and Wando High School; all other photos, including photos of teachers, by Sara Davis Powell.

Pearson Education Ltd.
Pearson Education Singapore Pte. Ltd.
Pearson Education Canada, Ltd.
Pearson Education—Japan

Pearson Education Australia Pty. Limited
Pearson Education North Asia Ltd.
Pearson Education de Mexico, S.A. de C.V.
Pearson Education Malaysia Pte. Ltd.

10 9 8 7 6
ISBN: 0–13–060090–3

To my husband, Rus, for his unwavering faith in me, for late night editing sessions on our front porch, and for a life filled with love and laughter.

To my four wonderful sons, Jesse, Cody, Travis, and Noah, through whom I relived adolescence over and over.

To middle school kids and their teachers, who grow and learn together every day.

Educator Learning Center: An Invaluable Online Resource

Merrill Education and the Association for Supervision and Curriculum Development (ASCD) invite you to take advantage of a new online resource, one that provides access to the top research and proven strategies associated with ASCD and Merrill—the Educator Learning Center. At **www.EducatorLearningCenter.com** you will find resources that will enhance your students' understanding of course topics and of current educational issues, in addition to being invaluable for further research.

How the Educator Learning Center Will Help Your Students Become Better Teachers

With the combined resources of Merrill Education and ASCD, you and your students will find a wealth of tools and materials to better prepare them for the classroom.

Research

- More than 600 articles from the ASCD journal *Education Leadership* discuss everday issues faced by practicing teachers.
- A direct link on the site to Research Navigator™ gives students access to many of the leading education journals, as well as extensive content detailing the research process.
- Excerpts from Merrill Education texts give your students insights on important topics of instructional methods, diverse populations, assessment, classroom management, technology, and refining classroom practice.

Classroom Practice

- Hundreds of lesson plans and teaching strategies are categorized by content area and age range.
- Case studies and classroom video footage provide virtual field experience for student reflection.
- Computer simulations and other electronic tools keep your students abreast of today's classrooms and current technologies.

Look Into the Value of Educator Learning Center Yourself

A four-month subscription to Educator Learning Center is $25 but is **FREE** when used in conjunction with this text. To obtain free passcodes for your students, simply contact your Merrill/Prentice Hall sales representative, and your representative will give you a special ISBN to give your bookstore when ordering your textbooks. To preview the value of this website to you and your students, please go to **www.EducatorLearningCenter.com** and click on "Demo."

Preface

Introduction to Middle School models the ideals of middle level education in that it is both academically rigorous and developmentally responsive. It is *academically rigorous* because it is comprised of a comprehensive body of knowledge concerning middle level philosophy and structure; student development and diversity; curriculum, instruction, assessment, and planning for the classroom; and the creation and maintenance of a positive learning environment. It is *developmentally responsive* because it approaches these topics without intimidating or boring the reader. As an experienced middle school teacher, I speak to other teachers whether they are teacher candidates completing bachelor or master degrees; career changers preparing to take their skills and backgrounds into the middle school classroom; elementary or high school teachers getting ready for the challenges and joys of spending their days with middle schoolers; or teachers who desire to dig deeper into their profession, seeking insights and refreshment. Writing a book allows me only to speak, not converse. My hope is that readers will talk to one another about middle grades education, prompted by my side of the "conversation."

Teachers are my heroes. They make the minute-by-minute decisions on which student success and well-being depend. If knowledge is power, and I believe it is, the more we understand about the nature of adolescence, with both its documented predictability and its absurd volatility, the more prepared we are to make both the relatively insignificant, and the life-changing decisions. Yes, experience is the best teacher. But opportunities to read, reflect, discuss, and speculate will sharpen our focus on, and widen our peripheral vision of, middle grades education and all that is involved in teaching young adolescents. This book provides such opportunities.

The tenets of *Turning Points* (1989 and 2000), *This We Believe* (2003), the underpinnings of the National Middle School Association, and the teacher preparation standards of NMSA permeate every page. This strong conceptual foundation focuses us squarely on students and learning. As a unique phase of human development, early adolescence deserves continued concentrated research and study that will further deepen our understanding of how best to meet the needs of the students in our charge. *Introduction to Middle School* addresses the issues of teaching, and learning with, the marvelous kids of early adolescence in commonsense ways that infuse practicality with theory.

This book is a work of nontraditional scholarship—scholarly by way of knowledge base, and nontraditional by way of personalization. It is written in first person. I believe I best serve teachers, in whatever career stage, by speaking from both a research base and my own and others' experiences in the classroom. I welcome all readers to the adventure of exploring the landscape of middle school.

ORGANIZATION

This book is comprised of 12 chapters. Separating the body of knowledge of middle level education into discrete chapters seems arbitrary, but it is efficient to do so. Given the limits of the written word, I have chosen to organize this book in a traditional way. However, just as multiple ripples on calm water are caused by one single tossed pebble, every aspect of middle level education influences every other aspect. Chapter 1 focuses on the history of middle school and the elements that have given it legitimacy and theoretical grounding. Chapter 2 is an overview of student physical, intellectual, emotional, social, and character development. Chapter 3 looks at the diversity among our students from cultural, to socioeconomic, to learning styles, and beyond. Chapter 4 probes the characteristics of effective middle school teachers. Chapter 5 delves into the structures of people, time, and place, including teaming, flexible schedules, and classroom/school facilities. Chapters 6 through 9 discuss curriculum, instruction, and assessment at the middle level, while Chapter 10 details all levels of planning for instruction. Chapter 11 deals with the important topic of the classroom environment and its management. Chapter 12 addresses family and community involvement, No Child Left Behind legislation, and the critical issues of transitioning into and out of middle grades.

 ## SPECIAL FEATURES

- *Meet the students and their teachers.*   The reader will meet ten students and eight teachers, complete with background information, personal details, and pictures. We will follow the growth of the students from sixth through eighth grade. The teachers also grow in their abilities and professionalism as they confront dilemmas in and out of the classroom. This cast of characters will be used to illustrate concepts and pose questions. They may also be used in group discussions as ready-made examples to which scenarios can be applied.

- *Professional Practice.*   At the close of Chapters 2 through 11 are mini case studies involving the students and teachers who come to life through this text. While the formats of the Praxis II exams change on a regular basis, the exams consistently ask teacher candidates to respond to scenarios. This is what the Professional Practice sections do. Each scenario is followed by questions and a constructed response item to contemplate, providing excellent preparation for taking certification exams and also for actual teaching in a middle grades classroom.

- *NMSA Standards.*   Throughout the book, the Performance-Based Standards for Initial Middle Level Teacher Preparation are boxed for easy reference. The knowledge, dispositions, and performance standards are placed within the context of the topics they address. Elements of all seven standards are found in the text.

- *Balance.*   Creating and maintaining balance is a major theme of *Introduction to Middle School.* Throughout the text, scales are used to illustrate balance as they stand on strong theoretical and practical foundations. These symbols serve as visual reminders that teachers have the power and the responsibility to maintain balance in its many forms in their classrooms.

- *Margin notes.*   The margin notes illustrate concepts and results that readily fit into an equation. Each concept or result is followed by an equal sign, and the elements that comprise the concept or lead to the result are the addends on the other side of the equation. The concepts and results used in the equations of learning do not necessarily address all of the most important features of the chapter, but rather those that lend themselves to the equation scenario.
- *Activities.*   Following each chapter are group activities requiring readers to work cooperatively to accomplish particular tasks. Individual activities give readers opportunities to explore middle level concepts in various ways on their own. The Personal Journal section asks readers to reflect on their own experiences.
- *Internet Resources.*   Selected Web sites are annotated to provide additional sources of information on topics in each chapter. Most of the sites are quite large with links to other worthwhile Web sites.
- *Glossary.*   There is an evolving common vocabulary among educators that allows us to talk about our profession with mutual understanding. In addition, there are words and phrases that have specialized meanings and nuances when used within a middle level education context. Many of these terms are explained in the glossary.

 ## ACKNOWLEDGMENTS

I want to thank the teachers, students, and principals who allowed me to wander the halls of their schools and take pictures of middle schools in action. These schools are Alston Middle School, Laing Middle School, Cario Middle School, McClellanville Middle School, Chester Middle School, and Goodwin Elementary, all in South Carolina. The teachers featured in scenarios throughout the book are portrayed by Alston teachers Bruce McDonald, Melissa Mitchum, Angela Palmieri, Monica Grundy, and Sinclair Deweese; Chester guidance counselor Steven Cummings; Goodwin teacher Suzanne Robinson; and Cario teacher Sharla Gould. Special thanks go to Pat McTeer and Martha Hoover, middle school administrative assistants who diligently helped me contact students and their parents concerning their inclusion in this text. Thanks to principals Sam Clark, Kathy Sobolewski, Carol Bartlett, and Lucy Beckham for giving permission for their schools' yearbooks to be sources of individual student pictures. My thanks also go to the graduate students and employees at the College of Charleston whose clerical assistance and technical skills helped put this book together. They include Mollie Hedden, Iris Nelson, Carrie Shannon, Angela Bolden, Caroline Smith, Elizabeth Keith, and Kim Andrews.

I appreciate my editor, Debbie Stollenwerk, for both her faith in me and her insightful guidance. Thanks to Kris Roach, Mary Morrill and Carol Sykes for their prompt responses to my questions and requests. My gratitude extends to those who reviewed *Introduction to Middle School* and offered thoughtful and useful suggestions. They include Bob M. Drake, University of Cincinnati; Lydia Carol Gabbard, Eastern Kentucky University; Connie Jones, Middle Tennessee State University; Cynthia G. Kruger, University of Massachusetts Dartmouth; Ruby Midkiff, Arkansas State University; Sara Moore, University of Kentucky; Michael Perl, Kansas State University; Noell Reinhiller, Concordia College; Cathy J. Siebert, Ball State University; and Darrin D. Sorrells, Oakland City University.

Brief Contents

Contents

CHAPTER 11   **Managing the Learning Environment 307**

NOTE: Every effort has been made to provide accurate and current Internet information in this book. However, the Internet and information posted on it are constantly changing, and it is inevitable that some of the Internet addresses listed in this textbook will change.

1

What Is Middle School?

The middle school movement is an educational success story unparalleled in our history. In little over three decades the face of American education has been remade; the intermediate level of education has been given a long overdue identity and has, in fact, been recognized as the level leading in instituting significant educational reform.

Lounsbury, 1997, p. xi

1

Use this diagram as an organizational tool. In the boxes beside the chapter headings, indicate the dates by which the readings should be completed.

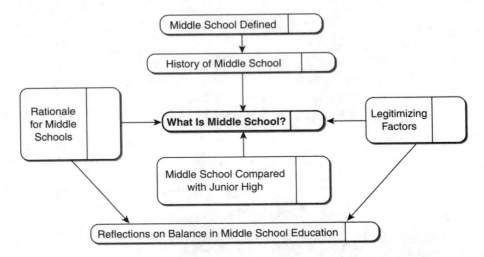

INTRODUCTION

If a poll were taken today of all middle level teachers, the great majority would possess a fictitious MSBA degree. No, this doesn't refer to some esoteric mix of a master's degree and a Bachelor of Arts. Instead, it's a tongue-in-cheek degree symbolizing the "Middle School By Accident" reality. This reality is how most of us landed in the midst of the young adolescent odyssey, and the "degree" quantifies our years of on-the-job training and experience. Many started out intending to teach elementary students; others majored in a subject area and became certified to teach high school students. But for a variety of reasons, including lack of our first teaching position choice, we found ourselves in a sort of "in between" school. In the 1960s and 1970s, these in-between schools were mostly junior highs, while in the 1980s and 1990s, and into the 21st century, most schools between elementary and high schools were, and still are, called middle schools. And most middle level teachers, whether in junior high or middle school, got there by accident.

As middle schools achieve the recognition they deserve on the educational landscape, the hope is that teachers will think of themselves as having a more relevant degree, an *MSBD—Middle School By Design*—rather than an *MSBA—Middle School By Accident*. With this purposeful choosing of the field of middle level education comes the cry for legitimacy. Teacher candidates now in programs to prepare them to enter the teaching profession more than likely attended middle school versus junior high. Granted, these schools may have been junior high in philosophy and practice, but chances are the sign out front reads "Middle School." So when the "teaching bug" hits, or the reasoned and thoughtful choice is made for a professional career in education, teachers most recently joining the ranks do so with an idea of what middle school is and who middle schoolers are. Most still enter with an MSBA, but they enter more prepared, having realized that there are three distinct levels of school, not just two.

Elementary schools conjure up images of eager children, full of curiosity and energy, adoring their teachers and revering them as wise and loving. High schools elicit images of maturing, sometimes smart-aleck, generally self-absorbed growing adolescents, often exhibiting adult-like tendencies and behaviors, who are capable of engaging in subject-specific discussions with teachers they consider experts. But what about middle schools? Is it possible to define the experience in such a way as to elicit testimonials of "Gee, I can't wait to become a middle school teacher"? Until we have a commonly held, legitimate identification of what a middle school is and what middle school students are like, entering the profession with an MSBD degree will be less common than entering with the nagging suspicion that the best use of our talents would be in an elementary or high school classroom.

In this chapter, we will explore both the concept and the institution of middle school. In Chapters 2 and 3 we'll concentrate on middle school students, and in Chapter 4 we'll take a look at the profession of teaching middle school. In Chapter 5, we will examine the structures of people, time, and place in a middle school context. Chapters 6 through 9 will look closely at curriculum, instruction, and assessment. In Chapter 10 we will discuss planning for instruction, and in Chapter 11 we'll explore the creation and maintenance of a middle grades learning environment. Chapter 12 will take a look at the involvement of family and community members and the future prospects for middle school education.

MIDDLE SCHOOL DEFINED

The National Middle School Association (NMSA) defines a *middle school* as one that is specifically structured to meet the developmental needs of young adolescents ages 10 to 15 (McEwin, Dickinson, & Jenkins, 1996). NMSA uses characteristics such as goals, activities, and organizational attributes rather than merely the school's grade configuration to designate a school as a middle school.

Let's look at the evolving definition of middle school according to some practitioners and authors considered experts in the middle school movement. Alexander (1968) defined middle school as "A school having at least three grades and not more than five grades, and including at least grades six and seven" (p. 1). Alexander and McEwin (1989) refined and expanded this definition of a middle school 20 years later by stating that schools with grades 6–8 are likely to feature the following:

1. An interdisciplinary organization with a flexible day.
2. An adequate guidance program, including a teacher advisory plan.
3. A full scale exploratory program.
4. Curricular provision for such goals and curriculum domains as personal development, continued learning skills, and basic knowledge areas.
5. Varied and effective instructional methodology for the age group.
6. Continued orientation and articulation for students, parents, and teachers. (pp. 84–85)

Kellough and Kellough (1999) defined middle school as

A school that has been planned and organized especially for students of ages ten through fourteen and that generally has grades 5–8, with grades 6–8 being the most popular grade-span organization. There are many variations, though; for example, a school might include only grades 7 and 8 and still be called a middle school. (p. 442)

Manning and Bucher (2001) defined middle school as

A school organization containing grades 6 to 8 (and sometimes grade 5) that, first, provides developmentally appropriate and responsive curricular, instructional, organizational, guidance, and overall educational experiences and, second, places major emphasis on 10 to 14 year olds' developmental and instructional needs. (p. 7)

Stevenson (1992) simply states that "Middle school refers to a school that is organized to include some combination of the grades between 5 and 9" (p. 13).

So, we get the general idea that middle schools serve students roughly between 10 and 15 years of age in grades 5–8. These are the students about which this book is written and this entire book will actually serve to define middle school philosophy. Keep these students and their needs as the focal point of the lens you use to read and reflect.

 ## A BRIEF HISTORY OF MIDDLE SCHOOL

"Knowing where we are now—the present—knowing where we came from—the past—and knowing what the trends are provide a solid basis for charting the course of middle level education. . . ." (McEwin, et al., 1996, p. xi). We won't spend a lot of time talking about the history of middle schools. The years involved are relatively few, with most accounts telling us the history is only about four decades old and that it began in the 1960s. There are some notable educators and writers who are responsible in great measure for catapulting the middle school concept/philosophy into our everyday lives. When we consider that most of the educators who invested their careers in the establishment and proliferation of middle schools are still with us, and are still inspiring our efforts, the history of the middle school movement comes alive as an ongoing progression of events. The pioneers of middle school have made, and continue to witness, significant progress.

Junior High

The first signs that a separate school organization was being established to bridge the gap between elementary and high schools began in 1909. These new schools were aptly named *junior highs* and were established to be preparatory schools for students going on to high school, where they would enter one of two defined tracks. The tracks had two broad purposes—to provide enriched curriculum for college bound students, or to provide vocational training for those preparing to enter the workforce (Manning, 2000). Even then, elementary schools were made up of self-contained grade level classes intended to provide consistency and security for young children, much as was experienced ideally in a family setting. As they are today, high schools at the beginning of the 20th century were basically departmentalized by subject area, with students changing classes four to eight times a day. The junior high resembled the high school in structure in 1909, but was generally smaller to allow for a greater sense of personalization, while functioning in a departmentalized fashion. Junior highs were intended to get students ready for high school, where serious study and/or job preparation was to take place. Even though there was little written research about early adolescence, the junior high concept met a recognized need that made it a widespread and rapidly growing part of public education. By 1960, approximately four out of five high school graduates attended junior high as part of a 6–3–3 grade configuration—6 years of elementary, 3 years of junior high, and 3 years of high school. By the mid-1960s, variations began to emerge resulting in middle level schools consisting of grades 5–8 or 6–8 (Alexander & McEwin, 1989).

As early as 1945, some educators were troubled by what they observed in junior highs. An early advocate for the junior high wrote about what he perceived as persistent problems. His list included the following (Anfara & Waks, 2000):

- Curriculum that was too subject-centered
- Teachers who were inadequately prepared to teach young adolescents
- Classrooms that were teacher-centered and textbook-centered
- Students who were tracked (p. 47)

These problems are very similar to the ones addressed by what is considered middle level philosophy today.

Middle Level Recognized

William Alexander broke ground for the establishment of what are now middle schools when he presented a "philosophy" of the characteristics needed in a transitional school at the Cornell University Junior High School Conference in the summer of 1963. Alexander urged the maintenance of the positive contributions of junior highs such as core curriculum, guidance programs, exploratory education, and vocational/home arts, and the elimination of high school practices such as competitive sports and subject matter orientation (Manning, 2000). He conducted a survey of middle level schools, then labeled junior highs, whose grade configurations had evolved into grades 5–8 or 6–8 from original 6–3–3, 6–2–4, and 6–6 grade structures. A total of 101 middle level schools were located by contacting state departments of education. The results of this study were published in *The Emergent Middle School* in 1968 by Alexander and Williams (Manning & Bucher, 2001). This book described middle school as a new concept, not merely a rearrangement of junior high.

Twenty years later, in 1988, a second major research study was conducted and the results published by Alexander. The grade configurations studied included the 5–8 and 6–8 schools of the 1968 study. The scope of this study was also expanded to include schools calling themselves middle schools containing three to five grade levels that included grades 6 and 7, schools with grades 7 and 8 only, and schools with grades 7–9 only. The last two organizational configurations were included to allow broad comparisons to be made. The identified middle schools in the 1988 study totaled 10,857. The data showed rapid acceleration in the establishment of middle schools after the early 1960s.

A third major study of middle schools occurred during the 1992–1993 school year. This study consisted of a random, national, stratified 30% sample of middle schools. Results were published in 1993. At that time, 80% of all seventh graders attended schools with grade configurations of 5–8, 6–8, 7–8, and 7–9 as opposed to 9% who attended K–8 schools (McEwin, Dickinson, & Jenkins, 1996).

The overwhelming conclusion to be drawn from the 1968, 1988, and 1993 studies is that middle schools with varying grade configurations grew in number at a tremendous rate. Other studies have been conducted over the course of the last half of the 20th century that have informed middle school practice, including studies by McEwin and Clay in 1983; Calweti in 1988; Epstein and McIver in 1990; and Valentine, Clark, Irwin, Keefe, and Melton in 1993. These studies documented various aspects of middle schools, from numbers of students to philosophical bents and forms of practice. Another comprehensive research study is planned for 2010, the results of which will be compared with the 1993 study (McEwin, et al., 1996). While it is important to have these aspects recorded and analyzed, it is perhaps more important to seek to understand the development and manifestation of the middle school qualities examined in separate sections of this book so that they may be considered in more depth and within the context of middle schools as we know them today.

What Current Research Says to the Middle Level Practitioner, edited by Judith Irvin and published in 1997 by the National Middle School Association, is an excellent source of information on the history of middle school. It is a collection of relevant research, merged with cumulative experiences of thousands of educators, with the sole purpose of furthering critical reform and improvements in middle level education.

RATIONALE FOR MIDDLE SCHOOLS

Middle school educators continue their quest for legitimacy that goes beyond mere numbers of schools. One sign of increasing legitimacy is the growing body of literature on the topic of middle level education. We find that the literature about middle school can be basically divided into two major categories—one justifies the rationale for, and existence of, the unique middle school organization; the second explores better ways of doing what we do within these schools.

You will notice that throughout this book, middle school is referred to in a variety of ways—middle level education, middle grades education, middle school, schools in the middle, and so on. By whatever name, we are referring to a philosophy of educating young adolescents that is different from elementary philosophy, high school philosophy, or junior high philosophy. This philosophy of viewing both the needs and ways of meeting these needs will permeate the chapters to follow.

A unique philosophy is necessary because we recognize that middle school should be far more than a "holding tank" for children who are too old for the traditional elementary school and too young for high school. The junior high mindset viewed preparation for high school as sufficient justification for a transitional school. Middle level education can be, and should be, much more. Kienholz (2001) wrote, "the middle school movement attempted to close the gap between what we know about young adolescents and what we do with them in schools, to narrow the chasm between theory and practice in our public schools" (p. 21). As Jackson and Davis (2000) wrote in *Turning Points 2000: Educating Adolescents in the 21st Century:*

> Just as middle grades teachers need to know how, specifically, young adolescents are different from young children and older adolescents, they also need to understand that middle grades schools are different from elementary and high schools. This difference is much more than the

sign on the front of the school; it lies in the philosophical foundations of middle grades education and the organizational structure that grows from and supports this philosophy. (p. 100)

Four major occurrences grew out of and at the same time helped shape the middle school movement. We will look at them in chronological order.

Contributors to rationale for middle schools = National Middle School Association + *Turning Points* + *This We Believe* + *Turning Points 2000*

National Middle School Association

The first major contribution to the growing rationale for middle school was the establishment of the *National Middle School Association (NMSA)* in 1973. This organization is dedicated exclusively to the education, development, and growth of young adolescents. The NMSA mission statement and contact information are in Figure 1.1. The organization provides a voice and a professional structure for middle level educators, and has grown to include members in all 50 states, Canada, and dozens of other countries. There are more than 50 affiliate organizations of NMSA that sponsor local, regional, and state activities focused on middle level education.

NMSA publishes a wealth of books and monographs, a variety of which are included in this book's reference section at the end of each chapter. In addition, NMSA publishes the *Middle School Journal,* a refreshing and informative compilation of articles that is highly regarded for both its topical and scholarly content. Alternating monthly with the *Middle School Journal* is *Middle Ground,* a very practical and entirely reader-friendly journal featuring regular columns written by practitioners. Membership in the National Middle School Association is accompanied by subscriptions to both the *Middle School Journal* and *Middle Ground.* NMSA also publishes *Research in Middle Level Education Online,* several general newsletters, and videos. In addition to periodicals, NMSA publishes the largest selection of books written specifically for middle school practitioners. These are available through NMSA catalogs and at middle school conferences.

One of the highlights provided by the National Middle School Association is the widely acclaimed NMSA annual fall conference. This conference draws more than 10,000 teachers, principals, central office personnel, university faculty, state department officials, parents, and community members, all vitally interested in the promotion of developmentally appropriate practices in our middle schools. It's an exciting conference that all teachers

---

The National Middle School Association is dedicated to improving the educational experiences of young adolescents by providing vision, knowledge, and resources to all who serve them in order to develop healthy, productive, and ethical citizens.

National Middle School Association
4151 Executive Parkway, Suite 300
Westerville, OH 43081
1-800-528-NMSA
www.nmsa.org

FIGURE 1.1   The National Middle School Association.

Source: *Middle School Journal* and *Middle Ground,* National Middle School Association, Columbus, OH: National Middle School Association. Reprinted with permission.

should have the opportunity to attend. Lasting 3 days, the main events include keynote speakers, concurrent sessions on topics of interest to adults who work with young adolescents, and site visits to local schools to view exemplary practices. Perhaps the major inspiration provided by this annual conference comes from the realization that we are not alone, the knowledge that hundreds of thousands of adults concerned with young adolescent development and education are represented by those who attend.

Turning Points

The second major factor shaping middle level education was the highly acclaimed document *Turning Points: Preparing American Youth for the 21st Century,* published in 1989 by the Carnegie Council on Adolescent Development. The Council's research showed that substantial numbers of American young adolescents were at risk of reaching adulthood inadequately prepared to function productively. As a result of this finding, the Carnegie Council developed a research-based document that has shaped middle school philosophy. This study continues to lead the way in both describing characteristics of young adolescents and prescribing ways to meet their needs within the school setting.

This groundbreaking work, which we will refer to simply as *Turning Points,* was undertaken because "A volatile mismatch exists between the organization and curriculum of middle grade schools and the intellectual and emotional needs of young adolescents" (*Turning Points,* 1989, p. 8). Authors of the study were spurred on by their belief that "for many youth 10 to 15 years old, early adolescence offers opportunities to choose a path toward a productive and fulfilling life. For others, it represents their last best chance to avoid a diminished future" (*Turning Points,* 1989, p. 7). More than 100,000 copies of the full report and more than 200,000 copies of the abridged version have been disseminated. The eight tenets of *Turning Points* summarized in Figure 1.2 provide a model of what a middle school can be. The tenets are interrelated elements that, when taken as a whole, provide a vision for teaching and learning appropriate for young adolescents.

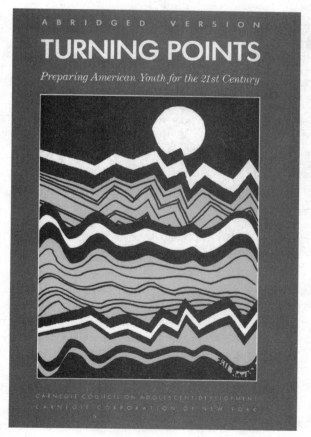

Source: Illustration by Jill Ryerson. Copyright Carnegie Corporation of New York. Reprinted with permission.

Turning Points: Preparing American Youth for the 21st Century Carnegie Council on Adolescent Development, 1989	
Creating a community for learning	Schools should be places where close, trusting relationships with adults and peers create a climate for students' personal growth and intellectual development.
Teaching a core of common knowledge	Every student in the middle grades should learn to think critically through mastery of an appropriate body of knowledge, lead a healthy life, behave ethically and lawfully, and assume the responsibilities of citizenship in a pluralistic society.
Ensuring success for all students	All young adolescents should have the opportunity to succeed in every aspect of the middle grade program, regardless of previous achievement or the pace at which they learn.
Empowering teachers and administrators	Decisions concerning the experiences of middle grade students should be made by the adults who know them best.
Preparing teachers for the middle grades	Teachers in middle grade schools should be selected and specially educated to teach young adolescents.
Improving academic performance through better health and fitness	Young adolescents must be healthy in order to learn.
Reengaging families in the education of young adolescents	Families and middle grade schools must be allied through trust and respect if young adolescents are to succeed in school.
Connecting schools with communities	Responsibility for each middle grade student's success should be shared by schools and community organizations.

FIGURE 1.2 *Turning Points.*

Source: From *Turning Points: Preparing American Youth for the 21st Century* (pp. 37–70), by Carnegie Council on Adolescent Development, 1989, Washington, DC: Author. Reprinted with permission.

This We Believe

The third major contributor to our understanding of why middle schools are unique and necessary is the 2003 revision of the National Middle School Association's position paper *This We Believe: Successful Schools for Young Adolescents*. This publication, which we will refer to simply as *This We Believe,* begins with a rationale for responsive middle level schools summarized here.

- Contemporary society represents different challenges than those faced decades earlier.
- Young adolescents consciously experience more rapid and profound changes between the ages of 10 and 15 than during any other period of their lives.

- Due to changing patterns in thinking and learning, middle level students require ongoing concrete, experiential learning to develop intellectually.
- Rapid physical maturation and accompanying concerns about appearance and body image require special attention.
- Multiple hazards of contemporary life pose serious mental and physical threats requiring decision-making skills.
- Students' search for personal identity is heightened during this unique period.
- Family structures are continually being refined.
- The need is greater than ever to cultivate responsible decision makers and wise consumers.

This We Believe seeks to isolate and quantify the unique aspects of young adolescents and identify the appropriate support, responses, and environment of a middle school. In doing so, it has provided both a mission statement and benchmarks for what the effective middle school should be and has contributed a framework within which decisions about programs can be made. This document outlines eight general characteristics of successful

Source: From *This We Believe: Successful Schools for Young Adolescents* by the National Middle School Association, 2003, Westerville, OH: National Middle School Association. Reprinted with permission from National Middle School Association.

This We Believe

National Middle School Association believes . . .

Successful schools for young adolescents are characterized by a culture that includes
- Educators who value working with this age group and are prepared to do so
- Courageous, collaborative leadership
- A shared vision that guides decisions
- An inviting, supportive, and safe environment
- High expectations for every member of the learning community
- Students and teachers engaged in active learning
- An adult advocate for every student
- School-initiated family and community partnerships

Therefore, successful schools for young adolescents provide
- Curriculum that is relevant, challenging, integrative, and exploratory
- Multiple learning and teaching approaches that respond to their diversity
- Assessment and evaluation programs that promote quality learning
- Organizational structures that support meaningful relationships and learning
- School-wide efforts and policies that foster health, wellness, and safety
- Multifaceted guidance and support services

FIGURE 1.3 *This We Believe.*

Source: From *This We Believe: Successful Schools for Young Adolescents* (p. 7), by National Middle School Association, 2003, Westerville, OH: Author. Reprinted with permission from National Middle School Association.

schools for young adolescents and identifies and describes six major program components that are widely regarded as characterizing the developmentally responsive environment. The characteristics and six program elements of *This We Believe* are summarized in Figure 1.3.

Turning Points 2000

The fourth major contribution to basic middle level philosophy was the publication of *Turning Points 2000: Educating Adolescents in the 21st Century*. While the original *Turning Points* (1989) provided a framework for middle grades education, *Turning Points 2000* gives us in-depth insights into how to improve middle grades education. Strong emphasis is placed on curriculum, instruction, and assessment. The point is made that organizational changes (teaming, flexible scheduling, schools-within-schools, etc.) may be necessary, but not sufficient, for major improvement in academic achievement.

Turning Points 2000, written by Anthony Jackson and Gayle Davis, traces the progress of middle schools, and the levels of implementation of middle school philosophy, since the publication of the original *Turning Points* in 1989. *Turning Points 2000* reports that as schools implemented more of the tenets of *Turning Points,* and with greater fidelity, their students' standardized test scores in mathematics, language arts, and reading increased significantly. These results occurred at both the low and high ends of proficiency scales. The report continues by stating that still to be reached are the schools that need improvement most—the high-poverty

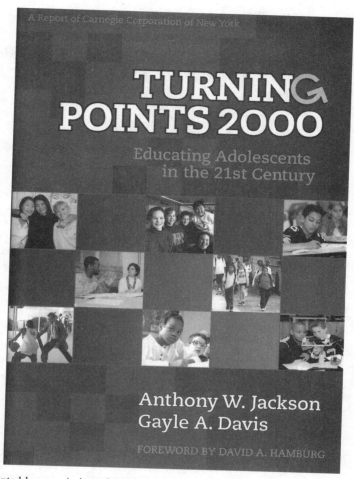

urban and rural communities where lack of achievement is rampant and pockets of excellence are few and far between. Middle school philosophy has achieved its greatest level of acceptance and success primarily in suburban and upper-income areas (Jackson & Davis, 2000). *Turning Points 2000* provides practical applications for implementing what research tells us is best practice for young adolescents. In doing so, it has made some alterations in the original eight tenets. The newer document contains seven recommendations that have at their core the goal of ensuring success for every student, reflecting the centrality of teaching and learning.

As you consider the recommendations of *Turning Points 2000* in Figure 1.4, keep in mind that there is no specific order in which a school must address improvements and make changes. As Jackson and Davis (2000) state:

Schools are not blank slates on which this design or any other can be drawn without restriction or concern for the unique nature and status of the school itself. The *Turning Points 2000* design,

Turning Points 2000 calls for schools that:

- Teach a curriculum grounded in rigorous, public academic standards for what students should know and be able to do, relevant to the concerns of adolescents and based on how students learn best.
- Use instructional methods designed to prepare all students to achieve higher standards and become lifelong learners.
- Staff middle grades schools with teachers who are expert at teaching young adolescents, and engage teachers in ongoing, targeted professional development opportunities.
- Organize relationships for learning to create a climate of intellectual development and a caring community of shared educational purpose.
- Govern democratically, through direct or representative participation by all school staff members, the adults who know the students best.
- Provide a safe and healthy school environment as part of improving academic performance and developing caring and ethical citizens.
- Involve parents and communities in supporting student learning and healthy development.

FIGURE 1.4   *Turning Points 2000.*

Source: Reprinted by permission of the publisher from Jackson, A. W., and Davis, G. A. *Turning Points 2000,* (New York: Teachers College Press, © 2000 by Jackson, A. W., and Davis, G. A. All rights reserved.), pp. 23–24

like instruction for students, should meet schools where they are and help take them to where they need to go to ensure success. (p. 25)

They point out that when one element in a school is changed, it inevitably affects other aspects of schooling. The recommendations are to be viewed as means to an end—improving classroom practice to lead to greater levels of student achievement. It is a continual process of change for the sake of improving, not just for the sake of change, as principals and teachers, and parents and communities embrace what is proving to be best for young adolescents.

LEGITIMIZING FACTORS

Legitimizing factors = NMSA Standards + Praxis Exams

While educators who were convinced of the legitimacy of middle level education as a distinct and vital part of the K–12 sequence were building the philosophical foundation and supporting practices, validation of their efforts grew. We will look at two major sources of legitimacy—the National Council for the Accreditation of Teacher Educators and the Educational Testing Service.

Middle Level Teacher Preparation Standards

A major step toward legitimacy occurred in 1995 when the *National Council for the Accreditation of Teacher Educators (NCATE)* recognized the need for the establishment of standards for the preparation of middle grades teachers. Most schools of education are either accredited, or are seeking accreditation, through NCATE. In 2000, NMSA and NCATE jointly established seven standards for middle level teacher preparation. Within each of the seven standards are objectives organized around teacher knowledge, dispositions, and performances. Figure 1.5 lists the standards that encompass adolescent development; philosophical underpinnings of developmentally responsive programs including curriculum,

NO

Standard 1 Young Adolescent Development

Middle level teacher candidates understand the major concepts, principles, theories, and research related to young adolescent development, and they provide opportunities that support student development and learning.

Standard 2 Middle Level Philosophy and School Organization

Middle level teacher candidates understand the major concepts, principles, theories, and research underlying the philosophical foundations of developmentally responsive middle level programs and schools, and they work successfully within these organizational components.

Standard 3 Middle Level Curriculum and Assessment

Middle level teacher candidates understand the major concepts, principles, theories, standards, and research related to middle level curriculum and assessment, and they use this knowledge in their practice.

Standard 4 Middle Level Teaching Fields

Middle level teacher candidates understand and use the central concepts, tools of inquiry, standards, and structures of content in their chosen teaching fields, and they create meaningful learning experiences that develop all young adolescents' competence in subject matter and skills.

Standard 5 Middle Level Instruction and Assessment

Middle level teacher candidates understand and use the major concepts, principles, theories, and research related to effective instruction and assessment, and they employ a variety of strategies for a developmentally appropriate climate to meet the varying abilities and learning styles of all young adolescents.

Standard 6 Family and Community Involvement

Middle level teacher candidates understand the major concepts, principles, theories, and research related to working collaboratively with family and community members, and they use that knowledge to maximize the learning of all young adolescents.

Standard 7 Middle Level Professional Roles

Middle level teacher candidates understand the complexity of teaching young adolescents, and they engage in practices and behaviors that develop their competence as professionals.

FIGURE 1.5 *NMSA Performance-Based Standards for Initial Middle Level Teacher Preparation.*
Source: From http://www.nmsa.org

instruction, and assessment; the need for content-specific knowledge and training; the value of collaborative relationships; and the importance of professional development of teachers. Each standard is addressed within this book. Familiarize yourself with the standards and recognize that many of the recommended areas of knowledge, dispositions, and performances are addressed numerous times and in a variety of ways, chapter after chapter.

Assessing Teacher Knowledge and Skills

The *Educational Testing Service (ETS)* has developed a series of assessments designed to test teacher candidates according to the standards established by most states in the areas of basic academic skills, subject knowledge, knowledge of teaching methods, and classroom performance. These assessments form the *Praxis* Series. ETS tells us that there are three basic uses for the Praxis results: universities may use them to assess the knowledge of teacher candidates; states use them for granting initial licensure; and professional organizations require their successful completion as part of the criteria for certification.

You may have taken the Praxis I exam in conjunction with entry requirements for your teacher education program. The Praxis I exam assesses basic knowledge in reading, writing, and math. The Praxis II Series is designed to assess specific knowledge and skills aligning with your chosen level of teaching and/or subject area. Exactly which tests are required varies from state to state. One of the most widely used tests in the Praxis Series is the Principles of Learning and Teaching (PLT). This assessment is now divided into grade levels, with middle level defined as grades 5 through 9, encompassing the ways in which middle level education is configured. Success on the test requires knowledge of young adolescent development, curriculum, instruction, assessment, and maintenance of an appropriate learning environment. The Praxis II Series also includes subject-specific middle level tests in mathematics, science, literature and language studies, and history/social studies.

MIDDLE SCHOOL COMPARED WITH JUNIOR HIGH

So now we have defined middle school, taken a brief look at its growth history and some major research studies, considered the rationale for this unique level of schooling, and examined four major forces that contribute to middle school philosophy. With this background information in mind, let's now compare characteristics of middle schools with those of traditional junior highs. This will serve to further define what is meant by middle school philosophy.

Figure 1.6 lists some major distinctions between middle schools and junior highs. The tenets on the list will all be discussed in detail in future chapters. While you may not yet fully grasp the impact of the distinctions that are made, this list gives you an idea of how different the two philosophies and organizational structures are.

REFLECTIONS ON BALANCE IN MIDDLE SCHOOL EDUCATION

The concept of balance will play an important role throughout this book. As we discuss student/teacher characteristics, curriculum, instruction, assessment, the learning environment, and family/community involvement in middle grades education, envision a balance

Junior High	Middle School
1. Subject-centered	Student-oriented
2. Emphasis is on cognitive development	Emphasis is on both cognitive and affective development
3. Organizes teachers in subject-based departments	Organizes teachers and students in interdisciplinary teams
4. Traditional instruction dominates	Experiential approaches to instruction
5. Six to eight class periods per day	Allows for block and flexible scheduling
6. Provides academic classes	Provides exploratory, academic, and nonacademic classes
7. Offers study hall and/or homeroom	Offers advisor/advisee, teacher/student opportunities
8. Classrooms arranged randomly or by subject or grade level	Team classrooms in close proximity

FIGURE 1.6   Differences between junior high and middle school.

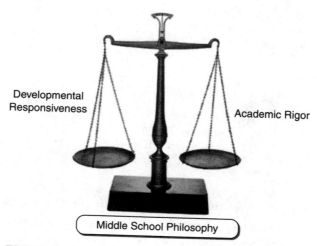

Developmental Responsiveness

Academic Rigor

Middle School Philosophy

FIGURE 1.7   Achieving balance: Philosophy.

scale resting on the foundational principles of middle school. As teachers we perform the all-important function of the pivot, as seen in Figure 1.7.

There are some aspects of middle level philosophy that we cannot overdo, aspects that actually make the scale more difficult to tip out of favor for young adolescents. Dispositions such as care, concern, and enthusiasm actually strengthen equilibrium. They serve to more firmly anchor the entire education process and should be generously applied and allowed to temper all our actions.

Arth, Lounsbury, McEwin, and Swaim (1995) tell us, "The most successful schools are those that understand the unique needs of their clients [students] and fill those needs quickly and effectively" (p. 20). Middle school philosophy is grounded in two areas—our understanding of the unique nature of young adolescents and how we choose to respond to their needs. Middle school philosophy is an attitude, a belief in possibilities. It's not necessarily quantifiable. It requires reflection and the renewal of resources, both physical and psychological. Middle school philosophy asks the adults who touch the lives of young adolescents to stretch and grow right along with their students.

With ongoing growth comes the ability to balance what we know and understand about young adolescents with how we respond to their needs. To maintain balance is to continually weigh what we know against what we do. Sound and reasoned judgment along with an eye for appropriateness will maintain this sensitive equilibrium.

Incorporation of Standards

For the remainder of the book, standards and accompanying knowledge, dispositions, and performances will be boxed and labeled in sections of the text where they are addressed. Please remember that even if you don't see a particular standard boxed, it may be addressed. There are some areas of standard knowledge, dispositions, and performances that are ongoing themes of the entire book. So far in Chapter 1 we have addressed a number of areas, specifically those listed in the box. By the time you work your way through this book, you will have a grasp of the enormity of our task and how our knowledge and dispositions are to be manifested through our performances as middle level educators.

Standard 1

Knowledge 4: Middle level teacher candidates understand the implications of young adolescent development for school organization and components of successful middle level programs and schools.

Standard 2

Knowledge 1: Middle level teacher candidates understand the philosophical foundations of developmentally responsive middle level programs and schools.

Knowledge 2: Middle level teacher candidates are knowledgeable about historical and contemporary models of schooling for young adolescents and the advantages and disadvantages of these models.

Knowledge 3: Middle level teacher candidates understand the rationale and characteristic components of developmentally responsive middle level schools.

Disposition 1: Middle level teacher candidates believe in the philosophical foundations that support developmentally responsive and socially equitable programs for all young adolescents.

Disposition 2: Middle level teacher candidates are committed to the application of middle level philosophical foundations in their practice.

Group Activities

1. Obtain a wall map of your city and/or county. Locate and mark each middle school in your surrounding area. This will help put your future discussions of local middle schools in context.

2. As a class, begin a paper file (or an electronic file) to which you all have access to be kept in your classroom or brought to each session by your instructor. This file should have a section designated for each local (city or county) middle school. As data and observations are collected, add them to the file.

3. Find all the middle schools in your community and assign each class member a school to research. Call each school and ask for the approximate number of students. Then ask for a copy of its mission statement. Whoever answers the phone may be able to quote or read it to you.

Individual Activities

1. Establish a three-ring Middle Level Education binder for your work concerning middle grades. Use dividers for sections containing group activities, individual activities, your personal journal, observation and interview notes, helpful handouts, newspaper clippings, and other sections as the need arises.

2. Clip items from your local newspaper(s) that deal with or impact middle grades education. Glue them to notebook paper, include the date of the clipping, and summarize your reactions. You may be surprised at how many issues surface that are relevant to middle grades. Continue to collect clippings during your course.

3. Choose a mission statement from a local middle school. Write a brief assessment of the statement as you examine it for elements of *This We Believe.*

Personal Journal

At the end of each chapter, there are questions and/or prompts that require you to draw on your own experiences. Use the designated section of your Middle Level Education binder to respond to the personal journal items. Feel free to react to any portion of the chapter beyond the items asked for. This part of your binder should be for your eyes only and should be shared at your own discretion.

1. Describe the grade structure of your K–12 school experience. Was any part of it called Middle School?

2. What do you recall about the facility you attended during the middle level years? How was it different from your elementary and high schools?

Internet Resources

Association for Supervision and Curriculum Development (ASCD)
http://www.ascd.org

ASCD is the nation's largest organization of educators interested in curriculum and supervision of instruction. The Web site offers valuable resources for teachers on multiple topics and features a wide variety of outstanding publications, conferences, and professional development opportunities.

Middle Web
http://www.middleweb.com

This large site, sponsored by the Edna McConnell Clark Foundation, is dedicated to increasing achievement for all middle school students. It features numerous articles and dozens of links, along with a teacher chat room.

National Forum to Accelerate Middle-Grades Reform
http://www.mgforum.org

This group is dedicated to promoting academic performance and healthy development of young adolescents. They work across organizations to promote common goals and strengthen efforts to improve middle grades schools.

National Middle School Association (NMSA)
http://www.nmsa.org

NMSA maintains this valuable Web site to inform members and all others interested in middle grades education about the organization's philosophy and focus. Information is available for teachers, administrators, state level officials, and higher education faculty concerning events, resources, and position statements of NMSA. Online shopping for NMSA publications is available, as is information on professional development and conferences.

References

Alexander, W. M. (1968). *A survey of organizational patterns of reorganized middle schools.* Washington, DC: United States Department of Health, Education, and Welfare.

Alexander, W. M., & McEwin, C. K. (1989). *Schools in the middle: Status and progress.* Columbus, OH: National Middle School Association.

Anfara, V. A., & Waks, L. (2000). Resolving the tension between academic rigor and developmental appropriateness. *Middle School Journal, 32*(2), 46–51.

Arth, A. E., Lounsbury, J. H., McEwin, C. K., & Swaim, J. H. (1995). *Middle level teachers: Portraits of excellence.* Columbus, OH: National Middle School Association and National Association of Secondary School Principals.

Carnegie Council on Adolescent Development. (1989). *Turning points: Preparing American youth for the 21st century.* Washington, DC: Author.

Irvin, J. L. (1997). *What current research says to the middle level practitioner.* Columbus, OH: National Middle School Association.

Jackson, A. W., & Davis, G. A. (2000). *Turning points 2000: Educating adolescents in the 21st century.* New York: Carnegie Corporation of New York.

Kellough, R. D., & Kellough, N. G. (1999). *Middle school teaching: A guide to methods and resources* (3rd ed.). Upper Saddle River, NJ: Merrill/Prentice Hall.

Kienholz, K. B. (2001). From Dewey to Beane: Innovation, democracy, and unity characterize middle level education. *Middle School Journal, 32*(3), 20–24.

Lounsbury, J. H. (1997). Foreword. In J. L. Irvin (Ed.), *What current research says to the middle level practitioner* (p. xi). Columbus, OH: National Middle School Association.

Manning, M. L. (2000). A brief history of the middle school. *The Clearing House, 73*(4), 192–195.

Manning, M. L., & Bucher, K. T. (2001). *Teaching in the middle.* Upper Saddle River, NJ: Merrill/Prentice Hall.

McEwin, C. K., Dickinson, T. S., & Jenkins, D. M. (1996). *America's middle schools: Practices and progress—A 25 year perspective.* Columbus, OH: National Middle School Association.

National Middle School Association. (2003). *This we believe: Successful schools for young adolescents.* Westerville, OH: Author.

Stevenson, C. (1992). *Teaching ten to fourteen year olds.* White Plains, NY: Longman.

Development of Middle Level Learners

Early adolescents are child-like and adult-like, mature and immature, sensitive and unaware, seekers of independence and clingers to dependence, concrete and idealogical, interested and detached. Sometimes all these characteristics are evident within a single individual and within a brief span of time. Adolescents are in a state of transition from a more predictable, prescribed, limited, and familiar place in the world to one less familiar, more unpredictable, more self-directed, and fuzzier in its boundaries.

Williamson & Johnston, 1998, p. 21

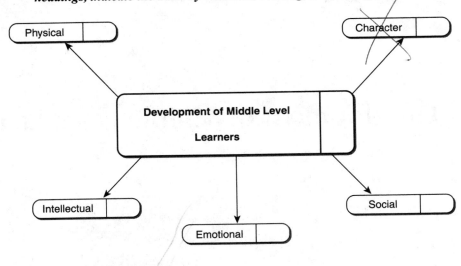

Use this diagram as an organizational tool. In the boxes beside the chapter headings, indicate the dates by which the readings should be completed.

INTRODUCTION

The middle school years represent a unique and significant period of human development (Caissy, 1994). Young adolescents are in a world of their own and yet are keenly aware of their surroundings—the places, people, and things that make up their world. By middle school, students have begun to develop diversified views of themselves (Strahan, 1997). They look beyond snapshots of accomplishment or failure and judge their self-worth in more general terms. This chapter will approach young adolescent development from five broad perspectives—physical, intellectual, emotional, social, and character development. Each of these perspectives interact with, and influence, all of the others. In the ever-changing world of young adolescence, it is artificial to separate these areas of development. Exploring them separately must be considered only an organizing tool. Let the perspectives flow in and out of one another as you read and reflect.

Keep in mind that while we "live with" young adolescents in the school setting, parents and other adults experience these kids in various settings within our communities and struggle with our students' developmental issues as well. In Chapter 12, we will explore parental and community involvement that is so vital to the "growing" of healthy bodies and minds of 10- to 14-year-olds.

PHYSICAL DEVELOPMENT

Familiarity with the physical and biological development of early adolescents is necessary before early adolescent behavior and other areas of change and development can be reviewed and understood.

Caissy, 1994, p. 9

Standard 1

Knowledge 1: Middle level teacher candidates understand the major concepts, principles, and theories of young adolescent development—intellectual, physical, social, emotional, and moral.

Knowledge 2: Middle level teacher candidates understand the range of individual differences of all young adolescents and the implications of these differences for teaching and learning.

"Mirror, mirror, on the wall, who's the fairest of them all?" Remember the days when self-consciousness took priority over everything else? Maybe you were one of the lucky ones who had looks that were enviable or self-esteem that gave you the confidence to be relatively free of trauma when it came to your physical appearance. But let's face it, even the cheerleaders and the coolest guy around had their moments of doubt. Perhaps the physical burden was never feeling quite good-looking enough. This desire to be physically attractive is part of the human condition and needs to be put in perspective. Easy to say as adults! However, we are concerned here with young adolescents who at times are completely devoid of perspective.

In the inconsistent world of young adolescence, there is one predictable factor. Physical development influences every other type of development that middle level students experience—emotional, social, intellectual, and character. Behavior often has its roots in whatever physical event is occurring at the time.

Mismatched Parts

If we held up a bag of male body parts and asked a blindfolded 12-year-old boy to reach inside, grab parts randomly, and become the young adolescent that is the composite of those parts, the result would be a middle level student in sixth or seventh grade. As discussed earlier, there is no such thing as "typical" because these newly double-digit-aged kids so often appear to be "Mister Potato Heads" in this awkward stage of life! Ears too big, arms too long, voices too squeaky. Girls, too, often resemble creatures of mismatched parts. Their hips may widen before their breasts develop, their noses may be too big for their faces. Their arms may stretch to their knees because their torsos haven't lengthened (Caissy, 1994). Schurr, Thomason, and Thompson (1996) tell us that the mismatched body parts result in a "disproportionate body framework" where "nothing ever seems to fit" (p. 18).

Growth spurts usually occur for boys between the ages of 12 and 14, but for some boys, rapid physical growth may be delayed well into high school and even into college. Growth is seldom even or gradual for young adolescents. Bones tend to grow more rapidly than muscles. So while weight gain generally accompanies bone growth, without equivalent development of muscle, awkwardness and clumsiness are inevitable! Joint pain, leg aches, restlessness, and fatigue may accompany these uneven periods of growth. Outer extremities, such as hands and feet, grow before arms and legs. With boys, all four of these tend to grow before shoulder width increases (Caissy, 1994). Have you ever heard someone say that you can predict the adult size of a puppy by looking at the size of its paws? Well, chances are that

if a boy needs a size 13 sneaker by age 12, 30 × 28 jeans will be history by age 14! So in his new 32 × 34 jeans, he walks into middle school to greet his eighth grade year as a remarkably different-looking young adolescent than his sixth and seventh grade teachers experienced. As a middle school teacher, I never tired of gasping (to the delight of many a boy!), "This can't be the same Cody who sat by the window in my third period class last year!"

Girls generally experience rapid growth a year or two before boys. Remember middle school dances when the tall, gangly girls giggled in one corner while shorter, "cutie pie" boys taunted each other to ask for a dance—only to find that their faces often matched up with developing breasts as they awkwardly tried to create the appearance of Fred and Ginger on the gym floor? (If this reference is too obscure, ask someone over 50 about this famous couple!)

Puberty

Outward growth spurts indicate big changes on the inside. Between childhood and the beginning of young adulthood is the transition period known as *puberty*. The word *puberty* often causes parent and teacher alike to shudder. If we think it's scary as adults to spend time around kids in puberty, let's try to recall what it was like to have puberty actually taking place inside us. For many of us, it's a time best left in the past. But we are survivors! During puberty biological changes that make us taller, heavier, and more muscular are accompanied by hormonal changes that forever alter our bodies in equally significant ways. Although testosterone, the male hormone, and estrogen, the female hormone, are present in all of us,

Standard 1

Knowledge 5: Middle level teacher candidates understand issues of young adolescent health and sexuality.

the balance of the hormones is broken during puberty so that one hormone takes over to influence sexual development. All of this is happening for some at the same time as those mismatched parts are appearing almost overnight. At this point, if you are thinking, "I'm supposed to teach these creatures subject-verb agreement and the Pythagorean theorem?" you are beginning to get the picture of some of the challenges of middle level education!

Other changes occur during puberty. Hair growth develops under arms, on legs, in pubic areas, and on the face. It may be darker and coarser than in other areas. The voice changes as the larynx grows larger. Girls' voices may become more mellow while boys' voices may go through those embarrassing falsetto-crack-bass-crack-falsetto moments. Oil and sweat glands may begin to function, resulting in all kinds of potentially embarrassing situations. Acne medication, soap, shampoo, and deodorant appear on shopping lists, while longer, more frequent showers become part of a daily routine.

So you think you want to spend your career behind closed doors with as many as 30 of these creatures at a time? Read on!

Sexual Maturity

With puberty comes sexual maturation. Yes, these awkward, funny-sounding, often aromatic configurations we call young adolescents have all the parts necessary to reproduce themselves. This is what sexual maturity is all about, at least in the physical sense. Biological growth generally comes before psychological and sociological maturation. Because the body often matures before mental and emotional decision-making skills, middle grades students are at high risk for either poor decisions or not thinking at all before acting. Ill-timed sexual experimentation can easily lead to multiple unfortunate consequences, only two of which are sexually transmitted diseases and pregnancy.

Timing

Perhaps at no other stage of life does timing play such an important role. Rapid physical changes, puberty, and sexual maturation generally take place, in starts and stops, between the ages of 10 and 14. Puberty, with all its miraculous changes, may qualify as a challenging period of life for many young adolescents. If we could say, "Okay, between March 20 and April 12 of the seventh grade year, you will all experience puberty. You will grow to full maturity and emerge April 13 as lovely, adjusted teenagers, all looking good in your 'Clearasiled' skin, wide-shouldered or B cup upper bodies, all deodorized and smelling of aftershave and perfume," what a wonderful world this would be!

However, we live in a less than perfect young adolescent world and the changes experienced by growing children happen sporadically, predictable only in the sense that there are growth patterns. These patterns happen rapidly and early for some, and slowly and haltingly for others. The "early bloomers" can be boastful but are often embarrassed. The "late bloomers" are almost always self-conscious. There are emotional consequences associated with physical changes that can lead to long-lasting and very memorable scars on the psyche that haunt for a lifetime. So let's look at some physical development issues that may accompany physical maturation and explore some ways we, as teachers, might make the "child-to-adolescent" passage a bit more tolerable.

Physical Development Issues

From nutrition to hygiene to exercise, the issues are many and often uncomfortable for teacher and student alike when it comes to physical development. Here are some of the reasons for concern, along with suggestions for how we can make a difference, both as individual teachers and on school and district levels.

Issue #1

Middle level students need information on physical development

A comprehensive health education curriculum is invaluable. National and state standards are available that outline what 10- to 14-year-olds need to know about wellness, puberty and sexual maturation, and the dangers of substance abuse. A health educator is needed in every school—someone who is honest, straightforward, trustworthy from a student perspective, and accessible. Boys and girls should be separated at times to allow for more honest and detailed questions and answers.

Issue #2

Physical changes affect behavior

Not only do middle level students have a hard time finding answers, they can rarely define the question or problem when it comes to physical growth and changes. What is clear is that physical changes often lead directly to behavioral problems. Teachers serve students well when they recognize and accept a variety of behaviors that may result directly from the turmoil caused and/or aggravated by the biological aspects of puberty. When opportunities arise to address the unspoken questions and resulting behaviors, teachers should reassure students that their anxieties are normal, and even expected.

Issue #3

Rapid growth requires increased nutrition

If that nutrition takes the form of balanced meals, terrific! But there are two problems when it comes to a balanced diet. Body image worries scream "thin" to many middle level students. And then, when they're hungry, their taste buds, along with peer pressure, often lead them to less nutritional food choices.

A comprehensive health program will include lessons on good nutrition. But the health educator can't do it alone. All of us need to emphasize healthy eating. When we have a snack, let's make it something nutritional like an apple or carrot. When we eat in the cafeteria, let's model healthy eating habits. Middle level kids are often hungry. If, as a faculty, a decision can be made to allow eating during the day other than at lunchtime, then find a way to let kids have snacks, perhaps mid-morning or mid-afternoon, provided the snacks follow healthy eating guidelines you and your team/administration have established.

Issue #4

Children at this age level should not be stereotyped according to physical characteristics

Some middle level students experience athletic success as they mature. Others find themselves lacking the coordination and stamina they may have had in elementary school. Bone growth, muscle formation, balance issues—so many growth issues factor into physical ability. Let's give middle level students the opportunity to explore athletics and find their talents and interests according to their own timing. Tall boys are not automatically talented at, or even interested in, basketball. Petite girls are not all gymnastics candidates. Keep in mind that while physical development may sometimes engender a child's interest in a particular activity or sport, mental development or interests can also guide, to a certain extent, an individual's physical development. An enlightened teacher will preserve those fragile egos from danger while encouraging the development of interests.

Plan ways to incorporate a variety of intramural opportunities that allow even less physically skilled students to participate in team and individual activities. Offer nongraded classes in exploratory time or after school that help students learn skills such as dancing, tennis, martial arts, and so on.

Issue #5

Many related arts curricular areas require physical development to master skills involved

Chorus quality depends on vocal cord development. Some activities in home economics and home/shop arts require dexterity, and some art forms require coordination/spatial sense. Remember, clumsiness can interfere in any situation involving cords, outlets, equipment, supplies, ingredients, appliances, and so forth. While we would like all middle level students to experience success in all areas, we need to understand that while the brain may be willing, biological development may not have caught up! Let's make sure we keep exploratory courses just that—opportunities to experience and experiment in broad areas that allow for, and accommodate, differences in development.

Issue #6

Many girls will experience the first signs of a menstrual period during the school day

This development alone will cause most girls to be upset and anxious, depending on the amount of information they have or the level of openness they have experienced among friends and family. The most common cause of absenteeism among young adolescent girls is menstrual pain. About two-thirds of girls experience cramping and discomfort (Caissy, 1994). Teachers need to be very sensitive to girls' requests to leave the classroom suddenly, as well as to girls who are late to class or stay in the restroom longer than expected. Of course, the key to knowing the legitimacy of these events is knowing our students. Not every tardy girl is menstruating. Just be aware that questioning tardiness or rest room requests in front of other middle schoolers is not appropriate. Make sure your school clinic has feminine hygiene products available. Menstrual discomfort is real, not psychosomatic, and can't simply be willed away. As with other physical aspects of life, some will use cramping as an excuse to miss activities in class when perhaps it's not necessary. We should try to err on the side of belief, however, rather than punishing sincere girls who need our understanding.

Issue #7

Middle level students are restless and uncomfortable much of the time

Because of varying growth rates and the excess energy that may accompany these periods of rapid growth, regulation desks arranged in rows do not always provide the physical setting students need. Providing a classroom with a variety of seating possibilities can prove very beneficial. Perhaps a couple of tables with chairs, desks of varying sizes, a few comfortable chairs, and a couch will provide ample choices. I realize that this gives students a lot of freedom, and many teachers are hesitant to build their classroom environments in this way. However, I have found that most middle level students respond positively when their needs are taken into consideration and when teachers do things that show respect for them.

Issue #8

Sitting for extended periods of time is likely to have negative effects on young (and even old!) bodies and on mental processing (Cranz, 1998)

The legitimate restlessness resulting from growing bodies may be exacerbated by long periods of sitting, regardless of the variety of chairs provided. It's no secret that active learning is more effective than passive learning. Movement stimulates the learning process. Howard Gardner (1999) tells us that the brain learns best when the body is actively involved in exploring physical sites and materials. Find ways to get students up and moving as part of instruction.

Issue #9

Some middle level students (and I'm not just talking about girls!) feel a compulsion to check themselves out visually on a regular basis

I found that having a full-length mirror in an out-of-the-way place in the classroom served a positive purpose. I also placed a smaller mirror on the wall by the pencil sharpener, so it was never obvious who needed visual reassurance and who simply had pencils with bad lead! These mirrors were up in August and were a natural part of the classroom setting. As a result, I had very few problems related to them.

Issue #10

Overactive glands may cause difficulties

Because glands of all kinds may be overactive or newly activated in young adolescents, by mid-morning a student may realize that he forgot to use deodorant, or perhaps he feels the need for just a touch of something that smells good. Consider having a brown paper bag in the pantry with spray deodorant and an inexpensive bottle of aftershave, along with a very light fragrance for girls. As with the mirrors, this may be an "extra" that some teachers may not be comfortable providing. Very few students will ever use these items, but you may save some 12-year-old a world of embarrassment. It's worth the effort!

If comfortable with both the issue and the students, we may have occasions to initiate a personal hygiene discussion with students who, for whatever reason, need our brown bags of smell-good items. A trusted guidance counselor may be a better choice than the classroom teacher for this kind of heart-to-heart. It all depends on the individuals involved.

 ## INTELLECTUAL DEVELOPMENT

The intellectual changes of young adolescence are equally profound but considerably more subtle than the more outwardly visible physical changes taking place at the same time.

Stevenson, 1992, p. 92

Prior to puberty, as well as in the beginning stages of this profound transformation, young adolescents' thinking capacities and mental abilities are more similar to a child's than a teenager's. Thinking capabilities become more adult-like as puberty progresses. Middle level students experience a transitional state between child-like thinking and adult-like thinking. Child-like thinking is characterized as concrete. This means that children organize information and experiences around things that are visible and familiar. They have difficulty visualizing concepts that they cannot see or touch. In the concrete stage, children have rigid patterns of thinking and are very much in the "here and now" (Caissy, 1994). Middle grades students who are concrete thinkers learn concepts much more readily when they are taught using manipulatives and hands-on activities that help bridge the transition from concrete to more abstract thinking and learning.

As puberty progresses, ways of thinking begin to expand. At this stage, children become capable of more abstract thinking. This is more adult-like and is sometimes referred to as formal thinking. The intellectual transition that occurs in puberty opens whole new worlds for children progressing to the teen years. They begin to think in more general terms. They begin to visualize events without having to see them; they can form mental connections; they can put things in perspective and predict in more complex ways.

Becoming

We must not lose sight of a very important word—**becoming**. As vital as it is to understand how the terms *concrete* and *abstract* apply to the thinking process, it is just as vital to understand the transition between the two distinct stages. Middle level students are generally concrete thinkers at age 10, and they may remain basically concrete through age 14. However, they may be concrete at age 10 and well on their way to abstract thinking capabilities by age 11. One thing is certain, they are becoming. Some researchers tell us that the complete transition into abstract thinking may not take place until the age of 17 or 18. As technology progresses, so do research capabilities. Research evidence now shows that some parts of the brain do not fully develop until the mid-20s.

While we may be able to identify and characterize stages of mental and intellectual growth, we must remember that the process of moving from concrete to abstract thinking is completely individual. In other words, becoming is idiosyncratic. It happens at different rates and at different ages for all of us. To complicate matters even further, the other areas of development impact this intellectual growth. By itself intellectual development is variable, but just think about how physical, emotional, social, and character development figure into the mix of progressing from childhood to adolescence and subsequently to adulthood. It's a complex and staggering period, to say the least! The National Association of Secondary School Principals' Council on Middle Level Education (1989) stated that

> The recognition that intellectual development is part of broad functions is a hallmark of middle level education. . . . It is grounded in the reality that the nurture and education of young adolescents must be an integrated venture; physical, social, emotional, and intellectual development are each inexorably woven together in the fabric of early adolescent life. (p. 1)

Intellectual Development Issues

We should be aware of the varied manifestations of intellectual development in the classroom and of the issues they present to the teacher. This awareness leads us to seek ways we can assist in this important growth process.

Issue #1

The attention span of middle level students may not be as great as it was in late elementary school or will be in high school

This issue has profound implications for instruction. Expecting a middle level student to sit through a 20-minute lecture, much less a 45-minute one, and gain a great deal of knowledge is ludicrous. We may be able to entertain students for that length of time, but their attention will wander and learning will be hit or miss at best. In Chapters 7 and 8, we will explore instructional strategies intended to hold attention for appropriate lengths of time. Breaking up blocks of time into manageable segments is a technique that should be mastered by middle level teachers.

Issue #2

Middle level students often have very vivid imaginations which can be linked to concepts as abstract thinking develops

The imaginations of children provide one of the greatest sources of pleasure afforded to humans. When this imagination can be purposefully channeled into learning experiences, the combination conjures up creativity that has not been possible before. Students are now capable of problem solving in creative ways that lead to their own discoveries. Encouraging students to use their imaginations and creativity to discover nuances and possibilities rather than simply to be fed information, helps them to take advantage of this imagination-meets-abstract-thinking stage of life.

Issue #3

Because intellectual development is so variable among middle level students, a group of 25 seventh graders may represent a whole spectrum of levels of development

This is one of the biggest challenges of middle level education. The question is, "How do we facilitate the learning of a prescribed curriculum, that is, state and national standards, in a classroom filled with students who are at very different places in development?" As teachers, we must be observers, constantly monitoring what's working and what isn't, and for which students at which times. In Chapters 7 and 8, we will discuss filling our "instructional toolboxes" to the brim with ways of teaching concepts and skills to students at variable levels of readiness. One size does not fit all!

Issue #4

As the shift from concrete to abstract thinking is ongoing, it is possible to lose opportunities to challenge middle level students

Observation is the key to this issue as we adjust and readjust our presentations, activities, and assignments to keep up with changes in development. We must watch closely and listen carefully to our students. Kellough and Kellough (1999) present a list of capacities gained through the shift into abstract thinking. Among them are:

- Ability to project into the future, to expect, and to formulate goals
- Analysis of the power of political ideology
- Consideration of ideas contrary to fact
- Insight into the sources of previously unquestioned attitudes, behaviors, and values
- Reasoning with hypotheses involving two or more variables (p. 38)

We need to vary our instructional approaches to make the most of these possibilities.

Issue #5

Physical development and intellectual development happen concurrently

Active learning should take precedence over passive learning. Let's get middle level students up and moving. They have a need to experience learning—to move, to touch, to manipulate, to search for meaning and understanding. The concept of inquiry, or discovery, learning should pervade what we do in the classroom. How to accomplish this will be discussed in Chapters 7 and 8.

Issue #6

A major shift in the intellectual development of middle level students is their newly acquired ability to think about their own thinking, or to experience metacognition

We "miss the boat" when it comes to helping students take charge of their own learning by failing to ask them to reflect on their learning processes. Knowles and Brown (2000)

tell us that the emerging possibilities to think about thinking may be a source of frustration for students. They may become confused about their ability to be reflective. We can help them explore how their thinking takes place and what happens inside and outside the classroom that increases comprehension and makes learning specific skills easier and faster.

Issue #7

Middle level students begin to understand what is meaningful and useful, with application to their lives

This intellectual development has major implications for what we teach, or the curriculum. In Chapter 6, you will find guidelines for a curriculum that weaves the knowledge and skills mandated by state standards with what interests and concerns middle level students. Framing our lessons in the context of real life makes learning a more natural process of satisfying intellectual curiosity that arises from this sense of purpose and usefulness.

EMOTIONAL DEVELOPMENT

Crossing over the line from childhood to adolescence is difficult because the line is not clear and there are inherent risks involved. It is an emotional leap as well as a physical one, and maintaining a balanced sense of self becomes increasingly difficult.

Milgram, 1992, p. 22

Parents, teachers, and even young adolescents themselves often refer to the roller coaster of emotions that accompany the middle grades years as difficult to understand and impossible to predict. If you have ridden a roller coaster, you can no doubt close your eyes and recall the exhilaration of expectation, the sheer terror of the actual descents, and brief moments of calm during leveling off sections. But even in those supposedly steady and "catch your breath" phases of the ride, there is an anticipation that keeps the adrenaline flowing and a sense of peace at bay. That's how young adolescence feels to most of us.

Dan Goleman, author of *Emotional Intelligence* (1995), says that emotional intelligence determines about 80% of a person's success in life. His understanding of emotional intelligence is based in part on Howard Gardner's interpersonal and intrapersonal intelligences that we will discuss in Chapter 3. Goleman tells us we need to include five dimensions of emotional intelligence into what we do in schools. These five dimensions are self-awareness, handling emotions, motivation, empathy, and social skills. He believes it is possible to raise the emotional intelligence of students by, among other things, being available to them with a sympathetic ear.

Describing Emotions

Numerous descriptors are used when referring to the emotional states of young adolescence. Of course not every 10- to 15-year-old experiences all the characteristics, and, when compared to the student next to him at lunch, none to the identical extent. Kellough and

Kellough (1999) tell us that among other emotions, young adolescents tend to be easily offended, erratic, restless, and self-conscious. Caissy (1994) characterizes the emotions of young adolescence as unstable, unpredictable, extreme, prone to moodiness, often angry, and fraught with fears, worries, and anxiety. Williams (1996) tells us that the emotions of young adolescents may involve embarrassment, feelings of awkwardness, depression, feelings of isolation, confusion, and disappointment.

While these descriptors seem to be negative in nature, my experience leads me to add hopefulness, optimism, and excitement to the list. I see these positive emotions exhibited every day by young adolescents. The message here is that variability makes for a wide emotional spectrum of middle school students. All of the descriptors are tied into the concept of self. Introspection is difficult for most of us, according to Milgram (1992), but when change occurs as rapidly as it does during young adolescence, it becomes particularly difficult. Introspection, or knowing one's self, is integral to self-esteem. The development of a positive self-esteem is crucial but often elusive. The sense of losing control over the environment contributes to self-consciousness (Knowles & Brown, 2000) and this self-consciousness often results in loss of self-esteem. The transition from elementary to middle school carries with it a myriad of changes that to a 10- or 11-year-old may seem overwhelming. Add this transition to the physical changes being continually experienced and it's entirely understandable that self-esteem would suffer. In *The Adolescent Views Himself,* Strang (1957) wrote about four variations of self-concept that young adolescents need to reconcile in order to achieve some degree of emotional stability.

1. General self-concept: An evaluation of self and abilities and roles
2. Temporary self-concept: Temporary evaluation based on a recent event or remark
3. Social self: The way we believe we are viewed by others
4. Ideal self: How we would like to be

Understanding these four variations may help us deal with self-concept and self-esteem issues. Helping our students understand them would be a valid topic for counseling and/or advisory groups. We'll talk more about advising in Chapter 5.

We should note that developing a positive self-esteem, while universally challenging for young adolescents, may prove to be especially difficult for minority students. Knowles and Brown (2000) posed the question "How does one develop a sense of self within a dominant culture whose values may be contradictory to those of one's personal culture?" (p. 30). As teachers we must create learning environments that account for cultural, ethnic, and racial differences. Chapter 3 deals with these, and other, differences.

Interrelatedness

Emotional development is interrelated with both physical and intellectual development. As various hormones are released at uneven rates during puberty, temporary chemical imbalances occur. Many of the stormy emotions of young adolescence can be attributed to this imbalance (Caissy, 1994). The physical changes already described in this chapter are enough to cause emotions to occasionally go haywire. Imagine going from 4 feet 11 inches to 5 feet 8 inches in the three short summer months between seventh and eighth grade. Or consider the creamy, smooth complexion that becomes embarrassingly blemished during first semester of the seventh grade. How about the unpredictable erections that occur while finding the surface area of a cylinder or discussing the merits of the Panama Canal? The list of physical changes that can provoke emotional responses could go on and on, with each of us adding our own personal traumas. Be keenly aware that each time you are in a classroom of 25 middle grades students in the process of becoming, there are potentially 25 cases of moodiness and insecurity and emotional distress in there with you. Dealing with the physical changes taking place in their bodies is a persistent emotional challenge for young adolescents.

Emotional development is also entangled with intellectual development in ways we are just now beginning to understand and document. Brain researchers tell us that emotions strongly influence our ability to pay attention and retain information (Wolfe, 2001). The implications of this for the way we approach teaching and learning are tremendous. Williams (1996) indicates that emotional and psychological concerns can impede academics unless middle school teachers know how to work with these factors and channel concerns into productive results by understanding the context of the student's world. "The affective side of learning is the critical interplay between how we feel, act, and think. There is no separation of mind and emotions; emotions, thinking, and learning are all linked" (Jensen, 1998, p. 71).

Worry

Middle grades students worry about almost everything. Their fears have changed from those of childhood to concerns about social and appearance issues. "Do I fit in? Do my jeans look like everybody else's? Is my hair right? Will they want me to sit with them at lunch? Did he notice my braces? Will I be in the 'right' group on the field trip?" It's a list that could go on forever. Worry, fear, and anxiety are common emotions of young adolescence. From an adult perspective, the sources of these negative emotions may seem trivial, but remember that perceptions form realities. To middle grades students, their worries are legitimate and quite real. To try to convince them otherwise is futile and potentially harmful. If we denigrate their concerns, we are, in fact, denigrating them and adding to their anxieties and uncertainties. Our responses should be tempered with understanding and the absence of judgmental attitudes. When a 12-year-old girl is crying because she found uncomplimentary notes written about her by kids she considered friends, the last thing she wants to hear is "It's no big deal, you'll find new friends." Instead, we should acknowledge that she is hurt. The gift of an understanding ear will allow her to express her feelings and know that someone cares. It won't take away the hurt, but it will legitimize her emotions and give her the opportunity to work through the grief of the moment.

Emotional Development Issues

As middle grades educators our goal regarding emotional development should be to help our students find their way toward emotional maturity. Caissy (1994) refers to emotional maturity as "the ability to control emotions that are socially disapproved of and to relieve emotions in a socially acceptable way" (p. 52). This task is compounded by the challenge of understanding what is socially acceptable. We'll take a closer look at this in the next section. Along with displaying emotions in socially acceptable ways, emotional maturity must include dealing with personal emotions in mentally healthy ways. Middle schools must provide opportunities for students to see that a wide range of emotions is normal.

Learning to balance negative emotions with thoughts and actions that create positive emotions is a lifelong task. Creating an environment that says "It's okay to feel the way you do" will enhance self-acceptance and allow emotional maturity to progress.

Issue #1

Because emotions occur suddenly and without warning, self-regulation is very difficult

A sensitivity to the emotions of our students should make us acutely aware of the volatility they are experiencing. When an outburst of emotion or some sort of personal affront is aimed at us, we have the perfect opportunity to model self-regulation. The sage advice of "take a deep breath and count to ten" has a lot of validity in a middle grades setting. Show how it's done and encourage students to do likewise. Speaking of the fluctuations of young adolescent emotions and the consequent behaviors, Knowles and Brown (2000, p. 33) conclude that "One never quite knows what to expect—except for the fact that if we wait awhile, it will change."

Issue #2

Emotional variability places young adolescents at high risk of making decisions that may have negative impact (Milgram, 1992)

We can help students recognize that many emotions are fleeting, that what they feel at one moment may change quickly and unexpectedly. Through thinking out loud when a decision needs to be made, we can model the difference between reacting and responding. Reactions are emotionally triggered while responses are the result of thinking through those emotions. We want our students to make decisions that are responsive to both emotion and rational thought.

Issue #3

There will be incidences and events that will trigger emotions to the point of disruption of the learning process

As individual teachers, but preferably as a team of teachers, we have a very beneficial tool for dealing with emotions. That tool is providing a psychologically safe environment in which concerns may be aired. This environment may include appropriate readings and videos that present possible solutions to emotionally charged dilemmas and situations. Encouraging students to role-play and involve themselves in simulations may be a vehicle for venting worries, anxieties, and emotional distress.

SOCIAL DEVELOPMENT

It has been suggested that the paramount reason young adolescents come to school is not for the education we offer but because school is where the other kids are. In my years of being a teacher and researcher with ten to fourteen-year-olds, I have come to recognize that both goals—companionship and learning—are powerful, complementary motivators.

Stevenson, 1992, p. 105

The emotion-laden search for personal identity integrates experiences with developing bodies, biological drive, new thinking capacities, and expanding social roles (Knowles & Brown, 2000). As young adolescents become aware of the unique aspects of themselves, they also become acutely aware of those around them—most specifically, their peers. They develop an exaggerated view of themselves as victims of what Elkind (1984) refers to as the imaginary spotlight that focuses everyone's attention on them, making them uneasy in social settings. As uncomfortable as it may be, socialization plays a major role in the psychological growth process, as it is influenced by, and interrelated with, physical, intellectual, and emotional development. The need for socialization is especially strong during young adolescence. Milgram (1992) refers to the absence of a healthy dose of socialization as *"undersocialization,"* a state in which learning opportunities are missed and some important developmental tasks of this life stage are neglected. As we explored in Chapter 1, middle level philosophy originated partially from the belief that the school can and should play a major role in both the cognitive and the affective dimensions of the development of the whole child.

Standard 1

Performance 9: Middle level teacher candidates deal effectively with societal changes that impact the healthy development of young adolescents.

Adult Relationships

Young adolescents often find themselves caught between their desire to be safe and secure (as in childhood) and their desire for freedom and independence. Because adults generally represent security, the struggle for change often revolves around relationships with them. In the middle school years, one's own parents are likely to be viewed as out of step with society (Caissy, 1994). While affirmation of parental love is secretly sought, young adolescents may act out in argumentative and rebellious ways against those closest to them, in many cases parents and guardians. This rebellion, in its many forms, is normal and even necessary, as attempts are made toward demonstrating that they have minds of their own. Considering the options, perhaps rebellion during middle school years is preferable to rebellion at other times in life, when even more dangerous options become available. Our hope is that rebellion will occur in "safe" ways that fall within reasonable parameters (Caissy, 1994).

Even as young adolescents tend to disassociate themselves from family, they may seek to emulate other adults (Knowles & Brown, 2000). They easily buy into fantasies about adults, often created in the media. This leads to hero formation, most likely of movie stars and sports figures. In fact, Mee (1997) found in a large-scale study that boys almost exclusively named sports figures as their role models. Both genders may fantasize that adult life can be (or is) glamorous; that money is easily made; that outward beauty equates to happiness; that TV sitcom life is realistic; that those successful, carefree people in the advertisements drinking beer and smoking do so with no consequences; that casual sex is desirable. . . . The list goes on.

Peer and Group Relationships

As young adolescents begin to discover that it is unlikely that they can always please the adults with authority over them as well as the kids they hang around with, a loyalty shift usually takes place. Friends take on greater significance and the "flock mentality" begins (Caissy, 1994). Their fear of being different, and therefore not accepted by peers, is a drive that for most is unavoidable. They adopt personalities and appearances that will win them placement in a group. I remember distinctly the groups that existed during my middle school (junior high) years, and I'm certain you remember yours too. "Natural selection" played a role in group formation. There were certain groups I knew I could not align with. The "cheerleader," for instance, was not a possibility for me because I didn't look the part, regardless of how I tried. I recognized the choices that were realistic and found my way into a group that was comfortable. Being part of a group provides security and is a source of feedback when experimentation and dilemmas occur. It seems that simply being part of a group is more important than which group. Since most of us don't choose our families or teachers, choosing friends and a peer group takes on importance as a factor in establishing identity and independence. It's a decision-making opportunity.

Group alignment creates peer pressure, the driving force created by the need/desire to conform. Although the roots of the power of peer pressure tend to lie in self-consciousness and insecurity (Caissy, 1994), giving in to peer pressure is absolutely normal at any age. Peer pressure can have a positive or negative influence. If peer pressure dictates that good grades, church attendance, and politeness are the norm, then most adults cheer the influence. However, if peer pressure leads to smoking, drinking, drugs, vandalism, or early sex, then it is viewed as negative. Most peer pressure is somewhere in between and varies according to circumstances and timing. Like it or not, the influence of peers on young adolescence is a phenomenon that is inevitable. Adults can and should attempt to influence the choices of friends and peer groups, but the truth is that young adolescents will assert their need for independence and make choices that only locking them in their rooms until age 21 could prevent.

In the beginning of young adolescence, around ages 10 to 12, same-sex friendships are the most vital. The need for a "best friend" to whom there is uncompromising loyalty and from whom the same is expected, is a driving force. Once the best friend status is achieved, the relegation to "second best friend" is a devastating prospect. This appears to be much more pronounced in girls than boys. Girls will bare their souls to best friends, while boys are often content to be in a group where they laugh at the same things and are physically active in the same interest areas. When and with whom opposite sex attractions occur occupies a place in young adolescent variability that exceeds most other aspects of the age. Some "puppy love" experiences influence 11-year-olds heavily, while in others opposite sex attractions do not wield a great deal of influence until age 16 or so.

The social development of young adolescence includes some notable paradoxes. In their quest for independence, adolescents will freely conform to fit in. They rebel against adult authority while doing what they can to become adult-like. Social development implies relationships with other people and yet this is an age of egocentricity and selfishness. These paradoxes exist as "young adolescents become aware of themselves not only as individuals, but also collectively as members of society" (Schurr, et al., 1996, p. 21).

Social Development Issues

If we do not allow for socialization time, we are depriving our students of growth opportunities. Kids are going to talk, pass notes, gather in groups, and so on. If we don't give them time for such activities, they will take the time from us. Showing that we understand socialization needs should be part of our visible attitude toward our students. Social validation is important.

Issue #1

Young adolescents have a very strong need to be part of a social group

Giving students "free time" during the school day allows for informal socialization. Students who are part of advisory groups (more about these in Chapter 5) often feel a bond of trust, or at least a sense that they know the others in the group. Clubs give students chances to get to know others with similar interests. At a minimum, we should adhere to the *Turning Points* tenet that calls for us to create small learning communities. This translates into teams, the basic organizational foundation of middle school. We'll explore teams and teaming in Chapter 5.

Issue #2

There are young adolescents who feel like targets

Caissy (1994) tells us that kids often pick on others as a way of diverting attention away from themselves, their differences, or their insecurities. Regardless of the reasons, it happens. As educators, we need to do what we can to stifle this activity. Be sensitive to the kids who seem to be the outcasts and never say things like "stop picking on Sam" in front of Sam or other kids who aren't involved. This will just make things worse for unfortunate Sam as students chide him because the teacher has come to his rescue. Instead, we need to find interests and activities that Sam does well and capitalize on them. Identify kids with similar interests/skills and arrange for Sam to get together with them. We should also encourage Sam not to react to teasing. Then it will no longer be fun for the perpetrators and it will lessen the occurrences. As strange as it may seem, some kids who become "targets" actually thrive on it in a perverse way. Attention, even though it's negative, gives a sense of identity.

Issue #3

Young adolescence is a prime time for shyness, given the self-consciousness of the age

Milgram (1992) tells us that shyness may be manifested in blushing, nervous stomach, sweating, and increased pulse rate. Adolescents may experience these symptoms, but the need to conform to group norms may cause them to hide the symptoms and appear to be confident. Whether shyness is obvious, or a hidden malady, it can be painful and viewed as a negative trait by peers and adults. As with Issue #1, providing a variety of outlets for socialization will help ease shyness. Offering activity opportunities that vary enough to appeal to a variety of students may help shy students find their talents and interests, and other students who share them.

Issue #4

Teachers' social backgrounds may be different from their students'

This is a very common phenomenon. We may teach students with whom we have difficulty relating. Mee (1997) tells us "it is essential that educators look seriously at the differences between the social realities of the teachers and those of the students and be willing to make needed adjustments in perceptions and in the way they conduct schooling" (p. 5). She continues by stating that student learning will be more meaningful if teachers understand young adolescent realities. Knowing student social realities will assist us in relating to them and connecting them more fully to school experiences.

 ## CHARACTER DEVELOPMENT

> *The characters of young people are determined by what they do and what happens to them. But these take place in a concrete social medium, a complex web of human relationships. The content and quality of this social medium as a whole plays a significant, formative role in shaping the character of students.*
>
> Dobrin, 2001, p. 275

The discussion of character development has the potential to become value-laden as we deal with morals and ethics. Rather than steering clear of the topic because of possible controversy, or embedding it in discussions of emotional and social development, let's take a look at what appear to be the characteristics of young adolescence in terms of character development and explore how "what they do and what happens to them" may be dealt with in healthy ways within our middle schools. The "concrete social medium" referred to by Dr. Dobrin is the 24 hour a day, 7 day a week life of students. Time spent in school accounts for a major chunk of this time. So the school is an influential part of the social medium that shapes the character of students.

Young Adolescent Character Traits

There are many generalizations that can be made about typical character traits of young adolescents. Here are some to consider. Young adolescents often

are concerned about fairness.

>   Telling a teacher "you're not fair" is a terrible rebuke. Middle grades students have definite ideas about what adults should be and should do. When adults disappoint them, the students are not quick to forgive and forget.

ask unanswerable questions.

>   Middle grades students want to know answers to major questions, such as the meaning of life and what their roles should be in society. They usually realize that adults don't have all these answers, but they at least want adults to treat their questions seriously.

need support, but seldom ask for it.

>   To make wise decisions about moral issues, young adolescents need us to be positive role models to help them with issues of right and wrong.

make poor decisions as a result of their strong need for peer acceptance.

During the middle grades years, students often value social approval over moral convictions. This may lead to decisions that have harmful, often life-changing consequences.

School Programs

Understanding that young adolescents are continually struggling with character development, we naturally ask ourselves how we can help them. Over the years, schools have institutionalized many character-development programs delivered to students in a variety of ways. Classes and/or occasional meetings devoted to character development are often plagued with controversy over exactly what values and aspects of character should be promoted in public schools. Even with the controversy, there is a renewed call for schools to address character issues, perhaps due to the increase in violent incidents in our schools at the end of the 20th century. We find groups of citizens and educators widely debating what character issues to emphasize.

From Aristotle's universal values of wisdom, courage, temperance, and justice, to C. S. Lewis's list that includes respect, responsibility, honesty, compassion, and fairness, we debate our own values, struggling to impart a sense of right and wrong that will not conflict with religious values or be politically incorrect. Communities attempt to come up with what they consider universally (or at least locally) acceptable values. Stevenson (1992) tells us that young adolescents, more than any other school age population, are in need of responsive schooling that accommodates the moral growth dimensions of their development. In their article "Intrinsic Goodness: Facilitating Character Development," Richardson and Norman (2000) identified 10 attributes that are necessary for character growth. Five are intrapersonal and five are interpersonal. These attributes, contained in Figure 2.1, may be used as the basis of a character education program.

Most character-building curricula will specify the qualities of good character. According to Gathercoal and Crowell (2000), the most commonly used terminology for the desired characteristics of many programs include

- Trustworthiness
- Respect for others
- Responsibility
- Fairness
- Caring
- Citizenship (p. 175)

They continue by stating, "If character education is to be successful, the teacher must display these attributes in his or her own learning and living" (p. 175). In other words, as teachers we have the capacity to **be** the character-building program. Actually, we have no choice. Whether they acknowledge it or not, students watch us and count on us to model exemplary character. So even if your district or school doesn't have an organized character-development program, your students are observing, and to some degree internalizing, the morals and values you exemplify.

As middle level educators, we can provide a welcoming experience to life by providing opportunities for students to explore and internalize attitudes and values that will promote a positive,

Intrapersonal Attributes:	**Interpersonal Attributes:**
1. Self-Discovery	1. Empathy
2. Self-Management	2. Altruism
3. Delayed Gratification	3. Problem Solving
4. Courage	4. Tolerance
5. Honesty	5. Social Deftness

FIGURE 2.1   Necessary attributes for character growth.

Source: Adapted from "Intrinsic Goodness: Facilitating Character Development," by R. C. Richardson and K. I. Norman, 2000, *Kappa Delta Pi Record, 36*(4), pp. 168–172.

productive, healthy, and fulfilling adult life. No other level of teaching has such an opportunity or responsibility. (Arth, Lounsbury, McEwin, & Swaim, 1995, p. 89)

Character Development Issues

The issues involved in character development tend to be more dependent on the context of home and community than those in other developmental areas.

Issue #1

Some students grow up in homes that emphasize a very strict moral code while others live in homes where there are few moral guidelines or restrictions

We need to be the first to understand that home life heavily influences the behaviors and attitudes of the kids in our classes. Through conscientiously being positive role models, understanding home influences, and finding ways to gently prod students toward what our communities consider good character, we will be teachers who make a difference. We cannot lose sight of the variability of influences outside the school. Individualizing our approach to character development is essential.

Issue #2

Students are continually faced with contradictions concerning character

We can't erase or deny contradictions. Creating a forum that allows students to candidly discuss their disappointments in adults, in their personal lives, or in the media will help them understand that they are not alone in their feelings. Through discussion comes opportunity for growth. We need to remember, however, that when kids come to us to talk about character, emotional, or social issues, sometimes they simply want to talk and need someone who will listen rather than talk back.

Issue #3

Middle grades students are especially vulnerable to falling into the "wrong crowd"

Before values are established, being accepted by a group may take precedence. As we've discussed, socialization is a major force during the middle grades years. When socialization leads to the acceptance of values, morals, or ethics that result in undesirable behavior, we have a problem. As middle grades educators, we have the responsibility of exposing kids to all kinds of relationships and groups. We can, in fact, act as engineers in our own classrooms as we build experiences that give our students social and value choices in a context that allows them to question and change their minds.

NMSA

Standard 1

Knowledge 6: Middle level teacher candidates understand the interrelationships among the characteristics and needs of all young adolescents.

Knowledge 7: Middle level teacher candidates understand that the development of all young adolescents occurs in the context of classrooms, families, peer groups, communities, and society.

Disposition 1: Middle level teacher candidates are positive and enthusiastic about all young adolescents.

Disposition 2: Middle level teacher candidates respect and appreciate the range of individual developmental differences of all young adolescents.

Performance 1: Middle level teacher candidates establish close, mutually respectful relationships with all young adolescents that support their intellectual, ethical, and social growth.

REFLECTIONS ON THE DEVELOPMENT OF MIDDLE LEVEL LEARNERS

Now that we have explored the wide variance possible in each of the five areas of development, let's consider possible flip-chart books that divide figures into their heads, torsos, and lower extremities. These books allow us to make bizarre configurations that form funny and preposterous new characters. We might add a muscle man torso to the head of a young girl and complete the picture with shapely female legs in high heels—or maybe "dress" a bearded lumberjack in a ballerina tutu and suit pants with loafers. Yes, this can be funny, and yes, so can the combinations possible in one 12-year-old. But it also can be not so funny, maybe sad, maybe "normal"; the possibilities are endless.

MEET THE STUDENTS

You are about to meet a group of students (and their teachers in Chapter 4) who will, throughout this text, introduce you to applications of a variety of middle grades education topics through scenarios involving themselves, their teachers, and their schools. Developing composite profiles involves the understandable risk of offending some who believe I am perpetuating stereotypes. My intent in presenting these students is to illustrate the variability inherent in individuality. Obviously, it would be impossible to present every combination of developmental characteristics.

The 10 students introduced here are all sixth graders. As you continue through the text, you will watch them grow and become. Their stories will unfold as they leave sixth grade, go through seventh grade, and then go on to eighth grade and beyond. You may have memories of kids with similar profiles. You may even see yourself in some of the students. Get to know them—they may mirror your future students.

Michael, *sixth grade*

Michael is a sixth grade boy who was retained in kindergarten and in third grade. That makes him 13 years old. He is 5 feet 10 inches, with 6 of those inches having been added between spring of the fifth grade and fall of the sixth grade. In spite of being retained 2 years, Michael still tries to achieve and his teachers report that he is cooperative and seems to want to learn. He consistently makes Cs and Ds but hasn't failed any classes since entering middle school. Michael doesn't hang out with the students in sixth grade. He has a steady girlfriend who is in eighth grade and who talks about dropping out of school when she turns 16. Michael is never in trouble while in school, but other kids say they have seen him hanging out with older kids at the mall or sitting outside on cars where he and his friends are often smoking.

Allison, *sixth grade*

Allison is a petite blonde with braces and a high, childlike voice. She's in sixth grade a year earlier than most. Her parents decided to promote her from kindergarten directly to second grade because they felt she had already mastered first grade objectives. The fact that she is barely 10 and physically immature compared to her friends doesn't seem to hinder her socially. She is very bright and precocious and appears to be readily accepted by her classmates. To her teachers this sociability is actually a liability. Allison talks nonstop.

Marvin, *sixth grade*

Marvin is the class clown. He is quite heavy and "throws his weight around" freely. He has learned to use his weight to what he perceives as his benefit. He has a habit of popping other kids on the backs of their heads as he walks down the hall or down a row of desks in the classroom. He does this with a grin, and the other kids don't seem to mind. They know they can count on Marvin to risk getting in trouble just to break the monotony of notetaking or silent reading with a well-timed belch or a loud sneeze followed by an insincere apology. Marvin is smart enough to know when he's on the verge of treading too heavily on the patience of most of his teachers.

Hector, *sixth grade*

Hector is short for 12, but very strong. He can throw a baseball with speed and accuracy. This makes him an asset on the field. Along with his physical prowess, he possesses equal intellectual strength. Hector is a straight-A student, to the delight of his teachers. To watch Hector in a group of students would be quite deceiving. He is painfully shy. The only thing that keeps the other kids from considering him a misfit is his athletic ability.

Jeanetta, *sixth grade*

Jeanetta is tall, thin, and lovely. She carries herself with confidence and is soft-spoken. Although she is 12, her sometimes provocative dress and mature mannerisms make her seem older. Her grades are acceptable and her personality is pleasing in class. Her teachers are concerned, however, because Jeanetta often seems withdrawn and seldom wants to express herself in class.

Barry, *sixth grade*

Barry's physical size hasn't quite caught up with his mouth. He has not entered puberty and appears to be much younger than 12. Despite his diminutive stature, his presence in the hallway and the classroom is never in doubt. He speaks without thinking and expends his overdose of energy in mischievous ways. The other kids tolerate Barry's antics only to a certain point. He often goes beyond that point. Teachers and classmates show their displeasure but he just keeps going until he is in trouble with adults or insulted, and sometimes ignored, by his peers. Although he's very smart, his behavior interferes with his achievement.

Mia, *sixth grade*

Mia spends a lot of time alone. She is virtually ignored by most kids, and seems to prefer it this way. She doesn't stand out in terms of physical size and never presents behavioral problems for her teachers. There are some subjects in which she excels, particularly literature and poetry units in language arts. When it comes to math and science she is an average achiever.

Mia is most often seen carrying a floral covered notebook in her hands even though she is wearing a backpack.

Anthony, *sixth grade*

Anthony is a good-looking boy of 12 with what his teachers describe as a "chip on his shoulder." Teachers, as well as students, know that Anthony can be charming when it suits him, and angry and aggressive when things don't go his way. He has a group of friends who hang out with him, or perhaps follow him. The sixth grade teachers have learned that when Anthony is happy, the mood of the class is brighter. But when Anthony is sullen, there is a classroom mood shift. So Anthony, at a young age, is a powerful force in group dynamics.

Darlene, *sixth grade*

Darlene has lots of friends, mostly girls in her neighborhood. She is the first to come to their aid with help and sympathy. Darlene has a smile that brightens a room. Her "bounce back" spirit is admired by her teachers. This admiration and enjoyment of Darlene is matched by concern that low test scores are shrugged off and missing homework assignments are dismissed with an "I won't forget again" reply, even after many such occasions.

Lee, *sixth grade*

Lee is small for 11. He never has much to say in class, but teachers notice that he has a group of friends with whom he sits at lunch and appears to fit in and enjoy himself. While he entered sixth grade with poor standardized test scores, he is making average grades and always has a book to read during the downtimes in class or when he finishes an assignment. He speaks in class only when questioned.

There are as many possible combinations of developmental traits as there are middle grades students. All of our students are evolving and becoming—they are not finished products. Our challenge as teachers is to accept them as they are and do what we can to help them grow in healthy ways physically, intellectually, emotionally, and socially, and with positive and productive character traits. Williamson and Johnston (1998) tell us that, while not a homogeneous group, middle level students are "bound together by common threads." The common threads in the physical, intellectual, emotional, social, and character development of young adolescents weave patterns that form the students we nurture in our classrooms.

Group Activities

1. In small groups, make bulleted lists of possible characteristics or descriptors of middle level students for each of the five developmental areas discussed in this chapter. Feel free to add to what this text covers. It would take volumes to be comprehensive! Share your lists with other groups.

2. How do movies and television shows portray middle level students? As a class, brainstorm about all the 10- to 15-year-olds we see on TV and in movies. What characteristics from your lists do these fictitious kids exemplify?

Individual Activities

1. Interview at least three of your friends and ask them to describe themselves as middle schoolers in the five developmental areas. Write brief sketches of them using your interview notes. Would you have predicted them to be as they are today given their self-described young adolescent personas?

2. Go to a place where you are likely to see groups of young adolescents. Try the mall, a fast food restaurant, a sporting event, or an afterschool hangout. Describe what you observe during a 10- or 15-minute period. Include their physical size/shape, clothing, accessories, hairstyles, socialization patterns, and so on. This exercise may bring back memories! Be prepared to share your observations with your class.

3. If you teach in a school that does not have a designated health/sex education teacher and/or class, are there ways you as an individual teacher might have a positive impact in this important dimension of young adolescent development? Write some notes on your own thoughts. Share them with fellow teacher candidates and your instructor to compile a list of possibilities that are both appropriate and within reasonable guidelines.

Personal Journal

1. Write an honest appraisal of yourself during young adolescence. Try to think about the span of sixth, seventh, and eighth grade rather than one particular time frame. Consider all five areas of development at each grade level.

2. Call at least two family members, if possible, to ask them to recall what you were like as a young adolescent. Assure them that you can remain objective about their comments because you are now a mature teacher candidate. Try the "if you'll be honest with me, I'll be honest with you" ploy. Of course, that tactic could backfire, as many of us would rather leave those years in the past! Compare your family members' observations to your own self-assessment.

Professional Practice

This is the first of the Professional Practice sections you will find at the end of each chapter. The scenarios, multiple choice questions, and constructed response items ask you to apply the knowledge in the text to classroom situations. The items are designed to provide practice for a variety of the Praxis II exams that may be required for certification. It is possible to write shorter scenarios than you might find on a Praxis exam because most of the students and teachers profiled in the Professional Practice scenarios are profiled throughout the book. For instance, the students in the Chapter 2 Professional Practice are Hector, Marvin, Mia, and Anthony—all students you know from the chapter and will meet again throughout the book. Here's the first of 10 Professional Practice sections.

Ms. Anderson teaches sixth grade math. Her classes have 16 to 27 students in each. This is her second year at Central Middle School and she feels relatively confident in her teaching abilities after what she considers to have been a fairly successful first year.

Ashley Anderson

She covered most of the material in the textbook by explaining concepts and doing examples on the board. She assigned homework each day and went over the problems the following day. She kept a tight reign on the students and wrote no more office referrals for discipline problems than the other teachers.

Ms. Anderson knows that middle school philosophy endorses heterogeneous grouping of students in most classes, and she treats all of her students basically the same way. As she watches the kids in her third period class take a quiz on a sunny October morning, she can't help but feel there's more going on under the surface of the quiet classroom than she realizes. She is just beginning to understand what a challenge this group is likely to present as she looks up and down the rows at the individual students. It occurs to her that maybe last year she was so focused on getting routines down and planning enough seatwork to keep the kids occupied that she hadn't really noticed how very different her students were from one another. She has one of those "wake up" moments when she realizes her view of her first year of teaching as relatively successful was based on the fact that her lessons were organized, she was diligent in controlling student behavior, and the grades she gave her students seemed in line with the grades given by other teacher team members.

Now Ms. Anderson begins to wonder how she could have missed what seems so crystal clear on this test day in October. She looks at her 23 students in this quiet setting and begins to really see them in their various stages of development. She watches Hector work deliberately and methodically through the problem solving required on the test. He is sitting behind Marvin who is too big for his desk and is tapping his foot on the back of Mia's desk while she stares out the window, her floral notebook in her lap. Marvin isn't quite finished with his test. He chooses to use his "almost finished" status to annoy Mia, and consequently the whole class with his foot tapping. Mia appears to have finished her test.

Ms. Anderson gets up from her chair and walks down a neat row of desks to where Anthony sits with his arms folded and his paper turned over. She picks up his paper. He looks the other way. On every item he has written, "I don't know and I don't care." She puts the paper down and continues to walk around the room.

1. What is the most plausible explanation as to why Ms. Anderson considered her first year a relatively successful one?

   (a) Her student teaching experience had been in a school where simply keeping order was a sign of a good day.

   (b) Central Middle School is in an area where achievement expectations are high.

   (c) She felt like she used a variety of instructional techniques to reach her students.

   (d) Her principal praised her at the end of the year for developing close relationships with several socially needy students.

2. Anthony's test paper is troubling. Which is the best explanation for his responses?

(a) He didn't learn enough during the unit to be able to find answers to the problem-solving items.

(b) He has little interest in succeeding.

(c) Something has happened to make him angry and he chooses not to concentrate any effort on his test.

(d) He is bored and wants Ms. Anderson to know it.

3. Mia is not responding to Marvin tapping on her desk. She is sitting quietly with no expression. It is likely that she

(a) is thinking about seeing all her friends at the mall after school.

(b) is a victim of "undersocialization" and has not experienced a healthy dose of social experiences.

(c) has finished her test and has the social skills to ignore Marvin.

(d) is about to turn around and slap Marvin.

Constructed Response

As Ms. Anderson observes Hector's conscientious efforts and Marvin's cavalier attitude, she is reminded of what she read in *This We Believe* concerning expectations and varied teaching and learning approaches. Briefly explain how these parts of the document apply to Hector and Marvin.

Internet Resources

Center for Adolescent and Family Studies
http://education.indiana.edu/cas/

The Center focuses on the biological, psychological, and social characteristics of adolescence. The site features Teacher Talk, an opportunity to learn about classroom strategies and lesson plans to enhance social and emotional growth.

Six Seconds
http://www.6seconds.org/

Six Seconds, a nonprofit service organization, provides information about emotional intelligence for schools, families, and communities.

Studies in Moral Development and Education
http://www.uic.edu/~lnucci/MoralEd/

This site brings together educators and others who are interested in research and practices in the area of moral/character development.

References

Arth, A. E., Lounsbury, J. H., McEwin, C. K., & Swaim, J. H. (1995). *Middle level teachers: Portraits of excellence.* Columbus, OH: National Middle School Association and National Association of Secondary School Principals.

Caissy, G. A. (1994). *Early adolescents: Understanding the 10 to 15 year old.* Reading, MA: Perseus Books.

Carnegie Council on Adolescent Development. (1989). *Turning points: Preparing American youth for the 21st century.* Washington, DC: Author.

Carnegie Council on Adolescent Development. (1996). *Great transitions: Preparing adolescents for a new century.* New York: Author.

Cranz, G. (1998). *The chair: Rethinking culture, body, and design.* New York: W.W. Norton & Co.

Dobrin, A. (2001). Finding universal values in a time of relativism. *The Educational Forum, 65*(3), 273–278.

Elkind, D. (1984). *All grown up and no place to go.* Reading, MA: Addison-Wesley.

Gardner, H. (1999). *The disciplined mind: What all students should understand.* New York: Simon & Schuster.

Gathercoal, P., & Crowell, R. (2000). Judicious discipline. *Kappa Delta Pi Record, 36*(4), 173–177.

Goleman, D. (1995). *Emotional intelligence.* New York: Bantam Books.

Jensen, E. (1998). *Teaching with the brain in mind.* Alexandria, VA: Association for Supervision and Curriculum Development.

Kellough, R. D., & Kellough, N. G. (1999). *Middle school teaching: A guide to methods and resources* (3rd ed.). Upper Saddle River, NJ: Merrill/Prentice Hall.

Knowles, T., & Brown, D. F. (2000). *What every middle school teacher should know.* Westerville, OH: National Middle School Association.

Mee, C. S. (1997). *2,000 voices: Young adolescents' perceptions & curriculum implications.* Columbus, OH: National Middle School Association.

Milgram, J. (1992). A portrait of diversity: The middle level student. In J. L. Irvin (Ed.). *Transforming middle level education: Perspectives and possibilities* (pp. 16–27). Needham Heights, MA: Allyn & Bacon.

National Association of Secondary School Principals' Council on Middle Level Education. (1989). *Middle level educators' responsibilities for intellectual development.* Reston, VA: Author.

Richardson, R. C., & Norman, K. I. (2000). Intrinsic goodness: Facilitating character development. *Kappa Delta Pi Record, 36*(4), 168–172.

Schurr, S. L., Thomason, J., & Thompson, M. (1996). *Teaching at the middle level.* Lexington, MA: D. C. Heath.

Stevenson, C. (1992). *Teaching ten to fourteen year olds.* White Plains, NY: Longman.

Strahan, D. B. (1997). *Mindful learning: Teaching self-discipline and academic achievement.* Durham, NC: Carolina Academic Press.

Strang, R. (1957). *The adolescent views himself.* New York: McGraw-Hill.

Williams, J. (1996). *How to manage your middle school classroom.* Westminister, CA: Teacher Created Materials.

Williamson, R. D., & Johnston, J. H. (Eds.). (1998). *Able learners in the middle level school: Identifying talent and maximizing potential.* Reston, VA: NASSP.

Wolfe, P. (2001). *Brain matters.* Alexandria, VA: Association for Supervision and Curriculum Development.

3

Diversity Among Middle Level Students

Diversity is the hallmark of middle level learners. . . . The middle school population includes both sexes, members of many cultures, students representing a panoply of interests, students with a full range of learning profiles, as well as students who struggle greatly with academics, and those for whom academics mirror advanced scholastic talent.

Tomlinson, Moon, and Callahan, 1998, p. 3

Use this diagram as an organizational tool. In the boxes beside the chapter headings, indicate the dates by which the readings should be completed.

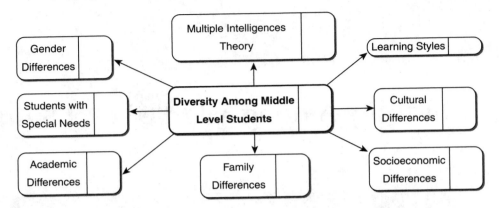

INTRODUCTION

Diversity may be viewed in a myriad of ways. We explore the differences inherent in middle school students not to place labels on them, but to understand them. Armed with knowledge and understanding of differences, we can make enlightened decisions (Stevenson, 1992). Tomlinson, Moon, and Callahan (1998) endorse middle school as the ideal place to recognize and utilize student differences when they write, "Perhaps more than any other segment of schooling, middle school must exemplify appropriate attention to student differences" (p. 10).

This chapter explores student differences in terms of gender, multiple intelligences, learning styles, family structures, academics, culture, socioeconomics, and special needs. These are by no means all the ways in which students differ, but, when viewed along with the five developmental areas discussed in Chapter 2, they provide an overview of some of the diversity you will likely encounter in your classroom. As you read, reflect on the characteristics of diverse populations as generalities rather than stereotypical images.

Standard 1

Knowledge 2: Middle level teacher candidates understand the range of individual differences of all young adolescents and the implications of these differences for teaching and learning.

Standard 6

Disposition 5: Middle level teacher candidates value and appreciate all young adolescents regardless of family circumstances, community environment, health, and/or economic conditions.

Disposition 6: Middle level teacher candidates value the enrichment of learning that comes from the diverse backgrounds, values, skills, talents, and interests of all young adolescents and their families.

GENDER DIFFERENCES

Teachers and schools are powerful influences on the lives of students. If we want boys and girls to have equal opportunities for success in school and outside school, we must create classrooms where all students feel valued for their . . . contributions.

Gober and Mewborn, 2001, p. 31

Girls and boys are different. Ask parents who have both. Chances are they'll tell you that differences are apparent from birth. Denying these differences isn't a healthy approach to coeducational settings. Mee (1997) cautions us to be sensitive to gender characteristics and the developmental differences between young adolescent girls and boys as we work with middle grades students. She presented 2,000 students from grades 5 through 8 with 53 open-ended statements. On Mee's "statementaire," each student identified his or her age, grade, gender, brothers and sisters and their ages, and her or his ethnic background, given the choices of American Indian, Alaskan Native, Asian or Pacific Islander, White Not of Hispanic Origin, Hispanic Origin, and Black Not of Hispanic Origin. She personally read the statements to almost 100 classes of students following an informal dialogue.

The students in Mee's study appeared to appreciate being involved. They wrote their responses after Mee verbalized the statements. After careful analysis of responses, Mee concluded, "The thoughts of young adolescents were clearly defined along gender lines. Although this study was not initially focused on gender, the findings emphatically indicated that the greatest differences in responses were gender based" (Mee, 1997, p. 12). She noted that geographic and cultural diversity factors were not as apparent as gender differences. On a humorous note, Mee tells us that overwhelmingly, for middle school boys, the best thing about being a boy is not being a girl!

If we accept that gender differences exist, both physiologically and psychologically, we come to the conclusion that it's okay, a part of the human condition. Most of us are very happy that there are differences! Much of our social lives revolve around these differences. For middle grades students, acquiring social acceptance is rooted in gender.

According to Milgram (1992), girls perceive being part of a prestigious social group as the most important asset leading to general social acceptance. Boys see athletic prowess as the main key to social acceptance.

Two excellent books on the subject of gender in adolescence are *Reviving Ophelia* by Mary Pipher (1994) and *Raising Cain* by Daniel Kindlon and Michael Thompson (1999). These authors delve deeply into the natural and societal forces that contribute to gender characteristics. The insightful material in both of these books provides food for thought and discussion with colleagues, and will help refocus your perspective regarding adolescent gender issues.

Media Impact

Acknowledging gender differences is not the same as perpetuating stereotypes that may result in unfair treatment. Print and electronic media often portray gender differences in exaggerated ways. In selling products and/or services, the media will shamelessly capitalize on gender differences. A proactive way to approach gender differences while giving students a sense of perspective on the subject is to acquaint children with the impact magazines, television, movies, and advertisements have on our society. Frank discussions of how we are influenced in terms of gender stereotyping provide a valuable service to developing young adolescents.

Standard 1

Knowledge 8: Middle level teacher candidates are knowledgeable about how the media portrays young adolescents and comprehend the implications of these portraits.

NMSA.

Gay and Lesbian Students

A discussion of gender differences could not be complete without acknowledging gay and lesbian students, whom Anderson refers to as the "invisible minority" (Anderson, 1997, p. 65). These students often find that the two places where they spend the most time and encounter adults most frequently—home and school—are often the places where they are most misunderstood. Just as we have a responsibility to meet the needs of students who differ in other respects, we also have a professional mandate to address the needs of the sexual minorities (Anderson, 1997). Edwards (1997) tells us that most gay and lesbian youth will acknowledge their sexual preferences in high school after spending their middle school years questioning their orientation. It is important that gay and lesbian students and their parents experience a school environment that is supportive. Taylor (2000) tells us that a supportive environment is particularly important for these students because of the increased safety and health risks they often encounter. He reports that young adolescent gay and lesbian middle grades students are more likely to be verbally and physically attacked, to be threatened, to skip school, to drop out of school, and to attempt suicide. As educators committed to meeting the needs of all students in developmentally responsive ways, we should not ignore or sidestep the needs of gay and lesbian youth.

Avoiding Differential Treatment

When it comes to unequal treatment of girls and boys in educational settings, we need to find ways to avoid what many of us do naturally as a result of social conditioning. We are often unaware of how we interact with students (Gober & Mewborn, 2001). Unintentionally treating boys and girls differently often leads to allowing boys to interrupt girls, and then at times going so far as to praise girls for their patience. Avoiding such discrimination may be difficult even when we are aware of it (Kellough & Kellough, 1999).

I don't think educators would intentionally create unequal opportunities for learning between girls and boys. But, many, myself included, have unintentionally treated them differently when it comes to expectations and classroom question/answer sessions. I became aware that I called on boys more frequently than girls when a practicum student kept a tally without my knowledge. She presented the results to me and I have worked toward balance for two decades. Figure 3.1 is a visual reminder of our obligation to create and maintain gender balance. Colleagues can help each other detect how we approach gender,

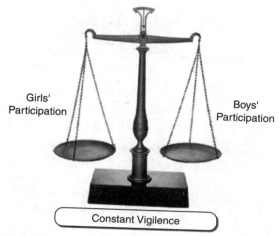

Girls' Participation

Boys' Participation

Constant Vigilence

FIGURE 3.1   Achieving balance: Gender issues.

or we can keep track of our own questioning using a seating chart on a clipboard. When we direct discussions, we can keep track of boy/girl talk time and try to achieve gender balance.

Three specific strategies can help us create balance. One is to give students a certain number of chips as they enter the classroom. The students "spend" a chip each time they speak, and the goal is to spend all the chips by the end of the class period. Another strategy is to use wait time between asking a question and calling on a student to answer the question. Research tells us that girls often take longer to respond to questions than boys. Consequently, not using adequate wait time may disadvantage girls. A third strategy is to use the Think-Pair-Share method. A question or situation is posed. Students are given an opportunity to think of their responses before being asked to share responses with a partner. This allows equal time for students to think before answering (Gober & Mewborn, 2001).

Equalizing Expectations

How well teachers cope with and compensate for gender differences, unequal opportunities, and stereotyping can have very real and lasting consequences by creating artificially different expectations in activities, social settings, or academic performance. Academically, differing expectations of boys and girls seem to be the most prevalent in science and math. Tests such as the *National Assessment of Educational Progress (NAEP)* and the *Third International Mathematics and Science Study (TIMSS)* reveal a gender gap in math and science that increases with age (Gober & Mewborn, 2001). How much our classroom practices and curriculum materials have to do with documented decline is not known, but common sense tells us that equalizing expectations and opportunities will have an influence on perpetuating interest and, consequently, achievement. We need to do all we can to encourage both girls and boys to participate fully in the education process.

MULTIPLE INTELLIGENCES THEORY

Definitions of intelligence abound. Consideration of the cognitive process continues to intrigue us. Many educators have changed their view of the concept of intelligence, as illustrated in Figure 3.2.

More Than One Intelligence

Is it possible to move beyond the "old view" of intelligence to the "new view" in ways that are operational in a school setting? Howard Gardner's Theory of Multiple Intelligences, first presented in 1983 in *Frames of Mind,* does exactly that. Gardner added an "s" to intelligence. In other words, he espoused that intelligence is not unitary, but rather could be exhibited in many ways. In Multiple Intelligences (MI) Theory he proposed a revolutionary revision of our thinking about intelligence by recognizing that through a unique relationship between nature and nurture, each person has a mix of intelligence strengths he labels "frames" (Willis & Johnson, 2001). Each of these "frames" is an intelligence.

Gardner conceptualizes intelligence as "a biopsychological potential to process information that can be activated in a cultural setting to solve problems or create products that are of value in a culture" (Gardner, 1999, p. 33). In other words, he sees intelligences as

---

Old View
- Intelligence was fixed
- Intelligence was measured by a number
- Intelligence was unitary
- Intelligence was measured in isolation
- Intelligence was used to sort students and predict their success

New View
- Intelligence can be developed
- Intelligence is not numerically quantifiable and is exhibited during a performance or problem-solving process
- Intelligence can be exhibited in many ways—multiple intelligences
- Intelligence is measured in context/real life situations
- Intelligence is used to understand human capacities and the many and varied ways students can achieve

---

FIGURE 3.2   How our definition of intelligence has changed.
Source: From *So Each May Learn: Integrating Learning Styles and Multiple Intelligences* (p. 7), by H. F. Silver, R. W. Strong, and M. J. Perini, 2000, Alexandria, VA: Association for Supervision and Curriculum Development. Copyright 2000 by Silver, Strong, and Associates, Inc. Adapted by permission.

potentials that can be mobilized and connected according to personal inclinations and cultural preferences (Gardner, 1999). The eight intelligences include the following:

- Verbal-Linguistic
- Logical-Mathematical
- Visual-Spatial
- Bodily-Kinesthetic
- Musical
- Interpersonal
- Intrapersonal
- Naturalist

How Intelligences Look

We want to briefly discuss how these intelligences "look" in the classroom. A widely accepted method involves considering *dispositional theory* based on the work of Perkins, Jay, and Tishman (1993), who tell us that good thinkers have dispositions that influence their ability to process and make sense of information. In *So Each May Learn*, multiple intelligences are linked to dispositional theory like this:

> Dispositional theory provides a productive means of looking at multiple intelligences. A sensitivity may lead to an inclination for using that intelligence and, in the right environment and under the right circumstances, an inclination can be translated into an ability to use the intelligence in a variety of contexts. (Silver, Strong & Perini, 2000, p. 10)

Figure 3.3 gives us ways of thinking about the intelligences in terms of dispositional theory.

A series of studies have found that all children profiled demonstrate abilities in at least one area, while none have exceptional abilities in all (Strahan, 1997). Individual differences arise when unique combinations of intelligences, and degrees of those intelligences, are manifested. Knowledge of the eight intelligences helps teachers recognize and appreciate student differences. To make the most of teaching/learning opportunities, teachers should help students discover and nurture their primary intelligences and foster the development of intelligences that may not be as "natural" to them.

Applying MI Theory

Program after program has evolved based on MI theory. Howard Gardner himself cautions us in terms of application and tells us "MI theory is in no way an educational prescription" (Gardner, 1999, p. 89). He views MI theory as an "endorsement of three key propositions: we are not all the same; we do not all have the same kinds of minds; and education works most effectively if these differences are taken into account rather than denied or ignored" (p. 91). In Chapter 7 we will explore instructional strategies that align with Gardner's view of differences. We must keep in mind, however, that superficial application of MI theory may not only be ineffective, it may actually harm students if labeling is all that occurs and measures to increase each student's capacity to perceive and understand are not implemented.

Disposition/ Intelligence	Sensitivity to	Inclination for	Ability to
Verbal-Linguistic Intelligence	Sounds, meanings, structures, and styles of language	Speaking, writing, listening, reading	Speak effectively (teacher, religious leader, politician) or write effectively (poet, journalist, novelist, copywriter, editor)
Logical-Mathematical Intelligence	Patterns, numbers, and numerical data; causes and effects; objective and quantitative reasoning	Finding patterns, making calculations, formulating hypotheses, using the scientific method, deductive and inductive reasoning	Work effectively with numbers (accountant, statistician, economist) and reason effectively (engineer, scientist, computer programmer)
Spatial Intelligence	Colors, shapes, visual puzzles, symmetry, lines, images	Representing ideas visually, creating mental images, noticing visual details, drawing and sketching	Create visually (artist, photographer, engineer, decorator) and visualize accurately (tour guide, scout, ranger)
Bodily-Kinesthetic Intelligence	Touch, movement, physical self, athleticism	Activities requiring strength, speed, flexibility, hand-eye coordination, and balance	Use the hands to fix or create (mechanic, surgeon, carpenter, sculptor, mason) and use the body expressively (dancer, athlete, actor)
Musical Intelligence	Tone, beat, tempo, melody, pitch, sound	Listening, singing, playing an instrument	Create music (songwriter, composer, musician, conductor) and analyze music (music critic)
Interpersonal Intelligence	Body language, moods, voice, feelings	Noticing and responding to other people's feelings and personalities	Work with people (administrators, managers, consultants, teachers) and help people identify and overcome problems (therapists, psychologists)
Intrapersonal Intelligence	One's own strengths, weaknesses, goals, desires	Setting goals, assessing personal abilities and liabilities, monitoring one's own thinking	Mediate, reflect, exhibit self-discipline, maintain composure, and get the most out of oneself
Naturalist Intelligence	Natural objects, plants, animals, naturally occurring issues	Identifying and classifying living things and natural objects	Analyze ecological and natural situations (ecologists, rangers), learn from living things (zoologist, botanist, veterinarian), and work in natural settings (hunter, scout)

FIGURE 3.3   Intelligences as dispositions.

Source: From *So Each May Learn: Integrating Learning Styles and Multiple Intelligences* (p.11), by H. F. Silver, R. W. Strong, and M. J. Perini, 2000, Alexandria, VA: Association for Supervision and Curriculum Development. Copyright 2000 by Silver Strong and Associates, Inc. Adapted by permission.

60

LEARNING STYLES

A most important characteristic of becoming an effective, caring educator is the ability and commitment to recognize individual learning differences among students.

Knowles and Brown, 2000, p. 65

Individuals have unique styles of learning. We adapt these styles, usually unconsciously, to varying circumstances according to the learning demand. Many psychologists and educators have observed, and attempted to label, the ways we learn.

Multiple intelligences and *learning styles* are linked in practical ways. Intelligences are "biological and psychological potentials and capacities" (Gardner, 1999, p. 82). Decisions about how to use these capacities may depend on style preference. Style determines our approach to intelligences. To clarify this concept, consider a person with strong musical intelligence. This intelligence may manifest itself in the careers of conductors, performers, composers, and music critics, or it may be manifested in a talent that is enjoyed as an avocation. Learner preferences and styles contribute to how intelligences are used and developed.

To use our understanding of learning differences to the benefit of students, we need to analyze our own inclinations as well as those of our students. Then we must help our students see how they can learn best so they can both use their dominant characteristics and enhance their less dominant characteristics. All this involves understanding of self. Carl Jung's (1923) work has contributed greatly to our ability to do just that. He divides all human behavior into two categories—perception and judgment. To perceive is to find out or discover. To judge (or process) is to decide, evaluate, and take action. Each of us spends time perceiving and judging, individually tending toward one over the other.

Imaginative, Analytic, Common Sense, Dynamic Learners

Bernice McCarthy (1997) describes four major learning styles: imaginative, analytic, common sense, and dynamic. She explains these styles, using Jung's conception of perceiving and judging. *Imaginative learners* perceive information in concrete ways and then process it reflectively. Imaginative learners prefer interaction and integration and sharing rather than the "sit and git" traditional classroom style. *Analytic learners* perceive information abstractly and then process it reflectively. They value established knowledge and detail. Because they prefer sequential, step-by-step learning, the traditional classroom approach works well for them. *Common sense learners* perceive information abstractly and then process it actively. They desire real life applications of learning and thrive with hands-on instruction. Traditional classroom instruction will frustrate them unless they can see immediate uses for the skills/knowledge presented. *Dynamic learners* perceive information concretely and process it actively. They do not care about order and sequential learning, but prefer to take risks and tackle new challenges. They are often frustrated by traditional classroom methods.

Given this theory of learning styles, it appears that traditional classrooms, generally recognized for material presentation, guided practice, and assessments, and characterized

McCarthy's learning styles =
Imaginative + Analytic + Common
sense + Dynamic

by lecture, notetaking, occasional demonstration, and testing, are places where analytic learners thrive most. In our chapters on instructional methods, we will explore ways to better motivate all learners, regardless of their learning styles.

Learning Modalities

Learning styles and learning modalities are often spoken of interchangeably. Modalities refer to how students use their senses in the learning process. We commonly consider four modalities: *visual* (seeing), *auditory* (hearing), *kinesthetic* (moving), and *tactile* (touching). As you might guess, the more senses or modalities we can activate, the more learning will take place.

Four basic learning modalities =
Visual + Auditory + Kinesthetic +
Tactile

The great majority of students can learn using all four modalities, but we all have preferences that can be capitalized on, as well as weaker leanings that can be enhanced. In our classrooms, we must provide an environment that is conducive to all four. Traditional classrooms rely heavily on auditory stimulation with lecture and discussion. Now that we have considered the developmental characteristics of young adolescence, we realize that visual, kinesthetic, and tactile modalities also play strong roles in adolescent lives. Figure 3.4 will help us understand characteristics we may observe in students who learn best through hearing, seeing, moving, and touching.

Auditory learners tend to . . .
  enjoy reading and being read to.
  be able to verbally explain concepts and scenarios.
  like music and hum to themselves.
  enjoy both talking and listening.

Visual learners tend to . . .
  have good spelling, notetaking, and organizational skills.
  notice details and prefer neatness.
  learn more if illustrations and charts accompany reading.
  prefer quiet, serene surroundings.

Kinesthetic learners tend to . . .
  be demonstrative, animated, and outgoing.
  enjoy physical movement and manipulatives.
  be willing to try new things.
  be messy in habits and surroundings.

Tactile learners tend to . . .
  prefer manipulatives when being introduced to a topic.
  literally translate events and phenomena.
  tolerate clutter.
  be artistic in nature.

FIGURE 3.4   Traits of auditory, visual, kinesthetic, and tactile learners.

Cognitive Type Theory

Cognitive type theory gives us ways of determining learning preferences and styles. Basing her work on Jungian theory, Carolyn Mamchur (1996) helps us understand eight psychological type preferences and how each relates to the learning process. Our look at type theory is an overview, a brief coverage of what can be an in-depth and valuable theory for educators. I encourage you to explore it more fully after reading this "in a nutshell" version. In Figure 3.5, the Eight Psychological Type Preferences are paired as four sets of opposites.

Using tests such as the Myers-Briggs Test Inventory, the one preferred by Mamchur (1996), we can determine 16 unique psychological profiles consisting of various combinations of four of the eight preferences. Figure 3.6 is an adaptation of Mamchur's conjectures concerning characteristics of learners whose profiles contain particular preferences. Applying this knowledge to what we know about our students will further emphasize the need for a variety of instructional strategies.

Self-Awareness

Most students (and many adults) appear to think that learning is some kind of magical process. If you ask students how they learn, most will not be able to tell you (Johnson, 1998). Self-awareness is a vital component of increasing learning capacities, so helping students identify their learning styles, modalities, and preferences should be one of our goals.

E	**Extroversion** An outward focusing of energy.		**I**	**Introversion** An inward focusing of energy.
S	**Sensing** Seeking immediately relevant and accessible experience through senses.		**N**	**Intuition** Making sense of the world by creating patterns and inventing hypotheses.
T	**Thinking** Valuing objective, analytical ways to make decisions and evaluations.		**F**	**Feeling** Valuing subjective analysis and empathetic understanding to make decisions and evaluations.
J	**Judging** Preferring to deal with the world by decisively acting to create order.		**P**	**Perceiving** Preferring to deal with the world by following one's curiosity and seeking understanding.

FIGURE 3.5 The eight psychological type preferences.

Source: From *A Teacher's Guide to Cognitive Type Theory & Learning Style* (pp. 11–54), by C. Mamchur, 1996, Alexandria, VA: Association for Supervision and Curriculum Development. Copyright 1996 by Carolyn Marie Mamchur. Adapted by permission.

The intuitive learner. . .
  likes to develop hypotheses, explanations,
    and ways of doing things.
  will put more energy into a project when
    encouraged to invent.
  gets bored easily and seeks variety.
  works unevenly in spurts and starts.
  pays attention to details only when viewed
    as important.

The thinking learner. . .
  values honesty and fair play.
  believes in following rules.
  can be competitive, driven, and independent.
  likes to win and appear confident.
  needs well-organized, logically developed
    courses.
  values, respects, and expects expert
    knowledge.

The feeling learner. . .
  needs harmonious environment.
  is very uncomfortable with criticism.
  desires respectful manners in the classroom.
  values cooperation, consideration, and
    consensus.
  dislikes competition.
  learns best when values are a motivating
    factor.
  wants to please in the classroom.

The extroverted learner. . .
  likes to "think out loud."
  learns by doing.
  prefers hands-on, action-oriented
    experiences.
  likes sharing ideas and tasks.
  enjoys variety.
  needs feedback on progress.

The introverted learner. . .
  needs to think things through.
  prefers to volunteer rather than be called on.
  sometimes surprises others with
    unexpected/intense responses.
  appreciates quiet, uninterrupted work time.

The sensing learner. . .
  learns best with step-by-step procedures.
  likes to stick to skills and knowledge he or
    she already possesses.
  dislikes abstractness and theory.
  needs to see practical application of
    learning.
  wants to see, hear, and touch as they learn.

The judging learner. . .
  likes to plan and schedule.
  wants to see definite structure in course.
  values completion of all tasks.
  expects a lot of feedback from teacher.
  wants everything to be evaluated and to
    count.

The perceiving learner. . .
  enjoys the process of discovery.
  doesn't necessarily see value in completing
    tasks.
  appreciates flexibility and freedom.
  needs help to succeed in a structured
    setting.
  will sometimes withdraw if pressed.

FIGURE 3.6 Type preferences as manifested in learners.

Source: From *A Teacher's Guide to Cognitive Type Theory & Learning Style* (pp. 11–54) by C. Mamchur, 1996, Alexandria, VA: Association for Supervision and Curriculum Development. Copyright 1996 by Carolyn Marie Mamchur. Adapted by permission.

Stevenson (1992) tells us, "In order to help students learn how to learn, we must understand as much as possible about the circumstances under which they learn most effectively" (p. 99). Then we must share our understanding with our students. David Strahan (1997) says that "Mindful learning begins with students thinking about how they learn best and gains momentum as students begin to 'own' more of their own instruction" (p. 69).

Mamchur (1997) advises us to discover as much as we can about how we, as teachers, learn. Because it is natural to teach in the same ways we learn, knowing our own styles, modalities, and preferences will help us recognize when we are doing that rather than teaching in a variety of ways to meet the needs of more of our students. We should first know ourselves as learners, and then discover the ways in which our students learn and help our students understand their own ways of learning. It is our responsibility to use a variety of instructional strategies to meet as many needs as possible.

CULTURAL DIFFERENCES

We believe that cultural diversity in schools and in the curriculum helps prepare students for living in a multicultural society and an interdependent world.

Hodges, 1995, vii

We are told that by the year 2050, the percentage of Latinos in the United States population will almost triple; Asian students will more than triple; and African Americans will increase about 3% (Carger, 1997). The American teaching force is heading in the opposite direction, with about 9% non-White in 2001, and predictions that fewer and fewer teachers in the future will be of ethnicities other than Caucasian (Jorgenson, 2001). Because the middle school is part of the public school system, these figures are, and will be, reflected there.

Culture, Ethnicity, Race, Linguistics

In most discussions concerning cultural similarities and differences, certain phraseology is used. As commonly used as the words *culture, ethnicity,* and *race* are, various scholars define them in different ways. We'll settle on what appear to be widely accepted definitions. *Culture* refers to specific shared values, beliefs, and attitudes (Rasool & Curtis, 2000). *Ethnicity* depends on "a sense of group identification, a common set of values, political and economic interests, behavioral patterns, and the culture elements that differ from those of other groups within a society" (Banks, 1991, p. 13). *Race* categorizes individuals into groups (such as White, Black, Asian) based on certain outward physical characteristics (Rasool & Curtis, 2000).

Along with differences in culture, ethnicity, and race often come linguistic differences. In 2000, as many as 42% of public school students were language minority students. "There is a wide gap between what they understand in English and what they can say in English . . . , between how they conceptualize in English and how they conceptualize in their native languages" (Teemant, Bernhardt, Rodriquez-Munoz, & Aiello, 2000, p. 30).

So what once was thought of as the majority is rapidly becoming the minority in American schools. Numerous books and articles address the topic of differences in culture, ethnicity, race, and language. This same topic permeates most teacher education and staff development programs. I encourage you to take advantage of growth opportunities dealing with this vital topic. What is offered here is only a brief discussion.

Desegregation

The 20th century was a time of extremes in how public education was delivered to a diverse cultural population. Segregation of Whites and Blacks (then the single largest minority population) was the norm until the 1954 Supreme Court decision of *Brown v. Board of Education* after which the United States began efforts "to dismantle entrenched racial segregation in public schools" (Kahlenberg, 2000, p. 17). Where desegregation occurred, Black achievement rose sharply and White scores did not decline. Unfortunately, in the 1990s a series of court cases stated that previous desegregation rulings were temporary and school districts were freed from federally mandated desegregation remedies (Kahlenberg, 2000). As we begin the 21st century, there appears to be a resurgence of segregation. Whether in racially segregated schools, or in schools where segregation is subtly accomplished, racism is ugly and detrimental.

Understanding Differences

As educators, we should avoid racism in any form. In order to do this, we need to examine our own ethnicities, deeply held beliefs, and prejudices. For many, this is a lifelong endeavor. The sooner we begin, the better able we will be to meet the diverse needs of our students. It is easy to misinterpret the behaviors of those from whom we differ. Because statistically most teachers in the United States are Caucasian and were raised in predominantly Caucasian communities, knowledge of other races is often limited. Figure 3.7 contains information from *Multicultural Education in Middle and Secondary Classrooms* (Rasool & Curtis, 2000, p. 61). The authors urge us to use caution as we consider generalizations in order to avoid racial/ethnic stereotyping. "Generalizations are statements supported by data, whereas stereotypes are general statements based on incomplete or missing data. . . . Stereotypes are often based on misperceptions and usually involve a negative judgment" (p. 61). The generalizations in Figure 3.6 represent compilations of learning characteristics that are often cited as typical. Please view them as such. It is important to note that while generalizations pertaining to learners can be made, many educators and researchers tell us that learning styles are not culturally, ethnically, or racially dependent. While these factors may affect student learning, " . . . there is no single or dual learning style for the members of any culture, national, racial . . . group" (Dunn, 1997, pp. 74–75).

Students of Mixed Race

Teachers need to be particularly aware of the unique concerns presented when adolescents of mixed race or mixed ethnic backgrounds are present in the classroom or school. Studies in the 1990s show that the number of biracial, multiracial/ biethnic, or multiethnic children has increased dramatically in the last decade, and these children are now populating our schools in statistically significant numbers. Since much of a child's self-identity and self-esteem are tied to a sense of pride in cultural or racial background, children of mixed heritage can experience significant pressure to identify with only one of their ethnic or racial backgrounds (usually the one of color). At the same time, our society serves to make them feel alienated, belittled, and often insignificant as they experience insensitivity from both mainstream and minority groups. Cultural and racial identity issues can intensify during the middle school years as a facet of the adolescent's search for self-awareness. Schools can and

African American learners . . .

are more global, focusing on the whole picture rather than on parts.
often approximate space, numbers, and time rather than being tied to
precise accuracy.
prefer inferential reasoning.
rely on non-verbal as well as verbal communication patterns.
sometimes distrust mainstream people and institutions.
prefer visual and aural cues.

Hispanic/Latino learners . . .

are more group-oriented and inductive thinkers.
are peer-oriented and more likely to perform well in small groups.
have a more external locus of control.
prefer more personal and informal relationships with authority figures.

Native American learners . . .

prefer sharing and cooperative learning versus competitive learning
environments.
have a different concept of time from the mainstream perspective.
frequently exhibit behaviors that seem to indicate a lack of interest in learning.
are more reflective than impulsive.
are more visually and imagery oriented than verbally oriented.
more often have an internal locus of control and are self-directed.
view teachers as facilitators of learning.

Asian American learners . . .

prefer formal relationships with teachers and other authority figures.
are autonomous and conforming.
are obedient to authority.
are usually conservative and reserved.
are more introverted.

FIGURE 3.7   Generalizations of learning characteristics.

Source: From *Multicultural Education in Middle and Secondary Classrooms: Meeting the Challenge of Diversity and Change* 1st edition by Rasool/Curtis, © 2000. Reprinted with permission of Wadsworth, a division of Thomson Learning: *www.thomsonrights.com* Fax 800-730-2215.

should be sensitive to these issues by including specific staff training in their agenda, reviewing curriculum for undue emphasis on any one cultural or racial group to the exclusion of others, and supporting an atmosphere of positive cross-cultural attitudes, perceptions, and behaviors (Wardle, 2000).

English as a Second Language

A controversial issue in education revolves around children whose first language is not English. As our nation becomes more and more diverse, the number of languages spoken in the homes of students increases. Minority language learners are often placed in low-ability groups where they are labeled as poor readers. They may be segregated in bilingual programs or mainstreamed into English-speaking content classes with only limited assistance in sporadic *English as a Second Language (ESL)* pull-out programs. At the other end of the spectrum are the total immersion programs that place non-English speakers in all-day programs where they concentrate only on the development of English language skills before they are assimilated into regular classes. The selection of a plan by a community depends on political and demographic profiles in the local population, as well as on what the district or state embraces philosophically. As "regular" classroom teachers, we may find ourselves in a variety of situations with regard to students for whom English is not their native language. Take advantage of whatever assistance is offered.

Multiculturalism

"Our goal should be to become culturally responsive teachers, to approach teaching in ways that . . . respect diversity; engage the motivation of all learners; create a safe, inclusive, and respectful learning environment; derive teaching practices from principles that cross disciplines and cultures; and promote justice and equity in society" (Wlodkowski & Ginsberg, 1995, p. 19). What a tall order! Fortunately, there is support for becoming a culturally responsive teacher, and there are schools that foster the concept. The *Association for Supervision and Curriculum Development (ASCD)* strongly endorses culturally responsive teaching as indicated by their stated value of Cultural Pluralism. They say, "We believe that cultural diversity in schools and in curriculum helps prepare students for living in a multicultural society and an interdependent world" (Hodges, 1995, p. viii).

There are numerous ways to tailor instruction to the specific needs of children from varied cultural groups and many blueprints are available to schools to help in the promotion of multicultural education. Dunn (1997) tells us that *multicultural education* has " . . . two broad goals: increasing academic achievement and promoting greater sensitivity to cultural differences in an attempt to reduce bias" (p. 74). James Banks (1990), a noted expert in multicultural diversity issues, tells us that there are some specific characteristics that multicultural schools share. He says that the adults in multicultural schools have high expectations for students and respond to them in positive ways. They make sure the curriculum and materials reflect a wide array of cultural perspectives. Language differences are respected and assessments are culturally sensitive. In the classroom teachers differentiate their teaching methods and styles to match the learning styles of their students.

In *Educating Everybody's Children* (1995), Carbo tells the story of Joe Sweeny, a middle school teacher in New York City. In his school, 58% of the students are Hispanic, 12% are Asian, and the other 30% represent 25 different countries. Sweeny organizes neighborhood workshops using volunteer interpreters. He assigns math problems that call for collection and analysis of data relevant to problems such as homelessness and graffiti, with some projects actually leading to social change for neighborhood residents. According to Sweeny, "School cannot be an isolated site that exists only from 9:00 to 3:00. The whole community must get involved with the school. If everyone works together, our schools will succeed" (p. 7). While Joe Sweeny has obviously found ways to communicate with the students and families he serves, we are all in danger of the miscommunication that can occur in culturally diverse settings. Multiculturalism requires teachers to understand the norms and preferences, along with the verbal and nonverbal patterns of alternative cultures (Chesebro, Berko, Hopson,

Cooper, & Hodges, 1995). Louanne Johnson (1998), author of the book that served as the basis for the film "Dangerous Minds," tells us that, "Cultural differences create many opportunities to put your foot in your mouth" (p. 157). She goes on to tell us that students will readily forgive us if they are assured that we genuinely care about and respect them.

 ## SOCIOECONOMIC DIFFERENCES

> *As communities across the United States abandon racial desegregation efforts, educators are finding a more effective way to insure quality of educational opportunities: socioeconomic integration.*
>
> Kahlenberg, 2000, p. 16

Let's look at the statistics. More than 35 million Americans are officially poor. Of our children, one out of every five lives in poverty. More than 10 million Americans live in high-poverty neighborhoods. Add to this the fact that minorities are poorer than the rest of Americans. About 30% of African Americans and 30% of Hispanics were classified as poor in 1995. Families in poverty are more likely to be headed by women with educational deficiencies themselves. Their children are home alone more often; siblings drop out of school more frequently; and children often lack social support. For the last two decades of the 20th century, the old saying—the rich get richer and the poor get poorer—was true (Wellstone, 1995). In *Hints for Teaching Success in the Middle Schools,* Rubenstein (1994) tells us that today's middle schoolers can expect to be the first generation in America that will have a lower standard of living than their parents.

Socioeconomic Integration

Kahlenberg (2000) proposes that if using race to promote integration is problematic, then perhaps we should promote integration through students' economic status. Given the strong correlation between race and socioeconomic class in the United States, *socioeconomic integration* would likely produce racial diversity. Many educators believe that access to education among a core of children of middle class families may be the best predictor of school quality. Therefore, socioeconomic integration would give all students access to quality schools.

Students who qualify for free or reduced price lunch provide a measure that our government uses to appropriate funds; hence, this statistic is kept by all schools, districts, and states. In some schools, as many as 98% of the students fall within free or reduced lunch guidelines. When these students are concentrated in a particular school, extra money in the form of Title I (government distributed) funds is given to the school. However, a congressionally authorized study of the Title I Elementary and Secondary Education Act found that extra funding in a "high poverty" school results in very few achievement gains (Puma, Karweit, Ricciuti, Thompson, & Vaden-Kiernan, 1997). Simply giving extra money to high poverty schools doesn't appear to have the desired effect of enhancing the quality of education offered.

Given the statistics concerning students who are poor and the below-average performance of most high poverty schools, even with additional funding, Kahlenberg's suggestion of socioeconomic integration may hold the key to giving every student the opportunities offered in basically middle class settings. It would mean redistricting and busing, and would require major legislation and bold moves by policy-makers. As educators, we need to voice our concerns and be part of the solution.

High Expectations

While a mandated attempt at a solution may be years away, individual teachers can make a difference in the lives of poor students. Given all we have explored in terms of young adolescent development, even middle school students with unlimited financial resources struggle with the passage from childhood to adolescence. Think about how much more difficult it may be for those young adolescents who qualify as poor. To add to their problems, many studies show that teachers expect less of students from lower socioeconomic strata than they do of middle class students. We must examine what part we play in the ongoing failure of poor students by communicating to them that they lack potential (Rasool & Curtis, 2000). Teachers must believe their students can achieve before they put forth their best effort to teach them. Likewise, students must believe that they can achieve before they are willing to try.

FAMILY DIFFERENCES

It is even more difficult to accurately depict a typical young adolescent's family structure than it is to correctly generalize about that kid's development, for there are so many deviations from the tradition of the two-parent nuclear family.

Stevenson, 1992, p. 101

Some of the family structures experienced by middle school students today are far different from what was considered "normal" during much of the last century. Regardless of what the family/home structure is like, it strongly influences a child's development. Likewise, as young adolescents try to figure out who they are within the family unit, their struggle affects the way family members interact with each other (Peterson, 1995).

> **NMSA.**
>
> *Standard 6*
>
> *Knowledge 1:* Middle level teacher candidates understand the variety of family structures.
>
> *Knowledge 2:* Middle level teacher candidates understand how prior learning, differing experiences, and family and cultural backgrounds influence young adolescent learning.
>
> *Disposition 1:* Middle level teacher candidates respect all young adolescents and their families.

Defining Family

With only about one-fourth of school age children living in traditional, two-biological parent homes, we need to examine the structures in which our students live. The U.S. Census Report for 2000 also tells us that our divorce rate exceeds 50% and is the highest in the world. The number of single-parent homes rose by 300% from 1980 to 2000, reaching an incredible 12 million homes. This translates into almost half of our students spending at least part of their childhood in homes with only one parent. Some studies reveal that as many as one-fourth of the babies born at the turn of the 21st century were born to unwed mothers. Add the staggering number of 45 million people (almost 20% of the U.S. population) who moved in 1999–2000 and it becomes obvious that there is a general lack of stability pervading families today. Young adolescents in middle schools may live with

- two biological parents
- one biological parent
- one biological parent and a stepparent
- one stepparent
- grandparents
- aunts and uncles
- adult siblings
- foster families
- other students in a group home

It is not uncommon for students to "time share" in two houses because their parents have joint custody following a divorce. These houses may have any number of others living there as well (stepparent, stepsiblings, halfsiblings, etc.). Our migrant family population is also significant. These families often move repeatedly according to the season and the available work, so that children are in several different schools during the year. A relatively new family structure for which there are no statistics as yet are same-sex partners who choose to be parents. And we must never forget the children, who by themselves or in a variety of family units, find themselves homeless. In Figure 3.8, Peterson (1995) discusses the many ways the concept of family may be experienced by our students.

Involving the Family

All of these different family structures carry with them inherent strengths and weaknesses in terms of the amount of support offered to our students. When we hear teachers complain that more and more is expected of the school when it comes to "raising" children, it's easy to understand why the roles we play have been altered. We may be the central stability and only consistent factor in a student's life. Only by knowing the home situations and understanding the challenges of students whose lives we touch, will we know best how to help our students grow.

Getting to know the adults with whom our students live is more difficult in middle school when parental involvement often plummets. The parents of middle grades students are only half as likely to attend parent conferences as the parents of elementary students. Overall, parent involvement drops around the sixth grade (Downs, 2001). Stevenson (1992) tells us that the developmental changes occurring during young adolescence not only affect the children themselves, but everyone else in the household, too. Caissy (1994) says that

"Family" includes anyone who lives (or lived) together and may include grandparents, aunts and uncles, cousins, married older siblings, and even pets. It may also include persons in more than one household in cases of divorce and remarriage, especially when a child's time is regularly divided among them. "Extended family" usually refers to whatever generations of the family are still living, whether or not they live near each other. "Nuclear family" usually refers to parent(s) and children, although in today's circumstances that term might have a variety of meanings.

Depending on their cultural heritage, family traditions, and family situation, group members may have different perceptions of what a family is and what "family" means. It is important to be sensitive to, and accepting of all group members' situations and perceptions of "family." Some may even speak of close friends as family and may not want to speak at all of blood relatives they feel cut off from.

FIGURE 3.8   Defining family.

Source: Excerpted from *Talk with Teens About Feelings, Family, Relationships, and the Future : 50 Guided Discussions for School and Counseling Groups* by Jean Sunde Peterson, Ph.D. © 1995. Used with permission from Free Spirit Publishing Inc., Minneapolis, MN; 1-866-703-7322; *www.freespirit.com*. All rights reserved.

parents/guardians are often caught off guard by the rapid and unexpected changes they see in their young adolescents. Adults in the home are confused and often look for faults on which to blame behavior changes, not recognizing that many of the changes have very little to do with them. As students strive for greater independence, the adults in their homes may interpret the struggle, rightly or wrongly, as a signal to disengage (Downs, 2001). When students enter middle school, they leave what many experience as the comfort zone of the self-contained elementary classroom. Schooling becomes more complex with class changes, course options, and larger numbers of students with which to contend. Middle school parents or guardians often feel as if they are lost in the maze. Their attitudes may turn to merely hoping to survive the middle grades.

Parents and other adults in the home play significant roles in the academic achievement of middle school students. Teachers often tell us that lack of home support is a major obstacle to raising student achievement (L'Esperance & Gabbard, 2001). So far, the picture I've painted of family and home structures of our middle grades students has been generally negative. We need to acknowledge, however, that there may be many adults in the lives of our students who are very supportive. There are whole schools that experience overwhelming support from the majority of parents and guardians, resulting in an environment conducive to increased student achievement. This valuable partnership should be nurtured so that we are not guilty of Fege's (2000) lament of, "Twenty-first century families attempting to partner with twentieth-century school organizations" (p. 40). He encourages us to accommodate parents/adults in our students' education by offering unique settings such as weekend and weeknight volunteer opportunities, child care, and transportation. In Chapter 12 we will explore ways to make the most of family and home structures to the benefit of our students.

ACADEMIC DIFFERENCES

All young adolescents should have the opportunity to succeed in every aspect of the middle grade program, regardless of previous achievement or the pace at which they learn.

Carnegie Foundation, 1989, p. 49

As discussed in Chapter 2, middle grades students experience intellectual development at varying rates and to varying degrees. This variance, along with other developmental changes taking place within the context of a student's world, contributes to academic success, or the lack of it. Stevenson (1992) cautions us against expecting all students to learn the same things in the same ways at the same rate.

Ability and Effort

Academic success is dependent on both ability and effort. In any heterogeneous middle school classroom, we may find IQ scores ranging from about 70 to 140 and beyond. In terms of effort, the variability would be just as wide. As shown in Figure 3.9, the wide variances in, and interplay between, both IQ and level of effort can lead to failure by very capable students as well as success by only marginally capable ones. Most students exhibit moderate levels of both IQ and effort. It is our responsibility as educators to attend to both ability and effort.

Self-Worth Theory and Underachievement

We have explored the role that developing self-esteem plays in the lives of young adolescents. Strahan (1997) tells us that how students perceive ability and effort is a critical factor in a student's academic self-esteem. He says that if students experience academic success, they will assign more importance to academic self-esteem. On the other hand, if students do poorly in school, they face a difficult psychological dilemma. In an attempt to preserve some measure of self-esteem, these students will discount academics. They may adopt a "school doesn't matter" attitude. Covington (1984) says that when children are young, they

High IQ	Low Effort	May or May Not Succeed
High Effort	Low IQ	May or May Not Succeed

Will Succeed   Will Not Succeed

FIGURE 3.9   Effects of IQ and effort on academic success.

see ability and effort as one and the same. If they try hard, they are successful. By middle grades, students tend to see the "smart" kids appearing not to try as hard for good grades. Assuming that if you have ability, effort isn't important, their logic leads them to believe that if you have to try hard, you must not be very "smart." In an attempt to avoid failure, students may appear not to try so they can get away from feeling unable. They may display lack of effort, procrastination, putting blame on others, and purposefully turning in wrong assignments. Strahan (1997) cautions us that if these behaviors are " . . . unchecked, these failure-avoiding tactics can become self-fulfilling prophecies and make it increasingly difficult for students to succeed" (p. 37).

We can equate one of Covington's sample behaviors, devaluation, to one of the causes of underachievement. Psychologist Sylvia Rimm (1997) tells us that when academically unsuccessful students complain that the work is boring, they may be masking feelings of inadequacy. Here's how she defines *underachievement:* "Underachievement is a discrepancy between a child's school performance and some index of the child's ability. If children are not working to their ability in school, they are underachieving" (p. 18). Our role as educators should include recognizing when our students are not working up to their potential, and then taking appropriate action.

Academic differences exist, whether stemming from levels of ability or levels of effort. Williamson and Johnston (1998) give us an appropriate challenge when they write, "High achieving schools, where all students succeed, embrace the conversations about achievement, about rigor and challenge, about raising standards, and about serving students more appropriately. They understand the importance of achievement and unabashedly promote it as their school's primary goal"(p. 8). Our mission is to meet students where they are in terms of ability and effort and then find ways to design/choose curriculum, instructional strategies, and assessments to move them forward.

STUDENTS WITH SPECIAL NEEDS

> *Including 'special needs' students in general education classrooms can be challenging for teachers, administrators, and students—but it is well worth the effort. . . . All students should have the opportunity to learn with their peers, not because it's required by law but because it's right.*
>
> Ruder, 2000, p. 49

More than 5 million students are receiving special services in American public schools. The delivery of these special services is the source of continual controversy regarding which students to serve, and how and where to serve them. This section is a broad overview rather than a comprehensive look at special services for students with special needs.

History of Services

The "official" history of special services delivery is very recent. Until 1975, a student with disabilities was accorded no federal rights to an education. Children with disabilities were often denied access to public education and placed in separate schools to be educated, often minimally, with other children with disabilities. The legislative act known as the 1975 Education for All Handicapped Act (PL 94–142) mandated, among other things, that all children with handicaps be given the right to a free and appropriate public education in the *Least Restrictive Environment (LRE)* guided by an *Individualized Education Plan (IEP)*. All handicapped children are entitled to a nondiscriminatory evaluation and parental participation in the development of the IEP (Rasool & Curtis, 2000).

In 1990, PL 94–142 was renewed as the *Individuals with Disabilities Education Act (IDEA)*. The disabilities listed in the 1990 law include autism, deafness, deaf-blindness, hearing impairment, mental retardation, multiple disabilities, orthopedic impairments, other health impairments, serious emotional disturbance, specific learning disabilities, speech or language impairments, traumatic brain injuries, and visual impairments. The 1990 legislation reiterated the principles of the 1975 law and added guidelines for transitioning of students. Grade-to-grade transitions for regular education students are generally uneventful, requiring minimal support. However, for students with developmental disabilities, transitions may be quite traumatic.

In 1997, the law was reauthorized with an emphasis on accountability, requiring districts and states to include students with disabilities in their assessment plans and to provide appropriate alternative assessments when needed. Other highlights included the mandate for schools to support professional development for all staff to better involve them in the IEP process and to raise academic expectations and performances of students with disabilities. The law also called for more involvement of students with disabilities in extracurricular activities (Rasool & Curtis, 2000).

Inclusion

Rather than focusing on who is served and how, the most hotly debated question may be where to serve students with disabilities. The Least Restrictive Environment in a school is the regular classroom. The assignment of students to the regular classroom for some or all of the day is known as *inclusion* (*mainstreaming* is a term often used interchangeably with inclusion). Because middle school philosophy espouses heterogeneity in learning settings, inclusion is a natural fit. Inclusion supports social development and awareness as it gives all students the opportunity to interact.

> The shift to inclusion profoundly affects both teachers and students, not only in classrooms, but throughout the school environment. . . . Thus, inclusion of special needs students implies more than a policy decision, it entails a profound shift in the ways people view themselves, their actions, and their peers in and around school. (Deering, 1998, pp. 12–13)

Students receiving special education services generally require an Individualized Education Plan. Since the writing of IEPs involves both special education and regular classroom teachers, placement of students in inclusive settings is a collaborative effort. While most general education teachers agree that inclusion can be a positive practice, they don't necessarily feel adequately prepared to serve the wide range of needs often accompanying inclusion. In fact, not all parents of children with disabilities believe that neighborhood schools are capable of providing the desired services for their children (Crockett & Kauffman, 1998). Ruder (2000) tells us that for teachers the two biggest enemies of successful inclusion are time and fear: time to plan, to search for resources, to assess needs, and so on, and fear of moving beyond their comfort zone and failing to meet the needs of all students. To be successful, inclusion requires close collaboration among staff members and, ideally, a special educator actually present in the regular education classroom.

Schools are required by IDEA to have a continuum of alternative placements available that vary in terms of restrictiveness since a particular level of inclusion is not mandated by law. The "where" of the delivery of services is based on the individual student's IEP and must be revisited annually. Placement decisions often pose scheduling difficulties, as well as staffing, planning, and resource dilemmas. No single model of services can be prescribed (Doelling, Bryde, Brunner, & Martin, 1998).

Learning Disabled

Many students with special needs are designated as part of the broad category of *Learning Disabled (LD)*. Having a learning disability does not imply a low level of intelligence. Students with learning disabilities may have great strengths in some areas and experience difficulties in others. LD students learn differently and in most cases benefit from instructional strategies that help them cope with whatever those differences may be in terms of perceiving, listening, remembering, organizing, generalizing, and conceptualizing. Since students are usually labeled as LD because they are not performing satisfactorily in the regular classroom setting, why would we identify them and then place them back in the regular setting exclusively? Recent studies show that many LD students are slipping behind at disturbing rates. Holloway (2001) reports a study showing that a combination of regular education and special education services yielded the highest achievement, while total inclusion showed the lowest achievement results. Most schools have teachers who work with students with learning disabilities during one or more class periods a day and are referred to as resource teachers.

Attention Deficit Disorder

Encountered more and more in the classroom, and only coincidentally assigned to any kind of special education setting, are those with *Attention Deficit Disorder (ADD)* and *Attention Deficit Hyperactivity Disorder (ADHD)*. Students are not considered disabled because of a diagnosis of ADD or ADHD. ADD students try to pay attention to everything rather than focusing attention on the task at hand. ADHD adds two dimensions to ADD—hyperactivity and impulsivity. Hyperactivity is defined as "age-inappropriate increased activity in multiple settings" while impulsivity refers to the "tendency to act rashly and without judgment or consideration" (Schlozman & Schlozman, 2000, p. 28). Most researchers say that ADD and ADHD have biological causes and behavioral symptoms. To be diagnosed with either, symptoms must be excessive and long-term. More than 3% of all children under 19 are on medication such as Ritalin in attempts to manage ADD and ADHD. In some schools, as many as 10% of the students are on medication for ADD and ADHD (Jensen, 1998).

Many educators and researchers think that ADHD is overdiagnosed and/or misdiagnosed. They say the causes of disruptive behavior often associated with ADHD may actually be from overcrowded classrooms, lack of self-discipline skills, or teachers who demand inappropriate amounts of attention. Still others bemoan the fact that many students whom they suspect have the disorder go undiagnosed and experience what Jensen (1998, p. 50) calls "a horror movie they can't escape."

The symptoms of ADD and ADHD may be mild to extreme within a class that includes a number of diagnosed students, or within a single day, with a single child. Schlozman and Schlozman (2000) tell us that "Tight budgets, large classrooms, and often multiple students with the same diagnosis who require different teaching strategies substantially challenge the educator's primary objective: to teach and inspire every student dynamically and efficiently" (p. 28). In addition to medication, behavioral treatments may be used in the classroom—social skills groups, daily report cards, positive reinforcement, preferred seating, "time out" arrangements, and so on. Jensen (1998) suggests a "rich balance of novelty and ritual" (p. 50). Of course, that's a good prescription for classroom instruction for all kids!

REFLECTIONS ON CELEBRATING DIVERSITY

We have explored a variety of diversity issues and should consider both the richness these differences represent, and the opportunities they lend, as we plan all aspects of our classrooms. Our responsibility is to affirm each individual and help all students appreciate each other both for what they have in common and for the diversity that is inevitable. The days of teaching homogeneous classes of students in our public schools may be in the past. As the demographics of the population of the United States shift and change, our classrooms will become more diverse places. Creating environments that go beyond tolerance of diversity in its many forms to a real celebration of diversity both in the classroom and in the school, should be a major goal of middle level education. "In a world in which we are trying to recognize, accept, appreciate, and champion differences, we must teach our children how their differences can be used to make a positive impact" (Caram, 2001, p. 73).

MEET THE STUDENTS

Let's take a look at how our 10 students from Chapter 2 exhibit even more diversity than was apparent when we were introduced to some of their developmental characteristics. It would be a good idea to reread each student's introduction in Chapter 2 before reading these additional descriptions.

Michael, *sixth grade*

Michael, our student who has already been retained 2 years, has a genuine love of the outdoors. His favorite activity is camping with his dad and two stepbrothers. He lives with them and his stepmom, because his mother died when he was nine. When camping, he is the trailblazer, enjoying "roughing it" and finding ways to survive in the wild. He is White and lives in the house where his dad was raised in a small town that is the center of activity for a rural community. He has never been diagnosed with learning disabilities. In fact, he hasn't really caught the eye of teachers so far, possibly because he has pleasant social skills and is not a behavior problem.

Allison, *sixth grade*

Allison, our younger than average sixth grader, has many advantages her classmates do not have. She is White and lives in an exclusive, almost all White neighborhood with her biological parents and three younger siblings. Her dad and mom are both attorneys, but her mom has chosen to be a full-time homemaker. Allison has traveled extensively. She is on her neighborhood swim team, takes ballet lessons, and speaks French almost fluently.

Marvin, *sixth grade*

Marvin, our class clown who employs humor as a compensation for his size, has talents most of his teachers have not experienced. He is endowed with a beautiful voice and sings in his church choir. Marvin is Black and is an only child. He lives with his grandma, and they share a small house with his aunt and three of her children. Their home is loving, but economically insecure. Marvin was designated as gifted when he was in second grade, but his achievement was not at the required level to allow him to stay in pull-out gifted/talented classes in fourth and fifth grades. In sixth grade, his name was off the list for consideration.

Hector, *sixth grade*

Hector, our physically and academically talented student, is Hispanic and spent his first 4 years of school in a migrant farm situation. He was in and out of school, depending on fieldwork. His dad has now found a permanent job and his mom works part time while his little sister is in half-day kindergarten. He lives in a trailer park adjacent to a city park where he spends much of his time participating in local recreation department sports.

Jeanetta, *sixth grade*

Jeanetta, our tall lovely student, is the youngest of three girls in an African American family of educators. Her dad is a principal, and her mom is a teacher. Jeanetta's two older sisters are both in college and are talented and successful. Jeanetta spends a lot of time alone in her room.

Barry, *sixth grade*

Barry, AKA "Motormouth," lives with his mom and dad and a younger sister in an older, but very nice, neighborhood. He was a real challenge in the primary grades—smart, hyperactive, a real "bounce-off-the-wall" kind of child. As an elementary teacher his mom recognized that his tendencies indicated Attention Deficit Disorder, but hoped he might grow out of it or find a way to channel what appeared to be extra energy. However, when his tendencies interfered with his learning, she had him tested. He was diagnosed with ADHD and began a regimen of Ritalin.

Mia, *sixth grade*

Mia, our quiet loner, is a third-generation Asian American with a distinguishing feature. She must wear a hearing aid to correct her hearing enough to function in school. Mia is an only child and has spent most of her time with her mom and dad. Her dad manages a small grocery store, and her mom stays at home. They live in an apartment above the store. Although they are a family of below-average income, they enjoy time together listening to classical music, visiting museums, and sharing books.

Anthony, *sixth grade*

Anthony, our sometimes-moody student, is Black. He lives with his mom and four brothers and sisters in a duplex in a government-supported housing project. Anthony's two older brothers dropped out of school when they were 16. They still live at home, at least part of the time. His two younger school-age sisters are his responsibility until his mom gets home about 7 p.m. each weeknight. Anthony helps them with their homework.

Darlene, *sixth grade*

Darlene, our friendly student with a bright smile, is Hispanic. Her parents were killed in a car accident when Darlene was two. She doesn't remember them, but her aunt and uncle and older sister with whom she lives keep their memory alive. They have a stable, loving home in a mostly Hispanic neighborhood.

Lee, *sixth grade*

Lee, our avid reader, is part of a large household. His mom and dad and grandparents moved to the United States from Cambodia while his mom was pregnant with him. Since then, his family has grown with the birth of two sisters and a brother. The adults in his home speak very little English. Lee's neighbor, a retired schoolteacher, has taken him under her wing and tutored him since he started school. She has instilled in him a love of books.

Group Activities

1. Refer to your class file of local middle schools. Divide them among class members to find the total number of students, the percentage of free and reduced lunch students, and a breakdown of racial identification in each school. All schools should have this data. They may refer you to the district office. If so, only one call may be necessary to acquire the information. Add the data to your class file.

2. Together, brainstorm ways that you as middle school teachers might help create an appreciation of diversity among your students.

Individual Activities

1. Why is it important for your students to understand their particular strengths in terms of multiple intelligences? Is there value in students understanding the areas where they have less strength?

2. Choose a subject area and a topic you can imagine teaching. Think of ways you might approach the topic that could address each of the four learning modalities. Write a brief description of each approach and be ready to share your ideas with your class.

Personal Journal

1. Describe yourself in terms of the diversity categories in Chapter 3.

2. Did you experience any kind of prejudice because of ways you may have been different from other kids in middle school? This may be painful to remember, but "reliving" it and writing about it may lead you toward a better understanding of your students.

3. Are there certain areas of diversity that make you more uncomfortable than others? Do you have personal experiences that contribute to your comfort levels?

Professional Practice

(It would be helpful to reread the descriptions of Allison, Jeanetta, Darlene, and Lee in Chapter 2.)

Mr. Duncan has taught science at Harvest Middle School for 22 years. He majored in biology in college and has a minor in secondary education. He had planned to teach high school but, like so many in the early 1980s, found science high school teaching positions few and far between. (Hard to imagine today!) So Mr. Duncan took a position at Harvest Middle School where he teaches sixth grade science.

Jeffery Duncan

Mr. Duncan is a subject area teacher first and foremost. He prefers organization around disciplines rather than what *Turning Points* refers to as "small learning communities." When Harvest Middle School abandoned ability grouping in science he was quite distressed. He was comfortable teaching a "high" group, two "middle" groups, and a "low" group. Then middle school philosophy hit his district, and hit it hard, in the early 1990s. The sign out front changed from Harvest Junior High to Harvest Middle School. The change brought heterogeneous grouping, and Mr. Duncan had to adapt. He really likes his students and sincerely wants to help each one learn, so he adjusted his teaching techniques and expectations, and took the loss of tracking in stride. Now his principal has some news that he's not quite sure he can handle. Students designated as those with special needs will join his science classes, now that these students are evenly distributed among all sixth grade teachers and not just placed with one team (small community of learners). He was told this in August, just 2 weeks before school began. As Mr. Duncan looks at the roll of his third period class, he sees 22 "regular" students, including Allison, Jeanetta, Darlene, and Lee. His list also includes a student with cerebral palsy who is confined to a wheelchair and a student with a hearing disability that will require Mr. Duncan to wear a voice amplification box around his neck during the class period. Mr. Duncan is apprehensive.

1. Mr. Duncan has been told that an aide will escort the student with cerebral palsy to and from his class. She will stay for at least part of each class period, but has another student to check on as well. Given what you know about his third period class, which student would you recommend that Mr. Duncan ask to help the student with special needs with lab activities?

(a) Darlene

(b) Allison

(c) Lee

(d) Jeanetta

2. Mr. Duncan is accustomed to relying on two basic methods of teaching—lecture and lab work. He has always felt that verbal directions for the labs were sufficient. Which of the following is least relevant to any changes Mr. Duncan may need to make in the planning process for the school year?

(a) The concept of Least Restrictive Environment will change the day-to-day operation in his classes.

(b) It appears Mr. Duncan has not been as conscious of learning modalities as he may need to be.

(c) Mr. Duncan has been asked by his principal to continue to make clear to students which state standards he is addressing in his lessons.

(d) The student with a hearing impairment will likely benefit from visual reinforcement.

Constructed Response

Mr. Duncan's team of teachers have decided to have all their students complete a questionnaire that will help determine their strengths in terms of multiple intelligences. You know a little about six of the students in Mr. Duncan's third period class. Choose the three students you think will benefit most from this initiative and tell why you chose them.

Internet Resources

American Medical Association

http://www.ama-assn.org/

This AMA web site focuses on adolescent health issues, including fighting unhealthy behaviors and information on preventive services. Parenting resources are included along with links to articles about adolescent health.

Council for Exceptional Children (CEC)

http://www.cec.sped.org

The CEC is an international professional organization dedicated to improving education outcomes for individuals with exceptionalities, students with disabilities, and gifted students. This site gives information about professional development, publications, and conferences along with links to articles and other organizations.

Inclusive Education
http://www.uni.edu/coe/inclusion/index.html

> This site gives practical information to teachers, administrators, and parents about how to implement inclusive practices. Resources are provided along with links to other sites about inclusive education.

Multiple Intelligences Development Assessment Scales (MIDAS)
http://www.angelfire.com/oh/themidas/index.html

> This site concentrates on characteristics of students as exhibited through Howard Gardner's theory of multiple intelligences.

National Institute on the Education of At-Risk Students
http://www.ed.gov/offices/OERI/At-Risk/

> This organization is supported by the U.S. Department of Education and sponsors a wide range of research and development activities designed to improve the education of students who are at risk for failure due to poverty, race, geographic location, socioeconomic status, and/or limited proficiency in English.

Texas Education Network
http://www.tenet.edu/halls/multiculturalism.html

> This site provides an extensive list of other web sites, many addressing issues related to multicultural education.

References

Anderson, J. D. (1997). Supporting the invisible minority. *Educational Leadership, 54*(7), 65–68.

Banks, J. A. (1990). *Preparing teachers and administrators in a multicultural society.* Austin, TX: Southwest Development Laboratory.

Banks, J. A. (1991). *Teaching strategies for ethnic studies* (5th ed.). Boston, MA: Allyn & Bacon.

Caissy, G. A. (1994). *Early adolescence: Understanding the 10 to 15 year old.* Reading, MA: Perseus Books.

Caram, C. A. (2001). The best-kept secret in at-risk education. *Kappa Delta Pi Record, 37*(2), 70–73.

Carbo, M. (Ed.). (1995). Educating everybody's children. In *Educating everybody's children: Diverse teaching strategies for diverse learners.* (pp. 1–7). Alexandria, VA: Association for Supervision and Curriculum Development.

Carger, C. L. (1997). Attending to new voices. *Educational Leadership, 54*(7), 39–43.

Carnegie Council on Adolescent Development. (1989). *Turning points: Preparing American youth for the 21st century.* Washington, DC: Author.

Chesbro, J., Berko, R., Hopson, C., Cooper, P., & Hodges, H. (1995). Strategies for increasing achievement in oral communication. In *Educating everybody's children* (pp. 139–165). Alexandria, VA: Association for Supervision and Curriculum Development.

Covington, M. V. (1984). The self-worth theory of achievement motivation: Findings and implications. *Elementary School Journal, 85,* 5–19.

Crockett, J. B., & Kauffman, J. M. (1998). Taking inclusion back to its roots. *Educational Leadership, 56*(2), 74–77.

Deering, P. D. (1998). Making comprehensive inclusion of special needs students work in a middle school. *Middle School Journal, 29*(3), 12–19.

Doelling, J. E., Bryde, S., Brunner, J., & Martin, B. (1998). Collaborative planning for inclusion of a student with developmental disabilities. *Middle School Journal, 29*(3), 34–39.

Downs, A. (2001). It's all in the family. *Middle Ground, 4*(3), 10–15.

Dunn, R. (1997). The goals and track record of multicultural education. *Educational Leadership, 57*(7), 74–77.

Edwards, A. T. (1997). Let's stop ignoring our gay and lesbian youth. *Educational Leadership, 54* (7), 39–43.

Fege, A. F. (2000). From fund raising to hell raising: New roles for parents. *Educational Leadership, 57*(7), 68–70.

Forte, I., & Schurr, S. (1993). *The definitive middle school guide: A handbook for success.* Nashville, TN: Incentive Publications.

Gardner, H. (1999). *The disciplined mind: What all students should understand.* New York: Simon & Schuster.

Gober, D. A., & Mewborn, D. S. (2001). Promoting equity in mathematics classrooms. *Middle School Journal, 32*(3), 31–35.

Hodges, H. (1995). Preface. In R. W. Cole (Ed.). *Educating everybody's children: Diverse teaching strategies for diverse learners.* Alexandria, VA: Association for Supervision and Curriculum Development.

Holloway, J. H. (2001). Inclusion and students with learning disabilities. *Educational Leadership, 58*(6), 86–88.

Jensen, E. (1998). *Teaching with the brain in mind.* Alexandria, VA: Association for Supervision and Curriculum Development.

Johnson, L. (1998). *Two parts textbook, one part love: A recipe for successful teaching.* New York: Hyperion.

Jorgenson, O. (2001). Supporting a diverse teaching corps. *Educational Leadership, 58*(8), 64–67.

Jung, C. (1923). Psychological types. (H. G. Baynes, Trans.) New York: Harcourt Brace.

Kahlenberg, R. D. (2000). The new economic school desegregation. *Educational Leadership, 57*(7), 16–19.

Kellough, R. D., & Kellough, N. G. (1999). *Middle school teaching: A guide to methods and resources* (3rd ed.). Upper Saddle River, NJ: Merrill/Prentice Hall.

Kindlon, D. J., & Thompson, M. (1999). *Raising Cain: Protecting the emotional life of boys.* New York: Ballantine Books.

Knowles, T., & Brown, D. F. (2000). *What every middle school teacher should know.* Westerville, OH: National Middle School Association.

L'Esperance, M. E., & Gabbard, D. (2001). Empowering all parents. *Middle Ground, 4*(3), 17–18.

McCarthy, B. (1997). A tale of four learners: 4 MAT's learning styles. *Educational Leadership, 54*(6), 47–51.

Mamchur, C. (1996). *A teacher's guide to cognitive type theory & learning style.* Alexandria, VA: Association for Supervision and Curriculum Development.

Mee, C. S. (1997). *2,000 voices: Young adolescents' perceptions & curriculum implications.* Columbus, OH: National Middle School Association.

Milgram, J. (1992). A portrait of diversity: The middle level student. In J. L. Irvin (Ed.). *Transforming middle level education: Perspectives and possibilities* (pp. 16–27). Needham Heights, MA: Allyn & Bacon.

Perkins, D., Jay, E., & Tishman, S. (1993). Beyond abilities: A dispositional theory of thinking. *Merrill-Palmer Quarterly, 39*(1), 1–21.

Peterson, J. S. (1995). *Talk with teens about feelings, family, relationships, and the future: 50 guided discussions for school and counseling groups.* Minneapolis, MN: Free Spirit Publishing.

Pipher, M. (1994). *Reviving Ophelia: Saving the selves of adolescent girls.* New York: G. P. Putnam's Sons.

Puma, M., Karweit, C., Ricciuti, A., Thompson, W., & Vaden-Keirman, M. (1997). *Prospects: Final report on student outcome.* Cambridge, MA: Abt. Associates.

Rasool, J. A., & Curtis, A. C. (2000). *Multicultural education in middle and secondary classrooms: Meeting the challenge of diversity and change.* Belmont, CA: Wadsworth/ Thomson Learning.

Rimm, S. (1997). An underachieving epidemic. *Educational Leadership, 54*(7), 18–22.

Rubinstein, R. E. (1994). *Hints for teaching success in middle school.* Englewood, CO: Teacher Ideas Press.

Ruder, S. (2000). We teach all. *Educational Leadership, 58*(1), 49–51.

Schlozman, S. C., & Schlozman, V. R. (2000). Chaos in the classroom: Looking at ADHD. *Educational Leadership, 58*(3), 28–33.

Silver, H. F., Strong, R. W., & Perini, M. J. (2000). *So each may learn: Integrating learning styles and multiple intelligences.* Alexandria, VA: Association for Supervision and Curriculum Development.

Stevenson, C. (1992). *Teaching ten to fourteen year olds.* White Plains, NY: Longman.

Strahan, D. B. (1997). *Mindful learning: Teaching self-discipline and academic achievement.* Durham, NC: Carolina Academic Press.

Taylor, A. T. (2000, March/April). Meeting the needs of lesbian and gay young adolescents. *The Clearing House,* 221–224.

Teemant, A., Bernhardt, E. B., Rodriquez-Munoz, M., & Aiello, M. (2000). A dialogue among teachers that benefits second language learners. *Middle School Journal, 32*(2), 30–38.

Tomlinson, C. A., Moon, T. R., & Callahan, C. M. (1998). How well are we addressing academic diversity in the middle schools? *Middle School Journal, 29*(3), 3–11.

Wardle, F. (2000). Children of mixed race: No longer invisible. *Educational Leadership, 57*(4), 68–72.

Wellstone, P. (1995). If poverty is the question . . . *Nation, 264*(14), 15–18.

Williamson, R. D., & Johnston, J. H. (Eds.). (1998). *Able learners in the middle level school: Identifying talent and maximizing potential.* Reston, VA: National Association of Secondary School Principals.

Willis, J. K., & Johnson, A. N. (2001). Multiply with MI: Using multiple intelligences to master multiplication. *Teaching Children Mathematics, 7*(5), 260–269.

Wlodkowlski, R. J., & Ginsberg, M. B. (1995). *Diversity and motivation.* San Francisco: Jossey-Bass.

4

Middle Level Teachers

Middle level teachers are special. Those who observe them day after day presiding over their volatile, active charges know they have a distinctive quality that sets them apart from elementary and high school teachers. Their example, their caring, along with the effectiveness of their instruction have enduring influence. Perhaps more than any other group of teachers, middle level teachers shape the future.

Arth, Lounsbury, McEwin, and Swaim, 1995, p. 1

Use this diagram as an organizational tool. In the boxes beside the chapter headings, indicate the dates by which the reading should be completed.

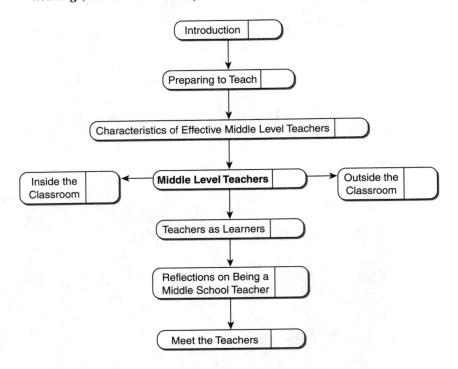

INTRODUCTION

As a young girl I vividly remember "playing school." Of course, I was always in the role of teacher. In my bedroom, I lined up my stuffed animals and dolls and held class on a regular basis. I loved school supplies (and I still do!). I was delighted by a new box of 64 crayons—who would not be thrilled by the sight of a periwinkle blue that had never touched a drawing pad! How about a new Big Chief tablet with freshly sharpened pencils? I liked school. The thought of being a teacher directed my behavior as a student. I wanted to please my teachers, to have them know they could rely on me to make their jobs easier. OK, so I was a geek. But I know there are others just like me who have come to realize—but perhaps won't admit it publicly—that the desire to teach may have its roots in utero!

While most middle grades teachers prepare for the profession in traditional university schools of education, there are a growing number of teachers who enter the profession as a second or third career. They have been successful engineers, full-time homemakers, business executives, factory workers, or military men and women—you name it, and we probably have teachers who have done it. Whether the "calling" to be a teacher comes early or later in life makes absolutely no difference. The enthusiasm of youth or the wisdom gained through life's experiences are both invaluable in the classroom. So from "always knowing it" to "I'm ready for a change," and every degree in between, we have teachers dedicating their professional lives to the welfare of children. Many elementary teachers report choosing the career of teaching because they love children. Many high school teachers report choosing the career because they love their particular subject area. Here we are between the two. We draw from the richness of both. A commitment to students in the middle grades entails caring for them as special individuals as well as both caring about, and knowing deeply, our chosen subject.

We come to the profession for a variety of reasons and with an even greater variety of perspectives. This diversity is strength. Fortunate are the middle school students who travel from class to class during the course of the day, greeted by men and women who present positive role models of adulthood garbed in personalities and life experiences. While we each have our own unique teacher fingerprints, we immerse ourselves in the lives of our students. Michael Fullan (1993), noted expert on the subject of educational change, tells us that "teaching at its core is a moral profession. Scratch a teacher and you will find a moral purpose" (p. 12). Public Agenda conducted an in-depth survey of more than 900 teachers who had been in the classroom for 5 years or less. The results, shown in Figure 4.1, are reported in *Educational Leadership*, May 2001. They reveal teaching to be a satisfying profession.

Eighty-six percent of the teachers in the Public Agenda survey believe that only those with "a true sense of calling" should pursue the profession of teaching. Overwhelmingly they pointed out that our profession requires a sense of mission; so although we express our individuality in the classroom, we seem to share a common notion of calling. In his insightful book *Meet Me in the Middle*, Rick Wormeli (2001) says, "It is a privilege to be in education. Not everyone is called to such a noble cause" (p. 1).

Teaching is a profession that just about everyone in the United States feels qualified to critique. We were all students, weren't we? We had good teachers and bad teachers, and those of every descriptor in between. Because we all went to school, sizing up the teachers in classrooms across the country is something that many feel

---

Percentage of teachers who have taught five years or less who say:

Teaching is work they love to do   **96%**

They would choose teaching again if starting over   **80%**

Teaching is a lifelong choice   **75%**

They get a lot of satisfaction out of teaching   **68%**

They fell into teaching by chance   **12%**

FIGURE 4.1   Why we teach.

Source: From "Why New Teachers Choose to Teach," by D. Wadsworth, 2001, *Educational Leadership, 58*(8), p. 25. Copyright 2001 by Association for Supervision and Curriculum Development. Adapted with permission.

obliged to do—and rightly so. Most of us have spent 12 years, many of us 16 years, and a considerable number 20 plus years in the classroom as students. We have been on the receiving end and can justifiably offer criticisms and suggestions. Public school teachers are paid with public funds collected from "we the people." Public engagement is to be expected, the more positively directed the better. We would be hard pressed to find a politician anywhere who has not placed education near the top of his or her agenda. Scrutiny, criticism, quickly formulated and loudly expressed opinions, and occasional greatly appreciated support all come our way.

Consider how teachers are portrayed in movies. This is a particularly good thing to do after a tough week in the classroom. On the flattering side, we have "Stand and Deliver" in which Edward James Olmos stars as Jaime Escalante who shows his dedication and skill in teaching kids at Garfield High School in East Los Angeles. And how about Michelle Pfiefer portraying the real life of LouAnne Johnson in "Dangerous Minds"? Pfiefer and Johnson, both knockouts in real life, show us how to tame some incorrigibles with the "you're not going to get the best of me" attitude that leads to student learning. Fictional teachers inspire us in "Mr. Holland's Opus," "The Prime of Miss Jean Brodie," "Up the Down Staircase," "To Sir, With Love," and "Goodbye, Mr. Chips." These movies resonate positively with most viewers. For laughs, there are a couple of movies I occasionally pop into the VCR that portray teachers in less than glowing light. "Fast Times at Ridgemont High" stars Sean Penn as a surfer dude who challenges his teachers at every turn. A movie that makes me smile at the very thought of it—and laugh out loud from the opening scene to the closing credits—is "Ferris Bueller's Day Off." Ferris, portrayed with sheer genius by Matthew Broderick, and his friends use every ploy imaginable to fool the system. After years of therapy (not really!) I have concluded that I am so enamored of Ferris because he is the opposite of my geekish self that I described earlier. What many people remember about teaching and teachers from "Ferris Bueller's Day Off" is the character played by Ben Stein, who attempts to illicit student responses concerning the Hawley Smoot Tariff Act with his monotone drone "Anyone? . . . Anyone?" While these last two movies should never be considered staff development tools, they do give us occasion to laugh and be good sports.

Any profession that calls for dedication, selfless giving, patience, and creativity will also necessitate renewal. In Chapters 2 and 3 we took an in-depth look at the students who fill our middle grade classrooms. If ever there was a challenging profession, teaching young adolescents is it! Later in this chapter, we'll discuss ways to bolster our resolve and renew our spirits through reflection and continual learning. While pep talks and chants, as seen occasionally in news magazine shows, seem to do the trick, at least temporarily, for Wal-Mart employees, auto manufacturing workers, and Mary Kay sales associates, they have little to do with the way we respond to students, parents, and administrators on a daily basis. Renewing our resolve as teachers must resonate in very personal ways. In *The Courage to Teach*, Parker Palmer (1998) tells us that the "self-hood of the teacher is key" (p. 7). He encourages us to recover continually "the inner resources that good teaching always requires" (p. 7). Maintaining inner balance is vital, but at times difficult, in this profession filled with ups and downs. Knowles and Brown (2000) exhort us, "Hold onto your hat. We believe working with young adolescents will be the most exhilarating ride you will ever take" (p. 7).

PREPARING TO TEACH

We come to the middle school classroom equipped with different knowledge, skills, and dispositions obtained in a variety of ways: some through a school of education four-year degree program, some through graduate programs in education, some through alternative programs necessitated most recently by the need for more classroom teachers. Teacher certification requirements vary by state.

Standard 7

Knowledge 1: Middle level teacher candidates understand their evolving role as middle level education professionals.

The NMSA Middle Level Teacher Preparation Standards discussed in Chapter 1 are based on an earlier set of standards outlined in 1995. These standards for middle level teacher preparation programs were validated in a 1999 study conducted by McEwin, Dickinson, and Hamilton (2000). Of the first 81 teachers to successfully obtain National Board Certified Young Adolescence/Generalist certification, 73 responded to open-ended questions concerning preparation. (National Board Certification will be discussed later in this chapter.) All of them responded "yes" when asked, "Are there important ideas, principles, understandings that an effective middle level teacher needs to know?" When asked to give examples, their responses included statements about the uniqueness of young adolescence, the importance of the learning environment, the value of active interdisciplinary instruction, the need to work cooperatively in teams, and the need to know content well. The authors note that "Clearly, the pattern of responses from these highly accomplished teachers offer further confirmation of the importance of specialized middle level teacher preparation programs" (p. 213).

The fact that you are reading this book indicates that you are likely to be part of a college class studying middle level education. Terrific! This may be the only course you take focusing exclusively on the education of young adolescents, or it may be part of a comprehensive middle level program. Keep in mind that while textbooks, and class discussions and lectures by middle grades experts provide background knowledge, most of the skills you will need to be successful teachers at the middle level will be learned on the job. David Berliner, a noted researcher in the area of teacher expertise, says that we cannot completely pre-train teachers and that a college degree prepares us to be beginners in the complex world of the classroom (Scherer, 2001). We hope to emerge from teacher preparation programs with understanding and skills, but knowing when and how to apply our learning takes real-life situations to see how to pull strategies apart and determine how best to use them to meet the needs of particular students (Tolan, 2001). The National Board Certified teachers referred to earlier recommend that middle level teacher preparation include, beyond "book learnin'," more real-life experiences with students and teachers in the classroom (McEwin et al., 2000). These experiences may be part of your preparation program. If not, I highly recommend that you pursue them on your own. You will not be alone in your pursuit. Scales and McEwin (1994) tell us that

Middle grades preservice teachers, cooperating teachers, and teacher educators comprise a system trying to become more effectively coordinated than ever before. As it develops, the system reveals both growing pains and its promise. . . . Through the difficult growth, a generation of comprehensively prepared teachers will emerge, teachers who feel they have been given an excellent start and the promise of continuing support so they can really make a positive difference in the lives of young adolescents. Our teachers and our youth deserve no less. (pp. 80–81)

CHARACTERISTICS OF EFFECTIVE MIDDLE LEVEL TEACHERS

I've come to the frightening conclusion that I am the decisive element in the classroom. It's my personal approach that creates climate. It's my daily mood that makes the weather. As a teacher, I possess a tremendous power to make a child's life miserable or joyous. I can be a tool of torture or an instrument of inspiration. I can humiliate or humor, hurt or heal. In all situations, it is my response that decides whether a crisis will be escalated or de-escalated, a child humanized or de-humanized. (Ginott, 1993, p. 15)

Being a teacher is an awesome responsibility. I purposefully focus on the Haim Ginott quote on a regular basis. It is posted in my office at the university and next to my desk at home. I give it to each of my students at the beginning of every semester. So how do we use this "tremendous power," accorded to us simply because we are teachers, in wise and positive ways? I firmly believe that teachers who understand that they have the power to make or break the experiences of young adolescents will seek out ways to be more effective. Once we understand that "we make the weather," the sobering reality of it should drive us to be the best teachers we can be.

From what we know about middle schoolers, we recognize that effectively teaching them requires us to do more than merely survive. We need to find ways to thrive. There are basic differences between surviving and thriving in the classroom—the main difference being the ability to balance conflicting demands of the profession. On one hand, we should teach "the whole child," nurturing their development in every way. On the other hand, we are held accountable for "covering" the curriculum and increasing test scores. Teachers who thrive, not merely survive, find ways to do both. They integrate their care for students as people with their efforts to enrich instruction and curriculum. John Lounsbury (1991) tells us, "There is no conflict between academic effectiveness and developmental responsiveness at the age of young adolescence" (p. 97). Supporting student development and structuring educational experiences in ways that promote success is what Strahan (1997) refers to as "caring in action."

In their book, *Middle Level Teachers: Portraits of Excellence* (1995), four major contributors to our knowledge of middle level education provide us with 16 research-based traits of effective middle level teachers. Al Arth, John Lounsbury, Ken McEwin, and John Swaim tell us that effective middle level teachers should strive to possess the characteristics listed in Figure 4.2.

As you continue reading this book, refer back often to this list of characteristics. You will be able to link them to structures within middle schools (Chapter 5), curriculum development (Chapter 6), instructional and assessment strategies (Chapters 7, 8, 9), lesson/unit planning (Chapter 10), learning environment creation and maintenance (Chapter 11), and relationships with parents and community (Chapter 12).

It is appropriate to listen to middle level students concerning their views of effective teachers. Ed Lawton, a respected expert in the field of middle level education, as well as my

1. Is sensitive to the individual differences, cultural backgrounds, and exceptionalities of young adolescents, treats them with respect, and celebrates their special nature.
2. Understands and welcomes the role of advocate, adult role model, and advisor.
3. Is self-confident and personally secure—can take student challenges while teaching.
4. Makes decisions about teaching based on a thorough understanding of the physical, social, intellectual, and emotional development of young adolescents.
5. Is dedicated to improving the welfare and education of young adolescents.
6. Works collaboratively and professionally to initiate needed changes.
7. Establishes and maintains a disciplined learning environment that is safe and respects the dignity of young adolescents.
8. Ensures that all young adolescents will succeed in learning.
9. Has a broad, interdisciplinary knowledge of the subjects in the middle level curriculum and depth of content knowledge in one or more areas.
10. Is committed to integrating curriculum.
11. Uses varied evaluation techniques that both teach and assess the broad goals of middle level education and provide for student self-evaluation.
12. Recognizes that major goals of middle level education include the development of humane values, respect for self, and positive attitudes toward learning.
13. Seeks out positive and constructive relationships and communicates with young adolescents in a variety of environments.
14. Works closely with families to form partnerships to help young adolescents be successful at school.
15. Utilizes a wide variety of developmentally appropriate instructional strategies.
16. Acquires, creates, and utilizes a wide variety of resources to improve the learning experiences of young adolescents.

FIGURE 4.2   The effective middle level teacher.

Source: From *Middle Level Teachers: Portraits of Excellence* (pp. 6–7), by A. E. Arth, J. H. Lounsbury, C. K. McEwin, and J. H. Swaim, 1995, Columbus, OH: National Middle School Association and National Association of Secondary School Principals. Reprinted with permission from National Middle School Association.

own personal mentor, wrote a monograph for the National Association of Secondary School Principals in 1993 titled *The Effective Middle Level Teacher.* In it he reports on comments of students at Prospect Heights Middle School in Orange, Virginia. Very simply, the students give us a clear picture of their views on good teachers and not-so-good teachers in Figure 4.3.

While lists of characteristics of effective teachers are important—the more traits we can claim as our own, the better—an important point must be made. Knowles and Brown (2000) tell us "any student will tell you that teachers cannot feign caring and believing in

Good Teachers . . .	Not-So-Good Teachers . . .
• make learning more fun	• are not prepared
• give clear instructions	• are always cranky
• give you ways to remember things	• make a lot of threats
• review before the test	• lecture students in front of the class
• let students know how they feel	• don't review tests
• change their tone of voice	• single kids out and make them feel bad
• don't take anger out on kids	• take it out on kids when they are in a bad mood
• demand students' attention	• don't say anything when you give a wrong answer
• care about students' feelings	• only teach one way
• are strict but not mean	• won't call on you
• treat kids with respect	• act like a kid
• get students involved doing projects and experiments	• spend too much time ragging on kids who don't do their work
• move around	• sit at desks and read magazines or books
• are organized, know what they are going to do	• tell students to read the chapter and don't give notes
• start classes right away	

FIGURE 4.3   Student perceptions of teacher effectiveness.

Source: From *The Effective Middle Level Teacher* (p.13), by E. Lawton, 1993, Reston, VA: National Association of Secondary School Principals. Reprinted with permission.

students. Your students know what you feel about them" (p. 54). Lawton refers to the genuine nature and sincerity of teachers as "authenticity" (p. 7). Our care and commitment should be nothing less than authentic.

 ## TEACHERS INSIDE THE CLASSROOM

Teaching is a profession that permeates who we are. At 4:00 p.m., we don't become frogs after being princes all day—and we certainly hope the opposite isn't true. Just like the poem says, a rose is a rose is a rose. And a teacher is a teacher is a teacher. This doesn't mean we have no lives outside the classroom. I do—and you will, too! However, your students, your lessons, your colleagues, your curriculum, and so on are never far from consciousness. The good things we do professionally, and the deep satisfaction that follows, give life a sweeter flavor. For organization's sake, I want us to think separately about life inside the classroom and life outside the classroom. When I say inside, I literally mean within the four walls. Outside the classroom will include other places—from the school hallways to the grocery store, from school board meetings to dozing in the overstuffed living room chair with a book in your lap and the TV blaring.

Most middle school teachers conduct three to six classes a day, each made up of 15 to 30 students. In Chapter 5 we will explore a variety of scheduling options that are frequently seen in middle school settings. Most elementary teachers teach the same 15 to 30 students all day in what we refer to as a self-contained setting. They have what some would consider the luxury of seeing the whole child as the day progresses, as moods ebb and flow, as subject areas intertwine, as progress is made or not made. The middle school teacher generally sees his or her students for 45 to 90 minutes a day, experiences a variety of moods and subject matter interests, and sees progress or lack of it—all limited to the time frame of class. Five minutes later there's another group of 15 to 30 students finding their places in the classroom. I can assure you of one thing—teaching in the middle grades is never boring!

So here's the challenge. We are to mold this group in ways that facilitate cognitive growth and meet the developmental needs of young adolescents. And we must do this four to six times every day. This requires more than classrooms with doors to contain our charges and bells to signal the beginning and end of each class period. For the effective teacher this issue, as portrayed in Figure 4.4, is another critical balancing point.

Community of Learners

"Educational researchers and policy makers have agreed that one of the most powerful factors in promoting accomplishment is the extent to which the classroom is a learning community" (Strahan, Smith, McElrath, & Toole, 2001, p. 46). The more we explore and articulate beliefs about teaching and learning, the deeper our definition of *community of learners* becomes. You have probably heard the phrase and/or discussed it in education courses. Sergiovanni (1996) tells us, "Communities are collections of individuals who are bonded together by natural will and who are together bound to a set of shared ideas and ideals. This bonding and binding is

Creation of community = Changing collection of "I"s to "we"

tight enough to transform them from a collection of 'I's to a collective 'we'" (p. 48). This is an inspiring definition, especially the last part about the results—the sense of "we" is a noble goal for the classroom.

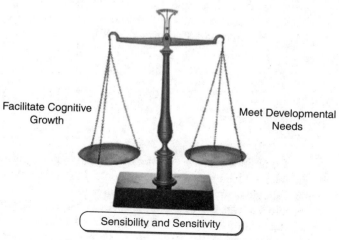

Facilitate Cognitive Growth

Meet Developmental Needs

Sensibility and Sensitivity

FIGURE 4.4   Achieving balance: Cognitive and developmental needs.

But let's face it, few middle school classrooms are made up of kids who come together 5 days a week out of what Sergiovanni refers to as "natural will." This fact makes our quest to create communities of learners more difficult. We are attempting to transform a captive audience of individual young adolescents into a "we," bound together by shared ideas and ideals. As difficult as this may sound, it is possible. I have seen it, I have experienced it, and I assure you it is happening all across our country.

The two operative words in "community of learners" are both vitally important. There are benefits in creating a sense of community; there are benefits in making sure learning takes place. When the two are combined, the whole is definitely greater than the sum of its parts. This is called *synergism*. Webster (1983) defines synergism as "the simultaneous action of separate agencies which, together, have greater total effect than the sum of their individual effects" (p. 1851). Authors of "The Caring Classroom's Academic Edge" refer to the "synergy of academic and social goals" (Lewis, Schaps, & Watson, 1996, p. 20). Bringing together a group of students with some, or all, of the diverse characteristics discussed in Chapters 2 and 3 for the purpose of studying a distinct body of content knowledge is what we do in middle school. Students may be in four or five, or up to seven, groups a day. How do we manage to create communities of learners so our young adolescents can experience this special synergism?

All the characteristics of effective teachers apply. The discussion of balancing the affective side of teaching with the curricular material of our subject areas is applicable, as is the reference to thriving versus surviving. Creating a community of learners is when the "big picture" of classroom teaching comes into focus. All the components are snapshots and when the snapshots are in their places, they form an album that showcases a community of learners.

A community of learners is characterized in *Turning Points* (Carnegie Council on Adolescent Development, 1989) as "a place where close, trusting relationships with adults and peers create a climate for personal growth and intellectual development" (p. 37). The authors of *Turning Points 2000* tell us that since the original document "an enormous amount has been learned from schools across the nation about how these kinds of middle grades learning communities can be created" (Jackson & Davis, 2000, p. 123). A recent study reports on two basic components that contribute to the creation of a community of learners: the teacher's personal commitment to the students which often results in students and teachers learning side by side, and the translation of this commitment into "procedures that fuse academic and social accomplishment" (Strahan et al., 2001, p. 46).

Standard 1

Performance 1: Middle level teacher candidates establish close, mutually respectful relationships with all young adolescents that support their intellectual, ethical, and social growth.

Commitment to the creation of a community of learners requires us to both recognize and increase the progress of our students. John Lounsbury (1991) tells us that our commitment should be manifested in ways that have the effect of multiplying, as well as adding, so we help students increase their knowledge while adding to their capacity to learn. We are helping to "grow" them and their abilities; that is, increase their capacities and expand their knowledge and skills. Think about water balloons—sometimes only about 2 inches by ½ inch empty. They look innocuous enough, but put them under the faucet and watch them

- Be pleasant to students.
- Call them by their first names.
- Greet them at the door.
- Smile often.
- Catch them doing something well.
- Crack a few jokes.
- Ask questions that show your interest.
- Applaud risk-taking.
- Share excellent homework or test responses with the rest of the class.
- Allow occasional democratic voting in the class.
- Refer one child who is an expert on something to another child who needs help, and make sure you rotate the expert's role.
- Ask students to tutor their peers after school.
- Give them responsible jobs in the classroom or school.
- Point out moments of caring among peers that occur in class.

FIGURE 4.5   Inviting students to participate in the classroom community.

Source: From *Meet Me in the Middle: Becoming an Accomplished Middle-Level Teacher* by Rick Wormeli, copyright © 2001, reprinted with permission of Stenhouse Publishers.

fill their original size and then continue to expand as the water flows in. Then watch out—they can pack quite a wallop. Commitment to students calls for us to see them as they are, help them fill up, and then be catalysts that stretch them.

Rick Wormeli (2001), a middle school teacher who regularly contributes to our profession with his insights, advises us on ways to invite students to be part of our community of learners (Figure 4.5).

Maintaining a classroom that is more than four walls with students and a teacher, a classroom that houses a community of learners, requires a teacher who has "a strong sense of self-awareness, a positive self-concept, and a controlled ego" (Lawton, 1993, p. 6). This kind of teacher passes the test of authenticity and is prepared to be a vital part of a community of learners.

TEACHERS OUTSIDE THE CLASSROOM

Let's take our assertion that "a teacher is a teacher is a teacher" outside the classroom walls. We are teachers within the school, within the sphere of education, in our homes and personal lives, and in the community at large. David Berliner, in an interview with Marge Scherer (2001), tells us,

Teachers need to provide more leadership, to be more politically active, and to show that they are concerned about the community. No one else can change the perception of the teachers except teachers themselves, but there are three million of them. And they ought to be out there—and much more active than they are now. (p.10)

Within the School

Wayside teaching.   Between classes, at lunch, at the bus departure/arrival areas, on the field—we are with our students at important times during the day outside our classrooms. While our encounters may not be planned, and certainly are not scripted, they are nonetheless very important. In the world of middle school, we teach as much by who we are as we do with our planned curriculum. So although we don't have lesson plans for passing periods or the lunchroom or the chance meeting on the way back to class from an errand, our attitudes toward our students dictate the interaction. John Lounsbury (1991) calls this *"wayside teaching"* (p. 29). It's not math or science or social studies or language arts, but it's teaching. Students are learning about life, about adulthood, about relationships. We can't fool them. Yes, they're wrapped up in themselves and their friends. So much is going on inside of them developmentally that it's only natural to be self-absorbed. That doesn't keep them from noticing us and paying attention to how we respond to them outside the classroom. Saying "How are you, Travis?" or "How's it going, Maresha?"—using names, showing concern, and demonstrating the simple fact that we actually like them—makes a difference to young adolescents.

Standard 7

Knowledge 2: Middle level teacher candidates understand the importance of their influence on all young adolescents.

Sometimes your classroom responsibilities will stretch outside your lesson plans and your classroom. You will have before school, after school, and lunch duties. Yes, these responsibilities may interfere with planning time and may require you to walk the halls or the field when you might rather have a second cup of coffee. Like everything else in life, attitude makes a difference. Try to view duty responsibilities as opportunities to interact with a student who needs an extra nudge toward cooperation, or maybe a "lost soul" who needs your caring touch.

As adults, we have a responsibility to model cooperation, respect, and, in general, healthy living. Exhibiting optimism and resiliency will be noticed and, hopefully, emulated.

Standard 1

Disposition 5: Middle level teacher candidates are enthusiastic about being positive role models, coaches, and mentors for all young adolescents.

Standard 7

Disposition 4: Middle level teacher candidates believe in maintaining high standards of ethical behavior and professional competence.

Adult relationships. Our relationships with fellow teachers weigh very heavily in terms of job satisfaction. Age and interests may determine the teachers we gravitate toward as "buddies," but paying attention to all the teachers in your building, noticing their composure and their attitude toward students creates learning experiences for us. We all have our own styles and individual characteristics, but there is a bond that people outside the teaching profession don't understand. We teach middle school. We're in this profession together. Take advantage of opportunities to observe and listen and learn. Be a team player when at all possible. Contribute and compromise—always for the sake of the kids.

The administrators in your building are important to you as a teacher. The role of principal is a difficult one; the buck often stops with them. They have the responsibility of coordinating and directing every aspect of their school; they answer to students, teachers, parents, district office personnel, school board members, the community, and their own conscience. Ideally, you will have a principal you respect and value, someone who makes the tough choices and puts the pieces together with the ultimate goal of serving students. As teachers, we may question decisions that principals make. That's healthy. Ask questions and make suggestions, but don't undermine. Because principals often see issues from different and wider perspectives, their decisions often reflect variables to which teachers are not privy.

Your school will have at least one guidance counselor and perhaps an assistant principal or two. These are valuable people with varying responsibilities. One thing's for sure—they're always busy with phone calls to return and students to see on top of the wide range of other duties assigned to them. Use their expertise and keep them informed of student issues from your perspective.

Two other important positions in the school are those of secretary and custodian. These are vital positions and the people who fill them deserve our respect and our gratitude. Without them the school would not function.

Within the System of Education

The district.   The school district is an important organizational entity. Many areas of policy-making, administration, services, coordination, programmatic issues, budget, and more are the functions of the district organization. I taught one year in Gilpin County, Colorado, where the district consisted of one school—a K–12 building with about 350 students. My duties, by the way, went from elementary music to senior Algebra II. The following year, I taught eighth grade math at Hill Middle School in Denver, a school district of 122 schools with more than 70,000 students. As you can imagine, the district offices looked very different. But each performed the responsibilities listed and each was governed by a school board. School boards are often very political groups made up of elected citizens who may or may not have any understanding of education or schools or teaching and learning beyond their own memories of "back in my day." Good or bad, like it or not, school boards have a great deal of power over the forces that shape what we do in our schools and in our classrooms. They can be supportive, positive influences that clearly understand their charge to keep the welfare of children uppermost in their decision-making, or they may become mired in special interests and be far removed from the realities of the classroom. As teachers, we need to be attentive to both thoroughly researched policy decisions and those made on what appear to be hunches or whims. We should be aware and active, with the faces of our students always in focus in the lenses we use to view decisions and directions.

Districts have superintendents, or Chief Executive Officers of schools, along with a wide variety of personnel who oversee curriculum, instruction, staff development, subject areas, personnel, testing, payroll, facilities, and so on. Get to know your district and the people who hold these administrative positions. If they are doing their jobs right, they will welcome your interest, questions, and opinions.

The district level provides common ground for middle level educators to talk and share with peers. No doubt there will be opportunities for you to get to know teachers at other middle schools near you. Take these opportunities to ask how things are done in their schools and to be an instigator of sharing. We all have so much to learn from one another.

Not only is it important for middle school teachers to talk to each other, it is also important for us to have ongoing conversations with teachers in the elementary feeder schools from which our students come, as well as the high schools our students will attend within our school districts. The transition into middle grades and then the transition into high school from middle school are big events in the lives of our students. We can gain insights from our students' former teachers and serve as resources for their future teachers. We'll consider transitions into and out of middle school in Chapter 12.

State and national. Because education is not addressed in the U.S. Constitution, it becomes an issue for states. Your state will have a State Department of Education with departments very similar to large school districts, plus departments that deal with certification and state political forces. Most states have established special committees charged with writing, updating, and overseeing curriculum standards. State oversight also includes departments that handle accountability issues we will address in Chapter 9 when we delve into assessment, and task forces too numerous to name. Most states also have their own affiliate of the National Middle School Association. Some of these affiliates are flourishing organizations with staff development opportunities, summer curriculum and instruction institutes, conferences, newsletters, and journals, all with the purpose of helping us to serve our students better. State middle school organizations provide camaraderie and growth opportunities that shouldn't be missed.

Although education is deemed a state right and responsibility, the federal government does have some influence. The Department of Education in Washington, DC is headed by a national Secretary of Education whose staff influences federal policy-making, program-funding, and goal-setting. However, federal funding for schools amounts to only about 5% of district budgets, while state and local funding often share the remaining 95% relatively equally. By the time federal policies trickle down to the classroom level, a new administration may be at the helm and priority shifts on the way. The broadest reform effort so far in the 21st century is the No Child Left Behind legislation, a product of President George W. Bush's administration (more on this in Chapter 12).

Standard 7

Disposition 3: Middle level teacher candidates believe that their professional responsibilities extend beyond the classroom and school (e.g., advisory committees, parent-teacher organizations).

Performance 4: Middle level teacher candidates engage in and support ongoing professional practices for self and colleagues (e.g., attend professional development activities and conferences, participate in professional organizations).

Universities. Many universities now offer courses leading to bachelor's and master's degrees in middle grades education. It would be to your benefit to explore what's available in your area. If you will soon student teach, or have already completed student teaching, you realize how important this on-the-job training is. Someday, you will be in a position to be a cooperating teacher for aspiring middle grades teachers. When you are ready, don't hesitate to do your part in assisting others. You don't need to have all the answers—none of us do. What's required is a genuine love of the profession and the students in your charge.

Within Our Personal Circles

The personal lives of teachers span all the possibilities within the general public. We may be young, middle-aged, or beyond; single or married; parents or not. We are individuals. After all my years in the teaching profession, there is one thing I can say with certainty—only those who have been classroom teachers understand what it's like. We can, and do, talk about our days with friends and families. While others listen to us with interest, and support us to varying degrees, they can't identify with the responsibility, the care, the exhilaration, and sometimes the depth of despair we experience unless they have done it themselves. Don't expect complete understanding, but keep talking and confiding in those you love.

Be good to yourself. You will find yourself thinking about your students, your lessons, your colleagues, and your school at times when you might rather concentrate on other areas of your life. In spite of this, treat yourself to personal interests. If you enjoy baseball, join a league; if you enjoy the water, swim or boat; if you enjoy travel, get away as often as you can. Go to movies, read what teachers often call "summer novels," take martial arts classes, begin guitar lessons, sing in civic or church groups, or learn to cook exotic foods. Do whatever makes you smile.

Remember the notion of balance? Figure 4.6 illustrates another application. Our profession is important and we are major players in the lives of our students. The old saying "we can't take care of others if we don't take care of ourselves" applies here. Taking care of ourselves keeps our profession and our personal lives in balance and better equips us to be our best in both areas. Our friends, our spouses, our extended families, our own children—all the people we love—deserve our attention and want to care for us. Enjoy yourself!

Within the Community

Schools exist in communities. Almost everyone has opinions about education and many voice those opinions freely and attempt to influence us. That's how it should be. Schools and teachers are vital components of communities and can contribute in monumental ways to the lifestyles of everyone in them. Some teachers choose to live in the communities in which they teach. They may be involved in civic organizations or choose not to be. Other

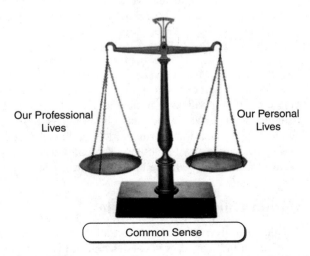

FIGURE 4.6   Achieving balance: Personal and professional lives.

Teacher in school = Public relations agent in community

teachers prefer to live in areas outside the immediate communities of their schools. They choose to drive longer distances to achieve some sense of anonymity, where they can separate their personal and professional lives to a greater degree, where running into students and their parents in the mall or a restaurant is less likely. It's a matter of personal choice.

Here is something we must take very seriously concerning our communities. We are our own best, or worst, public relations agents. To a large extent, we influence public opinion regarding education. What we say matters. The media, both print and electronic, will follow test score improvement or lack of it, violent acts as well as humanitarian ones within the schools, programs that succeed or fail. We have some control, but not much, over media coverage. What we do have total control over is how we portray our students and our profession. If things aren't going like you think they should on your team or in your school, keep your opinions within the system. Outsiders are not going to understand the variables we complain about, but you can be sure they will both sense our negative attitude and zero in on any issue that signals trouble within "their" schools.

Bottom line—be professional and be positive! Even if things aren't going the way you might like, remember whom we serve. Our young adolescents are our focus. Spread the news about what great kids they are, or can be. And spread the news that there are thousands of middle grades teachers who do the best they can for kids every day and in every community! Like any professional, we should strive to be a part of the solution, not the problem.

NMSA

Standard 6

Knowledge 4: Middle level teacher candidates know how to communicate effectively with family and community members.

Knowledge 5: Middle level teacher candidates understand that middle level schools are organizations within a larger community context.

Disposition 2: Middle level teacher candidates realize the importance of privacy and confidentiality of information when working with family members.

TEACHERS AS LEARNERS

We have explored preparation for entering the teaching profession, as well as characteristics of effective teachers. We know that graduation from a teacher education program or certification through an alternative route signals the beginning of a lifetime of learning that takes place through a dynamic combination of individual effort, teacher-to-teacher collaboration, and formal development opportunities. "We expect teachers to give their all to the growth and development of students. But a teacher cannot sustain such giving unless the conditions exist for the continued growth and development of the teacher" (Sarason, 1993, p. 62). In this section, we will look at some possibilities for professional growth.

Lifetime of learning = Individual effort + Teacher-to-teacher collaboration + Formal staff development

Standard 7

Disposition 1: Middle level teacher candidates value learning as a life-long process.

Learning Individually

We want students to take responsibility for their own learning; we want them to want to learn. As teachers, taking responsibility for our own learning is vital as well. We can model for students the value of questioning, examining, seeking answers and reasons, and allowing each learning experience to prompt new questions that send us off in other learning directions. It's an attitude, a state of readiness, an openness to new ideas. Not only will our students benefit from our modeling, they will also be the recipients of the insights and practices we learn about teaching—and life.

Reflection. Learning occurs when we actively analyze our actions. Individual *reflection* about teaching is not daydreaming or passive recollection of the day. It is purposeful and thoughtful. Keeping a journal of classroom events—some significant, some seemingly trivial—and our responses to them, will help frame reflections. This is likely to lead to insights that will be learning experiences for us. The style of your journal writing is your personal choice. Some teachers keep a notebook and vow to write reflectively about their day before leaving school each afternoon. Some days call for pages and pages, while others may boil down to a few sentences. The key is consistency. It's a habit that makes us better because as we write, situations will generally become clearer in our minds, and that clarity often leads to actions or changes in our practice. It may be helpful to establish a two-column journal with events and actions on the left, and our responses and thoughts about the occurrences on the right. This allows us the opportunity to go back later and respond as things "soak in."

Standard 7

Knowledge 8: Middle level teacher candidates understand the need for continual reflection on young adolescent development, the instructional process, and professional relationships.

I often recommend to student teachers, as well as practicing teachers, that they turn off their radios or CDs in the car after school and try to use the drive time to reflect on the day. Sometimes all we want to do is jump in the car, turn up the volume of our favorite music, and let our minds change channels from middle school to Mozart or Mariah Carey or Marvin Gay. Before going there, take some time to go back over your day, recalling what went right, what could use improvement, and what appeared at the time to be disastrous. Learn from your own experiences and resolve to grow.

Learn from others. In our determination to create a community of learners in our classrooms we shouldn't leave ourselves out. We are an essential part of the classroom learning cycle. Sure, we wear the name of teacher, but it's a two-way street—although some days

it may feel more like a 20-lane superhighway. We facilitate learning and, in turn, we learn from our students. Remember to include yourself in your community of learners.

There is a world of expertise in your building. None of us are perfect in the classroom, but we all have areas where we excel. Some of us are better than others at classroom management techniques, some are masters of class discussion, some use a sense of humor in marvelous ways, some are organized in ways we never dreamed possible. Many of us learn best by observing. We may read about strategies and techniques, but to see a teaching tool and its benefits in action makes it come alive. Teachers have reputations for certain attributes, which are usually apparent if you're observant. If your students come to you excited about a project they are doing in social studies, ask the teacher who assigned the project to explain it to you and reveal his "secrets" for motivating the kids. You may hear students simply say, "Ms. Newton is awesome!" Have a conversation with Ms. Newton. Look for her spirit. If your planning period allows, observe her in her classroom.

Many school districts have mentor-mentee programs. If you are fortunate enough to have an official mentor, take advantage of opportunities to ask questions, talk through dilemmas, express emotions, and rely on an experienced teacher to provide guidance in trivial, and not so trivial, matters. If you are not assigned a mentor formally, choose a teacher or two who seem to enjoy their jobs and like their students. Tell them you know you have a lot to learn and ask for advice. Most teachers are flattered and are willing to help in any way they can.

NMSA

Standard 7

Disposition 6: Middle level teacher candidates are committed to refining classroom and school practices that address the needs of all young adolescents based on research, successful practice, and experience.

Read, watch, listen.   A wealth of information is available on teaching. Reading "musts" for middle grades teachers are the two journals published by NMSA and discussed in Chapter 1, *Middle School Journal* and *Middle Ground*. The articles are current and practical, and I look forward to the journals arriving monthly in my mailbox. Most schools have institutional memberships in NMSA and should have the journals on hand. Soak them in— you are guaranteed to be a better teacher for it!

Video and audio tapes are available on the subject of teaching. Pop some popcorn, invite a teacher friend over, and watch a video about teaching practices in the middle school. No, I don't do this on Friday or Saturday nights, or at least not very often. But I do make it a habit to view tapes or listen to a cassette about teaching every month, or more often. There's so much to learn!

School as a Community of Learners

The section on "Teachers Inside the Classroom" earlier in this chapter was framed around the concept of a community of learners. In "Teachers Outside the Classroom" that followed we explored the adults who inhabit schools. These adults, plus the students, form the potential for a community of learners that encompasses everyone in a middle school.

In *Educators as Learners* (Wald & Castleberry, 2000) we find practical guidance on how to create and maintain a school-wide community of learners. The authors take us through the need for such a community, the changes necessary to create it, ways to identify the signs of learners coming together as a community, and methods to keep such a community vibrant. Books such as this open our eyes to possibilities. It is imperative that we understand the role of an individual teacher in supporting collaborative, collegial learning. Simple things like joining a discussion of curriculum and instruction, talking about solutions to dilemmas rather than just bemoaning their existence, sharing articles that spark your interest with other teachers—these build community and lead to learning.

A phrase I use often is "We are our own best teachers." It's true. When you have middle school teachers sitting around a table, you have collective knowledge and expertise that consultants and special seminars are hard pressed to match. Sometimes it takes a question or prompt to get the conversation going, but once middle level teachers become engaged in a topic, solutions and new ideas are not far behind. Listen, learn, and contribute.

One of the most effective vehicles of learning is the team organization. In middle school we have the privilege of working very closely with teachers with whom we share students. Some of my most valuable learning experiences have resulted from interactions with my teammates. In Chapter 5, we will look in-depth at the practice of teaming.

Formal Staff Development

All schools, school districts, and state departments of education provide staff development opportunities. Some of them are mandated, while others are voluntary. Some of them are very valuable, while others may seem like a waste of time. Even those that are less than thrilling will no doubt put you in situations in which you can interact with other teachers. When that happens, there's potential for learning.

Conferences and special institutes are generally available to teachers. The intense focus on teaching and learning has great potential, and the sense of camaraderie is inspiring.

Universities in almost every state offer graduate degrees in your content area and/or in middle grades education. If you have access to an appropriate graduate program, continuing your formal education may be a viable option.

Standard 7

Performance 5: Middle level teacher candidates read professional literature, consult with colleagues, maintain currency with a range of technologies, and seek resources to enhance their professional competence.

National Board Certification was mentioned earlier in this chapter. The *National Board for Professional Teaching Standards (NBPTS)* was formed in 1987. Its purpose is to establish high standards for teachers that will cut across state lines where certification requirements vary. The National Board process was always intended to be, and remains, voluntary. It is a nonprofit, nonpartisan organization governed primarily by classroom teachers. The five core propositions of the National Board are listed in Figure 4.7.

Teachers may apply in various categories, which are classified by developmental level and subject area. young adolescence Certification is available for Generalist plus four subject areas: Mathematics, Science, Social Studies-History, and English Language Arts. To qualify, candidates spend months creating portfolios that include lesson plans, student work samples, assessment measures, and videotapes of their teaching, as well as evidence of their work with colleagues, parents, and communities. Candidates also write extensive commentaries evaluating their goals for instruction, rationales for practice, and effectiveness in the classroom. When this work is complete, they must pass a 6-hour written examination designed to measure knowledge and skills in their certification category.

Rick Wormeli (2001) was in the first group to receive certification. He says that the benefits he appreciates most are those that helped him increase his professionalism and led him to be a better teacher. He learned how to more effectively view and improve his own teaching and how to discuss instruction and assessment in more productive ways. He also experienced greater influence on educational policy as his opinions were sought out by political leaders. Wormeli calls the certification process a "journey to excellence" (p. 186).

1. Teachers are committed to students and their learning.
2. Teachers know the subjects they teach and how to teach those subjects to students.
3. Teachers are responsible for managing and monitoring student learning.
4. Teachers think systematically about their practice and learn from experience.
5. Teachers are members of learning communities.

FIGURE 4.7   Five propositions of accomplished teachers.

Source: From the National Board for Professional Teaching Standards (NBPTS) at *http://www.nbpts.org* [August 2003].

REFLECTIONS ON BEING A MIDDLE SCHOOL TEACHER

We come to the profession of teaching for a variety of reasons and through a variety of paths. We prepare to teach in different ways. There is an abundance of literature on what it means to be a teacher, along with advice on how to be the best teachers we can be. Because there is diversity in our ranks and among our students, reading about and meeting teachers who appear to excel in diverse ways is valuable. If we desire to grow professionally, we must continually assess our own strengths and weaknesses, and seek professional development.

In the May 2001 issue of *Educational Leadership,* Jamie Sawatzky (Tell, 2001, p. 18) reflects on his entrance into the teaching profession. His sincere words as a new seventh grade U.S. History teacher speak volumes. Listen with both your head and your heart.

> I noticed the change in myself the first time I walked into my classroom. I was no longer Jamie. That was the name of the young man who had delivered pizzas or worked at the office. My new-found teaching life had metamorphosed me into "Mr. Sawatzky." My previous work experiences had taught me a variety of skills, but accepting the title of teacher brings with it responsibilities that do not appear on most job descriptions. Walking through the classroom door has cast me into a world where I am charged with the awesome responsibility of sculpting young minds and preparing students for positive participation in their community.
>
> When asked why they entered the profession, many teachers respond, "I wanted a chance to make a positive change in the world." In my case, perhaps selfishly, I wanted to be in a profession that would make a positive change in me. With my first year of teaching about to conclude, I can say that I am happy to be a teacher and happy to be "Mr. Sawatzky."

MEET THE TEACHERS

Let's get to know eight teachers. They are not portraits of real people, but rather compilations and configurations of backgrounds, personal attributes, education, teaching styles, and attitudes of teachers I have known, plus a healthy dose of imagination. We will meet the teachers now and learn from their experiences in the Professional Practice sections to come. They will interact with one another, with other teachers, and with the students you met in Chapters 2 and 3 and other students, as well as administrators, community members, and parents. As with the students we have met, pictures of the teachers are provided so you will feel even better acquainted with them. Here's who we'll meet:

- Jeffrey Duncan, sixth grade science, Caucasian American, age 45
- Marcus Hughes, science student teacher, African American, age 22
- Alicia Pruett, sixth grade language arts, African American, age 28
- Jennifer Blakely, language arts student teacher, Caucasian American, age 21
- Rita Lopez-Mitchell, seventh grade social studies, Hispanic American, age 42
- Maggie Chin, eighth grade math/science, Asian American, age 32
- Lester Jefferson, seventh/eighth grade language arts/social studies, African American, age 53
- Ashley Anderson, sixth grade math, Caucasian American, age 23

Jeffrey Duncan

I've taught middle school science for 22 years. I never planned to teach in a junior high, as Harvest was known in 1981. There were no science positions available in high school, so I figured I could still teach the science I love at a junior high school. When I started spending my days with middle grades kids, I have to tell you I wasn't ready for the challenges they presented. After more than two decades, I'm still often at a loss. Sometimes it's hard for me to get past the fact that they don't all understand what I present to them. Some understand right away, some take longer, and some never seem to get it.

I know my subject inside and out. I read science journals, I expand on what the textbook includes, and I view science as exciting. My lessons are well planned, and lab equipment is always ready. It's the kids who challenge me. Sometimes I just want to scream at them, "Why don't you get this?" In fact, I've done exactly that on occasion.

Since I came to Harvest, I've experienced some milestones. I've been married twice and divorced both times. I've had three stepchildren in and out of my home. I completed a master's degree in biology about 10 years ago. Rather than using the new degree to look at changing careers, I went into the lawn irrigation business with an old friend. My afternoons and weekends are spent outdoors. I'm in good shape physically and content with my two professions of teaching and small business ownership. I live alone and go out socially when the mood strikes me.

After all these years I've finally agreed to have a student teacher. Our principal, Mr. Jenkins, says this student is one he'd like to groom as a strong subject specialist. He's a young man and Mr. Jenkins thinks he will be comfortable with me. He added that there will be two student teachers on our team and that the four of us will actually "share" them in terms of responsibilities. So I agreed.

Marcus Hughes

I was one of those kids in an urban middle school who always had to have the last word with other kids, teachers, and my family. I went to school because I wanted to be around my friends. I guess I was a leader, but not in very positive ways. Schoolwork didn't interest me, but I got by. When I was a junior in high school I got in trouble with the law and was suspended from school for 2 weeks. Since I was 16, I just decided not to go back. Then Mr. Bailey came to see me. He was my earth science teacher. To make a long story short, he wouldn't give up on me. He convinced the principal that I had potential. The principal put him "in charge" of me. Rather than study hall, I helped Mr. Bailey with lab set-ups. He showed me so many really neat things and pushed me and pushed me, and pushed . . . and because of him I tasted real interest in science and a healthy dose of success in school. He turned me around.

So here I am—ready to student teach. I love science and I want kids to love it too. My degree will be in biology with a minor in education. My certification will be for both middle and high school. I'm glad my placement is in middle school. If I had met Mr. Bailey earlier I wouldn't have wasted so much time being a smart mouth. Last semester I took a course that concentrated on science methods in middle school and I had some practicum hours in Harvest Middle School where I'll student teach. It isn't like the one I attended, where more than 90% of the kids were African American and lived in the housing project near my family. The school where I'll be is in a nice neighborhood, and only about 20% of the kids are African American.

I feel ready for the challenge of teaching. In fact, I'm anxious. I know my stuff and kids think I'm cool and funny. I'm excited about putting what I've learned into practice.

Alicia Pruett

This is my sixth year of teaching. I started out at one of our feeder elementary schools teaching fourth grade. Then 3 years ago there was an opening for a sixth grade language arts teacher at Harvest Middle School. It worked out great for me. I resigned my fourth grade position in May when I was 5 months pregnant. The teacher I would replace at Harvest would be moving the following January when her husband transferred to another city. I had plenty of time to prepare for my new position and 7 extra months at home with baby daughter Shawntay.

I like teaching middle school, especially sixth grade. They remind me of fourth graders, just more unpredictable. They still have enthusiasm and want to please their teachers. (Well, most of the time.) I'm not sure I'd like seventh and eighth grades as much.

My degree is in elementary education and I'm certified for grades 1 through 8. My favorite subject was always language arts and I enjoy reading and writing stories and poems. When I was in college, I took a course in adolescent literature, and I couldn't get enough of the books written for young adolescents. I also took a course on middle grades organization and instruction. My professor was so enthusiastic about middle school and middle school kids. That experience assured me that I could teach middle as well as elementary school and adapt methods for either.

Last year I had a student teacher who wasn't very prepared for middle school. By the end of our semester together, he felt like he could handle it, but only if he had to. His real love was for the primary grades. Mr. Jenkins asked me to take another student teacher this year. I reluctantly agreed. My husband was not excited to hear this news because we both knew that the one last year actually took too much of my time because he had lots of needs and required late after-school sessions. He would rather my time be spent at home with Shawntay.

Jennifer Blakely

I'm going to be a teacher. I'm going to be a teacher . . . . I keep repeating these words to myself. The reality of student teaching is almost here. I've been assigned to a sixth grade language arts classroom at Harvest Middle School. I've visited there, but most of my practicum hours were completed at two urban schools, an elementary located in a housing project and a middle school "across the tracks," as my daddy would put it. Harvest is in a nice area and they have a mix of kids, most White and most middle or upper middle class in terms of socioeconomics. Daddy will approve when he sees it next month.

I was always a good student. I attended our local Catholic high school back home. We wore uniforms. My group of girls wore the shortest kelly green skirts we could get by with and outlandish socks, green of course, to set ourselves apart. I was a cheerleader, president of my senior class, and an officer in our honor society. My parents were proud and I had a very happy childhood. Daddy is an attorney and is a partner in a large firm. He always said I got the brains and the beauty and my brother, well, my brother got a knack for getting into trouble. So I went to college to major in English and planned to go to law school. By my sophomore year I knew that wouldn't happen. Some of the girls in my sorority were education majors, and they really seemed to enjoy the classes in their major. It's not that I didn't like my English courses, it's just that I didn't think I wanted to be a lawyer. I met with an advisor who told me about the degree in education that would lead to middle school certification. I signed up. I used my extra hours in English for a language arts content concentration and took three extra courses in social sciences for my other concentration. I felt right at home with my choice even though Daddy was a little disappointed. I told him I knew I wouldn't make as much money or join his firm, but I would have a career that I knew I would enjoy.

Rita Lopez-Mitchell

I have my own classroom now. It wasn't always that way. I met Brad when I was a freshman in college. He was a mechanic, and a good one. I got pregnant the summer before my sophomore year. We married in September and I was delighted to be a stay-at-home mom for 8 years until the youngest of our four daughters was in preschool. At that point I decided to be a teacher's aide at the elementary school our children attended. When Maria went on to middle school in sixth grade I decided to move up with her. Our local middle school was in need of someone to be a general aide in the mornings, going from class to class as needed, and to spend the afternoons in the BIR (Behavior Improvement Room) with students who had been kicked out of regular classes because they had misbehaved. To my delight, I found I could do both morning and afternoon duties quite satisfactorily.

After 14 years of marriage, Brad died of a heart attack. I won't take the time to explain, or try to explain, the trauma suffered by myself and my girls. What you need to know for the sake of this book is the action I took. Brad had enough life insurance to allow me to continue my work at the middle school and go back to school at our state university. The principal allowed me to arrange my work around my classes. In 4 years, I had my degree in middle grades education with concentrations in social studies and language arts. My girls were at my graduation ceremony. We hugged and cried and talked about how proud Dad would have been of me.

So now I have my own classroom for the fourth year. I've learned a lot in that time. I decided not to continue in my daughters' school. Instead I took a position teaching eighth grade social studies and a reading class at Central Middle School, an urban school in an almost deserted part of the city. The businesses around the school are boarded up. Our kids come from the old part of town that has not been revitalized like the northern side.

Maggie Chin

I went to college on a full scholarship and graduated in 3½ years with a degree in accounting. I was a dynamo in the School of Business. My advisor told me, "Maggie, you've got the brains, common sense, and aggressiveness to set Wall Street on fire!" Well, I took his words to heart, applied at a large firm, and successfully landed an enviable job uptown. Two years later my father died. About 6 months after his death my mother was diagnosed with uterine cancer. My grandparents on my father's side had lived with us since I was small. At the time of my mother's diagnosis, they were both in their 80s. I didn't feel like I had much choice. I could always pick up my career later. I moved back home to care for Mother and Grandmom and Grandpop.

At the time of my move I saw it as a duty. Now I view it as a great fortune. Let me explain. I grew up in a neighborhood where most of the Asian families lived in our community. I had a terrific group of friends who shared my heritage. When it was time to go to college, we separated. One day when I took my mom to the hospital for a radiation treatment, I ran into a dear old friend named Edward Chin. Well, we were married in 3 months. Ed was finishing his internship and planned to go into private practice.

To make a long (and very happy) story short, we wanted several children and I wanted a career that would allow me to be a mom with as much time for my children as possible.

Our local university has a Master of Arts in Teaching Middle School degree program, one of the first in the country. My "go getter" spirit propelled me to finish my master's degree, have our first baby, and care for my three needy relatives—all in 3 years. My "setting Wall Street on fire" determination was just redirected.

Two more children later, and with the death of my grandparents and my mom in remission, I'm in my fifth year of teaching math and science on a three-person team at our first-rate middle school, Hoyt River Middle School of the Performing Arts. It's a great place to be. One of my teammates teaches language arts and social studies, and the other teaches theater and French. When students are accepted at Hoyt by audition, they are assigned to a team with a performance arts specialty. One of my fondest hopes is that all three of my children will want to be part of this program, where students are grouped by interests and talents, regardless of age.

Lester Jefferson

I've never enjoyed teaching as much as I do now. The list of jobs I've had as an adult is fairly long, from my 4 years in the Navy to managing my brother's hardware store to teaching senior English at our local high school. The 12 years at the high school were busy ones. The senior class generally only had about 40 students. Besides teaching English, I was yearbook advisor, senior class sponsor, and part-time assistant principal. I liked it, but I often wished I could catch the kids earlier. By the time they got to me, their paths were pretty much set.

When the decision was made to turn our K–8 school into two schools—one K–6 and the other 7–8—and use an existing building next to the high school for the middle school, the community was concerned. A year was set aside for planning before the switch. We had a committee made up of elementary and high school teachers and a few parents who decided to research the issue and determine how best to serve our seventh and eighth graders. I knew this was my chance. As a member of the Association for Supervision and Curriculum Development (ASCD), I religiously read their journal *Educational Leadership*. I had learned about grouping options for middle schools and was enamored with a concept called looping that calls for teachers and students to stay together for 2 or more years in small learning communities called teams. I did more research and presented my ideas to the committee, and they liked them. Because we would only have about 50 students per grade we could have two-teacher teams, one teaching math and science and the other language arts and social studies. That's me! Sandra Henderson is my teammate and has been since we started this middle grades looping adventure 5 years ago. We have the same team of students for 2 years. It's a perfect transition from self-contained elementary school to six classes/six teachers a day in high school.

My wife says she's never seen me happier. Our own three children are grown. I plan to stay here at Marrington Middle School until I retire.

Ashley Anderson

I'm certain I was born to be a teacher. The only other profession I remember considering was missionary work overseas. I grew up in a parsonage, the only girl out of five children of a minister. Two of my brothers are now ministers. All of us went to college and remain very close.

After my first two practicum experiences in college, I knew I would look for a job where I felt I was needed the most. I'm drawn to the kids who have the least advantages. They break my heart. All I want to do is get better and better as a teacher. Every day is a real eye opener! By the time 4:30 rolls around, I'm beat. I drive to my apartment and hit the couch for an hour or so. I guess you could say I've learned to "power nap." By the time I'm getting my energy back, my boyfriend calls and we decide on dinner. Our plans depend on the amount of work I have to do for the next day. I use my planning time at school as efficiently as I can, but often I spend those 45 minutes with a student who's having a particularly bad day or a parent who returns my call or takes time off to come to school for a conference.

This is my second year teaching sixth grade math at Central Middle School. If you knew the backgrounds of some of my students, you'd understand what I mean when I say they break my heart. About 60% are Hispanic, 30% are Black, and the rest are mostly Caucasian and Asian heritage students. When I look at my classes, I see more of a homemade soup than a melting pot. I suppose they've "melted" and blended to some extent, yet there are definite cultural differences. The most obvious shared feature is poverty. All of my students qualify for free or reduced price lunch. I always thought teaching would make me feel needed—I just never dreamed how much.

I'm convinced that education is the way out for my kids. I tell them every day that they have the power. The opportunities are in our school building and they have the power to grab them and grow and flourish. I try to show them possibilities, but there is one possibility that frightens me. What if I get too discouraged or too tired or, worse yet, stop believing what I hear myself saying. . . .

Group Activities

1. To your school files, add the number of teachers for each school. School offices can give you this information. If possible, find out how many teach in each broad area—core subjects (math, language arts, science, social studies), related arts (P.E., art, music, etc.), and special education. These numbers can be estimates. Compare the ratios of teachers to the information on total number of students collected in Chapter 3.

2. Designate someone in your class to find information on your state NMSA affiliate. As a class, write a letter or send an e-mail to the organization asking for information concerning membership and activities.

3. In Chapter 2 you considered how middle level students are portrayed in the electronic media. Now consider how movies and television shows portray teachers. As a class, brainstorm all the instances you can think of in current or past productions. Are the majority of portrayals positive or negative? Do any appear to be realistic and, if so, in what ways?

Individual Activities

1. At what point in your life did you decide to be a teacher? Was it an "Ah-ha!" moment or a gradual realization? Be prepared to share your answers with other teacher candidates.

2. Briefly explain in your own words what the phrase "thriving versus surviving" means for middle grades teachers.

3. Pretend that the school at which you teach has recently received some very bad publicity involving unethical behavior of a teacher. What is your responsibility in terms of school image when you meet and are questioned by community members at the mall, in church, at a soccer game, etc.?

4. Why is an attitude of "I can't wait until graduation. No more learning for me!" inappropriate for teacher candidates?

Personal Journal

1. Reread the Haim Ginott quote at the beginning of the "Characteristics of Effective Middle Level Teachers" section. How do Ginott's words affect you? Reflect on the implications for teacher responsibility.

2. Refer to Figure 4.3. Think about a "good" teacher from your days in middle school. Which of the characteristics listed apply to this teacher? Now think of a "not-so-good" teacher you had in middle school. Which of the characteristics apply to this teacher?

3. Do you recall a teacher who did an exceptional job of what Lounsbury calls "wayside teaching"? Write about how the teacher accomplished this.

Professional Practice

(It would be helpful to reread the descriptions of Allison and Darlene in Chapters 2 and 3.)

Jennifer Blakely is in her fourth week of student teaching at Harvest Middle School with Alicia Pruett. They are both very pleased with the relationship they are establishing. Their personalities mesh and they feed off one another's enthusiasm in the classroom. Ms. Pruett brings more than 3 years of middle school teaching experience to the mix and Ms. Blakely brings explicit preparation from a middle grades university program. Ms. Blakely is teaching one language arts/reading class at the end of the day, so she can benefit from Ms. Pruett's modeling of the lesson twice earlier in the day. Their team rotates the three 90-minute core classes each week. By the time Ms. Blakely takes over two classes, she will have taught all of the students on the team. By week six she will be teaching full time.

Jennifer Blakely

Ms. Blakely is very impressed with the way Ms. Pruett plans lessons around literature. Ms. Pruett carefully outlines her lectures and questions and student prompts. Her expectations are high for her students. She puts thought and effort into what happens in the classroom.

Ms. Blakely hates to criticize Ms. Pruett, but for all her careful planning Ms. Pruett doesn't seem to enjoy students outside the classroom. Even though her teammates (teachers of science, math, social studies) urge her to stand in the hall during passing periods, Ms. Pruett doesn't see this as part of her responsibilities.

Alicia Pruett

The students notice the difference between Ms. Pruett and the other team teachers. They enjoy their language arts/reading class with Ms. Pruett, but are aware that she doesn't participate in their world outside the class. She will smile at them in the hall, but her enthusiasm for middle graders just doesn't carry over.

Allison and Darlene, sixth grade

Allison, a younger-than-most bundle of energy, has not only noticed that Ms. Pruett's enthusiasm ends at the classroom door, she has also verbalized it to Ms. Blakely. Darlene, another student, overheard her and immediately defended Ms. Pruett saying that she actually visited her at home when her aunt was ill. Allison said she has talked to the other team teachers, but Ms. Pruett still seems to be the only one who changes her attitude when she leaves the classroom.

1. Ms. Blakely is concerned by Ms. Pruett's apparent unwillingness to participate in her students' lives outside the classroom. Which of the following represents the least important reason for her concern?

   (a) Students are sensitive to interactions with teachers and Ms. Pruett is offending some of them who notice her lack of interest outside the classroom.

   (b) The other teacher team members are not pleased with Ms. Pruett's reticence to pull her weight outside the classroom. It is a source of team discontent.

   (c) Ms. Blakely is not getting the full benefit of Ms. Pruett as a role model and may be at risk for adopting a similar attitude toward students outside the classroom.

   (d) Ms. Pruett is missing out on teachable moments that happen between classes and in the lunchroom and the students are missing out on lessons in life she might be teaching them.

2. In her middle grades program at the university, Ms. Blakely learned about what John Lounsbury calls "wayside teaching," or teacher involvement outside the class. Which of the following is the most important reason for extending our lessons beyond the classroom door?

   (a) We all need to adhere to the duty roster as designated by the administration.

   (b) Middle grades students are learning about life inside and outside our classrooms.

   (c) Part of the fulfillment of teaching is embodied in our relationships with students.

   (d) The presence of teachers in the hallways helps the flow of student traffic and reduces between-class disturbances.

3. Allison is obviously disturbed by Ms. Pruett's lack of involvement with students outside the classroom. Using what we know about middle school development, how could Ms. Blakely best address the situation?

   (a) Remind Allison that Ms. Pruett has apparently involved herself in Darlene's life outside the classroom.

   (b) Talk with the other team teachers and convey what she observed as well as the comments by Allison and Darlene.

(c) Because she has a good relationship with Ms. Pruett, she could ask her about her view of responsibilities inside and outside the classroom.

(d) Encourage Allison to talk to other students and organize a group to confront Ms. Pruett.

Constructed Response

In the grand scheme of her student teaching experience, Jennifer Blakely is very satisfied. Her placement with Alicia Pruett is pleasing because of their growing mutual friendship and their shared appreciation for adolescent literature. Keeping NCATE Standard 7, Disposition 7 in mind (Middle level teacher candidates value collegiality as an integral part of their professional practice.), briefly describe an approach Jennifer might take if she chooses to speak with Alicia concerning "wayside teaching."

Internet Resources

Education World
http://educationworld.com

This large site has a section called First-Year Teachers. The section contains more than 100 subsections addressing the needs and apprehensions of new teachers. In addition, there are helpful strategies for planning the first days of school, organizing a classroom, communicating with parents, and much more.

National Board for Professional Teaching Standards (NBPTS)
http://www.nbpts.org

The NBPTS is a nonprofit organization responsible for the first nationally recognized standards for teachers. This site details the levels and subject areas in which board certification is possible, and provides specific information for teachers interested in applying for national board certification.

National Education Association (NEA) Resources for Teachers
http://www.nea.org

NEA is the largest national teacher union, with affiliate organizations in each state. Their mission is to advance the cause of public education. This site provides information on resources available to teachers, as well as information on current education issues and legislative efforts.

Public Education Network (PEN)
http://www.publiceducation.org

PEN is a nonprofit organization with the mission of promoting quality education for all children. Teachers can sign up to receive weekly updates on current issues in education with links to numerous articles on a wide variety of topics.

References

Arth, A. E., Lounsbury, J. H., McEwin, C. K., & Swaim, J. H. (1995). *Middle level teachers: Portraits of excellence.* Columbus, OH: National Middle School Association and National Association of Secondary School Principals.

Carnegie Council on Adolescent Development. (1989). *Turning points: Preparing America's youth for the 21st century.* New York: Carnegie Corporation.

Fullan, M. G. (1993). Why teachers must become change agents. *Educational Leadership, 50*(6), 12–17.

Ginott, H. G. (1993). *Teacher and child.* New York: Collier Books, Macmillan.

Jackson, A. W., & Davis, G. A. (2000). *Turning points 2000: Educating adolescents in the 21st century.* New York: Teachers College Press.

Knowles, T., & Brown, D. F. (2000). *What every middle school teacher should know.* Westerville, OH: National Middle School Association.

Lawton, E. (1993). *The effective middle level teacher.* Reston, VA: National Association of Secondary School Principals.

Lewis, C., Schaps, E., & Watson, M. (1996). The caring classroom's academic edge. *Educational Leadership, 54*(3),16–21.

Lounsbury, J. H. (1991). *As I see it.* Columbus, OH: National Middle School Association.

McEwin, C. K., Dickinson, T. S., & Hamilton, H. (2000). National board certified teachers' views regarding specialized middle level teacher preparation. *The Clearing House, 73*(4), 211–213.

National Board for Professional Teaching Standards. Retrieved June 20, 2003, from *http://www.nbpts.org.*

Palmer, P. J. (1998). *The courage to teach.* San Francisco: Jossey-Bass.

Sarason, S. (1993). *You are thinking of teaching.* San Francisco: Jossey-Bass.

Scales, P. C., & McEwin, C. K. (1994). *Growing pains: The making of America's middle school teachers.* Columbus, OH: National Middle School Association and Center for Young Adolescence.

Scherer, M. (2001). Improving the quality of the teaching force: A conversation with David C. Berliner. *Educational Leadership, 58*(8), 6–10.

Sergiovanni, T. J. (1996). *Leadership for the schoolhouse.* San Francisco: Jossey-Bass.

Strahan, D., Smith, T. W., McElrath, M., & Toole, C. M. (2001). Profiles in caring: Teachers who create learning communities in their classrooms. *Middle School Journal, 33* (1), 41–47.

Strahan, D. B. (1997). *Mindful learning: Teaching self-discipline and academic achievement.* Durham, NC: Carolina Academic Press.

Tell, C. (2001). Who's in our classrooms: Teachers speak for themselves. *Educational Leadership, 58*(8), 18–23.

Tolan, M. (2001). The new kid on the block. *Middle Ground, 5*(1), 10–13.

Wadsworth, D. (2001). Why new teachers choose to teach. *Educational Leadership, 58*(8), 24–28.

Wald, P. J., & Castleberry, M. S. (2000). *Educators as learners: Creating a professional learning community in your school.* Alexandria, VA: Association for Supervision and Curriculum Development.

Webster's New Twentieth Century Dictionary. (1983). New York: Simon & Schuster.

Wormeli, R. (2001). *Meet me in the middle: Becoming an accomplished middle-level teacher.* Portland, ME: Stenhouse.

5

Structures of Middle School

This We Believe *speaks to flexibility in grouping, scheduling, and staffing. Flexible structuring helps to create a responsive environment—in which needs can be recognized and adjustments made in form and function when necessary in order to maximize results. The best middle level schools are ever-changing, learning organizations.*

Jackson and Davis, 2000, p. 90

Use this diagram as an organizational tool. In the boxes beside the chapter headings, indicate the dates by which the reading should be completed.

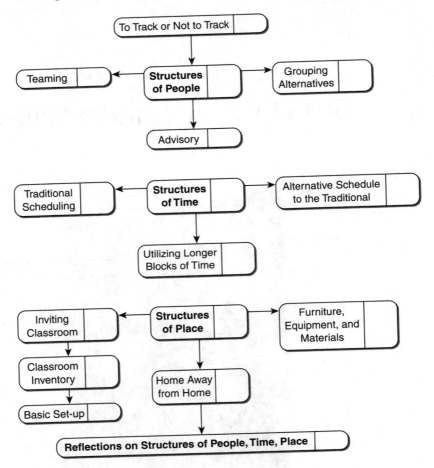

INTRODUCTION

Structure gives shape and support to middle level education. Developmentally responsive structures provide both framework and opportunity for the middle level educator to build on best practices with as few impediments as possible. However, assuming that putting certain structures in place will automatically lead to developmentally responsive middle grades education is a fallacy. For instance, organizing teachers and students into interdisciplinary teams is an organizational change and not a guarantee that the potential benefits of teaming will be realized.

This chapter looks at possible structures of people, time, and place that are believed to be appropriate for middle grades students. These are elements to look for when determining a school's degree of adherence to middle level philosophy as articulated in *Turning Points* and *This We Believe*.

Structures of middle school = People + Time + Place

Standard 2

Disposition 3: Middle level teacher candidates are supportive of organizational components that maximize student learning.

NMSA.

 ## STRUCTURES OF PEOPLE

As dynamic, living organizations, middle schools revolve around relationships that set the tone and determine the climate. Our challenge as teachers is to create structures of people that best promote learning and growth. In this section, we'll examine homogeneous and heterogeneous grouping, interdisciplinary teaming, multiage grouping, looping, schools-within-a-school, and advisory programs.

To Track or Not to Track

Perhaps the most controversial of all philosophical dilemmas concerning the structuring of people within the middle school is the homogeneous versus heterogeneous grouping debate. *Homogeneous ability grouping,* or *tracking* as it is commonly called, has been the norm in most levels of schooling for many years. It seems to make sense to test students and put them into classes based on their abilities and achievement levels so curriculum and instruction can be tailored to meet their specific needs. It appears reasonable to expect teachers to teach at their best when presented with groups of students who fall within narrow bands of intelligence and aptitude. What "makes sense" and "appears reasonable" dictates what often prevails in practice, in direct opposition to middle level philosophy.

Turning Points 2000 clearly calls for *heterogeneous grouping* of students, meaning that students in any given class represent the spectrum of ability levels in the school student population. Still, homogeneous grouping is prevalent in schools that otherwise follow the tenets of middle grades education. The arguments for and against ability grouping/tracking have been the same for decades (Pool & Page, 1995). It seems clear that ongoing research is needed on the topic of homogeneous versus heterogeneous grouping.

The case for tracking.   The literature available on the topic of tracking indicates that the case for *ability grouping* is based on the following propositions: tracking helps schools meet the varying needs of students; tracking provides low-achieving students with the attention and slower pace they require; high-achieving students are provided challenges when tracked; tracking is necessary for individualizing instruction; and tracking will prevent low-achievers from hindering the progress of high-achievers. Among the proponents of tracking are some administrators, teachers, and parents (mostly of high-achievers, as you might imagine).

It is easier to plan for instruction of a homogeneous class. Materials and teaching methods can be chosen specifically for the ability level of the students. High-achieving groups can sometimes "teach themselves." They often seem to thrive regardless of the curriculum and instruction. At the other end of the spectrum, teaching a class of low-achievers has been, and often still is, a matter of drill and practice in a worksheet-rich environment if the teacher is not committed to a type of instruction that is more interesting and challenging to students, and more difficult to plan. Perhaps it's not the grouping but the quality of instruction that makes a difference. We'll explore this later.

The case against tracking.   The literature available on tracking indicates that the case against it relies on the following propositions: tracking is <u>detrimental to young adolescent peer relationships</u>; it is harmful to the self-esteem of low-achievers; it <u>perpetuates class and racial inequities</u>; the grouping process is often <u>biased</u>; it <u>reinforces inaccurate assumptions about intelligence</u>; and the least experienced teachers are typically assigned to <u>low-achieving</u> classes. Those who oppose tracking again include administrators, teachers, and parents.

In *Beyond Tracking* (Pool & Page, 1995), author after author refers to the preponderance of research involving many schools and students that has failed to show positive effects of tracking for any subgroup of students, with the possible exception of the students considered to be gifted and talented (3% to 5% of the total student population).

Finding balance.   George (1995) contends that "the claims and counter-claims about the research are so confusing and contradictory that practitioners must come to their own conclusions about the most reliable generalizations that can be drawn" (p. 47). So while middle level philosophy in *Turning Points 2000* states that "<u>Classes should include students of diverse needs, achievement levels, interests, and learning styles, and instruction should be differentiated to take advantage of the diversity, not ignore it</u>" (Jackson & Davis, 2000, p. 23) the reality of what actually occurs in our schools often does not follow this philosophy. A major benefit of the team structure, which we will discuss later in the chapter, is that it supports heterogeneous grouping of students while allowing for grouping and regrouping

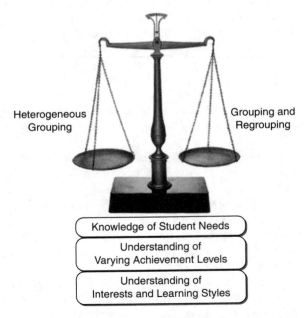

FIGURE 5.1   Achieving balance: Heterogeneous and homogeneous grouping.

as determined by individual student needs and the curriculum. The concept of balance becomes important once again as illustrated in Figure 5.1.

To make heterogeneous grouping successful, instructional practices need to respond to student needs. Chapters 7 and 8 deal with strategies that will enable us to differentiate instruction. There are numerous teaching practices that give students opportunities to learn in diverse ways. This variety of teaching practices is essential in creating a developmentally responsive classroom, one that embraces heterogeneous groups.

Some middle schools restrict grouping to subjects that are overtly hierarchical in nature. A common configuration of courses involves tracking in math and language arts with heterogeneous grouping in science and social studies. For those adamantly opposed to any kind of tracking, it may be difficult to accept this compromise. However, tracking is deeply embedded in our schools and is unlikely to be eliminated, regardless of the mounting evidence against it (George, 1995). Chances are you will encounter some form of it in your school, and may have no choice as to whether or not to practice tracking.

To track or not to track is a serious issue with potentially far-reaching consequences. It's therefore an issue that merits our best thinking and our most thoughtful actions. We've only scratched the surface; please take time to explore the homogeneous and heterogeneous grouping issue in greater depth. Keep in mind that a homogeneous middle school class is an oxymoron. There are not 2, much less 20, middle school students who respond in the same way and at the same time to any given scenario.

Magnet schools.   A *magnet school* is a public school that offers something different from traditional public schools. This difference may involve specialized curriculum, instruction, or both. Magnet schools may bring together academically gifted students, students with an expressed interest in a specific curricular area, or perhaps students with distinct career aspirations. Because students in a magnet school share aptitude and/or interests, they tend to be more homogeneous. In some cases, magnet schools represent overt tracking. The major growth in magnet schools occurred in the 1970s and 1980s. The courts approved them as acceptable methods of desegregation in 1975. By the mid-1990s, there were more than 1.2 million students in magnet schools across America (Yu & Taylor, 1997). During the 1970s, districts devised magnet plans to draw students from the suburbs into urban areas to create racially mixed populations. Magnet schools were, and still are, viewed as forces for integration that don't require mandatory student reassignment or forced busing (Smrekar & Goldring, 1999).

Magnet schools are considered by many to be vehicles for improving scholastic standards, providing a broad range of curricular choices, and allowing students to concentrate on distinct interests and talents. School districts generally have their own distinct magnet programs and entrance requirements. Some magnet schools require proof of academic achievement and aptitude through high scores on standardized tests. Once admitted, students must maintain high achievement levels to remain in the school. Some magnet schools require auditions in areas such as music, theater, and dance. Their programs then provide talented students in these areas with opportunities to enhance their skills and to use them in performance. Some middle schools declare a curricular focus such as math and science. They increase their resources and teacher expertise and invite students with interest in, and/or aptitude for, the chosen focus to apply. Still other magnet schools declare a focus on, for instance, military or career preparation. Interested students are asked to apply, and attendance is determined by lottery.

Magnet schools are more likely to have greater monetary and staff resources. They cost more to operate (Maranto, Milliman, Hess, & Gresham, 1999). So although magnet schools are part of public education, they are inherently unequal to non-magnet schools in what they can offer students. They often compete with private and charter schools to draw students and parents who are looking for alternatives.

Teaming

"No single educational idea has come to characterize the middle school concept as certainly as has interdisciplinary *teaming*" (Lounsbury, 1991, p. 58). Creating teams of teachers and students is vitally important to the development of a middle grades learning community. *Turning Points 2000* states this fact emphatically,

A Middle School Team = A distinct group of teachers and students learning together

"Large schools should be divided into smaller learning communities, with teams of teachers and students as the underlying organizational structure. To ensure strong teams, schools must pay attention to the nature and quality of interaction among teacher and student team members, ensuring that teams continually concentrate their efforts on achieving high standards for both teaching and learning. Schools should also attend to critical elements affecting team success, such as team size, composition, time for planning, and continuity."

This partnership of shared time, space, instructional and curricular emphases, and philosophy can make a large school feel smaller and reduce anonymity for young adolescents and adults alike. Within a team, a small group of teachers takes primary responsibility for facilitating academic and social growth of a specific group of students. I am convinced that the adage "An individual can make a difference: a team can make a miracle" is true!

As with any organizational structure, teaming is as powerful as the people involved choose to make it. The structure provides the opportunity, but teacher determination and creativity are necessary for successful implementation.

Standard 2

Knowledge 5: Middle level teacher candidates understand the team process as a structure for school improvement and student learning.

Team organization.   Teams in middle school are most often interdisciplinary. Each teacher on a team is responsible for one or more subject areas and, when a team is formed, they represent at least the subjects considered core areas—language arts, social studies, science, and math. Research indicates that positive results are achieved from a wide variety of team sizes. Teams commonly consist of as few as two teachers and 40 students to as many as four core teachers plus related arts teachers, special education, and resource teachers and more than 125 students. Research reported by Erb and Stevenson in 1999 indicates that instructional practices most closely linked to positive student outcomes occur more often when teams are not allowed to grow too large. They use a 120-student upper team limit. Other research indicates that teams with fewer than 90 students use desirable instructional practices most frequently (Flowers, Mertens, & Mulhall, 2000). Because "one size fits all" does not make sense when it comes to team configurations, many decisions are required about the composition of teacher expertise, space, time, student demographics, and other relevant variables. The goal is to create an effective organizational scheme that produces a learning environment that meets the needs of middle level students (Knowles & Brown, 2000). Smaller teams of two or three teachers are often created for fifth and sixth grade to more closely resemble self-contained classrooms, while larger teams are dominant in seventh and eighth grade. Figure 5.2 will give you an idea of some of the advantages and disadvantages of different-size teams.

NMSA

Standard 7

Knowledge 6: Middle level teacher candidates understand teaming/collaborative theories and processes.

Performance 3: Middle level teacher candidates work successfully as members of interdisciplinary teams and as part of the total school environment.

Recommendations for teaming.   Middle grades educators appreciate the concept of teams and have given lots of consideration to what elements contribute to team success. While effective teaming cannot be reduced to a checklist of components, there are guidelines that help promote successful functioning.

The choice of teachers and students who will comprise a team should not be random. Teams need to bring together teachers who have varying subject area expertise, different backgrounds to add diversity, and personalities that will combine to give the team collective power. Best friends do not necessarily make the best teammates.

The composition of students on a team is as important as the mix of teachers. A team should be a microcosm of the whole school, reflecting heterogeneity in terms of ethnicity, socioeconomic background, gender, special education status, and academic achievement. We should be careful not to weight a team heavily with either high-achievers or low-achievers (Jackson & Davis, 2000).

The quality of teaming is enhanced by staff development, both before implementing teaming and on a regular basis after teams are established to promote increased effectiveness. Learning how to set goals, provide consistent support, communicate openly, and collaborate willingly requires concerted effort and training (Schurr, Thomason, & Thompson, 1996).

A very effective form of staff/professional development is available to members of teaching teams as they meet in what Jackson and Davis (2000) refer to as the "daily professional development 'huddle' as teachers reflect critically on their purpose and approach to teaching" during common planning time (p. 141). The frequency and length of common planning time has a major impact on the effective functioning of teachers on a team. *Team planning* time typically occurs during students' related arts classes when all the core teachers

Two-Person Team

Advantages:
- Fewer personality conflicts; students and teachers know each other sooner and better
- Easier to find planning time and to integrate work in core subject areas
- May ease transition from elementary school organization

Disadvantages:
- Little team support or backup if one teacher on team is absent
- Students see only two different teaching styles and personalities

Three-Person Team

Advantages:
- More support, more diversity, more backup than two-person teams
- Each team member teaches one specific subject; all teach one common subject
- More opportunities to group and regroup

Disadvantages:
- Difficulties in agreeing on the common subject to teach
- Possible "two against one" problems in decision-making

Four- or Five-Person Team

Advantages:
- Increased diversity of teacher materials, delivery, personalities, and teaching styles
- Team members have only one major subject to prepare; they may specialize in the subject each is qualified to teach
- Ease in grouping and regrouping students for instruction; more flexibility and diversity in scheduling
- Transition easier to high school organization

Disadvantages:
- Difficulty in finding convenient planning time
- Difficulties in integrating the disciplines
- Greater number of possible personal and professional conflicts
- Teachers continue to specialize, encouraging tendency to departmentalize

FIGURE 5.2   Advantages and disadvantages of various team sizes.

Source: From *Teaching at the Middle Level:* A Professional's Handbook by Schurr et al. Copyright © 1996 by D. C. Heath and Company. Reprinted by permission of Houghton Mifflin Company. All rights reserved.

are available. A recent study indicates that teams of teachers that meet for 45 minutes four to five times a week function more effectively than teams that meet less frequently. This same study shows that there is a positive correlation between the frequency of team planning time and contact with other building resource staff. Teams that meet frequently have more interaction with counselors, resource teachers, and administrators. This is good news for students because of the active involvement of greater numbers of professionals in their education (Erb & Stevenson, 1999).

As team members, we should respect team planning time by being on time and focused. So much can be accomplished by teachers working together. Having an agenda for topics to be discussed and decisions to be made over the course of a week helps teachers stay on task. Team planning time should be separate from, and in addition to, individual planning time. A school and administration that values effective team functioning will arrange the schedule to accommodate both. Having to choose between using a planning period for individual planning or team planning is no choice at all. Both are vital to instructional effectiveness with young adolescents. Figure 5.3 gives you an idea of the variety of decisions and projects that teams of teachers confront. This list is by no means exhaustive. So many issues, so little time!

A recommendation that enhances the well-made choice of team members, staff development to help members grow, and efficient use of team planning time is the stabilization of team continuity for at least 3 years. Newly formed teams function differently than teams that have been together for a number of years. If norms have been established that foster effectiveness, then keeping teams together makes sense (Jackson & Davis, 2000).

Members of an effective team grow together and enhance one another. They establish a team name and motto. They build ownership and enthusiasm. Teachers spend time together in productive ways as they show care and concern for one another and for students. They come to consensus on a philosophy, and then they publicize and teach according to that philosophy. Effective teams take advantage of opportunities to alter their schedule within flexible blocks of time. They group and regroup students for instruction. They work together to accomplish all the items on their ever-growing, ever-changing agenda. They meet with students and confer with parents as a unit. They plan curriculum together and make connections among concepts and topics as they use varied instructional strategies. Student welfare guides all decisions and actions. Effective teams of teachers put students first.

- Upcoming thematic unit
- Student progress reports
- Scheduling of parent conference(s)
- Student disciplinary issues
- Overlapping curricular topics
- Special education referrals
- Field trip to museum
- Problem with graffiti in boys' bathroom
- Book fair approaching
- Bulletin board display rotation
- Choosing liaison to district committee
- Encouraging parent participation
- Rotating responsibility for student teacher
- Participation in writing competitions
- New rules during construction on field
- Use of computer lab time
- Discussing article given to team by principal
- Jointly grading unit projects
- Discussion of individual students as need arises
- Preparing for long-term substitute for teacher requiring maternity leave

FIGURE 5.3   Possible agenda items for team planning.

Team leadership and membership.   Every team needs a designated facilitator, usually called the team leader. This task is sometimes rotated among members for varying lengths of time. Being a team leader takes more time than being a team member. Agendas must be made, extra meetings are often required with school-wide leadership teams, communication among team members and school administrators generally falls to the team leader, and the day-to-day functioning of the team relies in great measure on the team leader's efficiency.

Being a good team member is a task to be taken seriously and that cannot be defined by one set of standards. However, there are some traits that are common among those who are valued team members. They include participating in discussions and sharing ideas; following through on decisions that are made; maintaining a spirit of trust, collaboration, and confidentiality; aiding in the achievement of team goals; and attending meetings on time, ready to work (Erb & Doda, 1989).

Benefits of teaming.   As you can imagine after reading the preceding discussion, effective teaming has far-reaching benefits. The benefits listed in Figure 5.4 will be referred to throughout the rest of this text.

In *Meet Me in the Middle,* Wormeli (2001) views subject integration as one of the major benefits of teaming. He tells us that subject integration works well when it helps students understand who and why and how. It's not about making forced connections, but rather looking for and being conscious of natural links. Teams of teachers can coordinate assignments, focus on larger skills and concepts, and progress logically through subject matter. Subject integration shows students that "real jobs are seldom separated into pure disciplines" (p. 137). In Chapters 6, 7, and 8, we will explore subject integration and interdisciplinary instruction.

Involving other school professionals.   Most middle school teams are limited to core curriculum teachers. Our students spend the majority of their school time with this group of two to five teachers. However, involving other school professionals makes the teaching/learning connection more viable.

Benefits for Teachers

Teachers get to know students well.

Procedures and routines are consistent.

Decisions are made collaboratively.

Collegiality and professionalism are enhanced.

Synergy is created by combining strengths.

Intellectual stimulation is the result of collaboration.

Instructional strategies may be shared.

Curriculum integration is easier to implement.

Assessment is enhanced by joint evaluation.

Classroom management is more consistent.

Benefits for Students

Teachers get to know students well.

Learning environment is more personalized.

Sense of belonging is created.

Connections among curricular areas are more obvious.

Support from teachers is comprehensive.

More opportunities for grouping and regrouping exist.

FIGURE 5.4   Benefits of teaming for teachers and students.

Standard 7

Knowledge 4: Middle level teacher candidates understand the interrelationships and interdependencies among various professionals that serve young adolescents (e.g., school counselors, social service workers, home-school coordinators).

Courses taught outside the core are sometimes called related arts, exploratory curriculum, wheel courses (referring to the fact that they are rotated), or encore courses. Perhaps the most generic term is *related arts,* so we'll stick with that. Related arts courses are vital to middle level philosophy. They provide skills training, use talents, and motivate students to pursue real-life activities.

As you will see in the next section of this chapter, related arts teachers and their courses are the main reason teams are able to benefit from common planning time. While appreciating related arts teachers for the valuable learning resources they provide to our students, we also realize that without them core teams could not function effectively.

The principal plays a pivotal role in the success of teaming. When first implemented, teaming requires fundamental changes in any school's organization. To make the logistics work, principals have to rethink staffing, time allocations, and use of facilities. To begin and then continue the structure of teaming requires the principal to understand and support the concept of interdisciplinary teams (Rottier, 1996).

As discussed in Chapter 3, the structure of special education in middle school is increasingly inclusive. This means that students who qualify for special services are part of both core and related arts courses. If the schedule can be arranged, everyone involved benefits from having special educators in the classroom alongside core and related arts teachers, all working in concert with students with special needs and any other students in need of assistance. Some schools have even arranged schedules that support co-planning and co-teaching. As teams of students reflect the school population, they also share equally the students who have physical and learning differences. Many schools designate special education teachers to be part of specific teams and serve the students of those teams. In smaller schools, the special educators may serve the entire population of special education students.

Guidance counselors can have a tremendous influence in middle school. As discussed in Chapter 2, middle grades students sometimes appear to be on social, emotional, and/or physical roller coasters. Counselors who are compassionate, committed, and specially trained to work with young adolescents have the potential to make significant differences in the life of a school. Teams of teachers should communicate regularly with guidance counselors about the students they serve.

Creating team identity.   The teachers' vision for their team leads the team to a unique persona, an identity that is recognizable. An element of "this is who we are" does much to unify and motivate both those who teach and those who are taught.

A team name is essential. Don't announce to students in August that they should be proud to be members of team 7B. Screams excitement, doesn't it? How about "Welcome to the Stargazers! Stargazers dream big and aspire to reach the stars," as the lights go out and stars are projected around the room. Some teams of teachers choose a name and a theme and stick with it year after year. They accumulate "stuff" that speaks to their theme. It grows with time. Other teams allow students to choose a name and theme each year. They let the students experience the democratic process and take ownership of team identity. There are pros and cons with each method. No matter how it's chosen, the team's name and theme should be proudly displayed in each team classroom and used in fun ways all year.

Choosing team colors and a team chant helps students feel that they belong. If fabric painting is part of art, then banners and T-shirts can be made. The music teacher may help students write a chant or song. Most sixth graders will participate willingly, while many seventh graders will consider it all pretty silly, although they may secretly take a good deal of pride in their team identity. Eighth graders will often take a renewed interest in team identity and relish being the "big guys" of the middle school. Students of each grade level will generally reflect the enthusiasm of the team teachers. Team identity will be as meaningful as teachers choose to make it.

Creative Grouping Alternatives

While the vast majority of middle schools are organized by grade level, there are other possible organizational structures. In some schools, more than one structure is operating and variations of basic organizational schemes can be found. It would be impossible to describe all the possibilities, so as we briefly discuss three of these structures, keep the basics of teaming in mind. The possibility of creating alternative structures is very real. "The knowledge and experience required for such organizational transformation to take place is available; only the will needed for more widespread implementation is lacking. For the sake of the education of young adolescents, it must be done" (George & Lounsbury, 2000, p. 113).

 Multiage grouping.   Do you remember reading about the one-room school in an introduction to education class? Maybe you've seen the reruns of "Little House on the Prairie." Some communities, like the village of Romulus, New York, have renewed interest in their local education history. The folks of Romulus actually restored their historic one-room schoolhouse and moved it to the campus of the current high school to celebrate their education heritage. Today we perceive the concept of the one-room school as a form of *multiage grouping.*

In middle schools, multiage grouping refers to students of two or more grade levels being placed on the same team and even in the same classroom as ability levels and interests dictate. If a school serves grades 6, 7, and 8, students spend 3 years with others who are their same age and students who are younger and/or older than they are. At the end of each year, one-third of the students in the multiage group go on to high school to be replaced by the incoming sixth graders the following fall. One-room schools were formed out of necessity due to the size of the communities and the economics dictated by limited population, resources, and qualified teachers. Today multiage grouping is driven by the benefits derived from long-term relationships. Discipline becomes much less of a problem as relationships are maintained over three years. Beginnings and endings of the year are much smoother. Parent relationships are more positive and productive. Interethnic relationships improve. When there are signs of difficulty of any kind, multiage problem solving and growth are possible. Teachers, students, parents, and administrators who practice multiage grouping have discovered that many school processes work better when more permanence is part of school relationships (George & Lounsbury, 2000).

More research is definitely called for concerning multiage grouping. This research needs to track students and teachers for 2 or more years to capture the complexities of this creative alternative. Affective outcomes appear to be positive, while the effects of multiage grouping on academic achievement are mostly unknown (McLaughlin, Irvin, & Doda, 1999).

Looping.   The rationale for this grouping alternative is that if teams of students and teachers have many benefits, why not extend those relationships, and consequently the benefits, over longer periods of time? A continuous year-to-year instructional plan involving the same team of students and teachers has been called teacher rotation, student-teacher progression, and, most recently, *looping.*

While research is sparse concerning achievement benefits, anecdotal accounts tell us that looping is a very positive experience. Some have reported that this gift of time is experienced in the second and third years when moving ahead instructionally is not hampered by the necessity of getting acquainted, becoming familiar with achievement status, and working out procedures. In *Making Big Schools Feel Small* (2000), a medical analogy is given. George and Lounsbury relate that the idea of finding a new dentist or doctor for a child every year makes no sense. If it's important for physicians to know their patients as they develop, how can we not see that it's equally important for teachers to know their students as they grow? This is a powerful argument.

Schools-within-a-school.   This third alternative method of grouping also takes advantage of long-term relationships. In large middle schools, separate community systems may be established composed of a sixth grade team, a seventh grade team, and an eighth grade team (or teams). *Schools-within-a-school* is also known as a house plan. The original *Turning Points* (Carnegie Council on Adolescent Development, 1989) document recommended that "The student should, upon entering middle grade school, join a small community in which people—students and adults—get to know each other well to create a climate for intellectual development. . . . One successful solution to unacceptably large middle schools is the schools-within-a-school or house arrangement" (pp. 37–38).

In this grouping, each *house* is a microcosm of the total school population. If facilities permit, each house has its own distinct area of the building(s), where at least the core classes are held. Ideally each house has its own administrative area, along with related arts classrooms. If this isn't possible, houses stay together for core classes and then join others on individual grade levels for related arts and intramural activities.

Schools-within-a-school have been around for years. The organization requires fewer alterations and less effort than multiage grouping and looping. Teachers remain with a team of students for one grade level. The benefits are derived from grade to grade by teams continuing to work together closely as a unit. They can plan for ongoing themes as they build a curriculum for a specific group of students. Sixth graders know who their teachers will be in subsequent years. They also know that the students on their team will remain constant. So the benefits of a small learning community can be realized without the complexities inherent in other arrangements (George & Lounsbury, 2000).

Advisory Programs

Turning Points (1989) directs middle schools to provide opportunities for each student to have a close relationship with an adult within the school.

> Every student should be well known by at least one adult. Students should be able to rely on that adult to help them learn from their experiences, comprehend physical changes and changing relations with family and peers, act on their behalf to marshall every school and community resource needed for the student to succeed, and help to fashion a promising vision of the future. (p. 40)

Middle grades educators have met the challenge of having every student known well by at least one adult by establishing advisor-advisee relationships. *Turning Points 2000* (Jackson & Davis, 2000) supports the intention of the original document and contends that the advisory period is important to the development of strong interpersonal bonds.

Standard 7

Knowledge 5: Middle level teacher candidates know advisory/advocate theories, skills, and curriculum.
Performance 2: Middle level teacher candidates serve as advisors, advocates, and mentors for all young adolescents.

Advisory defined.   A special time regularly set aside for small groups of students to meet with specific adults is known as *advisory* period. Some schools call it advisor/advisee or home-based guidance or teacher-based guidance. Typically advisory groups meet for 20 to 30 minutes, at least three days a week.

Organizing advisory.   Schools vary in their approaches to advisory. Some are quite structured with all advisory periods following basically the same plan—possibly a prescribed affective program using purchased materials to guide discussions and activities. Other schools leave advisory up to individual teams that decide how to best use the time. Some advisories are organized by day. For instance, Monday may be used for housekeeping activities, Tuesday for planned discussion, Wednesday for intramurals, Thursday for silent reading, and Friday for test preparation and homework completion. This kind of arrangement closely resembles the traditional homeroom and certainly does not best meet the developmental and affective needs of the middle school student. It does, however, afford the advisor a daily forum within which developmentally appropriate topics may be addressed if desired. Another approach might be for the team to decide on weekly or monthly themes that guide discussion and activities. Possible themes include self-awareness, respect, the dangers of substance abuse, healthy lifestyles, and celebrating differences.

The primary purpose for advisory is to meet the developmental and affective needs of students. Whatever schedule may be in place and regardless of the "plan," advisors should respond to crisis situations by giving advisees opportunities to ask questions, express fear or frustration, and, in general, draw comfort and guidance within the advisory setting. Incidents of school violence, crises of the 9/11 proportion, local happenings, or whatever is of concern to our students is appropriate advisory content.

Advisory discussions.   Given that the primary purpose of advisory is to create relationships that will help meet the developmental and affective needs of students, frank discussions should be regular features of the advisory schedule. In her book *Talk with Teens* (1995), Peterson outlines some descriptors that will be helpful for us to keep in mind when approaching discussions with our students, whether in small groups or individual sessions. These descriptors include:

1. All adolescents have a desire to be heard, listened to, taken seriously, and respected.
2. Some adolescents who are quiet, shy, intimidated, or untrusting will not spontaneously offer comments, but they, too, want to be recognized and understood as unique individuals.
3. All adolescents need support, no matter how strong and successful they seem.
4. All adolescents feel stressed at times. Some feel stressed most or even all of the time.
5. All adolescents are sensitive to family tension. Some are trying hard to keep their families afloat or intact. They may be unaware of it, but they might be using bad behavior to keep their parents focused on them—and together.
6. All adolescents feel angry at times.
7. All adolescents feel socially inept and uncomfortable at times.
8. All adolescents worry about the future at times.
9. All adolescents, no matter how smooth and self-confident they may appear, need practice talking honestly about feelings. (p. 3)

Some schools are implementing full-day advisory experiences to supplement their advisory program, or to supplant it. A study of full-day advisory sessions is in the works and the results so far are positive (Wormeli, 1999). Researchers are recommending occasional full-day experiences plus advisory lunches on campus and one-on-one student-advisor conferences each year. Sounds like a perfect match for the middle level philosophy we've explored so far.

Roadblocks to advisory.   While advisory by definition and in practice is a major tenet of middle grades philosophy, its widespread implementation remains elusive. Most middle schools have a nonacademic and nonrelated arts period during the day that serves as an administrative time, like a homeroom, but may have the label "advisory." Close examination is required to determine if the period is being used for purposes similar to those described in this section. As with so many concepts, having a designated period provides opportunity. What is done with the period makes the difference. Schurr et al. (1996) tell us that:

> . . . when schools are committed to respond to students' needs and teachers are willing to make the effort to provide a place and time in which long-term relationships between themselves and students can develop, the advisory program is a significant factor in making a middle level school a true middle school. (p. 89)

The "teachers are willing to make the effort" clause of this statement is critical. Many teachers view advisory as another preparation and are often unwilling to commit the time to make it valuable for students.

Please consider carefully how advisory can make a difference in the lives of middle grades students. You may find yourself in a school where advisory exists in name only. If you have the designated period, use it with your kids and for their direct benefit. The effort will be worth it. And remember that advisory is an attitude more than a program. It's an attitude that causes us to commit to know our students well, to advocate for them when possible, and to wear our advisor hats all day, every day.

STRUCTURES OF TIME

"Time is perhaps the most important but least available resource in American education" (Jackson & Davis, 2000, p. 131). We typically have 180 days with our students. That's a constant. How we choose to use these days is a critically important variable. As with other variables in life, there isn't just one right way. Fortunately, there are many options and variations to each. As educators, we have an awesome responsibility for organizing the time our students spend with us so optimal benefit is achieved. While some configurations appear to be more developmentally conducive than others, ultimately schools have to choose a schedule that facilitates their priorities (George & Alexander, 2003). In this section we will delve into how days can be scheduled for student movement through middle school.

This We Believe (2003) calls for flexible grouping, scheduling, and staffing, with teams designing and operating much of the program. *Turning Points* (1989) calls for teams to have the power to ". . . create blocks of instructional time to best meet the needs of students, rather than tailoring learning to fit a rigid schedule. Teacher control of scheduling can. . . make learning come alive for students" (p. 16). *Turning Points 2000* echoes this point by recommending that team teachers lengthen and shorten classes, as well as determine the frequency and order of classes to reflect instructional and student needs.

Sounds great, doesn't it? With flexible scheduling we can have team autonomy to use time in ways that respond to the needs of students. Reality? Rarely. As middle grades educators, we need to seize opportunities to fulfill the potential afforded us by 180 days a year with our students.

Traditional Scheduling

Although opportunity exists for flexibility and creativity in scheduling, the majority of middle school class periods remain 45 to 55 minutes long. Many schools schedule six or seven fixed periods a day, every day, all year long (Williamson, 1998). I'll be the first to say that a well-planned instructional period of 50 minutes is far preferable to a 90-minute period, half wasted. Limiting instructional time in each subject to an arbitrary 50 minutes is traditional, but perhaps not as effective as alternatives.

If we view time as a resource rather than an element of schooling to be managed, we see that perceived obstacles to using time in more constructive ways are worth overcoming. The good news is that "educators and administrators are focusing attention on the manner in which time is allotted to various subject areas during the day, seeking . . . a way to organize instruction more effectively and improve the quality of learning" (Kruse & Kruse, 1995, p. 1).

Alternatives to the Traditional Schedule

Dissatisfaction with both the limits of shorter classes and the inflexibility of traditional schedules has led increasing numbers of schools to reconfigure the way students and staff spend their days. No schedule is perfect, nor should any schedule be considered permanent. There are advantages and disadvantages to each that grow or recede in importance based on numerous variables. It's not necessary—and indeed prohibitive and downright impossible—to wait until all the anticipated kinks are ironed out of any given plan. While schedules need to stay fixed for given periods of time, they should be evolving and moldable from semester to semester, year to year.

The May 1998 issue of *Middle School Journal* is a theme issue called "What's New on the Block?" One of the articles by Hackman and Valentine (1998) gives six guidelines to consider when looking at scheduling alternatives. These guidelines are outlined in Figure 5.5. Ideally, administrators and teachers should examine alternatives, visit schools together, talk with practitioners actually using the alternatives, and spend time examining restrictions and absolutes as they look for ways in which they can be flexible.

The word "block" is used in many ways when discussing schedules. A block of time is a chunk of time—a longer period than the traditional 50-minute period. A *block schedule* is any schedule that allows for more time in class. It is important to understand that whatever the configuration of a block schedule, there are three major distinctions to be considered. Some forms of block scheduling increase the time spent in a given class period, but because the class may not meet every day the total minutes allotted to the class over the course of the year don't change. Other forms not only increase the time in a particular class, but also the total minutes for the year by increasing the number of times the class meets. Both of these differ from what is referred to as the flexible model where time is divided by teachers as appropriate for the day's academic plan.

4 × 4 semester block model.   The 4 × 4 is used in many high schools, and some middle schools are adapting the basics of the plan. In this model, four courses are completed during

1. The schedule should support interdisciplinary team organization.
2. The schedule should support an appropriate curriculum.
3. The schedule should support quality instruction in the disciplines through expanded and flexible uses of time.
4. The schedule should promote student development and supportive relationships.
5. The schedule should promote quality teacher collaboration.
6. The schedule should promote teacher empowerment.

FIGURE 5.5   Guidelines for schedule creation.

Source: From "Designing an Effective Middle Level Schedule," by D. G. Hackman and J. W. Valentine, 1998, *Middle School Journal, 29*(5), p. 3–13. Copyright 1998 by National Middle School Association. Reprinted with permission from National Middle School Association.

Sample of schedule for one student on a team

	Semester I	Semester II
8:00–9:30	Math	Math
9:30–11:00	Language Arts	Language Arts
11:00–12:00	Lunch and Advisory	Lunch and Advisory
12:00–1:30	Science	Social Studies
1:30–3:00	Related Arts	Related Arts

FIGURE 5.6 4×4 semester block model.

each semester. Figure 5.6 illustrates a variation for middle schools. In this sample, the student would have 90 minutes of math and 90 minutes of language arts every day of the year, but 90 minutes of science or social studies every day for only a semester. This plan would work well for a three-teacher team—one math, one language arts, and one science/social studies.

Alternating day model.   This model is also popular in high schools where it's often referred to as the A/B schedule. In middle school this model allows for three related arts periods or a course repeated daily. Figure 5.7 illustrates the basics of this model using eight periods on a 2-week cycle. Like the 4×4, a benefit of this model is that students change classes only four times a day and thus spend more minutes in each period.

A variation of the previous model is the alternating day model that follows a weekly cycle as illustrated in Figure 5.8, allowing for each class to meet three times a week rather than some two times and some three.

Daily plus alternating day model.   Some schools declare curricular emphasis in a certain subjects such as science and math. Others have a "back to basics" approach that invests more time in math and language arts. The daily plus alternating model in Figure 5.9 shows how a schedule can create time frames to accommodate some classes having twice as much time as others. This model still provides the benefit of longer class periods for all subjects.

Flexible block model.   The schedules presented so far provide longer class periods and, for some courses, considerably more total time. What the schedules don't provide for is flexibility. The model that best approximates the vision for scheduling in *This We Believe* and *Turning Points* is the *flexible block* schedule. This model provides large blocks of time allotted to teams to be used for instruction. A sample flexible block schedule is shown in Figure 5.10. Grade levels, and therefore interdisciplinary teams, have two large blocks to use as they deem appropriate. Early in the section, I wrote that even when given the opportunity to use flexibility in scheduling, most middle school periods remain fixed. Examining Figure 5.10 will reveal how easily a team could take their 250 minutes and divide them into five neat periods—math, language arts, science, social studies, and reading. Or they might divide them into four periods of 60+ minutes with one split around lunch or related arts. That is OK to do as a base schedule. It is not OK to do every day for 180 days.

Time	Monday	Tuesday	Wednesday	Thursday	Friday
8:00–9:25	1	5	1	5	1
9:25–10:50	2	6	2	6	2
10:50–12:10	Lunch/Advisory/Recess				
12:10–1:35	3	7	3	7	3
1:35–3:00	4	8	4	8	4

Time	Monday	Tuesday	Wednesday	Thursday	Friday
8:00–9:25	5	1	5	1	5
9:25–10:50	6	2	6	2	6
10:50–12:10	Lunch/Advisory/Recess				
12:10–1:35	7	3	7	3	7
1:35–3:00	8	4	8	4	8

Time	Sixth Grade	Seventh Grade	Eighth Grade
10:50–11:15	Advisory	Recess	Lunch
11:15–11:40	Lunch	Advisory	Recess
11:40–12:10	Recess	Lunch	Advisory

FIGURE 5.7 Alternating day model (2-week cycle).

Time	Monday	Tuesday	Wednesday	Thursday	Friday
8:00–8:45	1	1	5	1	5
8:45–9:30	2				
9:30–10:15	3	2	6	2	6
10:15–11:00	4				
11:00–12:00	Lunch/Advisory/Recess				
12:00–12:45	5	3	7	3	7
12:45–1:30	6				
1:30–2:15	7	4	8	4	8
2:15–3:00	8				

FIGURE 5.8 Alternating day model (weekly cycle).

Time	Monday	Tuesday	Wednesday	Thursday	Friday
8:00–9:30	1	1	1	1	1
9:30–11:00	2	2	2	2	2
11:00–12:00	Lunch/Advisory/Recess				
12:00–1:30	3	5	3	5	3
1:30–3:00	4	6	4	6	4

FIGURE 5.9 Daily plus alternating day model.

Time	Sixth Grade	Seventh Grade	Eighth Grade
7:35–8:00	Homeroom/Advisory	Homeroom/Advisory	Homeroom/Advisory
8:00–8:25	Related Arts/ Exploratory	Instructional Block	Instructional Block
8:25–8:50			
8:50–9:15			
9:15–9:40			
9:40–10:05	Instructional Block		
10:05–10:30			
10:30–10:55		Related Arts/ Exploratory	Lunch
10:55–11:20			Recess
11:20–11:45	Lunch		Instructional Block
11:45–12:10	Recess		
12:10–12:35	Instructional Block	Lunch	
12:35–1:00		Recess	
1:00–1:25		Instructional Block	Related Arts/ Exploratory
1:25–1:50			
1:50–2:15			
2:15–2:40			

FIGURE 5.10 Flexible block model.

Standard 2

Knowledge 6: Middle level teacher candidates understand that flexible scheduling provides the context for teachers to meet the needs of all young adolescents.

To make optimal use of the flexible block, teams of teachers should spend time devising about five different ways the schedule might be altered and brainstorm reasons for making the alterations. For instance, the science teacher plans to have students conduct a lab experiment that requires more than 50 minutes. The schedule is altered so that one science class meets for 150 minutes each day. The other teachers divide the remaining students (in the case of a four-person team, that would be 75% of the students) and rotate them through their subjects. Perhaps the team wants to see a special exhibit at the local museum. They would have 150 minutes for the trip without interrupting related arts schedules.

When teams have the autonomy to use their time, it is possible to rotate classes from day to day. We discussed the changeability of middle level students, how they may behave very differently from one day to the next. In fact, a student may approach school at 9:00 a.m. very differently than at 1:30 p.m. Teachers who rotate student schedules on a regular basis report that students respond differently to their teaching depending on the time of day. Not surprisingly, they find that their teaching styles and attitudes also vary—some are "morning people" and others function more enthusiastically as the day goes on. Thus, there are benefits in rotating classes of students to spread out the advantages, and to share the low moments equitably. On Monday, you may see groups A, B, C, and D in that order (ABCD). On Tuesday, you would see them in BCDA order and then on Wednesday in CDAB. Given uninterrupted team time, rotation is possible without interrupting schedules outside the team.

Perhaps the greatest benefit of the flexible block is that it accommodates *interdisciplinary instruction.* We'll explore this concept in detail in Chapters 6, 7, and 8. With the flexible block, time is available for large group experiences, uninterrupted video viewing, co-teaching, grouping/regrouping, guest speakers, joint projects—the list can go on and on.

Utilizing Longer Blocks of Time

Two elements are absolutely necessary to make longer blocks of time the effective instructional tools they can be. One element is continuing staff development. A 90-minute lesson is not two 45-minute lessons back to back. "Block scheduling requires teachers to rethink how they work. More time does not mean more of the same" (Gallagher, 1999, p. 15). Teachers need strategies appropriate for longer class periods. George and Alexander (2003) tell us that the most frequently reported outcome of longer blocks is better teaching—teaching that is more creative and innovative. More hands-on learning is possible with time for projects and opportunities for active student participation.

Making longer blocks work = Continuing staff development + Planning

The second necessary element is planning. With adequate staff development, teachers are equipped to open their instructional toolboxes and apply varying strategies to longer blocks of time. To do so in effective ways, both individual and common team planning time are necessary.

Both traditional and alternative scheduling can provide opportunities for curricular and instructional improvement. Maximizing the potential of any structure requires commitment, energy, and ever-developing expertise.

STRUCTURES OF PLACE

An important feature in the life of a middle school team is shared space. The core classes should be as close together as possible—either next door to one another, or at least on the same hallway. Proximity means fewer minutes lost in changing classes, fewer discipline problems in the hallways, and more opportunities for informal teacher-to-teacher contact (Jackson & Davis, 2000). Having an identifiable part of the building to call our own is a vital aspect of teaming. This is generally a built-in feature if a facility is constructed to accommodate middle level philosophy. Ideally there is a pod of classrooms including a science lab and a teacher workroom. With flexible scheduling, teams need to be free to move from classroom to classroom without disturbing other teams.

While we may have little control over the existence or location of shared team space, we have a great deal of control over our individual classrooms and the environments we create. What do we do inside our classrooms to make them livable, pleasant, and efficient? To answer this question requires thought and planning. There are multiple variables involved in the creation of our classroom environments including monetary resources of the school, actual size of the room, and creativity of the teacher. There's not a lot we can do about the amount of money the school district has, or chooses to spend, for physical amenities, and the size of the classroom is rarely a matter of choice. Sometimes the only variable within our sphere of influence is our own creativity.

The Inviting Classroom

We want our rooms to serve as an initial and continuing invitation to students. The environment should say to students "Welcome. This is a place where you are wanted." The amount of effort we put into the classroom environment is evident to our students.

First impressions are crucial. Having your classroom ready to go on the first day of school with a big WELCOME banner to greet your students will set the tone. Try standing by the doorway and shaking each student's hand as she enters and saying a personal "Welcome! I'm _____." Most 10- to 14-year-olds are not used to being greeted in such an adult way. It will make a lasting impression! Most of them will look away and giggle and give you what my daddy used to call a "deadfish" handshake. After a week or so, you can talk about the greeting. Ask students how it felt to be welcomed with a handshake. Talk to them about exuding self-confidence, a firm handshake, and eye contact. Repeat the greeting every few weeks.

Students need to feel safe and secure and comfortable. For some, these three factors don't exist outside the classroom. Their home and/or neighborhood environments may be less than desirable. You may bear the responsibility of providing one of the only inviting atmospheres they are currently experiencing. What a burden—and what an opportunity!

Standard 5

Performance 6: Middle level teacher candidates establish equitable, caring, and productive learning environments for all young adolescents.

NMSA.

Classroom Inventory

If you have the luxury of being hired in early summer for a position that begins in late August or September, you will have plenty of time to prepare your classroom. Unfortunately, some of you may be hired after school has already started because the enrollment allows the principal to add a position, or perhaps an emergency has led to the need to replace a teacher. Preparation may mean nights and weekends—whatever it takes to create a desirable environment.

It is vital to begin the creation of your classroom environment with a thorough inventory. Find and list the items available. Figure 5.11 will give you an idea of things to look for.

Once you know what you have, list any standard or basic items that are missing. They may be available somewhere in your building. Share your list of needs with your team, the custodial staff, and the main office staff. Don't be afraid to ask.

- Chalk/dry erase boards—don't cover them
- Assignment board (don't use valuable chalkboard space)
- Two trash cans
- Class work/homework baskets
- Podium on table or music stand
- Materials—appropriate for subject(s)
- Bulletin boards
- Place for posting rules
- Pets, plants
- Audiovisual equipment
- Computer(s)
- Windows/blinds/curtains
- Lighting accessories
- Desk
- Filing cabinet
- Shelves
- Bookcases
- "Cubbies," lockers, coat racks

FIGURE 5.11 Classroom inventory.

Planning the Basic Set-up

The kind of environment we create may depend on the subject(s) we teach and on our personal preferences. There are two imperatives for basic room arrangement. When setting up desks or student tables, we must provide for teacher **access** to all students and ways for students to **transition** from individual to small group to whole class instruction.

Access.   You need room to walk. You need to be able to reach each student in your classroom quickly. Proximity to students has both instructional and management advantages. Having a walking loop is an important way to accomplish proximity (Wolfgang, Bennett, & Irvin, 1999).

The configuration of desks in a row was typical in the recent past, and this configuration still persists in many classrooms. If lecture is the most frequently used form of instruction, then rows will work. Rows are easy to keep orderly. However, desks in rows also confine the teacher to the front of the room in the traditional power position. For standardized testing days or days dedicated to whole class lecture or strictly individualized work, desks in rows may be advantageous. But on typical days in a middle school classroom filled with active involvement, there are other configurations that allow for greater teacher access to all students. Students always need to feel the teacher's presence.

Transitions.   Whether you have 45- or 90-minute classes, your students will have *transitions* to make while following your lesson plans. If you are fortunate enough to have a large classroom that allows for easy movement, there are many room configurations that will work. If you are cramped for space by either a small classroom or a large number of students, your options may be limited.

Arranging desks or tables in small groups is the most usable and flexible configuration. If space permits the seating arrangement to be changed for transitions to individual and whole class work, that's terrific. If not, students can work individually or as a whole class from small group configurations.

When tables or desks are in small group configurations, make sure students understand your expectations for individual work. They may simply pull their desks apart or may turn them so they are not directly facing one another. For transition to whole class instruction, be sure all students can see and hear what's going on.

Efficient room arrangement =
Access + Transitions

Furniture, Equipment, and Materials

Once you have a basic set-up of desks or tables, it's time to plan the rest of the room. Your desk is an important feature of the classroom for you, but not for the students. As we will discuss in Chapters 7 and 8, students should see you sitting at your desk infrequently. It is an organizational tool for you where you may want to lay out materials you plan to use and keep information to which you need to refer. But the teacher's desk is not the focal point of a middle grades classroom. I suggest you choose a corner for a file cabinet, your desk, and a chair. It is your space and students need to respect that. Don't sit behind it and allow it to be a barrier between you and your students.

Learning centers are locations in your classroom where topics can be explored by individuals or small groups. Designate a table and shelves for a learning center. We'll talk more about setting up and maintaining these centers in Chapter 8.

A classroom library is appropriate regardless of the subject(s) you teach. Having interesting books, both fiction and nonfiction, on shelves for students to peruse and check out encourages reading.

If you have a computer(s) in your classroom, provide easy access and a method students follow for using technology. Frequency of use will depend on the subject you teach, the software available, and your encouragement. Do not allow your computer area to become a dumping ground for books and newspapers and jackets. If you are fortunate enough to have computers, by all means use them with your students.

As you plan for instruction, there will inevitably be materials involved. Maybe you'll use graph paper, newspapers, markers, maps, and so forth. Having materials organized and readily accessible will save valuable instructional time. Plastic crates and boxes that stack neatly work well. Teaching students good organizational habits will pay off. They need to know how to access and how to put away instructional materials. There's a knack to making all this organization work. The key is habit. Instill efficiency and respect for materials in your students from day one. It will pay off for each of the other 179!

Bulletin boards can be teaching tools in themselves. Many teachers merely purchase an assortment of posters, put them on the walls and bulletin boards, and then leave them all year. This is boring, and the posters rapidly become wasted instructional space once students have lost interest. You may have a few favorites that seem appropriate for the entire year, but choose carefully. Class/team/school rules may be left up and some inspirational posters are acceptable to use as permanent displays, but changing bulletin board displays is a creative and efficient way of bringing new information into the classroom. Bulletin board displays need to correspond to what's being learned. Make them interesting and interactive. Have groups of students design and make displays. Use student art or class work and display projects. Classroom wall space can be a dynamic teaching tool.

There should be a designated area where assignments and necessary books/materials are posted. This should be in a consistent location. Each afternoon before leaving for the day get into the habit of posting information for the following day. You do not necessarily need to write out the exact assignment, but have the space ready so you only have to fill in the details when it's appropriate.

You may want to add personal touches like plants to your classroom (let students rotate the responsibility for their care), couches, comfortable chairs, lamps, and so on. These items are a matter of space and availability and your own style. If time for individual reading is part of your day, seating options are enjoyed by students. Again, if they are in the habit of moving about the room in respectful ways, they will not abuse the privilege of sitting on a rug or in an overstuffed chair occasionally to enjoy silent reading.

Home Away from Home

The total time we as teachers spend in our classrooms is a considerable chunk. Think about it—at least 7 of every 24 hours of every school day are spent mostly within the walls of our classrooms. If we are in the school building from 7:30 a.m until 4:30 p.m., we may spend

1 1/2 to 2 of those hours in the halls, cafeteria, workroom, other classrooms, or on the field, and the remaining 7 in our own designated spaces. If we get up at 6:00 a.m. and fall asleep about 11:00 p.m., then 5 days a week we spend about 40% of our waking hours in our classrooms. "Home away from home" truly applies here!

Let your classroom reflect you, your care for students, and your interest in learning. Chances are you will experiment with configurations and move things around as the year goes by. You will learn what works best for your students in terms of your access and their transitioning. Learning centers will change and bulletin boards will develop in direct proportion to your creativity and the time you spend to make it happen. Remember that students are watching. Their curiosity and subsequent motivation depend on your keeping an organized and comfortable environment as part of your instructional planning. Use your classroom as a haven of security, a motivator of interest, and a workshop for organizational habits.

REFLECTIONS ON STRUCTURES OF PEOPLE, TIME, AND PLACE

How we choose to structure people, time, and place in the middle grades affects school climate and academic success. Some of the effects have been verified through research, while others are reported anecdotally. While many structures fall within an acceptable range, some follow more closely the tenets of *Turning Points* and *This We Believe*.

Creating smaller learning communities is a hallmark quality of middle level philosophy. The middle grades teacher/student team is most widely accepted as the optimum people structure. As we've seen in this chapter, there are many possible team configurations, some incorporating tracking, and some that group entirely heterogeneously. Some are quite small, and some are large. Some teams stay together for 1 year, others for 2 years, and, in extreme cases of looping, some stay together for 3 years.

Time, as a tremendous resource, is ours to use every school day. Arranging our structures of people within the school day and the school year is a responsibility that should not be taken lightly. There are so many variables in middle grades education that seem to be outside our control. Time is not such a variable. As educators, we are obligated to make the most of the 180 or so days we spend with our students. Longer blocks of time in classes provide opportunities for complete cycles of introductory experiences, inquiry, understanding, practice, reflection, and assessment. Putting blocks of time together for optimal learning and then incorporating flexibility both serve vital functions in the middle grades.

Manipulating our physical environments may be an ongoing process of working toward efficiency and comfort. In buildings designed for middle grades, arrangement of team classrooms and common areas are ideal for smaller learning communities. In traditional buildings, team classrooms can be grouped on one hallway. Beyond the configuration of classrooms and common team spaces, our responsibilities include our own areas where we meet with students. Choices of desk/table arrangements, use of wall space, walking and storage areas, and the atmosphere we create are all ours to make. The total effect of place relies in great measure on our efforts.

While the structures described in this chapter suit middle grades philosophy, there are schools all across America that are successfully educating young adolescents through responsive dispositions without many of the structures we have discussed. Understanding and appreciating the developmental processes of young adolescents and framing curriculum, instruction, and assessment around their needs and unique qualities will produce an atmosphere that fosters healthy physical, intellectual, emotional, social, and moral growth. It is possible for a school for middle grades students to be subject-area based with six classes a day and without clustering of classrooms, and still meet the needs of the students. It's possible, but certainly more difficult than if structures are in place that accommodate middle level philosophy. Keep in mind that structures aligning with middle level philosophy provide opportunities. They don't guarantee success. It's up to us to take full advantage of the opportunities provided by developmentally responsive structures of people, time, and place.

Group Activities

1. In groups of two or three arrange to visit with teachers from a school in your file. Your instructor will give you guidelines for arranging the visit. Your group will want to spend about 30 minutes with the teacher you visit to find out about their structures of people, time, and place. Using this chapter as a reference, work with your class to formulate questions/prompts that will lead to an understanding of the degree to which the teachers and students team, if and how tracking is used, the format of advisory, the schedule, and the physical layout of the building as it is used by teams and/or grade levels. The results of the school visits will be added to your school file.

2. Divide your class into four groups. Each group will be assigned one of the following structures of people: grade level teams, looping, multiage grouping, and schools-within-a-school configurations. Each group will formulate their best reasoning in support of their structure. They will present their reasoning to the class as "panels of experts." If possible, invite other students (education majors and others) to listen to the panels and then allow the audience, even if it's only your classmates, to critique the panel discussions.

Individual Activities

1. Knowing what we do about the development of middle grades students, write a description of what you would consider to be the most appropriate use of a week of daily 30-minute advisory periods.

2. Given the classroom inventory in Figure 5.11, draw an overview diagram of a classroom arrangement you might want for the subject area you plan to teach. Be prepared to explain (and possibly defend) your arrangement choices.

3. How do you feel about the "to track or not to track" debate? Specifically, what kind of grouping (and regrouping) do you feel might be most appropriate for your chosen subject area?

4. Explain in your own words the statement, "An individual can make a difference: a team can make a miracle."

Personal Journal

1. Think back to your days in middle grades. Was tracking used at your school? Was it formally orchestrated so that it was obvious to everyone, or was it more covertly arranged and just understood by students? Were you in a particular track in certain subjects? How did you feel personally, and how do you think you were perceived?

2. Do you remember classrooms that seemed to "invite" students? If so, what qualities did the classroom have? Was it a function of the physical amenities or of the teacher's personality? Was it a combination? If you don't remember any of your classrooms as obvious "invitations," what elements might have created this kind of atmosphere?

3. Do you think you have the personal skills to function as a cooperative and effective member of a teaching team? If so, what personal qualities give you this ability? If not, and if you want to be part of teaming, what personal qualities do you want to cultivate to allow you to participate productively on a team?

Professional Practice

(It would be helpful to reread the description of Lester Jefferson in Chapter 4, as well as the descriptions of Michael in Chapters 2 and 3.)

Lester Jefferson is in his fifth year of teaching on a two-teacher team with Sandra Henderson at Marrington Middle School. Mr. Jefferson was introduced to us in Chapter 4. Marrington is a small school with about 100 students. Mr. Jefferson and Mrs. Henderson and the other two-person teacher team at the school loop with their students who become a team in seventh grade and stay together in eighth grade. So each of the two teams of teachers have a group of about 50 students for two grades, seven and eight. The students come from a K–6 setting about three miles from Marrington Middle, which is a separate building on the edge of the high school campus. All three schools are focal points for the small rural community they serve.

Lester Jefferson

If you ask Mr. Jefferson and Mrs. Henderson to tell you about their Marrington experience, you'll hear high praise for everything from the planning phase of the middle school to the community support they continue to enjoy. No doubt they will tell you about how much they enjoyed creating their shared space. When a new high school was built on the same property as the old one, the former art/industrial tech/home economics building was saved. This building became the middle school. It has a wide hallway from one end to the other with a restroom on each side. Because of its previous use, water lines and faucets were already installed on each side, so two science lab areas were possible. Each team decided to occupy a side. Mr. Jefferson and Mrs. Henderson divided their space with an accordion wall so they could have separate classrooms or work together with all their students at once. They have separate doors into the hallway and can leave a doorway width opening in the accordion wall for easy access. Because it is an older building, they have high ceilings and large windows. It's perfect for them.

Michael, seventh grade

Michael is a seventh grader assigned to Mr. Jefferson and Mrs. Henderson. We met him in Chapters 2 and 3 as a sixth grader. Because he was retained twice, he is a physically mature almost 15-year-old. Michael was anxious to get out of the K–6 elementary; he just didn't fit in. At Marrington the kids are the same ones he has grown up with, but being with just seventh and eighth graders on the edge of the high school campus is more of a relief than he expected it to be. Mr. Jefferson has taken a personal interest in Michael. He knows Michael enjoys the outdoors and doesn't like being cramped up in a classroom. It's not that Michael rebels against school, he'd just rather not be there.

1. Mr. Jefferson is good for Michael for a number of reasons. Which of the following aspects about Mr. Jefferson probably matters least when it comes to his influence on Michael?

(a) He is an adult role model for Michael.

(b) He is personally secure and confident.

(c) He spent time in the Navy.

(d) He seeks to have personal relationships with his students.

2. Michael appears to enjoy school more at Marrington Middle. Getting up in the mornings and making it to school on time is not quite the chore it was in elementary school. Given what we know about Michael, which of the following probably has the greatest effect on his change of attitude?

(a) Michael feels more comfortable in a setting where he is not around children much younger and smaller than he is.

(b) Michael likes having two different teachers rather than just one.

(c) Michael's girlfriend who is in the ninth grade is on the same campus.

(d) Michael likes the fact that he will have Mr. Jefferson for two years in a row.

3. The space shared by Mr. Jefferson and Mrs. Henderson seems to be ideal for their needs. One thing that isn't mentioned is the dilemma over offering classes other than the core four of science, math, language arts, and social studies. The first 4 years, the Marrington teachers used their personal interests and talents to offer physical education, art, and beginning Spanish. This year, arrangements have been made with the high school for the Marrington students to be part of some of their related arts courses. Which of the following is most likely the greatest benefit for Mr. Jefferson and Mrs. Henderson?

(a) Mrs. Henderson took primary responsibility for art and Spanish while Mr. Jefferson taught physical education. Neither was certified in these areas, so they are relieved not to have the responsibilities.

(b) The students get to be around older students in related arts courses.

(c) When Mrs. Henderson had the students in art and Spanish, Mr. Jefferson had planning. When he had the students in physical education, Mrs. Henderson had planning. Now that the students go to the high school for related arts,

Mrs. Henderson and Mr. Jefferson have time for common planning.

(d) The students now have the opportunity to meet teachers they will have when they get to high school.

Constructed Response

The apparent success of Marrington Middle School can be attributed to many factors. Given what you know about the structures of middle school, what are some of the primary contributing factors to the school's success?

Internet Resources

Ability Grouping
http://www.indiana.edu/ ~eric_rec/ieo/bibs/ability.html

The current research on, and practices of, ability grouping are the focus of this Web site. The information is derived from Web sites, libraries, bookstores, and other sources.

Block Scheduling
http://www.education.umn.edu/carei/blockscheduling

The University of Minnesota College of Education maintains this site featuring research and information on block scheduling.

Design Share
http://www.designshare.com

The characteristics of an ideal middle school facility are featured on this site. Floor plans that support middle level philosophy of structures of people, time, and place are displayed.

References

Carnegie Council on Adolescent Development. (1989). *Turning points: Preparing America's youth for the 21st century.* New York: Carnegie Corporation.

Erb, T. O., & Doda, N. M. (1989). *Team organization: Promise-practices and possibilities.* Washington, DC: National Education Association.

Erb, T. O., & Stevenson, C. (1999). From faith to facts: *Turning Points* in action—What difference does teaming make? *Middle School Journal, 30*(3), 47–50.

Flowers, N., Mertens, S., & Mulhall, P. (2000). What makes interdisciplinary teams effective? *Middle School Journal, 31*(6), 53–56.

Gallagher, J. (1999). Teaching in the block. *Middle Ground, 2*(3), 10–15.

George, P. S. (1995). Untracking your middle school: Nine tentative steps toward long-term success. In H. Pool & J. A. Page (Eds.), *Beyond tracking; Finding success in inclusive schools* (pp. 141–154). Bloomington, IN: Phi Delta Kappa Educational Foundation.

George, P. S., & Alexander, W. M. (2003). *The exemplary middle school.* Belmont, CA: Wadsworth/Thomson Learning.

George, P. S., & Lounsbury, J. H. (2000). *Making big schools feel small: Multiage grouping, looping, and schools-within-a-school.* Westerville, OH: National Middle School Association.

Hackman, D. G., & Valentine, J. W. (1998). Designing an effective middle level schedule. *Middle School Journal, 29*(5), 3–13.

Jackson, A. W., & Davis, G. A. (2000). *Turning points 2000: Educating adolescents in the 21st century.* New York: Teacher College Press.

Knowles, T., & Brown, D. F. (2000). *What every middle school teacher should know.* Westerville, OH: National Middle School Association.

Kruse, C. A., & Kruse, G. D. (1995). The master schedule and learning: Improving the quality of education. *NASSP Bulletin, 79*(571), 1–8.

Lounsbury, J. H. (1991). *As I see it.* Columbus, OH: National Middle School Association.

Maranto, R., Milliman, S., Hess, F., & Gresham, A. (1999). *School choice in the real world: Lessons from Arizona charter schools.* Boulder, CO: Westview Press.

McLaughlin, H. J., Irvin, J. L., & Doda, N. M. (1999). Crossing the grade level gap: Research on multiage grouping. *Middle School Journal, 30*(3), 55–58.

National Middle School Association. (2003). *This we believe: Successful schools for young adolescents.* Westerville, OH: Author.

Peterson, J. S. (1995). *Talk with teens about feelings, family, relationships, and the future: 50 guided discussions for school and counseling groups.* Minneapolis, MN: Free Spirit.

Pool, H., & Page, J. A. (Eds). (1995). *Beyond tracking; Finding success in inclusive schools.* Bloomington, IN: Phi Delta Kappa Educational Foundation.

Rottier, J. (1996). *Implementing and improving teaming: A handbook for middle level leaders.* Westerville, OH: National Middle School Association.

Schurr, S. L., Thomason, J., & Thompson, M. (1996). *Teaching at the middle level.* Lexington, MA: D. C. Heath.

Smrekar, C., & Goldring, E. (1999). *School choice in urban America: Magnet schools and the pursuit of equity.* New York: Teachers College Press.

Williamson, R. D. (1998). *Scheduling middle level schools: Tools for improved student achievement.* Reston, VA: National Association of Secondary School Principals.

Wolfgang, C. H., Bennett, B. J., & Irvin, J. L. (1999). *Strategies for teaching self-discipline in the middle grades.* Boston: Allyn & Bacon.

Wormeli, R. (1999). Teacher advisories: Full day experiences are the way to go! *Middle Ground, 2*(4), 17–18, 40.

Wormeli, R. (2001). *Meet me in the middle: Becoming an accomplished middle-level teacher.* Portland, ME: Stenhouse.

Yu, C., & Taylor, W. (1997). *Difficult choices: Do magnet schools serve children in need?* Washington, DC: Citizens' Commission on Civil Rights.

6

Middle Grades Curriculum

Curriculum is the primary vehicle for achieving the goals and objectives of a school. As commonly conceived, curriculum refers to the content and skills taught. In developmentally responsive middle level schools, however, curriculum embraces every planned aspect of a school's educational program.

National Middle School Association, 2003, p. 19

Use this diagram as an organizational tool. In the boxes beside the chapter headings, indicate the dates by which the reading should be completed.

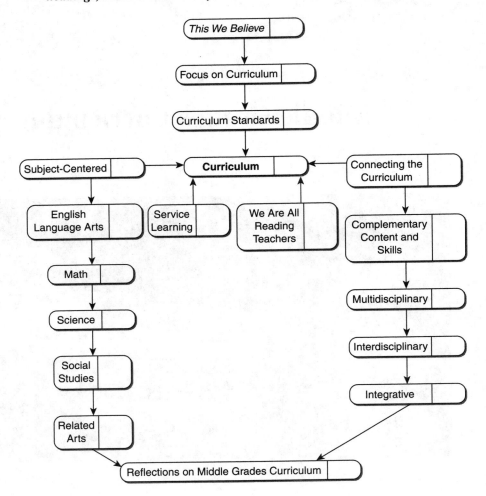

INTRODUCTION

Writing a chapter on middle level curriculum is complex and vexing. At first, it seems straightforward, even simple. After all, curriculum is the "what" of teaching. It's the meat, the content. We should simply discuss language arts, math, science, social studies, and related arts. Yes, indeed, that's the curriculum . . . according to one all too common level of thought. However, so simplistic a discussion is inadequate and unfair to you. Books, articles, and conversations about curriculum run the gamut from shallow coverage to deeply insightful. What you will read in this chapter is an overview. It will, however, give you a glimpse of just how complex and challenging the issue of curriculum, and in particular, middle level curriculum, is.

Chapter 1 helped us build a rationalization and a foundation for middle level education. In Chapter 2, we examined the development of our students. In Chapter 3, we discussed how our students may embody diversity. We looked at ourselves in Chapter 4. In Chapter 5, we considered how we might put middle level education together in organizational contexts.

Understanding who we are and how, where, and when we come together (Chapters 1 through 5) is essential before going on to examine what we do when we are together (Chapters 6—curriculum, 7 and 8—instruction, and 9—assessment). While in many ways separating curriculum, instruction, and assessment is artificial, it serves our purposes to explore the various aspects of each before attempting to understand their complex union. Let's begin our discussion of curriculum with the guidelines provided by the National Middle School Association, the organization that is both the result and the voice of our dedication to middle level students.

Standard 3

Middle level teacher candidates understand the major concepts, principles, theories, standards, and research related to middle level curriculum and assessment, and they use this knowledge in their practice.

THIS WE BELIEVE ABOUT CURRICULUM

Our guiding document tells us "curriculum embraces every planned aspect of a school's educational program" (p. 19). So *curriculum* consists of specific classes, core and otherwise, as well as guidance, advisory, activities of all kinds, and provided services. Whatever is intentionally designed to support and accomplish the mission of the school is curriculum. A developmentally responsive middle level school will embrace a curriculum that is challenging, integrative, and exploratory, finely tuned to the characteristics and needs of young adolescents.

This We Believe (National Middle School Association, 2003) tells us that we all share the responsibility of developing curriculum. As educators we must

> Cultivate the disposition and skills of scholarship and provide learning experiences that draw from and integrate the disciplines. The rapid expansion of knowledge constitutes the ongoing and difficult task of selecting content that is at the same time relevant, challenging, integrative, and exploratory. No other phase of designing a successful middle school is as important as creating a developmentally responsive curriculum. (p. 24)

Middle level curriculum = Relevant + Challenging + Integrative + Exploratory
---

To begin our discussion, let's summarize *This We Believe* as it pertains to curriculum. Following this summary, the remainder of the chapter will "flesh out" the concepts of *This We Believe* and add others. In this section, all page numbers after quotes refer to the *This We Believe* document.

Standard 3

Knowledge 1: Middle level teacher candidates understand that middle level curriculum should be relevant, challenging, integrative, and exploratory.

NMSA.

Relevant

"Curriculum is relevant when it allows students to pursue answers to questions they have about themselves, content, and the world" (p. 20). A relevant curriculum will result in student understanding of the connected, "holistic nature of knowledge" (p. 20). A relevant curriculum will be "rich in personal meaning" (p. 21). By creating new interests, a relevant curriculum will stretch "students to new levels of learning" (p. 21).

Relevant curriculum = Holistic + Personal meaning = New levels of learning

Challenging

To be challenging, a curriculum must address three issues. Let's look at them separately.

A challenging curriculum must include "substantive issues and skills . . . " (p. 21). Substantive issues are those that are worthwhile in the eyes of both adults and students. They are issues that are important enough to study in depth. This in-depth study uses basic principles along with alternative points of view involving skills that are contextually based. A challenging curriculum addresses both why and how things happen.

Challenging curriculum = Substantive + Multileveled + Responsibility building

Given the diversity exhibited by middle level students, implementing a curriculum that is appropriate for their varying levels of understanding is a daunting task. Finding ways to meet our students where they are, build on prior knowledge and experiences, and continue to challenge them should become our daily ritual.

The third issue requires that the curriculum enable students to take responsibility for their learning. Exercising decision-making must be a component of a developmentally responsive curriculum that is challenging.

Integrative

"Curriculum is integrative when it helps students make sense of their lives and the world around them . . . " (p. 22). To be integrative, *This We Believe* tells us curriculum must be coherent, must connect school to students' daily lives, and must encourage students to grasp the totality of their experiences. Applications, connections, construction of knowledge—making sense of content and experiences is what *integrative curriculum* is all about. "Intellectual, social, physical, communication and technical skills are learned and applied in context" (p. 23).

Integrative curriculum = Connections + Sense-making

Exploratory

"The entire curriculum at this level should be exploratory" (p. 23). Exploratory, then, does not refer to a set of courses, but rather an attitude and an approach. Discovery and choice are embedded in the disposition that encourages exploration.

Exploratory curriculum = Discovery + Choice

This We Believe states that "Exploration, in fact, is the aspect of a successful middle school's curriculum that most directly and fully reflects the nature and needs of young adolescents" (p. 23).

FOCUS ON CURRICULUM

In 1997 Edward Brazee wrote, "Only in the last few years has the curriculum become a focal point of study as reformers recognized the limitations of concentrating on school climate and school organizational issues to change the middle school" (Brazee, 1997, p. 196). This quote indicates that middle schools, in their inevitable coming-of-age, moved beyond structure to more difficult and less tangible areas of concern. The debate over curriculum led to the stand taken in *This We Believe*. As definitive as it appears, the debate continues as we strive to define options for curriculum that address the goals of middle level philosophy.

What we teach in the middle grades is influenced by a number of factors. For decades, school districts and states used curriculum guides for each subject and grade level that were only occasionally altered. Changes in accountability have precipitated changes in how we view and use curriculum guides of all descriptions. States now use subject area standards to determine curriculum.

Keep in mind that in middle level we view curriculum as more than just what is taught/learned in the classrooms, whether determined by district guides or state standards. Don't lose sight of the broader view of curriculum as everything that is planned for students in our schools. But for the sake of the discussion that follows, we will deal with that part of the curriculum that is planned by classroom teachers for students. Listing the topics to come will help us organize our discussion. We will look at

- Curriculum standards
- Subject-centered curriculum
- Levels of curriculum connections
- Service learning
- Shared responsibility to teach reading

CURRICULUM STANDARDS

Perhaps the most profound influence on what is taught/learned in schools is wielded by standards set by subject area organizations and states. Very simply, *standards* define what students should know and be able to do. Schmoker (1999) tells us that "The kind of significant, sustained improvement that we need in schools will not occur in an isolated, freelance culture, where no one knows what anyone else is doing" (p. 111). Standards openly reveal what others are (or should be) doing to promote learning and

Standards = What students should know + What students should be able to do achievement. "Standards are a balanced, coherent articulation of expectations for student learning" (Carr & Harris, 2001, p. 19). *Turning Points 2000* (Jackson & Davis, 2000) is very clear about recommendations for standards:

> Teach a curriculum grounded in rigorous, public academic standards for what students should know and be able to do, relevant to the concerns of adolescents and based on how students learn best. Considerations of both excellence and equity should guide every decision regarding what will be taught. Curriculum should be based on content standards and organized around concepts and principles. (p. 23)

NMSA

Standard 3

Knowledge 4: Middle level teacher candidates are knowledgeable about local, state, and national middle level curriculum standards and of ways to assess the student knowledge reflected in those standards.

Performance 2: Middle level teacher candidates use current knowledge and standards from multiple subject areas in planning, integrating, and implementing curriculum.

It's rare to pick up an education journal dated 1998 or later and not find numerous references to standards. Standards are here to stay (Schmoker, 1999). Standards documents will not be effective if we fail to make them living documents, subject to our best thinking, over time. While they won't (and shouldn't) be stagnant, the concept of standards will endure. *Turning Points 2000* provides criteria for excellent standards in Figure 6.1.

National and State Standards

In the 1980s, the National Council of Teachers of Mathematics introduced us to standards for teaching and learning math in prekindergarten through grade 12. In the 1990s, national

---

Academic standards should be
. . . concerned with the essential ideas.
. . . useful and clear.
. . . rigorous, accurate, and sound.
. . . brief.
. . . feasible, taken together.
. . . accessible.
. . . developmental.
. . . selected and modified or supplemented by consensus.
. . . adaptable and flexible.

FIGURE 6.1   Criteria for identifying excellent standards.

organizations for language arts, science, and social studies followed suit. The related arts—physical education, health, performance arts, and others—have now formulated standards. These subject area organizations have used groups of experts to determine essential knowledge and skills in the disciplines that students should master. Familiarity with these standards is essential for middle grades teachers as we specialize in one or two subject areas.

All 50 states now have standards documents that are followed by school districts. Most state documents are very similar to the national standards. Most states have developed their own assessment criteria aligned with these standards. I can't overemphasize the impact of state assessment standards. You will no doubt be handed copies of the standards for your teaching area(s) and grade level(s) and urged by your administrators and mentors and teammates to make the standards the guide and dominant "playbook" in your classroom. Your state standards will be the basis of your curriculum—perhaps the standards will actually BE your curriculum.

Standards in the Classroom

Wormeli (2001a) states without hesitation that we need standards in the classroom. Among his reasons are that standards

- Help us consistently move every child ahead
- Spell out what our communities consider essential and enduring knowledge
- Provide a guide rope that we can return to if we swim too far away during our investigations
- Give us a plan to follow as we create intellectually rigorous and developmentally responsive experiences (p. 65)

With rationale like these and others we move forward, embracing what has come to be called the standards movement. Classroom teachers were asked in the September 2001 issue of *Educational Leadership* to respond to the question of how standards had changed their lives. When asked whether standards had made their teaching better or worse, they answered without exception that standards had enhanced their professional performance. What a testimonial to the value of clear, accessible standards to guide our classroom practice. "With standards as guidelines, a teacher can work from the ground up—knowing where the students have been and the steps necessary to advance their skills and understanding" (Galus, 2002, p. 77).

Standards should be viewed as empowering. They give us structure and consistency, without dictating instruction. All of the instructional strategies in Chapters 7 and 8 can be used to teach standards. Standards are not restrictive. Standards don't necessarily dictate sequence. We are still free to take a set of standards for our subject(s) and grade(s) and move them around to match our classroom and team goals. They can be introduced in one unit, emphasized in another, practiced in another, and assessed and reinforced as often as desired. Within the structure of curriculum standards, we can create learning experiences that are developmentally responsive for middle grades students. "Every teacher deserves clear, manageable, grade-by-grade sets of standards and learning benchmarks that make sense and allow a reasonable measure of autonomy. Anything less is frustrating, inhumane, and counterproductive" (Schmoker & Marzano, 1999, p. 21).

Practical advice on the use of standards in the middle school classroom, and in whole schools and districts, is found in a very useful resource titled *Figuring It Out: Standards-Based*

Reforms in Urban Middle Grades, published by The Edna McConnell Clark Foundation. The author, Ann Lewis (1999), suggests that standards-based teaching is best implemented when content standards are augmented by three major types of support:

- Performance standards that tell teachers and students how good is good enough when attempting to meet the content standards;
- Articulate, sane assessment policies; and
- Assistance for teachers in analyzing their teaching, preparing lessons and assessments, and developing on-site and local networks of expertise. (p. 35)

Creating a standards-based classroom in the middle grades should be a collaborative effort, contributed to by teammates, administrators, central office personnel, curriculum leaders, and so on. Lewis makes this analogy:

> For many teachers, shifting to standards-based teaching is a bit like learning to eat calamari. Someone else orders it off the menu, then everyone gives it a try. The adventurous eaters may relish it immediately, while others need to taste it a few more times before willingly ordering it themselves. (p. 34)

A reality check must be included at this point. The recent proliferation of standards is often overwhelming. They provide not only the skeletal structure of a body of knowledge, but also the detailed fleshing out of a discipline. Rather than fit and efficient, we often seem to have an obese body of prescribed knowledge that simply won't fit in a 180-day school year. Our best judgment tells us that something must be trimmed in order to spend ample time on more foundational aspects. Perhaps the best way to put our curriculum standards on a diet is thoughtful and ongoing discussions with colleagues about what to emphasize and what to minimalize.

 ## SUBJECT-CENTERED CURRICULUM

As we discussed in Chapter 5, most middle school teams structure their days around subject areas—some very distinct, others blended to various degrees. While standards are typically organized by disciplines, this in no way prevents the blending of subjects. Both discipline-based curriculum and curriculum based on connections among disciplines are not only possible, but desirable. Concepts "can 'function' both within disciplines and across them" (Jackson & Davis, 2000, p. 48).

As a matter of practicality, we'll initially examine major subject areas separately. Keep in mind that in the previous section we established that on a national level, as well as on state and local levels, the curriculum for subject areas, or disciplines, is heavily influenced by standards documents. Later in this chapter, we'll discuss disciplines that are referred to as related arts, subjects that are important to middle grades philosophy but that may not be part of a school's required curriculum.

Each core subject area has its own national organization. These organizations are made up of educators from all aspects of education: teachers, administrators, subject experts, and others with keen interest in the discipline represented. The organizations have governance structures, position statements, multiple conferences, publications, resource guides, and Web sites. They have also taken on the responsibility of formulating standards. Middle school teachers derive numerous benefits from membership in these organizations. I urge you to go online and explore the organizations that represent the subject(s) you want to teach.

English Language Arts

Major Organization: National Council of Teachers of English (NCTE)
Web site: *http://www.ncte.org*
Student membership: $20/year (includes one journal)
Regular membership: $40/year (includes one journal)
Journals for middle grades:

Language Arts (for elementary and middle level)

Voices from the Middle (middle level)

Special feature: Middle Web

- Browse middle grades news
- Download curriculum guides
- Chat all year long with teachers
- Examine student work
- Take visual tours of high-performing schools

Standards

The English language arts standards were written in 1996 through a joint effort of NCTE and the International Reading Association (IRA). The standards articulate a consensus that has grown out of actual classroom practice. The standards are designed to be suggestive, not exhaustive. States have used the national standards to create more specific criteria to influence curriculum at the state, district, local, and classroom levels. There are 12 content standards that are interrelated and should be considered as a whole. The standards address, among other things

- range of materials students should read
- importance of students' knowledge of language use, variation, and conventions
- reading strategies
- knowledge needed to use language in writing, speaking, and making visual representations
- connections between reading and writing
- research and inquiry
- technology-driven modes of research and data synthesis (from *http://www.ncte.org*, 2003)

Position statements

NCTE has designated specific position statements for middle grades. The general areas addressed include selection of materials, gender-balanced curriculum, and incentives for excellence, tracking, and writing. General position statements address topics including reading, censorship, assessment, storytelling, drama, class size, and culturally/linguistically diverse students. These statements can be accessed through the NCTE Web site.

Mathematics

Major Organization: National Council of Teachers of Mathematics (NCTM)

Web site: *http://www.nctm.org*

Student membership: $34 (includes one journal)

Regular membership: $68 (includes one journal)

Journal for middle grades: *Teaching Mathematics in the Middle School*

Special feature: Illumination Web site with interactive multimedia investigations

Standards

The standards proposed by NCTM are based on members' core beliefs about students, teaching, learning, and mathematics. Recognizing that decisions made about content of school mathematics have important consequences for both students and society, the document *Principles and Standards for School Mathematics* was published in 2000 to provide guidance. One of its six principles is the Curriculum Principle that states, "A curriculum is more than a collection of activities: it must be coherent, focused on important mathematics, and well articulated across the grades" (NCTM, 2000, p. 14). Following this principle, NCTM developed 10 basic standards categories. Five of the standards are process-oriented: problem solving, reasoning and proof, communication, connections, and representation. Five of the standards are content-based: number and operations, algebra, geometry, measurement, and data analysis and probability. The standards are detailed for grades PreK–2, 3–5, 6–8, and 9–12.

NCTM prefaces the special section for grades 6–8 of *Principles and Standards for School Mathematics* (2000) with strong statements concerning the development of middle level students. Sample statements include:

> Middle grades students should see mathematics as an exciting, useful, and creative field of study. . . . In the middle grades mathematics classroom, young adolescents should regularly engage in thoughtful activity tied to their emerging capabilities of finding and imposing structure, conjecturing and verifying, thinking hypothetically, comprehending cause and effect, and abstracting and generalizing. . . . An ambitious, focused mathematics program for all students in middle grades is proposed in these standards.
> (From *http://www.nctm.org*, 2003, p. 211)

Position statements

NCTM provides an extensive list of position statements on content topics and grade level issues. They propose that all teachers of math at the middle level have extensive preparation in content to create an atmosphere of confidence where the process standards of NCTM are emphasized—problem solving, reasoning and proof, connections, communication, and representation. We are urged to work with other teachers and to be sensitive to students and parents from diverse racial and cultural backgrounds.

Science

Major Organization: National Science Teachers Association (NSTA)

Web site: *http://www.nsta.org*

Student membership: $30 (includes one journal)

Regular membership: $65 (includes one journal)

Journal for middle grades: *Science Scope*

Special feature: The Middle School Science Classroom—a Web link of articles, resources, teacher interactive section, discussion board

Standards

The National Science Education Standards outline what students need to know and be able to do in order to be scientifically literate. They promote excellence and equity for all students in science. The standards state that science should be an active process for students. In other words, science is something students do, with inquiry central to science learning.

Position statements

NSTA offers statements on a broad range of topics. The statement pertaining to middle grades addresses five major areas—needs of young adolescence, model programs, model teachers, necessary resources, and professional interactions. (From *http://www.nsta.org*, 2003)

Social Studies

Major Organization: National Council for the Social Studies (NCSS)

Web site: *http://www.ncss.org*

Student membership: $29 (includes one journal)

Regular membership: $55 (includes one journal)

Journal for middle grades: *Social Education*

Special feature: "Middle Level Learning" (three annual supplements with *Social Education*)

Standards

The standards developed in 1997 for social studies encompass 10 strands:

- Culture
- Time, continuity, and change
- People, places, and environment
- Individual development and identity
- Individuals, groups, and institutions
- Power, authority, and governance
- Production, distribution, and consumption
- Science, technology, and society
- Global connections
- Civic ideals, and practices

The integrative nature of social studies is a big factor in middle grades education. Most of the themes used in interdisciplinary instruction and integrative approaches are derived from social studies. No longer a subject where memorizing dates and names is paramount, social studies in the middle grades can and should be an exciting and worthwhile learning adventure. NCSS tells us that the primary purpose of social studies is to help students make informed decisions with the public good in mind as they actively support a democratic society with a culturally diverse population.

Position statements

The position statements of NCSS are rich with detail. The categories include ability grouping, citizen education, commercialism, democratization of schools, multicultural and global education, and testing, all of which can be accessed online (From *http://www.ncss.org,* 2003).

Related Arts

We established in Chapter 5 that most middle schools consider English language arts, math, science, and social studies to be the core subjects. A variety of other courses are typically offered, which I have chosen to call "related arts." In an article titled "The Evolution of Middle Schools," Paul George (2001) tells us that these related arts (or exploratory or elective) courses have been an "important part of the curriculum since the early days of the junior high school" (p. 41).

Related arts courses may include art, physical education, health, vocal music, instrumental music, technology, home/consumer arts, industrial arts, foreign language, and more. While middle grades teachers and schools openly acknowledge the value of related arts to student development and learning, there often appears to be a gap, real or perceived, between core and related arts teachers. Related arts areas of the curriculum sometimes are "on the fringes of middle school innovations, especially interdisciplinary teaming" (Doda & George, 1999, p. 32). We are warned against using a term such as "core" when it is used opposite the word "noncore" to refer to related arts, or classifying courses as academic and nonacademic. This kind of terminology can be inflammatory if personal and professional relationships are not strong. Scheduling restricts many related arts teachers from fully participating in team meetings and functions and makes contributing to interdisciplinary teaching and units difficult.

How can we attempt to close the gap? Doda and George (1999) give us some ideas:

1. Related arts teachers can be given advisory groups or co-advise with a core area teacher.
2. Related arts teachers can be placed on teams or assigned to teams on a rotating basis.
3. Related arts teachers can form their own teams and share common planning.
4. Related arts courses can contribute content for ongoing and specific assessment.
5. Administrators should make sure related arts issues and concerns are included in faculty meeting agendas.
6. School personnel such as administrators and counselors can take related arts concerns to team meetings.
7. Considerations should be made for related arts classes when teams decide to take students out of school for part of the day or when they attend core team meetings.
8. The schedule should allow for equal amounts of planning time for all teachers.
9. Related arts subjects should be included in interdisciplinary and integrative curriculum planning.

Sometimes relationships among subject areas and teachers can be improved simply through honest dialogue and awareness. Principal leadership plays a pivotal role in school climate issues such as these.

What follows is a very brief discussion of some of the related arts areas.

Arts education.   This is a broad category that includes related arts courses typically available in middle school. Major arts-related organizations joined to create standards in 1994 that apply to what the Consortium of National Arts Educators Association considers the four categories of arts disciplines: visual arts, music, theater, and dance. The Music Educators National Conference (MENC) developed goals for arts education that focus on understanding, appreciating, and being able to communicate within and through the arts.

Most middle schools offer an art course that is primarily visual arts. Some actually require students to take art for varying lengths of time each year, while others are grade level specific. In some schools, art is a choice for students. Teachers of core subject areas should regularly visit art classes and be aware of student displays. Visual arts courses very often allow students to discover and demonstrate talent that hasn't yet become evident in other areas. Students with artistic talent can be encouraged to use and expand their talent in other courses.

Vocal and instrumental music courses are available in most middle schools. Both types of music courses are most likely to be attended by choice, rather than as required fare. In elementary school, students are exposed to vocal music on a regular basis attributing to students choosing chorus or choir as an option in middle grades. In middle grades, students who take private instrumental music lessons may form the backbone of those courses. While some students will experience instrumental music for the first time in a middle grades course, programs of instrumental music that tend to thrive rely in some measure on communities where music lessons and easy access to instruments exist. Music programs in some middle schools serve primarily to give students awareness of the art form, while in others musical groups present entertainment on occasion and participate in competitions. The preface statement for the music standards for grades 5–8 tells us that the middle grades are critical to how music will be perceived and used in adulthood.

Health and physical education.   Most middle schools require students to be part of physical education classes each year. Health education is approached in a variety of ways. The curriculum for health courses varies by state and by district. Elements of health education are sometimes incorporated in science, but most frequently they are part of physical education. Some middle schools even contract with outside organizations to provide health education.

In 1995, the Joint Committee for National School Health Education Standards developed guidelines for school health standards. The topics include health promotion, disease prevention, healthy behaviors, influence of media on young adolescent health, goal setting, and decision-making.

Experts in the field of health education have identified 10 content areas as necessary for a comprehensive school health education and recommend a developmentally appropriate program based on community needs, with at least 50 hours per year of instruction in health-related areas. The 10 content areas are community health, consumer health, environmental health, personal health and fitness, family life education, nutrition and healthy eating, disease prevention and control, safety and injury prevention, prevention of substance use and abuse, and growth and development.

Technology education.   The broader phrase associated with technology is "information literacy." We all know that there is absolutely too much information in any discipline for any of us to "know it all." Not only is there a wealth of information, the information is constantly changing. The old adage that says "Give me a fish and I'll eat for today. Teach me to fish

and I'll eat for a lifetime" applies here. All teachers in all disciplines should be instructors of "fishing" techniques.

Our libraries are now media centers. Simply learning how to use the computerized systems that lead to information is a major coup. Regardless of the subject, we are all responsible for introducing students to resource generators and requiring that they use them.

Many middle schools offer specific courses that are basically technology-centered. Courses in keyboarding are prevalent, as are courses that relate to software programs and how to use them. The categories of the standards developed by the International Technology Education Association include the nature of technology, technology and society, design, and recommended abilities.

Industrial, home arts, and consumer education.   When I was in middle school (junior high), courses in this general category were simply called "shop" and "home ec." With advancements in technology and added sophistication, we have changed both names and content. Middle schools now offer courses with titles like "Family and Consumer Science," "Trade and Industrial Arts," and "Technology and Design." The classes are co-ed, with girls and boys learning similar information and skills. By virtue of their content, the classes are interactive and hands-on in nature, ideal attributes for courses for young adolescents.

Foreign language.   Typically there are two levels of foreign language instruction in middle school. Foreign language classes with curriculum equivalent to what students encounter in courses for which they receive high school credit (generally referred to as Carnegie Units) are usually offered to eighth graders who show promise and/or interest in languages.

Many middle schools have language classes that expose students to the culture of one or more countries and give minimal exposure to the associated language. Courses of this nature are often short in duration, possibly 6 weeks, allowing a student to become familiar with a number of cultures and languages. For instance, a seventh grader may have 6 weeks of Spanish culture and 6 weeks of French culture interspersed with other brief related arts courses.

The American Council on the Teaching of Foreign Languages (ACTFL) developed a vision statement that includes the philosophy that all Americans should be proficient in at least one language and culture in addition to English.

In Chapter 1 we recognized that the purpose of middle level education involves both academic and affective domains. The middle grades receive criticism both in philosophy and practice based on less than optimal progress of middle level students on standardized assessments such as the National Assessment of Educational Progress (NAEP) and the Third International Math and Science Study (TIMSS). In our efforts to strengthen this level of schooling, our focus must continually rest on what we teach and how we teach it—in both the four core subjects and the related arts. Strong programs require teachers who are competent and confident in the disciplines—all the disciplines. Schmoker (1999) tells us "The current interest in interdisciplinary learning still leaves room for emphasizing the disciplines. As Howard Gardner points out, we must not be in a rush to toss out the disciplinary baby with the bath water; a good grounding in disciplines is the best basis for interdisciplinary success" (p. 89). The next section discusses connections among the disciplines, not with the intent of "watering down" content but rather of strengthening the disciplines by giving them heartier context.

Standard 4

Performance 1: Middle level teacher candidates use their depth and breadth of content knowledge in ways that maximize student learning.

CONNECTING THE CURRICULUM

Most of us who have taught middle grades have realized the benefits of connecting curricular areas to whatever extent is feasible and appropriate. Concerning these connections, however, researchers tell us that it is imperative that we move toward clarity in defining our practices in middle level curriculum. In doing so, research studies can help us determine which approaches to connecting the curriculum yield the most positive results in student learning (Powell & Faircloth, 1997). The practices referred to include, among others, interdisciplinary, multidisciplinary, thematic, and integrative curriculum. Pick up any book or article dealing with middle level curriculum and you'll find these and other related terms. A brief discussion of semantics will be helpful here to identify and explain nuances that have developed as the body of literature on connecting the curriculum has grown. The terms "connecting" and "integrating/integration" are often used interchangeably in defining the process of looking for bridges or commonalities between historically distinct subject area curriculum strands. However, the writings of James Beane and others have redefined an integrated curriculum to encompass a much more sophisticated and comprehensive approach to connecting curriculum strands referred to as "integrative" curriculum. In the interest of clarity, when we discuss the various approaches to connecting curriculum, the four most widespread methods are described briefly in Figure 6.2.

			Comprehensive
Simple →			
Complementary Content and Skills	**Multidisciplinary**	**Interdisciplinary**	**Integrative**
• may alter timing	• alters timing	• alters timing	• alters timing
• uses content mapping	• uses content mapping	• uses content mapping	• uses content mapping
• subjects separate	• subjects separate	• subject boundaries blurred	• subjects interwoven
• teacher driven	• teacher driven	• teacher driven	• student and teacher driven
	• content-based	• content-based	• themes derived by student-teacher interaction and are based on student concerns and societal issues

FIGURE 6.2 Connecting the curriculum.

Regardless of definitions, procedures, and components, helping our students see and study connections within, between, and among subject areas can bring content alive, increase understanding, and more closely link "school learnin'" to real life. Coming to a common understanding of terms so that specific research concerning results is possible may or may not happen on a large scale. As teachers, however, it is our responsibility to determine approaches to curriculum that work best for our students.

Standard 3

Knowledge 2: Middle level teacher candidates understand the interdisciplinary nature of knowledge and how to make connections among subject areas when planning curriculum.

Disposition 5: Middle level teacher candidates are committed to implementing an interdisciplinary curriculum that accommodates and supports the learning of all young adolescents.

Three benefits derived from making connections among curricular areas that enjoy widespread acceptance, according to Weilbacher (2001), include

1. Teacher/student and student/student relationships are formed and fostered in positive ways.
2. Learning is made more relevant.
3. Connections are made not only among disciplines, but also within the community and students' own experiences.

What you're about to read represents both a compilation of what others have said about curricular connections and how I have come to understand and practice the broad concept.

Standard 4

Knowledge 2: Middle level teacher candidates know how to use content knowledge to make interdisciplinary connections.

Complementary Content and Skills

Curriculum mapping, a process developed and promoted by educators such as Heidi Hayes Jacobs (1997), is an effective way for teachers to plan a year of instruction and then share their plans and alter sequencing of three major elements:

- Process and skills
- Essential concepts and topics
- Assessment products and performances

Individual teachers arrange these elements on a calendar in sequences so the elements build on one another. A team of teachers then share their calendars. Carefully, they view the curriculum of their fellow teachers. They look for gaps and repetitions in individual calendars and complementary fits among subject areas. When natural connections are spotted, teachers negotiate timing so that a cohesive plan emerges that makes sense for student learning. The process is referred to as curriculum mapping. It may be accomplished in broad, simple ways, or it may involve details to any extent desirable. Curriculum mapping is a form of communication that allows teachers to make informal decisions about curriculum (Jacobs, 1997).

Through curriculum mapping, it is possible for teams of middle school teachers to recognize content topics and skills emphases that naturally fit together. For example, the science teacher may plan to use pendulum swings the second week in October as part of a 6-week study of physics. This would be an ideal time for the students to study circles, radii, and arcs in math. The language arts teacher may plan to study the elements of short stories, including Edgar Allen Poe's "The Pit and the Pendulum." The three teachers don't change their lesson plans. They alter the timing of topics. Pendulums do not constitute a theme, merely a focal point around which multiple content areas and skills fit.

Multidisciplinary Approach

The *complementary content and skills* approach requires little extra effort on the part of teachers. A curriculum map makes tweaking timing a relatively simple thing to do. The multidisciplinary approach also uses curriculum mapping, but in a more complex way. As teachers share their maps they do so with the intent of choosing a theme around which complementary content and skills may revolve, a theme that unifies topics and concepts in two or more subject areas. Teams will typically determine a theme and then decide what each subject area can contribute and when and for how long the theme will guide and unite their disciplines.

Along with curriculum mapping, a process called *webbing* is valuable. In a thematic web used in multidisciplinary instruction (see Figure 6.3), the theme is in the middle and the subject areas form the web. In *multidisciplinary instruction,* the subject areas remain distinct, and through the theme, students see connections. They see content learning in one area applies to another area (Knowles & Brown, 2000).

Multidisciplinary, or theme, teaching will only serve its purpose of enriching the curriculum through connections if those connections are not artificial or forced. Just as connections should be meaningful, so should the choice of themes. Knowles and Brown (2000) warn against choosing themes that are popular and fun but not significant and relevant.

Standard 3

Performance 4: Middle level teacher candidates develop and teach an integrated curriculum.

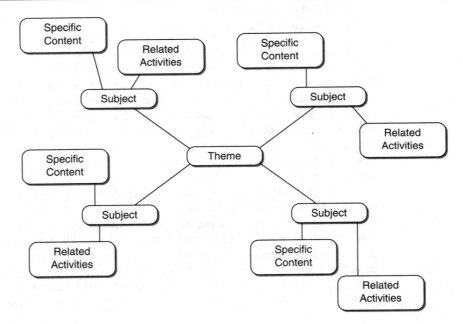

FIGURE 6.3 A multidisciplinary approach web.

Interdisciplinary Approach

An interdisciplinary approach is generally considered a more involved strategy for connecting curriculum than a multidisciplinary approach. Themes tend to be more conceptual in nature rather than content-based. For example, multidisciplinary teaching may revolve around "seasons," while an interdisciplinary approach might have "change" as the theme. A theme of seasons is more limited with fewer avenues to explore than a theme of change.

When teachers work together to explore a concept such as change by connecting multiple subjects, subject area boundaries are often blurred. Figure 6.4 lists some themes that are more concept-based as opposed to content-based.

Both curriculum mapping and theme webbing are excellent tools for planning interdisciplinary instruction. In Chapters 7 and 8, we will discuss how to use both tools to enhance curriculum through effective instruction.

Integrative Curriculum

Of all the terms used to describe connecting the curriculum, "integrative" elicits the most controversy. Not only do practitioners and researchers use it to mean different degrees of connections, but when defined by the most prolific of all writers about integrative curriculum, the concept itself is controversial. The concept of integrative curriculum as defined by author James Beane attracted much attention in the 1990s middle school scene with the publication of his book *A Middle School Curriculum: From Rhetoric to Reality* (1993). We're going to spend more time here than we did on the other three varieties of curriculum connections because what Beane proposes is the most prescriptive of all the published versions of how the curriculum might be connected. I'm not using "prescriptive" to mean recipe-like, but rather as a way of saying that there are guidelines in integrative curriculum that are not part of the other versions of connecting the curriculum.

I had the privilege of being present for what is considered a landmark event in the development of middle level curriculum. In November 1995, at the National Middle School Association annual conference in New Orleans James Beane presented his version of integrative curriculum. Following Beane's presentation, Paul George outlined possible dilemmas

• Activism	• Innovations
• Beginnings	• Interdependency
• Celebrating differences	• Journeys
• Change	• Justice
• Conflict resolution	• Prejudice
• Conservation	• Self-awareness
• Freedom	• Societal dilemmas
• Heroes	• Symbolism
• Independence	• Wellness

FIGURE 6.4   Conceptual themes.

and/or problems with Beane's approach. Listening to these two giants of middle school philosophy influenced me, as has reading their works over the years. The September 1996 issue of *Middle School Journal* includes the transcripts of the two speeches along with other articles about curriculum. Tom Erb (1996), editor of the journal, says that "Not until Paul George raised a plethora of concerns . . . had any serious challenge been posed to the notion that there are no legitimate alternatives to a fully integrated curriculum" (p. 2).

NMSA

Standard 3

Disposition 4: Middle level teacher candidates realize the importance of connecting curriculum and assessment to the needs, interests, and experiences of all young adolescents.

Performance 3: Middle level teacher candidates incorporate the ideas, interests, and experiences of all young adolescents in curriculum.

Beane (1993) proposes an integrative curriculum that he says should become "the whole, planned curriculum of the middle school" (p. 105). A major distinguishing factor of this curriculum is that the themes chosen for study should result from the intersection of problem-based student concerns and large social issues. Students and teachers determine themes jointly and plan the direction of study together. Skills needed to conduct this kind of study go beyond those normally promoted in middle grades such as communication, computing, and researching. Beane suggests a broader range, including those in Figure 6.5.

---

1. Reflective thinking, both critical and creative, about the meanings and consequences of ideas and behaviors.
2. Identifying and judging the morality in problem situations; that is, critical ethics.
3. Problem solving, including problem finding and analysis.
4. Identifying and clarifying personal beliefs and standards upon which decisions and behaviors are based; that is, valuing.
5. Describing and evaluating personal aspirations, interests, and other characteristics; that is, self-concepting and self-esteeming.
6. Acting upon problem situations both individually and collectively; that is, social action skills.
7. Searching for completeness and meaning in such areas as cultural diversity.

FIGURE 6.5   Skills for integrative curriculum.

Source: From *A Middle School Curriculum: From Rhetoric to Reality, 2nd ed.* (pp. 60–62), by J. Beane, 1993, Columbus, OH: National Middle School Association. Reprinted with permission from National Middle School Association.

Beane envisions a curriculum with core and related arts subject areas blended in the study of meaningful themes. He says the curriculum he proposes is conducive to heterogeneous grouping and accommodates individual differences. Teachers are facilitators who are also learners right along with students.

There are schools that have adopted Beane's integrative curriculum, but by most accounts they are rare. Their stories can be found in the literature. The most widely publicized school is Brown Barge Middle School in Pensacola, Florida. The principal of Brown Barge says her biggest concern is that fully implementing Beane's vision is very hard work requiring daunting amounts of teacher time and energy. She says, "Having the vision and creating and implementing it are one thing, but none of that compares to maintaining and sustaining it" (Powell, 1999, p. 29). A study conducted by Weilbacher (2001) echoes the concerns of Principal Camille Barr. He reports that "teachers who want to organize their curriculum in an integrative manner are having difficulty maintaining their commitments . . . the time it requires to plan, implement, assess, and defend takes a toll in emotional and familial ways" (p. 25). Of course, just because it is hard to do doesn't mean we shouldn't attempt to develop integrative curriculum if we have the knowledge and support to do so. We simply need to have a realistic picture of what is involved and set our self-expectations accordingly.

Paul George (1996) responds to claims that integrative curriculum is superior to subject-centered curriculum. Although his response directly followed Beane's proposal, he also includes the broader forms of connecting the curriculum—multidisciplinary and interdisciplinary. He prefaces his points by saying, "I do not believe there is an educational silver bullet. . . . I believe that IC [Integrated Curriculum] designs have great value, but that IC has not proven to be of greater value than other designs" (p. 13). He says there is little evidence that integrated curriculum accomplishes any of a list of desired outcomes "more effectively than exciting teaching of a well-prepared traditional curriculum" (p. 13). His list of outcomes is composed of elements we should all strive for, including opportunities for real problem solving, independent learning, in-depth learning, application, differentiation, transfer, and retention. George also says that he is not "opposed to innovation in, or integration of, the middle school curriculum" (p. 12). Instead he wishes "to assist middle school educators in the development and implementation of relevant, realistic, and rigorous curriculum experiences whenever possible" (p. 12).

Once again we return to the notion of balance as illustrated in Figure 6.6. George (1996) states that all curriculum designs rest with well-prepared, committed teachers. With strong subject foundations and connections among disciplines established to any degree considered appropriate, curriculum in middle grades will foster learning and motivate interest and achievement.

Standard 3

Performance 1: Middle level teacher candidates successfully implement the curriculum for which they are responsible in ways that help all young adolescents learn.

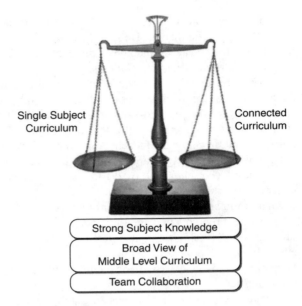

Single Subject
Curriculum

Connected
Curriculum

Strong Subject Knowledge

Broad View of
Middle Level Curriculum

Team Collaboration

FIGURE 6.6   Achieving balance: Curriculum.

 ## SERVICE LEARNING

"Service learning should be at the core of every school's curriculum because it gives young people purpose and nurtures their spirit as few experiences can" (Krystal, 1999, p. 61). We often think of *service learning* as a nice addition to what we do in middle school, if time permits. That's a very different approach compared to making service learning an embedded part of a school's curriculum. These are two ends of the spectrum with most middle schools somewhere in between.

Service learning and volunteerism are not the same. Volunteerism has benefits to the volunteer and the person/group receiving the help. Service learning takes the service connected to volunteerism and adds the dimension of learning. "Although it is related to both community service and volunteerism . . . , service learning is unique in that it links community service and volunteerism with academic learning" (Fertman, White, & White, 1996, p. 3). The authors of *Service Learning in the Middle School: Building a Culture of Service* continue by saying that service learning is not an add-on to programs that exist, but rather "a methodology that infuses service into the school's curriculum" (p. 3). "Service learning is a method by which young people learn and develop through active participation in thoughtfully organized experiences led by qualified adults" (Krystal, 1999, p. 58).

Middle schools generally incorporate occasional service projects. Young adolescence is the ideal age for service experiences. When *Turning Points* (1989) called for connecting schools to the community, service opportunities certainly filled the bill then, and they con-

Standard 1

Performance 7: Middle level teacher candidates engage young adolescents in activities related to their interpersonal, community, and societal responsibilities.

NMSA.

tinue to do so now. In the outline of the moral development of young adolescents, *This We Believe* (National Middle School Association, 2003) says that they

- are generally idealistic, desiring to make the world a better place and to make a meaningful contribution to a cause or issue larger than themselves.
- often show compassion for those who are downtrodden or suffering and have special concern for animals and the environmental problems that our world faces.
- are increasingly aware of, and concerned, and vocal about inconsistencies between values exhibited by adults and the conditions they see in society. (pp. 47–48)

As teachers, we can capitalize on these characteristics and provide a mechanism for the design and implementation of service learning.

> Service learning = Preparation + Service + Reflection + Celebration

There are four major elements of service learning: preparation, service, reflection, and celebration. Each element is vital and none should be omitted.

Dundon (2000) advises that teachers listen to students before beginning a service learning project and putting the model in place. She suggests that we ask students what they care about rather than arranging projects ourselves. The payoff can be profound. Once the students have spoken concerning their priorities, the preparation part of the cycle can begin.

Perhaps the greatest impact of service learning comes in viewing how the roles of students change from the traditional views held by youth to the views held by youth involved in service learning. Fertman et al. (1996, p. 4) tell us that young adolescents go from being "users of resources" to "resources"; from "passive observers" to "active learners"; from "consumers of service" to "producers of service"; from being "in need of help" to "helpers"; from "recipients" to "givers"; and from being "characterized by a feeling of helplessness" to "leaders of social change." Who wouldn't want young adolescents to experience this kind of growth? There are books that detail the "how to's" of service learning. If you have opportunities to facilitate the service learning model with your students, please do so. If your school doesn't already provide opportunities, creating the opportunities for service that lead to learning is a worthwhile mission.

WE ARE ALL READING TEACHERS

"Helping children to understand what they read might be the single most important skill a teacher can impart—at any grade level and in any subject" (Wormeli, 2001b, p. 17). I agree completely with this statement and hope that if you haven't thought about it yet, you will become a believer in the importance—and necessity—of teaching reading in a variety of meaningful ways in the middle grades. A shocking statistic that should motivate us comes from a study that reveals 30% of young adolescents leave elementary grades without basic reading skills (Showers, Joyce, Scanlon, & Schnaubelt, 1998). In *Turning Points 2000*,

Jackson and Davis write "both equity and excellence would seem to suggest that adolescents should have an inalienable right to read" (p. 87).

We often hear that children learn to read by third grade and then read to learn from then on. If only that were true. Two misconceptions exist. One is the expectation that students who enter middle school are proficient readers, particularly readers for literary experiences, including short stories and simple novels. The second is that students who have mastered reading for literary experiences will naturally read for information and for learning how to do something without direct instruction and guided practice in how to do so. The solution to the first misconception may be best accomplished through reading specialists. In the absence of funding (or the fact that reading instruction is not a priority), it is up to all of us to teach the basics of decoding and comprehension. Many of us are not prepared to do this. Staff development is essential to accomplish the task. "It no longer is acceptable to complain about the poor skills of students entering the middle grades or to dump them into remedial classes and forget about them" (Lewis, 1999, p. 49).

Standard 4

Knowledge 4: Middle level teacher candidates understand how to integrate state-of-the-art technologies and literacy skills into their teaching fields.

Disposition 4: Middle level teacher candidates value the integration of state-of-the-art technologies and literacy skills in all teaching fields.

Performance 5: Middle level teacher candidates integrate state-of-the-art technologies and literacy skills into teaching content to all young adolescents.

The second misconception implies that all types of reading are the same. We must address this misconception if our students are to be successful in any of the disciplines. They must be able to read with comprehension, regardless of the subject area. Reading a math book requires rereading. Once through is rarely sufficient. Students may need to read a paragraph, consider examples, and then reread. Reading a science text often involves calling up prior knowledge to provide context. Social studies material is often laden with names of people and places that are difficult to decipher. We must help students understand how to get beyond pronunciation to substance, to envision an event and get the big picture of a sequence. When we use opportunities provided in the content we teach to reinforce reading skills, then reading has purpose and relevancy. "Sole emphasis on content leaves students with isolated information and without strategies for learning new content; sole emphasis on the reading process leaves students with little about which to think or write" (Irvin, 1998, p. 241). We could tweak the reading adage to say "We read in middle grades to learn content and as we learn content our reading skills improve." After all, is there a content area that doesn't rely heavily on reading proficiency? Take a look at any standardized assessment and you'll find that only middle grades students with adequate reading skills can do basic or above work in social studies, science, and math.

Before, During, and After Reading

There are numerous reading programs and strategies available, some quite involved and others that can be applied with a little awareness and a minimum of effort. Be sure to find out what is already in place in your school. English language arts teachers are typically the best sources of information and advice. Regardless of what is in place that will allow us to involve ourselves in reading instruction, all of us can keep some basics in mind as we plan lessons. "Having a clear, relevant, and interesting purpose for reading is a necessary starting point" (Wilhelm, 2000, p. 7). We can do this by realizing that there is a "before, during, and after" to reading, regardless of the material we are reading. Before reading, we can help

---

Teaching reading = "Before reading" strategies + "During reading" strategies + "After reading" strategies

---

students understand the purpose of the reading they are assigned. During reading, there are many ways to help students succeed. Asking pertinent questions, encouraging discussion of the material, providing journal prompts, and so on will all move the process along. After the reading, it is important to debrief and help students see the major concepts and applications.

Reading Skills

Schurr, Thomason, and Thompson (1996) present some common sense tips for increasing reading skills within all subject areas and advancing understanding in all disciplines. The tips include

- Teachers presenting/modeling strategies for making sense of print
- Teachers reading quality literature to students
- Teachers and students sharing book experiences
- Teachers using guided reading with summarizing
- Students engaged in silent sustained reading
- Content and journal writing daily
- Emphasizing expository (content, text) reading strategies (p. 167)

Writing

A discussion of reading would not be complete without mention of writing. Reading is, of course, a prerequisite for writing. But more than a prerequisite, the two are inextricably linked. Good readers have most of the skills necessary for good writing, but instruction is necessary for students to successfully engage in the different genres of writing. Both reading and writing are necessary to succeed in our increasingly literacy-based society. Whether for pleasure, for information, or for knowing how to do something, reading and writing are essential skills. Reading and writing will be addressed in more detail in Chapters 7 and 8. As middle grades teachers we are all teachers of reading.

REFLECTIONS ON CURRICULUM FOR MIDDLE GRADES

According to *This We Believe* (National Middle School Association, 2003), "curriculum embraces every planned aspect of a school's educational program" (p. 19). As middle level teachers, this is a concept we must be aware of at all times. Curriculum is more than textbooks, district guides, and lists of facts, and even more than standards. Curriculum involves all the aspects of students' interactions with teachers, with each other, with specific discipline-based knowledge, with connections among concepts, and with their worlds and beyond. Middle grades students are with us for a few brief years. During that time they grow and change and become. Our daunting responsibility is to frame a curriculum that will bring out all their potential and catapult them forward with knowledge, skills, awareness, a sense of responsibility—all those positive and healthy attributes called for in *This We Believe.* You may hear the phrase "curriculum wars" referring to what some seem to perceive as conflicting viewpoints of curriculum—academic and affective. There is absolutely no need for conflict here. Developmental responsiveness does not adversely affect high academic expectations and vice versa. They should work in concert and complement one another.

Teachers with strong content knowledge coupled with understanding of young adolescent development are prepared for discipline-based and connected curriculum designs. Balanced curriculum includes core and related arts subjects, service learning, support of affective growth—a wholistic approach to middle grades. In all these areas, our curriculum is to be "relevant, challenging, integrative, and exploratory" (National Middle School Association, 2003, p. 19).

Group Activities

1. In groups, acquire your state standards for each of the disciplines for grades 5, 6, 7, and 8. All states will have math and language arts, most will have science and social studies, and many will have standards for related arts disciplines. Add these standards to your class files. You will use them in future activities.

2. Add to your school files by finding out what related arts courses are offered at each school. Are any of them required? Are any offered only at certain grade levels? Do any require auditions or other qualifications?

3. In pairs, go to a place where middle level students hang out—mall, theater, skate park, fast-food restaurant. With a clipboard in hand (makes you look official) tell the kids you're taking a survey to see what middle schoolers say are their favorite classes and why. This is far from a scientific survey, but rather an indicator of preferences. If you find they respond with only the core four, ask about related arts so they'll know they're free to consider all their classes. Talk with at least 10 students and then compile your findings as a class. Discuss possible implications.

4. In groups of three to five, choose a theme from Figure 6.4. Draw a web similar to Figure 6.3. Write your chosen theme in the middle and fill in the core four subjects plus at least two related arts areas. Now spend 15 minutes brainstorming concepts that could be explored in the core and related arts areas to support the theme. You should have no problem filling a page. Conceptual themes invite so many interesting topics. Be prepared as a group to share an overview of the results of your brainstorming with other groups.

Individual Activities

1. Consider the subject area(s) you want to teach. Was anything discussed in this chapter pertaining to that subject new information to you? If so, what?

2. Choose a subject area organization Web site to visit. Prepare a brief report of what's included to share with classmates.

3. Think of one related arts course that particularly stands out in your memory. Write at least five attributes of this course to share with your class.

Personal Journal

1. What was your favorite subject in middle school? In retrospect, was it your favorite because of the subject/curriculum or did other factors weigh more heavily? (teacher, instructional approach, time of day, cute boy/girl sitting in front of you, etc.)

2. Why have you chosen the particular subject area(s) you want to teach? What influences led to your decision?

Professional Practice

(It would be helpful to reread the description of Maggie Chin in Chapter 4, as well as the description of Barry in Chapters 2 and 3.)

We first met Barry in sixth grade when he was characterized as physically small with a "motormouth" that interfered with achievement. By the end of sixth grade his mom, a teacher, had taken him to the doctor for testing. He was diagnosed with ADHD and put on Ritalin. His mom decided to explore school options. Barry had been overly dramatic practically since birth. He was consistently cast in roles that required lots of dialogue in church and Boy Scout productions. He would be the first to jump up and propose a "toast" with his Kool-Aid at birthday parties. So the logical choice for Barry was Hoyt River Middle School of the Performing Arts (HRPA).

A unique feature of the planning process at HRPA is that not only do grade level teams have common planning, but each school-within-a-school is afforded the opportunity to plan together, as are subject area department groups on Monday afternoons. Students are dismissed at 1:00 p.m. each Monday to allow three hours of planning. For example, Maggie Chin, an eighth grade math/science teacher, plans with her eighth grade team every day, with all the teachers in her drama school-within-a-school from 1:00 to 2:30 p.m. on Mondays, and with all of Hoyt River's math/science teachers from 2:30 to 4:00 p.m. on Mondays.

Barry, seventh grade

HRPA is the proud home of schools-within-a-school. There are four of these schools, each focusing on a performance art—drama, vocal and instrumental music, and dance. Each school has sixth, seventh, and eighth grade teams. The team teachers teach language arts/social studies, math/science, and a performance art. Barry joined the seventh grade team in the drama school. When the teachers looked at Barry's history, they discovered he did well in language arts and acceptable in social studies, but barely passed math and science.

Maggie Chin

Ms. Chin enjoys the students at HRPA. She finds that their personalities are often marked by enthusiasm and a self-starter attitude. What she finds the most challenging is communicating to them their need for math and science. She is continually challenged to make math and science not only relevant, but also motivating. She often jokes with the language arts/social studies teacher with remarks such as, "Sure these kids want to read plays and poems and historical documents. They imagine themselves playing all of the parts to a packed house!

It's hard to imagine an extra curtain call for a particularly inspirational implementation of the Pythagorean theorem!"

1. What is the most likely reason Barry is having more success at Hoyt River than at the traditional middle school he attended as a sixth grader?

   (a) Being put on Ritalin for ADHD is an almost sure remedy for the behavior and focus problems experienced by some young adolescents.

   (b) HRPA is staffed with teachers who have proven their abilities to use classroom management techniques effectively.

   (c) Seventh grade is a year when most middle level students begin to take school and studying more seriously.

   (d) Barry has found his niche at HRPA where his talents can be channeled productively.

2. What characteristics of Hoyt River's unique structure of people would place Ms. Chin, an eighth grade teacher, in a position to affect Barry, a seventh grader, academically?

   (a) In a magnet school, there is necessarily a closer relationship among students and teachers.

   (b) Hoyt River provides departmental planning that would mean Ms. Chin has an opportunity to work closely with Barry's seventh grade math/science teacher as they plan Barry's success during his 2 years at HRPA.

   (c) Barry probably knows he is deficient in his understanding of math/science and chooses to stay after school for extra help.

   (d) Ms. Chin and Barry are both part of the drama school-within-a-school and may be in a production together.

Constructed Response

The planning opportunities for the teachers at Hoyt River Middle School for the Performing Arts are unique. Briefly explain why the three different opportunities—grade level, subject area, and schools-within-a-school—are important. Include an idea of a purpose each group might have for meeting.

Internet Resources

Education World
http://www.educationworld.com

This large site includes links to national subject area standards as well as state-by-state subject area standards information.

National Subject Area Organizations:

American Council on the Teaching of Foreign Languages (ACTFL)
http://actfl.org

Association for Supervision and Curriculum Development (ASCD)
http://www.ascd.org

International Society for Technology in Education (ISTE)
http://www.iste.org

International Technology Education Association (ITEA)
http://www.iteawww.org

Music Educators National Conference (MENC)
http://www.menc.org

National Art Education Association (NAEA)
http://www.naea-reston.org

National Association for Sport and Physical Education (NASPE)
http://www.aahperd.org

National Council for the Social Studies (NCSS)
http://www.ncss.org

National Council of Teachers of English (NCTE)
http://www.ncte.org

National Council of Teachers of Mathematics (NCTM)
http://www.nctm.org

National Middle School Association (NMSA)
http://www.nmsa.org

National Science Teachers Association (NSTA)
http://www.nsta.org

References

Beane, J. (1993). *A middle school curriculum: From rhetoric to reality* (2nd ed.). Columbus, OH: National Middle School Association.

Brazee, E. N. (1997). Curriculum for whom? In J. L. Irvin (Ed.), *What current research says to the middle level practitioner.* Columbus, OH: National Middle School Association.

Carr, J. F., & Harris, D. E. (2001). *Succeeding with standards: Linking curriculum, assessment, and action planning.* Alexandria, VA: Association for Supervision and Curriculum Development.

Doda, N. M., & George, P. S. (1999). Building whole middle school communities: Closing the gap between exploratory and core. *Middle School Journal, 30*(5), 32–39.

Dundon, B. L. (2000). My voice: An advocacy approach to service learning. *Educational Leadership, 57*(4), 34–37.

Erb, T. O. (1996). Following the bandwagon of curriculum integration: Beautiful music or deep ruts? *Middle School Journal, 28*(1), 2.

Fertman, C. I., White, G. P., & White, L. J. (1996). *Service learning in the middle school: Building a culture of service.* Columbus, OH: National Middle School Association.

Galus, P. (2002). How standards enhanced my teaching style. *Educational Leadership, 59*(4), 77–79.

George, P. S. (1996). The integrated curriculum: A reality check. *Middle School Journal, 28*(1), 12–19.

George, P. S. (2001). The evolution of middle school. *Educational Leadership, 58*(4), 40–44.

Irvin, J. L. (1998). *Reading and the middle school student: Strategies to enhance literacy* (2nd ed.). Needham Heights, MA: Allyn & Bacon.

Jackson, A. W., & Davis, G. A. (2000). *Turning points 2000: Educating adolescents in the 21st century.* New York: Teachers College Press.

Jacobs, H. H. (1997). *Mapping the big picture: Integrating curriculum and assessment K–12.* Alexandria, VA: Association for Supervision and Curriculum Development.

Knowles, T., & Brown, D. F. (2000). *What every middle school teacher should know.* Westerville, OH: National Middle School Association.

Krystal, S. (1999). The nurturing potential of service learning. *Educational Leadership, 56*(4), 58–61.

Lewis, A. C. (1999). *Figuring it out: Standards-based reforms in urban middle grades.* New York: The Edna McConnell Clark Foundation.

National Council of Teachers of Mathematics. (2000). *Principles and standards for school mathematics.* Reston, VA: Author.

National Middle School Association. (2003). *This we believe: Successful schools for young adolescents.* Westerville, OH: Author.

Powell, R. R. (1999). Reflections on integrative curriculum: A conversation with Camille Barr and Molly Maloy. *Middle School Journal, 31*(2), 25–34.

Powell, R. R., & Faircloth, C. V. (1997). Current issues and research in middle level curriculum: On conversations, semantics, and roots. In J. L. Irvin (Ed.), *What current research says to the middle level practitioner.* Columbus, OH: National Middle School Association.

Schmoker, M. (1999). *Results: The key to continuous school improvement.* Alexandria, VA: Association for Supervision and Curriculum Development.

Schmoker, M., & Marzano, R. J. (1999). Realizing the promise of standards-based education. *Educational Leadership, 56*(6), 17–21.

Schurr, S. L., Thomason, J., & Thompson, M. (1996). *Teaching at the middle level.* Lexington, MA: D.C. Heath.

Showers, B., Joyce, B., Scanlon, M., & Schnaubelt, C. (1998). A second chance to learn to read. *Educational Leadership, 55*(6), 27–30.

Weilbacher, G. (2001). Is curriculum integration an endangered species? *Middle School Journal, 33*(2), 18–27.

Wilhelm, J. D. (2000). When reading is stupid: The why, how, and what to do about it. In E. Close & K. D. Ramsey (Eds.), *A middle mosaic: A celebration of reading, writing, and reflective practice at the middle level.* Urbana, IL: National Council of Teachers of English.

Wormeli, R. (2001a). *Meet me in the middle: Becoming an accomplished middle-level teacher.* Portland, ME: Stenhouse.

Wormeli, R. (2001b). Reading between the lines. *Middle Ground, 5*(2), 17–19.

7

The Big Ideas of Instruction

Instructional practices in the middle school should focus on what we know about the learning needs of young adolescents coupled with what we know about how learning occurs.

Knowles and Brown, 2000, p. 108

Use this diagram as an organizational tool. In the boxes beside the chapter headings, indicate the date by which the readings should be completed.

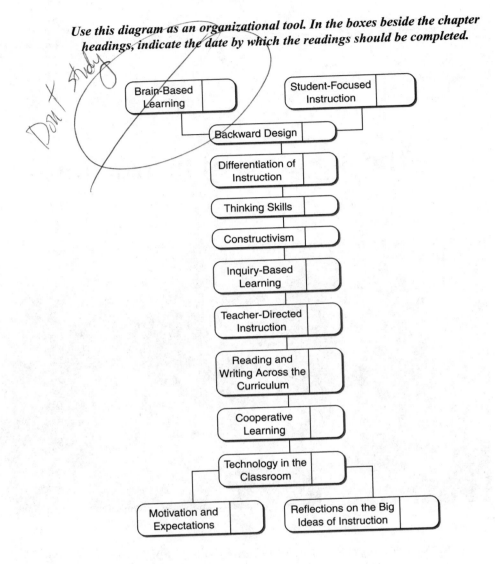

INTRODUCTION

If a tree falls in the forest but no one is there to hear it, does it make a sound?

Riddle of unknown origin

The emergence of standards-based learning is focusing the attention of teaching on outcomes, not the process itself. Although it's entertaining to ponder the "If a tree falls . . ." riddle, the laws of science make the answer obvious. The answer to its educational parallel—If a teacher teaches but learning does not occur, does the teaching have value?—may not be as obvious.

We can "teach our hearts out" in the middle school classroom but if students are not learning, then our efforts have little or no meaning. We haven't always viewed instruction this way. Some still don't. It's time to determine the success of instruction based on measures of student learning, not on teacher performance.

As the title of this chapter indicates, we are going to explore instruction, but by now I hope that you are realizing that curriculum, instruction, and assessment are all interwoven.

Standard 5

Disposition 6: Middle level teacher candidates realize the importance of basing instruction on assessment results.

We spent time on curriculum in the previous chapter. Measuring student learning would seem to fall neatly into a chapter on assessment. Separating curriculum, instruction, and assessment is artificial, but expedient in a textbook. Through Chapters 6, 7, 8, 9, and 10, I hope your appreciation for the interdependence of these three fundamental components of teaching will be further enhanced. Think of curriculum, instruction, and assessment as ingredients in a stew. Our spoons can pick them up one at a time. We can look at them, taste them, and experience their texture. Better yet is to put all three in a spoon and experience how they complement one another to create a rich, distinctive flavor.

When we talk about instruction, one chapter isn't enough. I have chosen to discuss the big ideas—the underlying concepts of instruction—first. These big ideas are supported from a practical standpoint by multiple instructional strategies that put the concepts in motion. A balanced and effective strategy is likely to encompass a number of big ideas. Some of these strategies are discussed in Chapter 8.

Turning Points 2000 includes recommendations around which to organize instruction. Each of these points will be considered in this chapter. Jackson and Davis (2000) recommend that educators

- Meet students where they are, since people learn best by connecting new information to old.

- Center classrooms on the students, not the teachers, since people also learn best when they exercise some control over their learning.

- Provide rich learning environments, since intelligence is fluid, not fixed, and will increase, given access to a diversity of materials, opinions, and options.

- Organize content around concepts, since the brain searches for meaningful patterns, connecting parts to wholes.

- Engage students in challenging work, grounded in higher-order thinking, since people learn best when they have to stretch to succeed.

- Connect what happens in the classroom to the students, either directly or by helping them discover links to the world beyond the classroom since people learn best when what they are learning has relevance to themselves or their society. (pp. 83–84)

Before exploring some big ideas of instruction, we'll discuss what brain-based research tells us about how we learn. Following the discussion of the big ideas, we'll look at the roles of motivation and expectation. As you read and reflect, keep in mind our discussions of young adolescent development, student diversity, middle school organization, and elements of curriculum design.

Standard 5: Middle Level Instruction and Assessment

Middle level teacher candidates understand and use the major concepts, principles, theories, and research related to effective instruction and assessment, and they employ a variety of strategies for a developmentally appropriate climate to meet the varying abilities and learning styles of all young adolescents.

Knowledge 1: Middle level teacher candidates understand the principles of instruction and the research base that supports them.

BRAIN-BASED LEARNING

Research on how our brains work is a dynamic area of science. Eric Jensen (2000), noted researcher and author concerning brain functioning, tells us that the field is new and should not be considered a " . . . magic bullet that will solve education's problems. It is not yet a program, a model, or a package for schools to follow" (p. 79). However, to ignore what we know about how the brain works is irresponsible and reckless. Jensen (1998) advises us to use what we know about brain functioning to guide our decisions about what is good for student learning.

Renate and Geoffrey Caine are major contributors to the field of brain research and its implications for learning and teaching. They developed 12 principles based on facts about the human brain that warrant our attention. These principles will probably seem like common sense to you, as they do to me. But having them written down, organized, and recognized by researchers gives them enhanced validity. Read each principle in Figure 7.1 carefully.

Understanding how the brain works when it comes to learning can help us better use our time with students in the classroom. The potential benefits of using Caine and Caine's (1994) principles of *brain-based learning* are in direct proportion to our willingness to apply them to instruction and enrich the experiences of the learner. Enrichment has two critical ingredients—the learning must be challenging, and interactive feedback must be present. Challenge may come through problem solving and critical thinking opportunities, relevant projects, and complex activities. We are urged to be aware that too much challenge may lead students to give up, while too little challenge will lead to boredom. Determining the right amount of challenge calls for us to know our students and to individualize levels of challenge to maximize enrichment. This definitely fits middle level philosophy of developmental responsiveness. Jensen (1998) tells us the brain is "self-referencing," meaning that it "decides what to do based on what has just been done" (p. 33). This is why interactive

1. *The brain is a parallel processor.* The implication for instruction is that good teaching "orchestrates" the learner's experience of many things—what the learner sees, what the learner hears, and so on—simultaneously.

2. *Learning engages the entire physiology.* The implication for instruction is that teachers must take "creature comfort" into account when planning and orchestrating learning, must control those factors that can be controlled, and must do whatever possible to take advantage of, or alleviate, other factors.

3. *The search for meaning is innate.* Learning is necessarily an active brain process, and the activity can be called "meaning making." The implication for teaching is *not* to transmit knowledge directly to the learner, but to engage with the learner in an active, collaborative construction of meaning. . . .

4. *The search for meaning occurs through patterning.* The implication for teaching is that the teacher may facilitate learning by exploring connections and categorizations with learners through a process of sorting and classifying.

5. *Emotions are crucial to patterning.* The implication for teaching is that the teacher must take students' attitudes and dispositions into account in planning instruction.

6. *The brain processes parts and wholes simultaneously.* The implication for teaching is that the teacher must help learners keep perspective: Teach the big picture and the parts that make it up, both at the same time.

7. *Learning involves both focused attention and peripheral perception.* The implication for teaching is that the teacher must pay almost as much attention to what students will experience indirectly as to what they will experience directly.

8. *Learning always involves conscious and unconscious processes.* The implication for teaching is that because understanding takes time, time for reflection and contemplation should be built into instructional plans.

9. *We have at least two different types of memory: a spatial memory system and a set of systems for rote learning.* The implication for teaching is that where rote knowledge is required, the teacher will want to provide plenty of time for rehearsal and application so that information will be firmly remembered. Spatial learning, so called because it occurs in three-dimensional space, requires no rehearsal and relies on no conscious learning.

10. *We understand and remember best when facts and skills are embedded in natural, spatial memory.* Imagine that all reading, writing, and discussion stemmed from the questions that arose from observations that learners made about the world around them. This exists in many classrooms today, where teachers have grasped the implication that what a learner can experience spatially, in three dimensions, can be understood in the abstract.

11. *Learning is enhanced by challenge and inhibited by threat.* The difference between challenge and threat results from how the brain responds, not from what actually occurs. The implication for teaching is that there is no risk in what students are asked to learn. Yet, mistakes are natural in the early stages of learning, and learners need to feel comfortable about making such mistakes.

12. *Each brain is unique.* The implication for teaching is that teachers need to be completely open to infinite possibilities in learners; that is, they should expect that there will be great diversity in understandings of what they teach.

FIGURE 7.1 Principles of brain-based learning.

Source: From *Instruction: A Models Approach* (pp. 6–8), by M. A. Gunter, T. H. Estes, and J. Schwab, 1999, Boston: Allyn & Bacon. Reprinted with permission.

feedback is the second ingredient of enrichment. Feedback from teachers, cooperative groups, partners—it all matters. To be most effective, Jensen states that feedback should be specific and immediate. The implications for curriculum, instruction, and assessment are tremendous. As we proceed through this chapter and into Chapter 8, keep challenge and feedback in mind. These two elements should be infused in every facet of our classroom environment.

Enrichment = Challenging learning + Interactive feedback

 ## STUDENT-FOCUSED INSTRUCTION

Teacher in a student–empowered classroom = Climate designer + Skills coach + Task designer + Learning coach + Standard setter

---

Shifting our focus to learning as a means of measuring instructional effectiveness naturally calls for us to view instruction from a student perspective. To do so changes what we do and how we view our responsibilities. *Student-focused instruction* calls for us to create opportunities that empower students to be self-directed learners. According to Vatterott (1999), "Student empowerment requires the teacher to be intensely involved in creating the right emotional climate and designing the right experiences that allow it to happen" (p. 18). She continues by describing five roles of a teacher in a student-empowered classroom. The roles are climate designer, skills coach, task designer, learning coach, and standard setter. Have you thought about yourself in these roles? What will your classroom look like if it is student-focused? Figure 7.2 gives us a comparison of teacher-focused and student-focused instruction. Remember that student-focused instruction requires teacher planning and direction.

Standard 1

Performance 5: Middle level teacher candidates use developmentally responsive instructional strategies.

Standard 2

Performance 4: Middle level teacher candidates implement developmentally responsive practices and components that reflect the philosophical foundations of middle level education.

Teacher-Focused Instruction	Student-Focused Instruction
Curriculum is presented part-to-whole, with emphasis on basic skills.	Curriculum is presented whole-to-part, with emphasis on big concepts.
Strict adherence to fixed curriculum is highly valued.	Pursuit of student questions is highly valued.
All content decisions are made by teacher.	Students are allowed to make some content decisions.
Teacher asks questions of students.	Students generate questions they want to answer.
Curricular activities rely heavily on textbooks and workbooks.	Curricular activities rely heavily on primary sources of data and manipulative materials.
Teacher generally behaves in a didactic manner, disseminating information to students.	Teacher generally behaves in an interactive manner, mediating the environment for students.
Teacher talks to teach.	Students talk to learn.
Assessment of student learning is viewed as separate from teaching and occurs almost entirely through testing.	Assessment of student learning is interwoven with teaching and occurs through teacher observation . . . student exhibitions and portfolios.
Written tests determine what students learn.	Projects require learning to complete.
Learning activity is different from the test.	Learning activity is often the assessment.

FIGURE 7.2   Differences between teacher-focused and student-focused instruction.

Source: From *Academic Success Through Empowering Students* (p. 45), by C. Vatterott, 1999, Columbus, OH: National Middle School Association. Reprinted with permission from National Middle School Association.

BACKWARD DESIGN

Having stated the unnaturalness of separating curriculum, instruction, and assessment, the philosophy and practice of *backward design* bring the three together. The link among the three has traditionally focused on the order just stated—we decided what to teach, we developed ways to teach it, and then we found ways to determine if the material was learned. Backward design changes that order. When Wiggins and McTighe (1998) published their book *Understanding by Design,* the seminal work that promotes backward design, some teachers said the authors had put into words the way they go about planning for instruction. So they were **affirmed**. Other teachers read the book and said they often think the way the authors do about instruction, but the book helped them learn about changes to their processes that would make their lessons

more effective. These teachers needed to **adjust**. The majority of teachers probably said, "Hey, this makes sense. I want to know more." So they felt the need to drop **anchor** and rethink instructional planning. Whether **affirming**, **adjusting**, or **anchoring**, we can all benefit from considering the philosophy and practice of backward design. Wiggins and McTighe (1998) tell us to brace ourselves for the fact that they ask us to think differently about "time-honored habits and points of view about curriculum, assessment, and instruction" (p. 6).

Stages of the Backward Design Process

Many teachers begin planning for instruction with textbooks, activities, and unit/lesson plans they've used before. Backward design calls for us to reverse our thinking and first consider our desired results. Next we determine what evidence would assure us the results are accomplished. Once these two decisions are made, we plan the experiences and instruction that will achieve the results and provide evidence of success.

Stage One of backward design involves identifying desired results. There is generally more content within the national, state, and district standards than can be reasonably addressed, so we have to make choices about what to include. To help us make our decisions about priorities we are encouraged to view content in three ways. The authors ask us to consider

1. " . . . The 'enduring' understandings. . . . The big ideas, the important understandings that we want students to 'get inside of' and retain after they've forgotten many of the details" (p. 10)
2. The essential knowledge and skills that require mastery as the result of a unit or course
3. What is " . . . worth being familiar with" (p. 9)

Stage Two of backward design calls for us to determine what evidence will tell us that students have achieved the desired results. Wiggins and McTighe are not just referring to culminating exams, but to a wide range of assessment methods, including informal checks for understanding, observations/dialogue, quizzes/tests, academic prompts, and performance tasks/projects.

Stages of backward design = Identify desired results + Determine evidence of achievement + Plan instruction to achieve and demonstrate results

Stage Three of backward design involves planning learning experiences and instruction to give students the opportunities to achieve desired results and to demonstrate those results with appropriate evidence.

What It Means to Understand

The whole purpose of backward design is to facilitate understanding. Wiggins and McTighe tell us that when we truly understand, we can explain, interpret, apply, have perspective, empathize, and have self-knowledge.

They advise us to organize lessons and units around essential questions that help us focus on desired results. They endorse turning standards and outcome statements into questions, and then designing assignments to find answers to the questions. They tell us that essential questions go to the heart of a discipline, recur naturally throughout one's learning and in the history of a field, and raise other important questions.

Backward design is a very important concept to consider as we continue to discuss other big ideas of instruction. Wiggins and McTighe have provided a framework for understanding how assessment, curriculum, and instruction are inextricably linked.

DIFFERENTIATION OF INSTRUCTION

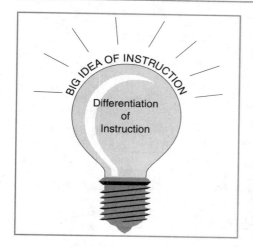

BIG IDEA OF INSTRUCTION

Differentiation of Instruction

Perhaps at no other level of schooling is *differentiation of instruction* more important than in the middle grades. *This We Believe* (2003) states that "The distinctive developmental and learning characteristics of young adolescents provide the foundation for selecting teaching strategies. . . . Teaching approaches should enhance and accommodate the diverse skills, abilities, and prior knowledge of young adolescents" (p. 25). Now that's a tall order!

Differentiating instruction calls for us to meet our students where they are, to accept them as learners with differing strengths and weaknesses, and to do all that we can to help each and every student grow as much as possible. Since the mid-1990s the words "differentiating instruction" have caused us to examine classroom practices in a new light. Just as backward design is linked to Wiggins and McTighe, the concept of differentiated instruction is linked to Carol Ann Tomlinson (1999) and her book *The Differentiated Classroom*. Tomlinson makes a common-sense case for the importance of differentiating instruction, describes the philosophy and ways to begin, and provides classroom scenarios (many in middle level) that give us vivid pictures of what a classroom looks like when the instruction is differentiated to meet the needs of students. I recommend that you add this book to your "must read" list.

Elements to differentiate = Content + Process + Product

Tomlinson tells us that we can differentiate content, process, and product according to students' readiness, interests, and learning profiles (see Figure 7.3). According to Tomlinson, **content** includes both what a teacher wants students to learn and the materials/mechanisms to accomplish the learning. **Process** includes activities that require students to use skills to make sense of ideas and information. **Products** allow students to demonstrate what they have learned. **Readiness** is where students are in their journey toward understanding or skill acquisition. **Interest** is a student's leaning toward, or passion for, a topic or skill. **Learning profile** refers to how a student learns and includes many of the variables discussed in Chapter 3. Tomlinson emphasizes that there is no one right way or time to differentiate.

Elements on which to base differentiation = Readiness + Interest + Learning profile

Tomlinson acknowledges that whole-class instruction is entirely appropriate in many instances. She tells us, "Teachers may adapt one or more of the curricular elements (content, process, product) based on one or more of the student characteristics (readiness, interest, learning profile) at any point in a lesson or unit" (p. 11). She continues by advising us to "Modify a curricular element only when (1) you see a student need and (2) you are convinced that modification increases the likelihood that the learner

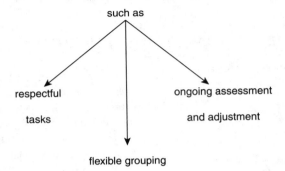

Differentiation of instruction

is a teacher's response to learner's needs

guided by general principles of differentiation,

such as

respectful

tasks

ongoing assessment

and adjustment

flexible grouping

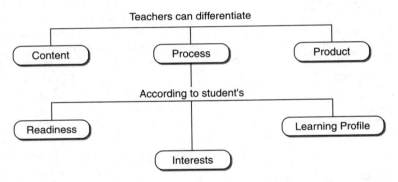

Teachers can differentiate

Content   Process   Product

According to student's

Readiness   Learning Profile

Interests

FIGURE 7.3   Differentiation of instruction.

Source: From *The Differentiated Classroom: Responding to the Needs of All Learners* (p.15), by C. A. Tomlinson, 1999, Alexandria, VA: Association for Supervision and Curriculum Development. Reprinted with permission.

will understand important ideas and use important skills more thoroughly as a result" (p. 11). Tomlinson cautions us to "not try to differentiate everything for everyone every day" (p. 14). Attempting to do so could destroy a sense of wholeness for the class. (And besides, there aren't enough hours in the day.)

In order to begin to differentiate instruction according to readiness, interests, and learning profiles as Tomlinson suggests, we must know our students well. At the heart of middle level education is the premise that doing schooling right requires us to have knowledge of, and closeness to, our students. Wormeli (2001) tells us that knowing our students well is like "taking their temperature," not just once in August, but often as they grow and change (p. 87). Tomlinson (1999) says that in a differentiated classroom the teacher is a diagnostician. In this way, instruction and assessment are inseparably linked. On this very important point, backward design and differentiated instruction are loudly singing the same song. In Chapter 9 we'll explore many forms of assessment used to measure what students know and are able to do. Assessment can be extended to help us determine not only readiness, but also interests and the ways in which students learn best. From assessment, we know best when and how to differentiate instruction.

Figure 7.4 shows Tomlinson's view of the characteristics of a traditional classroom compared with a differentiated classroom. Each bullet deserves pages of explanation

Traditional Classroom	Differentiated Classroom
• Student differences are masked or acted upon when problematic	• Student differences are studied as a basis for planning
• Assessment is most common at the end of learning to see "who got it"	• Assessment is ongoing and diagnostic to understand how to make instruction more responsive to learner need
• A relatively narrow sense of intelligence prevails	• Focus on multiple forms of intelligences is evident
• A single definition of excellence exists	• Excellence is defined in large measure by individual growth from a starting point
• Student interest is infrequently tapped	• Students are frequently guided in making interest-based learning choices
• Relatively few learning profile options are taken into account	• Many learning profile options are provided for
• Whole-class instruction dominates	• Many instructional arrangements are used
• Coverage of texts and curriculum guides drives instruction	• Student readiness, interest, and learning profile shape instruction
• Mastery of facts and skills out-of-context are the focus of learning	• Use of essential skills to make sense of and understand key concepts and principles is the focus of learning
• Single option assignments are the norm	• Multi-option assignments are frequently used
• Time is relatively inflexible	• Time is used flexibly in accordance with student need
• A single text prevails	• Multiple materials are provided
• Single interpretations of ideas and events may be sought	• Multiple perspectives on ideas and events are routinely sought
• The teacher directs student behavior	• The teacher facilitates students' skills at becoming more self-reliant learners
• The teacher solves problems	• Students help other students and the teacher solve problems
• The teacher provides whole-class standards for grading	• Students work with the teacher to establish both whole-class and individual learning goals
• A single form of assessment is often used	• Students are assessed in multiple ways

FIGURE 7.4   Comparing classrooms.

Source: From *The Differentiated Classroom: Responding to the Needs of All Learners* (p.16), by C. A. Tomlinson, 1999, Alexandria, VA: Association for Supervision and Curriculum Development. Reprinted with permission.

and expansion. Each presents a concept that begs for discussion. My hope is that your interest will be sparked and goals for your classroom will include further study of the aspects of differentiated classrooms. Tomlinson (1999) tells us in the conclusion of *The Differentiated Classroom* that "The ideas presented in this book are ambitious, maybe even visionary" (p. 119). While it is possible to achieve a classroom that looks like the "Differentiated Classroom" column in Figure 7.4, I must tell you that it is a lofty goal and a daunting measuring stick. In her advice on how to begin thinking and planning to differentiate instruction, Tomlinson advises us to start small with a differentiated task that takes a limited block of time. She says it's fine to grow slowly, as long as we continue to grow in our awareness and implementation of differentiated instruction.

When all the students in a classroom are completing the same assignment in the same way on the same timeline, a large percentage of our students probably aren't "getting it." Tomlinson (1999) suggests what a teacher might say to her students in a differentiated classroom.

> "Here's where we're headed. That we all learn and grow and work hard in the process is not negotiable. How we reach the destination is. Some of us may move more rapidly than others. Some begin further ahead. Some may succeed better with Plan A, others with Plan B. Sometimes I as a teacher will make some decisions. Sometimes you as students will make them. Often we will make them together. We will always try to make them in ways that help us all achieve the goal of maximum growth." (p. 111)

📖 THINKING SKILLS

Bloom's taxonomy = Knowledge + Comprehension + Application + Analysis + Synthesis + Evaluation

There are probably as many definitions of thinking as there are thinkers. Thinking and using thinking skills are cognitive acts that may simply involve awareness of surroundings or may be as complex as making judgments that lead to actions. Bloom's taxonomy (1956) presents six levels of thinking: knowledge, comprehension, application, analysis, synthesis, and evaluation.

I keep these six words in mind when I make decisions about curriculum, instruction, and assessment. Each level can be accessed through the use of active verbs and questions (Figure 7.5). I strongly urge you to explore the levels fully, to read books and articles about them, to internalize them. Regardless of the content area, we can provide thinking opportunities at all six levels. Teach them to your students. Then occasionally ask "Which level of Bloom's taxonomy are we using here?" The flower in Figure 7.6 is a fun way to keep the levels visible in your classroom.

Level	Explanation	Key Words	Question Stems
I. Knowledge	Recall basic facts/concepts	Name, tell, list, define, match, find	When did _____ ? Who was _____ ? Where is _____ ? Why did _____ ? Can you list four _____ ?
II. Comprehension	Demonstrate understanding	Compare, contrast, explain, summarize, classify	How would you compare _____ to _____ ? What is the main idea of _____ ? What is meant by _____ ?
III. Application	Apply knowledge to solve problems	Use, plan, model, solve, build	How would you use _____ to _____ ? What approach would you use to _____ ? Can you _____ by _____ ?
IV. Analysis	Examine critically to support/make inferences	Categorize, find relationships, conclude	What evidence can you find to conclude that _____ ? What does _____ have to do with _____ ?
V. Synthesis	Combine or rearrange to develop alternatives	Adapt, formulate, invent, create, modify, improve	How would you change _____ to form _____ ? Can you propose a different way to _____ ? How would you design _____ to _____ ?
VI. Evaluation	Make judgments, defend, validate	Debate, decide, conclude, prove, recommend	What is your opinion of _____ ? How valuable is _____ for _____ ? Why would you recommend _____ ?

FIGURE 7.5 Bloom's taxonomy.

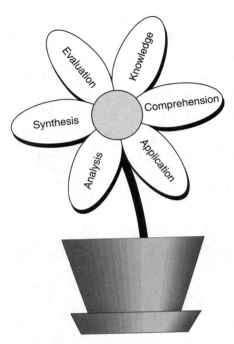

FIGURE 7.6 We're bloomin'!

Standard 5

Knowledge 3: Middle level teacher candidates know that teaching higher order thinking skills is an integral part of instruction and assessment.

Teaching Thinking Skills

Teaching students thinking skills can be accomplished through focused instruction outside a specific content area. Modeling is vital. We can model, for instance, the difference between reading and recalling the steps required to successfully learn to juggle two balls and actually doing it. We can read the steps out loud, close the book and recite them (knowledge), paraphrase the steps (comprehension), and then hold two balls and ineptly toss them into the air, bungling the process. We explain to our students that knowing and comprehending are quite different from applying. We would then ask our students to analyze what went wrong (analysis) and create (synthesis) a plan for us to learn to juggle. The final step would be to ask the students to predict the success of our attempts, or perhaps the value of learning to juggle (evaluation).

While it is possible to teach specific thinking skills in isolation, teaching thinking skills within the context of the curriculum should be ongoing. To extend a skill presented in isolation, such as categorization (analysis), a math teacher might give a small group of students a bucket of attribute blocks and ask them to develop categories in which the blocks might be divided and lists of blocks that fit each. A language arts teacher might ask students to read an essay, write a summary (comprehension), organize the main points (application and analysis), compose an essay on the same topic (synthesis), and then examine both essays critically to defend the value of each (evaluation). A science teacher might ask students to name the parts of an insect (knowledge), ask students to illustrate the parts (comprehension), dissect an insect into basic parts (application and analysis), and build a model out of clay (synthesis).

Critical and Creative Thinking

Critical thinking is more complex than ordinary thinking. It requires objectivity and consistency and involves the higher order thinking levels of Bloom's taxonomy. Lipman (1988) argues that for students to think critically they must be taught, among other things, to change their thinking from guessing to estimating, from preferring to evaluating, from grouping to classifying, from believing to assuming, from offering opinions without reasons to offering opinions with reasons, and from making judgments without criteria to making judgments with criteria.

Creative thinking calls for a major dose of Bloom's synthesis level. To think creatively is to use imagination and ingenuity to come up with solutions—to discover alternatives using what is given in unique ways. Some would say that creativity can't be taught. If that's the case, we can, at a minimum, provide activities and opportunities for our students to "get outside the box" and experience creating poems, songs, and roles, to brainstorm and invent.

Thinking Skills Activities

Moore (1999) purports that teaching thinking skills requires open-ended activities, ones that don't necessarily need or have a single answer. He lists brainstorming, flexible thinking, forecasting, inductive/deductive thinking, inference, and decision-making as thinking skills activities we should encourage in the middle grades. Because young adolescents are experiencing rapid cognitive development and moving from concrete to abstract in their thinking abilities, now is the time to explicitly lead them into critical and creative thinking through these activities. Rubenstein (1994) tells us, "As teachers, we do not teach students to think. Studies show that from birth, perhaps earlier, the human brain thinks. What we can do is help students access and use their natural ability to think and help them learn to organize" (p. 31).

 # CONSTRUCTIVISM

Constructivism as a teaching/learning process is just what the word implies, teacher facilitation of students using higher order thinking skills to construct their own learning. The last two decades have seen constructivism go from books of philosophy to teacher manuals on instruction. Teaching in constructivist ways means a variety of things. Perkins (1999) writes about constructivism as having many faces. In terms of the learner, he says there are three distinct roles: the active learner, the social learner, and the creative learner. Given this view, constructivism seems to be a perfect fit for the middle grades classroom.

Constructivism in the classroom =
Discovering + Inventing +
Reassembling knowledge

Young adolescents prefer active learning; they are generally very social creatures, and they have the capacity to be quite creative.

Constructivism takes emphasis off the teacher and places it squarely on learning and the learner. The goals of constructivism include helping the learner become an autonomous thinker, encouraging the learner to explore important questions, and facilitating the learner in building deeper understandings (Richetti & Sheerin, 1999). To encourage constructivism in our classrooms requires that we take time to promote active involvement of our students in the processes of discovering, inventing, and reassembling knowledge in individual and collaborative settings. Many teachers find that constructivist teaching techniques are appropriate only for certain topics at certain times. This balance in the classroom is referred to by Perkins (1999) as pragmatic constructivism, or using a constructivist approach when we want learners to grasp big or troublesome concepts.

When we look at the 12 descriptors of constructivist teacher practices that help students become discoverers and inventors, we see that most are good common sense. We can all incorporate these practices often in our classrooms. Brooks and Brooks (1993) tell us that constructivist teachers

1. encourage and accept student autonomy and initiative.
2. use raw data and primary resources, along with manipulatives, interactive and physical materials.
3. use cognitive terminology such as classify, analyze, predict, and create.
4. allow student responses to drive lessons, shift instructional strategies, and alter content.
5. inquire about students' understandings of concepts before sharing their own understandings of those concepts.
6. encourage students to engage in dialogue, both with the teacher and with one another.
7. encourage student inquiry by asking thoughtful, open-ended questions and encouraging students to ask questions of each other.
8. seek elaboration of students' initial responses.
9. engage students in experiences that might engender contradictions to their initial hypotheses and then encourage discussion.
10. allow wait time after posing questions.

Standard 5

Performance 2: Middle level teacher candidates create learning experiences that encourage exploration and problem solving so all young adolescents can be actively engaged in learning.

11. provide time for students to construct relationships and create metaphors.

12. nurture students' natural curiosity through frequent use of the learning cycle model. (pp. 103–118)

INQUIRY-BASED LEARNING

Inquiry-based learning is just what it sounds like—learning from questions and investigations. The process of inquiry is open-ended, beginning with a topic or scenario and involving a brief exploration or in-depth research. There are many levels of inquiry. A quick check in a reference book or a telephone call or an informal interview constitutes inquiry. Inquiry-based learning may involve a well-planned project with multiple levels. It is not passive, not characterized by middle grades students in straight rows taking notes as the teacher lectures. Inquiry-based learning is good for middle grades students because it cultivates students' responsibility for their own learning.

Standard 5

Knowledge 5: Middle level teacher candidates understand ways to teach the basic concepts and skills of inquiry and communication.

TEACHER-DIRECTED INSTRUCTION

Lecture, notetaking, textbooks, worksheets, whole-class instruction, content not based on student interests, use of curriculum guides, and so forth all have their place in a balanced classroom. While I encourage you not to allow any of these components to dominate your style, they are appropriate for certain content and at certain times in our classrooms. Take a look back at Figure 7.5 in which Tomlinson compares the traditional classroom with the differentiated one. Also review Figure 7.2 that compares teacher-focused instruction with student-focused instruction. The descriptors on the left side of the figures are not necessarily bad, they simply represent a more traditional view of schooling. In Chapter 8 we'll look at ways to implement teacher-directed methods to facilitate learning.

READING AND WRITING ACROSS THE CURRICULUM

A critical obstacle to fulfilling the *Turning Points* vision is the lack of reading skills (Jackson & Davis, 2000). In Chapter 6, we established the need for all middle grades teachers to be teachers of reading. In this chapter, we'll examine some basic components of teaching both reading and writing within the content areas.

Elementary school is generally considered the place where kids learn to read. But if reading is not mastered in elementary school, then it should be mastered in middle school. "Middle grades schools should teach reading across the curriculum as part of a system of supports to improve students' reading skills and enhance their enjoyment of reading" (Jackson & Davis, 2000, p. 88).

Two Approaches—Explicit Instruction and Whole Language

Reading and writing are intertwined and interdependent. If a person can read, composing thoughts into a format that may be written is possible. When viewed as processes that enhance both one another and learning, we see the necessity of finding ways to teach both reading and writing, either through explicit instruction or with a whole language approach.

Explicit instruction in reading and writing entails the teacher knowing and telling—using direct teaching strategies. With explicit instruction, reading and writing skills are often taught in isolation. *Whole language* instruction emerged in the 1970s and emphasizes learning to read and write within an authentic context. In other words, reading and writing skills are integrated into a real and purposeful learning situation.

When only the whole language approach is used, gaps in skills may exist (Morretta & Ambrosini, 2000). A combined approach to teaching reading and writing makes sense. Because the reading and writing required for each subject area varies, some explicit instruction is necessary. For the same reason, a whole language approach is appropriate since reading and writing occur within the context of a discipline being studied.

Content Area Reading and Writing

The ability to use reading and writing to acquire new content in a discipline is often referred to as content literacy (McKenna & Robinson, 1997). Each content area, or discipline, presents its own reading and writing demands. However, some reading skills are common to all disciplines, such as comprehension, vocabulary building, use of textbooks, understanding directions, and thinking skills development (Abbott, 1999). As middle grades teachers, we share the responsibility of helping our students grasp these common skills along with the skills unique to the discipline(s) we teach.

Vocabulary Acquisition

Reading requires understanding words to comprehend meaning, and writing requires using words to convey meaning. Every discipline has its own unique vocabulary. Words that appear in different contexts may take on different meanings. Explicit instruction is needed to give specific meaning to general vocabulary. Take the simple word "table." We can use a table of contents to locate a topic, we can table a bill in Congress, and we can set a table for dinner. There's joy in learning words and their meanings and nuances! Our students can discover this joy if we help them see and appreciate vocabulary and understand that, as a subject area becomes more complex, so does the vocabulary that accompanies explanations and contextual usage.

There are lots of ways to bring vocabulary alive for our students. We no longer need to perpetuate the drudgery of writing an assigned word and indicating part of speech, then writing a dictionary definition along with a sentence that may or may not illustrate meaning, followed by reading this structure over and over to memorize it. Far more interesting and productive strategies are available to us. We'll explore some of them in Chapter 8.

COOPERATIVE LEARNING

BIG IDEA OF INSTRUCTION

Cooperative Learning

There's cooperative learning . . . and then there's cooperative learning. The words can be a catch-all for any instance of students working together . . . or they can represent an instructional strategy with definitive guidelines and requirements. We'll examine both viewpoints.

Cooperative Learning, Loosely Defined

On any given day, in any given middle school, you will probably hear teachers referring to *cooperative learning* or cooperative groups or simply group work. Just as many say Kleenex for any brand of tissue, teachers say cooperative learning for any kind of group work. While proponents of stricter definitions may wince, my opinion is that any time middle level kids work together, they experience both cooperation and learning. This has to be good for them. So rather than debating guidelines or correcting one another concerning the use of the words "cooperative learning," let's encourage any and all attempts to create a sense of communal learning.

In Chapter 8 we'll begin to fill our instructional toolboxes with group work strategies. By reading about and experiencing many strategies, we have at our fingertips ways of teaching and learning to fit almost any scenario and a vast variety of student needs and styles.

Cooperative Learning, More Strictly Defined

Many school districts conduct professional development sessions based on the Johnson and Johnson (1987) method, which proposes that cooperative learning must incorporate five basic elements in order to realize all the potential of students working together. These elements are

1. Positive Interdependence

   This element requires students to depend on one another in order to achieve the desired results. It involves setting group goals rather than individual goals, joint rewards, shared resources, and roles that require each group member to play a vital part in success.

2. Fact-to-Face Interaction

   Students in cooperative groups have to work together to explain, discuss, complete assignments, problem solve, and so on.

3. Individual Accountability

   Students are required to be accountable for individual tasks that contribute to the group goals.

4. Interpersonal Skills

   Students are encouraged to learn to collaborate with each other in socially acceptable ways.

5. Group Processing

   This element requires students to think and talk about how their group functioned as they accomplished their tasks through the use of the first four elements. They analyze what they experienced and give feedback to each other and the teacher in an effort to improve group functioning.

Cooperative learning = Positive interdependence + Face-to-face interaction + Individual accountability + Interpersonal skills + Group processing

---

When these five elements are planned for in a lesson or project, students will experience a host of benefits. The presence of these elements, according to many researchers and teachers, sets "true" cooperative learning apart from more loosely constructed group work.

Implementing Cooperative Learning

Most definitions of cooperative learning state that cooperative groups are heterogeneous. This heterogeneity may be in achievement levels, interest and experience levels, or other areas that affect student differences. However, there may be instances when the goals of cooperative learning may be best accomplished with homogeneous groups. There are times when teachers designate groups and purposely put particular students together. Other times, students are grouped using random strategies, or they are allowed to choose their own groups. This is another situation where teacher judgment and balance come into play.

The length of time groups remain intact will vary. If you assign a group project, the groups of students will remain constant for the duration of the assignment. Changing the size and composition of your groups depends on the activity or task. Some teachers have great success with forming heterogeneous cooperative groups that stay together for a quarter, or longer. The philosophy behind this is that students in stable groups, with appropriate guidance, develop trusting and nurturing relationships along with social skills and commitment. They are better able to successfully handle multiple and diverse tasks when working in the kind of permanence that long-term grouping provides. For balance, you may want to thoughtfully and purposefully create permanent, or semi-permanent, groups who periodically work with other students in temporary groups for specific tasks.

The participants in cooperative groups are often assigned specific roles to help the groups function effectively and efficiently. The roles may include a facilitator to keep things moving, a recorder to take notes, a timer to keep members on schedule, a gatherer of materials, an encourager to ensure everyone provides input, and an artist to illustrate for the group.

The benefits of cooperative learning include growth in the following areas: racial and gender tolerance and friendship, understanding of children with disabilities, self-esteem, achievement, problem-solving abilities, comprehension, recall, and transfer (Vermetti, 1998). With benefits like these, the practice of cooperative learning is a must in our middle schools. The steps in Figure 7.7 will help you begin and maintain cooperative learning in your classroom.

1. Read about and experience cooperative learning in university classes and staff development opportunities.

2. Determine to implement cooperative learning in your own classroom.

3. Give several simple tasks to students in random groups that will show them the benefits of working together. Make sure success is built into the tasks.

4. Define a task for cooperative groups in your classroom.

5. Make decisions about grouping students, roles for the task, materials needed, time guidelines, and desired results of cooperative work.

6. Plan for positive interdependence, fact-to-face interactions, individual accountability, interpersonal skills, and group processing.

7. Talk with your students about the process of cooperative learning. Include your expectations, guidelines for interactions, and how work will be assessed.

8. Assign roles to students in groups.

9. Observe closely as groups work together. Take notes on what you see.

10. Involve students in debriefing the cooperative learning experience.

11. Plan your next venture into cooperative learning!

FIGURE 7.7   Getting started and maintaining cooperative learning.

TECHNOLOGY IN THE CLASSROOM

Technology of all kinds is pervasive in today's schools. According to Franklin (2001), our classrooms have been permanently altered by the proliferation of technology in the 1990s. *Turning Points 2000* refers to technology as an instructional resource that requires our vigilance (Jackson & Davis, 2000). Proponents and nay-sayers alike agree on one thing—technology will be an even greater part of our classrooms in the future. So our dilemma is not **if** we'll use technology, but rather **how** we'll use technology.

There are so many instructional tools available to us—textbooks, chalkboards, overhead projectors, manipulatives, videos, television, computers, distance learning, Internet. . . . Each tool has advantages and disadvantages. We make our choices according to lesson objectives, availability, our expertise in using the tool, and the appropriateness of the tool to the particular situation. Any tool that we use should be a means to an end (student learning), not an end in itself. Because new technologies arrive on the scene frequently, some teachers find themselves using technology for technology's sake. Although learning the skills that are required for new technology has value, that value is greatly enhanced if the skills are learned within the context of our planned curriculum. Our challenge is to mesh curriculum, our students and their needs, and instructional tools to foster effective learning opportunities. "The most important consideration should be to make sure that technological decisions are based on sound educational principles" (Moore, 1999, p. 176).

The use of calculators, videos, audiotapes, and other tools considered "lower tech" in the 21st century is common. Most classrooms have computers. Middle schools typically have computer labs. The future will doubtless bring wireless, handheld information gathering and communication tools into common use that many of us can only begin to imagine. Articles and testimonials tell us that students spend more time reading, writing, and problem solving when technology is involved. Students are often more enthusiastic if a project involves working on a computer. Access to information provided by the World Wide Web changes how we approach research in all content areas. The interactive nature of Web sites allows for simulations where students manipulate variables and receive immediate feedback. The possibilities are tremendous.

The "rabbit-like proliferation of computers in the school" (Roberts, 1999, p. 77) does not necessarily signify widespread or appropriate use. "The question should not be how many computers there are, but how well our schools make use of what they have" (Zelchenko, 1999, p. 78). As teachers we must learn how to use the technology to impact learning positively.

Tom Carroll (2000), executive director of the National Commission on Teaching and America's Future, expresses a vision for how technology can alter our current paradigm of schooling. He says that bringing together the technology available and what we know about cognition and learning can dramatically change the learning environment. He tells us that technology has the potential to be transformative—to replace our notion of the school as the center of learning where the learner is brought to the knowledge, with the notion of the school becoming an organizational tool for what he terms a "networked learning community" (p. 122).

I suppose we could consider most of our middle schools to be in transition to accepting and using technology, or to be on the verge of doing so. Available resources, whether in the form of money, hardware, or promoting the necessary teacher expertise, will determine where and when we experience the transformative powers of ever-burgeoning technology.

Standard 3

Knowledge 5: Middle level teacher candidates are fluent in the integration of technology in curriculum planning.

Standard 4

Knowledge 4: Middle level teacher candidates understand how to integrate state-of-the-art technologies and literacy skills into their teaching fields.

Disposition 4: Middle level teacher candidates value the integration of state-of-the-art technologies and literacy skills in all teaching fields.

Performance 5: Middle level teacher candidates integrate state-of-the-art technologies and literacy skills into teaching content to all young adolescents.

Standard 7

Knowledge 10: Middle level teacher candidates are fluent in the integration of a range of technologies (e.g., film, computers) in their professional roles with curriculum, instruction, and assessment.

MOTIVATION AND EXPECTATIONS

We began this chapter with the concept that teaching has value only if learning occurs. We then proceeded to examine the implications of brain-based learning followed by a look at some of the big ideas of instruction. In each idea was the implicit, and sometimes explicit, assumption that our goal is to make learning more accessible to our students. Focusing on the desirable result of teaching—learning—means that we understand the need to increase learner receptivity. In other words, we must do all we can to motivate our students to be learners. We want to engage their minds so that motivation is high.

Motivation may be defined as "processes or behaviors that initiate, direct, and sustain goal-oriented behavior" (Shalaway, 1998, p. 94). For some students, goal-oriented behaviors are directed by external forces, while others may be nurtured by internal forces.

Standard 1

Disposition 4: Middle level teacher candidates believe that all young adolescents can learn and accept responsibility to help them do so.

External or extrinsic motivators include grades, praise, and recognition. There are some who say that extrinsic motivation is not appropriate, and may even be harmful. I urge you to look for balance. Much of our world revolves around social reinforcement for hard work and success. Extrinsic motivation has its place in middle school.

Let's look specifically at the role of praise as a motivator for middle grades students. We have to be very careful about when and how we praise our students or it can backfire big time. We know that young adolescence is a time of self-conscious sensitivity. We also know that what might be positive in terms of public praise one day may be embarrassing the next. I believe in praising middle school students as a group in public ways. When it comes to praising individual students, doing so privately seems to be the most effective (and safest) way. As adults, public praise is usually valued and sought. For a 12-year-old, public praise, more often than not, brings unwanted attention. To a seventh grader the words "Sean's project is an excellent example of . . ." may be considered the same as "Hey, look everybody. Sean has no social life, he spends all his time on homework because nobody calls him, and he's a goody-goody wimp." Will Sean's next project be of equal quality? Maybe, maybe not. Generally, praise is most effective when it is specific, sincere and private, and focuses on individual accomplishment that does not rely on comparisons with others (Brophy, 1981).

Internal, or intrinsic, motivation is certainly the most valuable and long-lasting. If we can help instill in our students a love of learning, a desire to learn because it satisfies their curiosity or they find it inherently interesting and can derive a sense of accomplishment and confidence through learning, then motivation becomes self-dependent rather than others-dependent. Intrinsic motivation is something we can model. As lifelong learners ourselves, we should display our passion for concepts and topics, our sense of pride in accomplishment, our joy associated with learning. Young adolescents watch us; our enthusiasm influences them. Shalaway (1998) urges us to capitalize on our students' "innate motivation to learn" when she suggests that we

- stress the value of the task by pointing out how knowledge and skills can bring pleasure and satisfaction

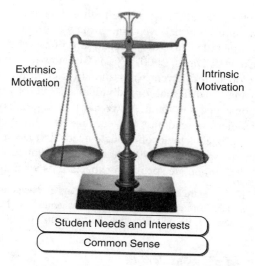

FIGURE 7.8   Achieving balance: Motivation.

- personalize by expressing beliefs, attitudes, or experiences that illustrate the task's importance
- be enthusiastic by stating a liking for the task
- state positive expectations by telling students they will enjoy the task and do well
- explain personal relevance by tying the task to students' lives and interests (p. 96)

While acknowledging that intrinsic motivation is more valuable than extrinsic motivation, I do not agree with some who say that extrinsic motivation is not appropriate, and may even be harmful. Again, I urge you to strive for balance in your search for ways to enhance student motivation as illustrated in Figure 7.8.

The role of expectations in motivation is crucial. The phrase "high expectations for all" is sometimes glibly thrown into presentations by administrators, staff development speakers, and politicians. What does it mean? Can we do it? *This We Believe* (2003) tells us that having high expectations for all is an imperative for the developmentally responsive middle school. There's a big difference between putting these words in a mission statement and actually demonstrating high expectations for each student in our classrooms. It's an attitude that takes constant and conscious effort.

"Positive expectations promote positive attitudes and motivation to achieve; negative expectations lead to alienation, discouragement, and lack of effort" (Arnold, 1997, p. 51). What a responsibility. To have high expectations for middle grades students needs to begin with ridding ourselves of negative stereotypes. Arnold reminds us that given opportunity and support, young adolescents are extremely capable. If our expectations become self-fulfilling prophecies for our students, then keeping our expectations high, tempered with realism, is a key factor in motivating learning.

The "for all" part of the high expectations phrase is tricky. "The hard fact is that many educators believe some groups of students are less able to achieve academically than others because they see these groups achieving less than others on a daily basis" (Jackson & Davis, 2000, p. 13). We know our students display different intelligences—developed in different ways and at different rates. So while we hold high expectations, they may be different for individual students at various times. That's what developmental responsiveness is about. As we saw in Chapter 3, our students come to us with significant differences in readiness for learning. While the challenges vary greatly, we must adjust our approaches to accommodate needs, but never lose sight of student potential to learn. Thomas Armstrong (1998) has written a wonderful book titled *Awakening the Genius in the Classroom*. He speaks to expectations when he writes,

> if you regard each one of your students as true genius—each in his or her own way—and create a classroom environment where that genius can be identified, nurtured, and made available to others, there's no telling how far the impact of your teaching may go. (p. 69)

Standard 1

Disposition 3: Middle level teacher candidates hold high, realistic expectations for the learning and behavior of all young adolescents.

NMSA.

 ## REFLECTIONS ON THE BIG IDEAS OF INSTRUCTION

To be effective, instructional practices must pass numerous tests—developmental responsiveness, research-based, content/skill appropriateness, time efficient, standards supporting. It takes time to build a repertoire of strategies and experience to make decisions about the what, how, and when of approaches. Backward design tells us to plan with results in view. Differentiation allows us to meet the varying learning needs of young adolescents. We encourage higher-order thinking skills as we create opportunities for our students to inquire about and construct meaning, sometimes individually and sometimes cooperatively. Reading literacy, writing literacy, and technological literacy are vital components of learning, regardless of the subject.

It is necessary that we be totally convinced that each and every one of our students can and will learn. Our expectations must be that each young adolescent in our classrooms has his own particular genius. Finding ways to motivate these very special young people to grow and learn is our challenge.

 ## Group Activities

1. In small groups (three or four), agree on a broad topic that would be taught in middle school. Refer to Figure 7.6 and brainstorm aspects of the topic **content**, **process** of learning, and **product** that might be differentiated. Then think of ways to determine student **readiness**, **interests**, and **learning profiles** concerning the topic chosen. Or-

ganize your best collective thoughts for the six bolded areas and be prepared to share with your whole class.

2. In pairs, make an appointment to talk with a middle school teacher. Ask how he approaches heterogeneous classes. How often and in what ways does he differentiate instruction? Add your findings to your school files.

3. In groups made up of teacher candidates who plan to teach different subjects, discuss ways each teacher might teach reading and writing skills within a variety of contexts. Put your ideas in writing and post on the class wall to be discussed with the whole class.

4. So far in this class you've had numerous cooperative learning experiences. As a class, discuss the experiences that seemed more successful than others. Can you determine the factors that may have affected the relative success of the experiences? List the factors and then classify them into the five categories as defined by Johnson and Johnson on page 198.

Individual Activities

1. Choose a topic within the subject you plan to teach. Write a narrative explaining how you might address each of the categories in Bloom's taxonomy as stated in Figure 7.5.

2. In this chapter you read the statement "Constructivism takes emphasis off of teaching and places it squarely on the learning and the learner." What are the implications of this statement for our work as teachers?

3. Some teachers and teams regularly use rewards systems in their classrooms that consist of candy, homework passes, popcorn parties, "free" time, and so on. What place, if any, do these types of extrinsic motivators have in middle grades?

Personal Journal

1. Do you recall cooperative learning experiences in your middle grades years? Write about your participation in, and reactions to, the experiences.

2. Did you ever have that "lost" feeling in a middle grades class? What topic in what subject? Now that you know more about differentiation, explain how your teacher could have done more to meet your needs?

3. Have you experienced technology in a class setting that you felt was used as "technology for technology's sake" rather than to enhance learning? If so, write about the experience. How comfortable are you with classroom technology?

4. Do you think your teachers in middle school had high expectations for you? If so, how were they expressed? If not, what attitudes or actions gave you the impression that their expectations were low?

Professional Practice

(It would be helpful to reread the description of Ms. Mitchell in Chapter 4, as well as the descriptions of Marvin and Anthony in Chapters 2 and 3.)

Rita Lopez-Mitchell, an eighth grade social studies teacher at Central Middle School, knows that her experiences working with students in a behavior improvement room (BIR) were valuable to her in terms of learning to be patient, direct but nonconfrontational, and encouraging when interacting with students. Her kids at Central are challenging, but she is respected for her consistency and what her students perceive as a genuine caring attitude.

Rita Lopez-Mitchell

Recently Ms. Mitchell attended an inservice workshop designed to create awareness of how teacher-focused and student-focused methods of instruction differ. She has attended other workshops during her 4 years of teaching where she has learned about cooperative learning and the importance of differentiating instruction. Even though some other eighth grade teachers at Central have attended the same staff development sessions, she feels isolated in her attempts to implement some of the strategies because the eighth grade is not teamed.

Ms. Mitchell decided to plan and implement a cooperative learning project that would take about 4 weeks to complete. Because the project will require significant monitoring and she wants to "work out the bugs" before implementing it with all 107 students she teaches, she decides to pilot the project in her first period class. She forms heterogeneous groups of five students each. She gives them an overview of the project and reminds them of the basics of their recent class study of media influences and the importance of an informed citizenry. Students will be given the individual task of watching television news and reading newspapers for a week with the purpose of choosing one local, one national, and one international issue on which they would like their group project to be based. They are to be ready to defend their choices using notes that Ms. Mitchell will collect. The groups will decide on an issue and together write a statement justifying their decision. They will create a poster. One side will include newspaper articles, summaries of television news reports, and personal commentaries that explain the issue. The other side will be used to follow up on other related events and/or solutions as they unfold over a period of 2 weeks.

1. One eighth grader who has warmed up to Ms. Mitchell is Marvin. Every once in a while he shines in social studies. He's not as funny as he was as a sixth grader. His classmates no longer see his antics as reason to laugh. Ms. Mitchell seems to understand and helps him use his creativity in productive ways. How might this project be most positive for Marvin's self-esteem?

Marvin, eighth grade

(a) Marvin will have an opportunity to use his creative streak to design a good poster.

(b) In the role of facilitator, Marvin could prove to other kids that he can be a leader and do more than pull silly stunts.

(c) From what Ms. Mitchell has heard, Marvin's behavior is most reasonable early in the day, so being a student in first period is a real plus.

(d) Marvin may develop an interest in a current events topic.

2. Anthony rarely participates in class. He is sullen and quiet most of the time. Ms. Mitchell knows he is likely to drop out of school in a year or so if he isn't somehow "hooked" on learning. Which one of the following would be the least beneficial aspect of this project for Anthony?

Anthony, eighth grade

(a) He may find an issue that sparks his interest.

(b) He may feel a sense of belonging as a result of being part of a small learning group.

(c) He will be expected to do some individual work.

(d) Because there is an element of choice involved, he may find the project inviting.

3. As part of the information presented to Ms. Mitchell on student-focused instruction, she learned that using primary sources of data is desirable. Which one of these responses illustrates this concept?

(a) As an authority in the class, Ms. Mitchell should give an overview of local, national, and international issues.

(b) The posters will result from the work of the students in each group.

(c) Students can ask the adults in their homes for opinions about the issues.

(d) The project requires students to get information directly from newspaper articles.

Constructed Response

If Ms. Mitchell were part of an interdisciplinary team, how might this project be enhanced? What characteristics of effective teams might help facilitate a project like the one described?

Internet Resources

Middle Web Writing/Reading Workshop Project
http://middleweb.com

This large site has a link for the Writing/Reading Workshop Project to assist with literacy instruction.

NCREL Instruction
http://www.ncrel.org/sdrs/areas/in0cont.htm

This part of the North Central Regional Educational Laboratories site is specifically geared to assist teachers by providing a synthesis of the research on issues of instruction along with practical classroom strategies.

Teachers Network
http://teachnet.org

This site, with the motto "By Teachers, For Teachers," is filled with ideas for the classroom including lesson plans, resources, professional development opportunities, and grant-writing information.

References

Abbott, S. (1999). *Teaching reading in the middle grades.* Westminster, CA: Teacher Created Materials.

Armstrong, T. (1998). *Awakening the genius in the classroom.* Alexandria, VA: Association for Supervision and Curriculum Development.

Arnold, J. (1997). High expectations for all. *Middle School Journal, 28*(3), 51–53.

Bloom, B. S. (1956). *Taxonomy of educational objectives, handbook I: Cognitive domain.* New York: Longman, Green.

Brooks, J. G., & Brooks, M. G. (1993). *In search of understanding: The case for constructivist classrooms.* Alexandria, VA: Association for Supervision and Curriculum Development.

Brophy, J. (1981). On praising effectively. *Elementary School Journal, 81,* 269–278.

Caine, R. N., & Caine, G. (1994). *Making connections: Teaching and the human brain.* Menlo Park, CA: Addison-Wesley.

Carroll, T. G. (2000). If we didn't have the schools we have today, would we create the schools we have today? *Contemporary Issues in Technology and Teacher Education, 1*(1), 117–140.

Franklin, J. (2001, Fall). Teachers and technology: Turning the corner on training. *Curriculum Update.* Alexandria, VA: Association for Supervision and Curriculum Development.

Gunter, M. A., Estes, T. H., & Schwab, J. (1999). *Instruction: A models approach.* Boston, MA: Allyn & Bacon.

Jackson, A. W., & Davis, G. A. (2000). *Turning points 2000: Educating adolescents in the 21st century.* New York: Teachers College Press.

Jensen, E. (1998). *Teaching with the brain in mind.* Alexandria, VA: Association for Supervision and Curriculum Development.

Jensen, E. (2000). Brain-based learning: A reality check. *Educational Leadership, 57*(7), 76–79.

Johnson, D. W., & Johnson, R. T. (1987). *Learning together and alone.* Englewood Cliffs, NJ: Prentice Hall.

Knowles, T., & Brown, D. F. (2000). *What every middle school teacher should know.* Westerville, OH: National Middle School Association.

Lipman, M. (1988). *Philosophy goes to school.* Philadelphia: Temple University Press.

McKenna, M. C., & Robinson, R. D. (1997). *Teaching through text.* White Plains, NY: Longman.

Moore, K. D. (1999). *Middle and secondary school instruction methods.* Boston, MA: McGraw-Hill College.

Morretta, T. M., & Ambrosini, M. (2000). *Practical approaches for teaching reading and writing in middle schools.* Newark, DE: International Reading Association.

National Middle School Association. (2003). *This we believe: Successful schools for young adolescents.* Westerville, OH: Author.

Perkins, D. (1999). The many faces of constructivism. *Educational Leadership, 57*(3), 6–11.

Richetti, C., & Sheerin, J. (1999). Helping students ask the right questions. *Educational Leadership, 57*(3), 58–62.

Roberts, G. (1999). Lessons from Sisyphus in a technological age. *Educational Leadership, 56*(5), 75–77.

Rubenstein, R. E. (1994). *Hints for teaching success in middle school.* Englewood, CO: Teacher Ideas Press.

Shalaway, L. (1998). *Learning to teach . . . not just for beginners.* New York: Scholastic Professional Books.

Tomlinson, C. A. (1999). *The differentiated classroom: Responding to the needs of all learners.* Alexandria, VA: Association for Supervision and Curriculum Development.

Vatterott, C. (1999). *Academic success through empowering students.* Columbus, OH: National Middle School Association.

Vermetti, P. J. (1998). *Making cooperative learning work: Student teams in K–12 classrooms.* Upper Saddle River, NJ: Merrill/Prentice Hall.

Wiggins, G. P., & McTighe, J. (1998). *Understanding by design.* Alexandria, VA: Association for Supervision and Curriculum Development.

Wormeli, R. (2001). *Meet me in the middle: Becoming an accomplished middle level teacher.* Portland, ME: Stenhouse Publishers.

Zelchenko, P. (1999). Exploring alternatives to hype. *Educational Leadership, 56*(5), 78–81.

8

Strategies of Instruction

The distinctive developmental and learning characteristics of young adolescents provide the foundation for selecting teaching strategies. . . . Teaching approaches should enhance and accommodate the diverse skills, abilities, and prior knowledge of young adolescents, cultivate multiple intelligences, and draw upon students' individual learning styles. . . . Since young adolescents learn best through engagement and interaction, learning strategies involve students in dialogue with teachers and with one another. They participate in decisions about what to study and how best to study the topics selected. While direct instruction is still important, varied approaches are needed.

National Middle School Association, 2003, p. 25

Use this diagram as an organizational tool. In the boxes beside the chapter headings, indicate the date by which the readings should be completed.

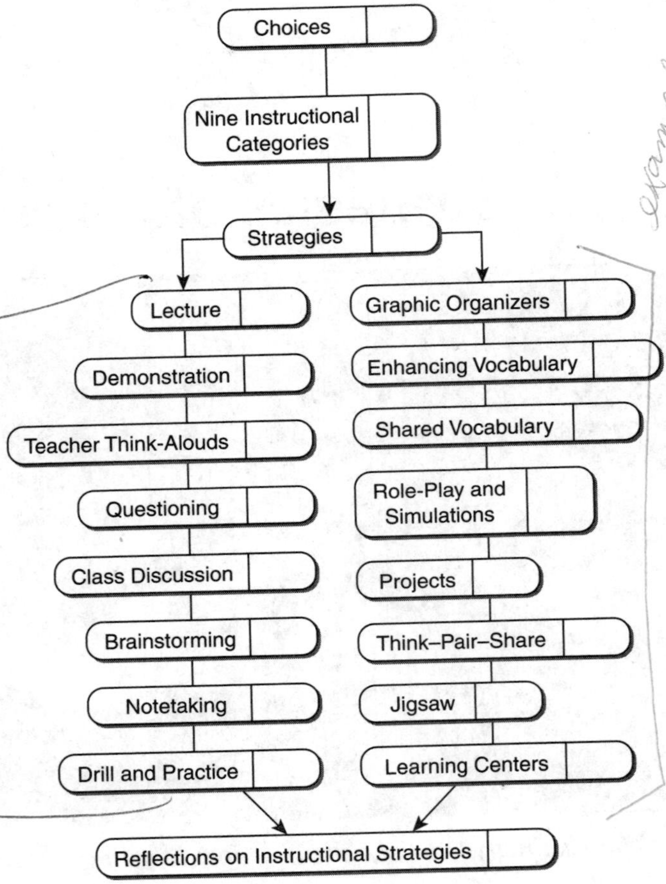

```
                    ┌─────────────────┐
                    │  Choices    │   │
                    └────────┬────────┘
                             │
                    ┌─────────────────┐
                    │ Nine Instructional │ │
                    │   Categories    │   │
                    └────────┬────────┘
                             │
                    ┌─────────────────┐
                    │  Strategies │   │
                    └────────┬────────┘
```

(handwritten annotations: "give 2 examples of each", "example given → you fill in one → choose")

Lecture		Graphic Organizers	
Demonstration		Enhancing Vocabulary	
Teacher Think-Alouds		Shared Vocabulary	
Questioning		Role-Play and Simulations	
Class Discussion		Projects	
Brainstorming		Think–Pair–Share	
Notetaking		Jigsaw	
Drill and Practice		Learning Centers	

Reflections on Instructional Strategies

INTRODUCTION

When selecting instructional strategies, the issues to consider are many and diverse. The most widely recognized issues include young adolescent development and all the implications involved, learning styles and multiple intelligences, and individual differences attributed to the variability inherent in 10- to 14-year-olds living in a multitude of settings. Add heterogeneity within the classroom to this mix and the absolute certainty about teaching strategies is that one size does not fit all. Our instructional toolboxes must be overflowing with strategies in order to best address the learning needs of each student. To be developmentally responsive means that we accommodate the needs of students in our classrooms who are by virtue of being young adolescents "developmentally unequal" (Stevenson, 1992, p. 122).

Standard 5

Knowledge 1: Middle level teacher candidates understand the principles of instruction and the research base that supports them.

Disposition 1: Middle level teacher candidates value the need for a repertoire of teaching/learning strategies that are appropriate for teaching all young adolescents.

Disposition 7: Middle level teacher candidates appreciate the importance of teaching strategies that are current and supported by research and successful practice.

Performance 1: Middle level teacher candidates use a variety of teaching/learning strategies and resources that motivate young adolescents to learn.

Standard 6

Performance 3: Middle level teacher candidates connect instruction to the diverse community experiences of all young adolescents.

 ## CHOICES

The ability to choose is a powerful motivator for both teachers and students. Having a full toolbox both motivates us and allows us to choose carefully with knowledge and insight those strategies that are appropriate for the audience, as well as for the content, skill, and/or standard to be addressed.

While hammers, saws, screwdrivers, and vise grips have differing uses for a carpenter, they are all of value in the building process. The effective carpenter knows the capabilities of each tool, can decide which tool is most appropriate, and realizes when to use each in the various stages of construction. This analogy will apply to your classroom as well. Instructional strategies are tools. Teachers must "rely on their knowledge of the students, their subject matter, and their situation to identify the most appropriate instructional strategies" (Marzano, Pickering, & Pollock, 2001, p. 9).

Standard 1

Knowledge 3: Middle level teacher candidates know a variety of teacher/learning strategies that take into consideration and capitalize upon the developmental characteristics of all young adolescents.

Tomlinson (1999) tells us that there is nothing inherently good or bad about instructional strategies. She refers to them as "the 'buckets' teachers can use to deliver content, process, or products" (p. 61). Keep in mind that even though an instructional strategy may require much teacher direction to be implemented effectively, it can still be student-focused as described in the previous chapter's Figure 7.2. The following sections provide information on a variety of instructional strategies. Some are obvious matches to the nine categories of effective instruction, while others may encompass combinations of categories or be more conspicuously linked to principles in Chapter 7. You have a lot of "lenses" through which to view the strategies.

Passing along the motivation of choice to our students as often as possible is good for them. The students in your classroom may often experience the same basic strategies. But within each strategy are ways to differentiate that will allow for student choices. Within parameters of what makes sense, the more choices the better. When students are allowed to make some decisions, the instruction is more student-focused. Choice is not only motivational; it is developmentally responsive and will pay off in increased learning.

NINE INSTRUCTIONAL CATEGORIES

In a meta-analysis of many studies of instruction, Marzano and colleagues (2001) found nine categories that correlate positively, and most often, with learning. Armed with information from the analysis about effective strategies and the knowledge that the most important factor in student learning is the teacher (Wright, Horn, & Sanders, 1997), the responsibility for implementing appropriate strategies falls squarely on our shoulders.

The nine identified categories of instructional strategies that positively affect student achievement are listed in Figure 8.1. While all nine were shown to be highly effective, note that

---

Identifying similarities and differences—involves identification of important characteristics and then comparing, classifying, and creating metaphors and analogies.

Summarizing and notetaking—powerful study skills for identifying and understanding the most important aspects of what students are learning.

Reinforcing effort and providing recognition—techniques that address students' attitudes, beliefs, and motivations concerning the connection of effort and success.

Homework and practice—provide opportunities for students to refine and extend knowledge.

Nonlinguistic representations—graphic representations and physical models that elaborate on knowledge.

Cooperative learning—flexible and powerful tool for grouping students to promote collaboration.

Setting objectives and providing feedback—process of establishing a direction for learning and then providing an explanation of what students are doing that is correct and what they are doing that is incorrect.

Generating and testing hypotheses—process of understanding a principle, making a conjecture, and applying the knowledge to see if it holds true.

Cues, questions, and advance organizers—techniques that activate prior knowledge and/or set the stage for, and bridge the way to, new knowledge.

FIGURE 8.1   Categories of instructional strategies that affect student achievement.

Source: From *Classroom Instruction That Works* (p. 7), by R. J. Marzano, D. J. Pickering, and J. E. Pollock, 2001, Alexandria, VA: Association for Supervision and Curriculum Development. Copyright 2001 by McREL. Adapted with permission.

the categories are listed in descending order of effectiveness. As we examine individual strategies throughout Chapter 8, refer back to Figure 8.1 to see how each strategy might fit into one or more categories.

INSTRUCTIONAL STRATEGIES

Each of the big ideas of instruction in Chapter 7 provides a theoretical basis for the great variety of instructional strategies available to middle grades teachers. From teacher-directed to student-driven, the strategies abound. Each is rich in possibilities, allowing us to differentiate instruction to accommodate the readiness, interests, and learning profiles of our students. This chapter consists of brief explanations of instructional strategies that may fit in more than one of the nine categories and may meet the needs of some or all of our students at varying times and in different subject areas. Consider each one carefully as you add to your instructional toolbox.

Lecture

Lecture has gotten a bad rap for quite a while. Like almost anything else, overuse and misuse of the lecture format, along with some of our own memories of fighting to stay awake through the Prussian Wars or the contributions of automation to the industrial revolution, have left many of us with a bad taste. However, with certain guidelines the lecture, or mini-lecture, can be a valuable teaching strategy to introduce a lesson, describe a problem, and/or provide information in concise ways.

A mini-lecture is simply a brief lecture. Inattention may fill a middle school classroom after 10 to 15 minutes of one person talking. Keeping the lecture format brief will allow it to be used effectively and as often as appropriate.

When planning a mini-lecture, identify the main points you want to include. Consider an attention-grabbing opener (advance organizer) that will set the stage for the content to come. Then decide on examples to include that will illustrate the main points you will make. Finally, develop a summary of the content that refers back to the advance organizer and main points with examples.

Wormeli (2001) tells us that using lecture as the dominant strategy appeals to only about a fourth of middle grades students. He says lecture "relies on symbolic and abstract thinking when the majority of middle grades students still think concretely" (p. 82). In spite of this, he acknowledges that mini-lectures used in conjunction with other strategies during a class period are effective instructional tools.

Lecture = Attention-grabbing opener + Illustrative examples + Summary

Demonstration

A demonstration is a way of showing students something that would be difficult to convey through words alone. Whether showing steps in solving a math problem, describing the symbols for editing and their applications, or conducting a science experiment, demonstrations can be very effective instructional tools that are applicable in every subject area. When coupled with a mini-lecture, a demonstration complements auditory learning with visual stimulation.

There are a number of reasons for choosing to use demonstrations and just as many levels of complexity in what they involve. Perhaps the most frequent reason to use demonstration is to detail the steps in a procedure. This can be as simple as writing on a chalkboard. Another reason to use demonstration is to get a point across that isn't easily expressed in words. While words can express the form of a volleyball serve, showing what it actually looks like will have much more benefit. When something needs to be shown, but it would take too long for every student in the class to experience it, the teacher or a student might complete the task while the class watches. Demonstrations can show the proper use of equipment or materials. Certainly if the possibility of danger to either students or materials exists, a demonstration by the teacher is appropriate (Moore, 1999).

Demonstration = Showing + Telling

Demonstrations of any kind can help focus attention. Young adolescent curiosity is more likely to be piqued by watching and listening, and the possibility of doing, than by listening alone.

Teacher Think-Alouds

Modeling is what we do all day long, whether purposefully or inadvertently. Modeling thinking processes through *teacher think-alouds* shows our students how they might go about solving a problem, approaching a task, or processing new information. We have learned through experience and maturity how to think our way into, through, and out of scenarios. "Think-alouds make invisible mental processes visible" (Wilhelm, 2001, p. 26).

Here are examples of think-alouds.

Math Problem

Margo purchased a CD on sale that had an original price of $15.00. All the CDs on the rack were 20% off. The sales tax was 8%. How much change did Margo receive from a $20 bill?

Think-Aloud:

"Ummmm . . . Let's see what I know. The CD is on sale so she's not going to pay $15.00. Does she pay 20%? No, that's the discount. So I have to find 20% of $15.00. I remember that "of" usually means to multiply. So I'll multiply 20% times $15.00. Twenty percent is the same as .20 so it will be .20 × 15 (write on board and multiply). That's 3. Do I add or subtract it? I should subtract it because the CD is on sale. Okay, that's $12.00. Now I need to add the tax. I have to multiply again (write .08 × 12 on board and multiply). I subtracted the $3.00 but now I have to add the $.96 (write on board 12.00 + .96). That means she paid $12.96 for the CD. She used a $20 bill so I have to subtract $12.96 from $20 (do this on board). So she got $7.04 back in change."

Note: This is very different from saying "Here are the steps" and then doing the computation almost silently on the board.

Language Arts Item

Directions: Choose the word that best completes each sentence.

1. Marcus and _____ decided to skateboard until dark.

   (a) myself

   (b) us

   (c) me

   (d) I

Think-Aloud:

"I remember learning that it's a good idea to leave out the words before the 'and' and see what sounds right in the blank so I'm going to try it. *Myself* decided to skateboard . . . No, that's not right. *Us* decided to skateboard . . . Sounds bad. *Me* decided to skateboard . . . kind of like "Me Tarzan, You Jane." How about *I* decided to skateboard . . . Hey, that's it."

Think-alouds can demonstrate to students how to bring personal background and prior knowledge into reading. Try reading an article or passage in a short story and then stop to verbalize an experience you may have had that relates to the text or some information you know that makes the reading more relevant. In this way, you are showing your students how to internalize what they read.

Think-alouds = Organized thought + Verbalization

Aside from academics, try using the think-aloud strategy when you hear students arguing or you become aware of a friendship rift, or when students have decisions to make. Think aloud about how you might deal with the situation. For young adolescents this is much more effective than "preaching" or talking "at them."

Questioning

Effective questioning takes thought and planning. We can prompt our students to think on all six levels of Bloom's taxonomy on any topic in any subject by asking relevant questions. The next time you have an opportunity to observe a middle school class (or even a university class), listen carefully to each question posed. Determine which level of the taxonomy is required to answer the question, and keep a tally. Chances are the knowledge category will have the most tally marks by far at the end of the class. That's not necessarily bad, depending on the lesson. However, finding that to be the case day after day is definitely a problem.

Questions may be convergent and tend to have one best answer. These questions lead to exercising Bloom's knowledge and comprehension levels. Divergent questions are those that are open-ended and that often have many possible responses. When we are looking for application in thinking, our questions should allow for a number of correct responses. Analysis is often personal and based on prior knowledge, so answers will vary. Synthesis can be almost a free-for-all because we are asking our students to come up with something new based on what they know. The responses to questions aimed at evaluative thinking can take many directions. Figure 8.2 contains very practical guidelines for using questioning as a thoughtfully planned instructional strategy.

Classroom questioning = Convergent + Divergent

1. Plan key questions that are clear and specific to provide lesson structure and direction. Ask spontaneous questions based on student responses.

2. Adapt questions to student ability level. This enhances understanding and reduces anxiety. Phrase questions in natural, simple language.

3. Ask questions at a variety of levels. Keep Bloom's taxonomy in mind.

4. Respond to students in ways that encourage them to clarify initial answers and support their points of view and opinions.

5. Give students time to think before requiring an answer. Wait time after asking a question should be 5 seconds or more to both increase the frequency of student responses and to encourage higher level thinking.

6. Encourage a wide range of student participation. Call on nonvolunteers, being careful to consider difficulty levels of questions.

7. Encourage student questioning. Prompt students to phrase questions that stimulate higher cognitive levels of thought.

FIGURE 8.2   Questioning techniques.

Questioning is a two-way street in a developmentally responsive, interactive classroom. One of the best ways we can help our students learn a concept deeply is to guide them in framing good questions. After a reading assignment or an activity, rather than requiring students to write a summary or an outline, have them write questions. Without guidance you will likely get a lot of "When did . . . ?" "Who was . . . ?" "What happened when . . . ?" —all knowledge and maybe a smattering of comprehension. To make the strategy effective, use question prompts, sometimes referred to as question stems. For instance,

"How does _____ compare to _____ ?"

"What is the major difference between _____ and _____ ?"

"How might we classify _____ similarly to our classification of _____ ?"

"How does _____ affect _____ ?"

"In what ways does _____ depend on _____ ?"

"How would you prioritize _____ ?"

"What conclusions can we draw from _____ ?"

"How is _____ an example of _____ ?"

"What can we predict given _____ ?"

As a homework assignment you might ask students to read a particular text and develop three questions using these prompts. The next day, form groups and have students exchange and answer each other's questions.

Be purposeful in both questioning and in teaching the art of questioning. An obvious skill that accompanies questioning is listening. To effectively question based on responses to previous questions requires concentration and an in-depth grasp of content. Questioning allows us to capitalize on those teachable moments that gratefully bombard us every day in our classrooms.

Class Discussions

Class discussions occur every day in almost every class in every middle school. It is the nature of most young adolescents to like to talk and voice opinions. Most want to be heard and have great things to contribute. Framing and orchestrating class discussion in positive ways requires us to be on our toes. We have to focus the discussion to keep it on track and ensure that everyone participates. This requires our complete attention as we employ the questioning techniques just discussed. Keep in mind that a discussion is a conversation, not just a question and answer session. Ideally the students talk far more than the teacher, asking and answering questions, offering responses, giving opinions, and making suggestions.

Given the wide variety of personalities in any middle grades classroom, it is a fact that there will be students who are always willing to discuss almost anything as well as those who are reticent to contribute for any number of reasons. When planning for a discussion of more than just a few minutes, consider writing a few major issues or questions on the board. Help your students learn to frame their thinking along conceptual, as well as concrete, lines the first time you try this by seizing the opportunity to model notetaking techniques. Choose an initial discussion topic that is certain to be of interest to students and, after a few brief blackboard notes, let the discussion proceed. As questions arise and important issues surface, fill in your blackboard outline and have the students parallel your efforts on individual cards. In no time, the blackboard and student note cards will be filled with both concrete and conceptual points that provide the framework for your expectations and student thinking patterns in future discussions. Once successfully modeled, ask students to think about possible points or responses and jot them down on index cards. In this way, students formulate their views and think about what will be discussed. The more reticent among them will be more prepared to contribute. In Figure 8.3, Schurr (1995) includes a tip about tossing a ball (preferably a soft, light one!) from student to student to promote participation. I've done this often in the classroom, and I know it works. Giving some upfront thinking time helps all students feel they can catch the ball and contribute.

Class discussion = Focus + Broad participation

It's hard to have a conversation when some of the people involved have their backs to one another. Similarly, straight rows in a classroom are not conducive to open discussion. Come up with a configuration that can be created quickly by students. It might be a matter of turning desks, having some students sit on tables or in perimeter chairs, or even clearing the center of the room and letting the students who wish to sit on the floor move to the middle, while others stay in desks. If you have enough space, an ideal configuration is a circle.

Brainstorming

The goal of brainstorming is to produce as many responses as possible. All thoughts are allowed without judgment (of course, within guidelines of good taste as established in your

1. **Initiate** a discussion by having students respond to an open-ended question individually and then share their ideas with a partner before discussing responses with the whole group.

2. **Organize** a discussion by having each student or small group of students write out a question or concern they have about the topic for discussion on individual file cards. Collect the cards and use these student-generated ideas as the sole basis for the discussion session.

3. **Stop** the large group dialogue at several points during a discussion and instruct students to discuss this "last major point" with a partner or small group.

4. **Pause** during a discussion session and survey students to determine how they feel about a question that has just been answered or a point that has just been raised by a peer. For example, you might ask: "How many of you agree with the answer just given by John?" or "Raise your hand if you think this point made by Susan is an important one to consider."

5. **Provide** each student or pair of students in a discussion group with a response tool such as a set of prescribed Yes/No cards, individual chalkboards, or a set of A, B, C, D multiple choice sheets of paper. After asking a question, instruct students to signal their answers by showing you the best "response" on their prop or response manipulative tool.

6. **Keep** students on their toes during discussion by tossing a ball to a student after asking a question. Whoever catches the ball must respond to the question.

FIGURE 8.3 Class discussion strategies.

Source: From *Prescriptions for Success in Heterogenous Classrooms* (pp. 9–10), by S. L. Schurr, 1995, Columbus, OH: National Middle School Association. Adapted with permission from National Middle School Association.

classroom). We want students to think in divergent ways as they contribute. The results of brainstorming can be recorded in many ways using the chalkboard, chart paper, and so on.

Brainstorming can be used to list all the things a class of students collectively knows about a topic. For instance, if you are beginning a unit on the U.S. Constitution, you could ask the class to brainstorm everything they know, or think they know, about the Constitution. While only one student may know a particular bit of information, it is important to include it to validate the student and to say, "Great! When we come to that part of the unit, we want you to help us understand more about _____." Brainstorming sets the stage by creating interest for what's coming, getting kids actively involved, and letting you get a feel for students' prior knowledge.

Brainstorming is also the first stage of a very popular and useful instructional tool—the K–W–L chart. Figure 8.4 shows a K–W–L chart and an example of how it might be used. The **K** stands for what we **KNOW**. Brainstorming fills that column. From the brainstorming will come questions, perhaps about things listed in the K column. The **W** stands for what we **WANT** to know, so the W column will be filled with questions. The **L** stands for what we **LEARNED**. The K–W–L chart should be displayed for the duration of the study of a topic so you and your sudents can continue to add to the columns.

Brainstorming = Creating interest + Getting kids involved + Assessing prior knowledge

U.S. Constitution		
K What we know	**W** What we want to know	**L** What we learned
• Written in 1700s • Tells how to run our country • Displayed in Washington • Fancy penmanship • Signed by a bunch of men • Has amendments	• Who actually wrote it? • Can it be changed? • What are some things that we hear about that are "unconstitutional"? • What do we do about things that aren't covered in the Constitution?	This column is for students to record answers to their questions and other things of interest learned in their study. Have a way of adding lots of paper for a long list.

FIGURE 8.4   K–W–L chart.

K–W–L = What we know + What we want to know + What we learned

Another important use of brainstorming is to begin the writing process. To write an essay, students can brainstorm all the things they might possibly want to include. Then they examine all the things they have written to find the things that seem to fit together. They group them, and the groups become logical paragraphs. The paragraphs are then sequenced and an introduction is written followed by the body paragraphs and then a conclusion. This is somewhat simplistic, but the structure works.

When a class decision is needed, perhaps to choose a field trip location or a topic to be studied in more depth than others, brainstorming is a valuable tool to allow everyone to participate. Once students have experienced the process, it can be student-led rather than teacher-led. Brainstorming is an effective way to create ownership of decisions.

Notetaking

Taking notes is part of our everyday lives. We make lists of groceries and things to do, notes to help us follow directions to a location, instructions for how to order something we see on television, and so on. You might want to have your students brainstorm when they use notetaking in their everyday lives. Of course, this isn't the same as taking notes on a lecture or a reading assignment, but the reasons for notetaking are similar. Notetaking, whether practical or academic, helps us remember and saves time.

Ernst (1996) calls notetaking "listening with your pencil" (p. 71). It requires both listening skills and critical thinking skills. We must decide what is important to remember, organize information to write, and determine if it's enough or if further clarification is needed. This is a lot to ask of a 10- to 14-year-old, so we must model the process. A good way to do this is to use the overhead projector. As you lecture, question, and/or conduct a class discussion, return to the projector and make notes of the most important points. Ask your students to write in their notebooks what you write on the transparency. After the notetaking is finished, go over the notes to organize them, put them in diagram or graphic form, consider what might be unnecessary, or decide where gaps in the information might exist. In this process, ask for student input. After modeling notetaking several times, ask the students to take notes on their own. For their first few solo ventures it's a good idea to collect the notes and give feedback. This will also let you know what your students perceive as important.

Learning to take notes on a reading assignment requires more than simply telling students to do it. Again, modeling is necessary. A good way to accomplish this is to write notes in whatever format makes sense, assign the reading, and give students copies of your notes.

Notetaking = Listening + Deciding what's important + Writing

Then go back through the reading and explain how you chose the concepts and information to include. If outlining is your chosen style, then modeling will need to be followed by extensive practice.

We can give students a framework for notes and have them fill in details as they listen to a lecture, participate in a discussion, read text, or watch a video. The outline format works, or you may want to simply write statements with key words and phrases omitted. Allow time for students to read through the guided notes before the lecture, discussion, or video so they will be reading or listening for specific information. This strategy focuses attention and also provides a study guide.

In an inclusive classroom you will likely have students for whom notetaking will be difficult. Try providing carbon paper for several students who are willing to share their notetaking abilities with students who need assistance. I have had great results with this technique. The able students are flattered to be asked to help and feel a sense of accomplishment, and positive relationships are often forged.

Drill and Practice

Drill and practice can be characterized as "systematic and repeated 'workouts' in the intended skill areas, with the purpose of achieving automatic accuracy and speed of performance" (Moore, 1999, p. 240). Clarifying and consolidating material already learned and then repeating the information or skill is what the drill and practice strategy is all about. The process helps with long-term retention and aids in developing speed and accuracy (Burden & Byrd, 1999).

Drill and practice = Clarifying + Consolidating + Repeating

When you use drill and practice, always make sure the material is familiar enough that students won't have to stop to look up something or ask questions. Students should be able to work independently and always have a way of knowing quickly how well they did. Software is available in almost every middle grades subject and on virtually any topic. Using the computer to practice skills and recall information is both efficient and effective. Use drill and practice in moderation, but don't fail to employ it when there are obvious benefits.

Graphic Organizers

Graphic organizers are very powerful instructional tools that help us think critically to visualize knowledge and comprehend relationships in organized ways. Shalaway (1998) tells us that graphic organizers "encourage active learning, demonstrate that knowledge is interconnected, facilitate group work, accommodate individual learning styles, and engage students in higher-order thinking" (p. 124). Any tool that can do all that is certainly valuable! Graphic organizers are flexible, with so many possibilities and uses. I started regularly using graphic organizers in my classroom after I had been teaching for 10 years. After this

Graphic organizers = Thinking critically + Visualizing knowledge + Comprehending relationships

somewhat tardy start, I now actually organize my thoughts and lesson plans by visualizing a graphic organizer that fits what I have in mind. I quickly sketch the organizer and, as I do, I never fail to come up with more ideas. What began as teaching and learning tools for my students have now become permanent organizational tools for me. So, be prepared to get hooked!

Graphic organizers can enhance teaching and learning in any subject area by allowing you to sequence events, prioritize actions, categorize information, compare and contrast ideas and objects, show part/whole relationships, illustrate connectivity, show cause and effect—you name it, and a graphic organizer can enhance it.

Following a brainstorming session, students can take all the random, scattered information generated and make sense of it using a graphic organizer. A simple web design (Figure 8.5) works well for this purpose where supporting ideas radiate from a central topic or theme, like spokes on a wheel. Talking students through the creation of such a web is the best way for them to understand the process.

After reading a story or novel, an effective way to review the events is to use a sequencing organizer (Figure 8.6). You can do this as a whole class a few times, then assign the task to small groups of students who can post their graphic organizers for others to view.

You'll find that many students will start to really catch on to the significance of concepts such as recognizing similarities and differences when they understand the use of Venn diagrams. You may remember from the beginning of this chapter that this is the top-ranked category of instructional strategies in terms of student learning. Figure 8.7 shows a simple Venn diagram, one of the most useful graphic organizers.

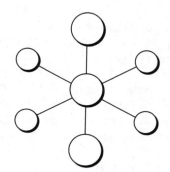

FIGURE 8.5   Simple web.

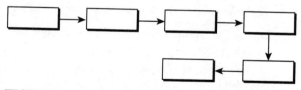

FIGURE 8.6   Sequencing organizer.

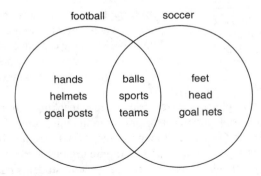

FIGURE 8.7   Venn diagram.

Enhancing Vocabulary

Enhancing the vocabulary of our students should be a major instructional goal. The more words students own, the higher their comprehension levels will be and the easier learning and conceptualizing will become. A word can be "an instrument of learning, a vehicle for information, and a changer of history. . . . If we accept the importance of words, then a broad and comprehensive vocabulary has power" (Powell, 2000, p. 14).

> Enhancing vocabulary = Creating a word-rich environment + Giving opportunities to use words

Creating a text-rich environment will immerse our students in vocabulary. When a new word surfaces in class readings, videos, discussions, and so on, have a student write the word on an index card along with a definition that is appropriate for the context. Then have the student put the card in a classroom pocket chart that has a pocket for each letter in the alphabet. In this way we create our own classroom dictionaries full of relevant words. Encourage students to use the words in the pocket chart in their writing. As the words increase, occasionally pull out all the cards in one letter pocket and review the words with students. Ask them to recall the context of the creation of each card. The words can also be used in games and exercises.

Graphic organizers can be very effective in vocabulary study. Knowing that visual stimulation promotes learning, graphically portraying words makes sense. Figure 8.8 shows two visually pleasing ways for students to study new words.

Shared Vocabulary

Every subject has a unique vocabulary. One of the richest benefits of the team structure in middle school is the possibility of sharing the vocabulary used in all our subjects all day long.

Team vocabulary sharing can be accomplished in a very simple way. Here are the steps:

1. Devise a rotation system that designates one team teacher to be in charge of vocabulary each week.

2. On Thursday, pass a clipboard with a page on it that is similar to Figure 8.9 among team teachers.

3. Each team teacher writes a brief description of the next week's content/plans and five or six key vocabulary words. Include related arts teachers who teach students on your team.

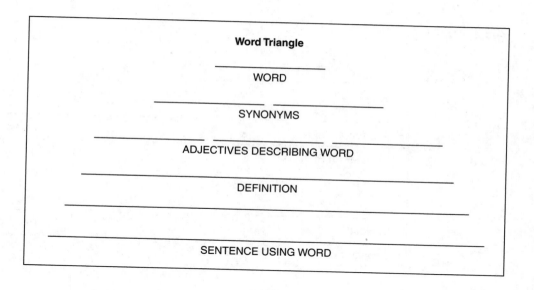

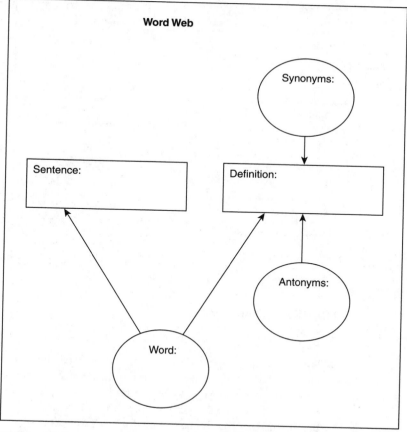

FIGURE 8.8 Vocabulary approaches.

Team _____

Week of _____

Subject:	Key Vocabulary
Overview of Plan:	
Subject:	Key Vocabulary
Overview of Plan:	
Subject:	Key Vocabulary
Overview of Plan:	
Subject:	Key Vocabulary
Overview of Plan:	
Subject:	Key Vocabulary
Overview of Plan:	

FIGURE 8.9   Shared vocabulary.

4. By Friday, the designated teacher should have the clipboard. This teacher makes a wall chart of the words for each classroom the team students use, including the gym, cafeteria, art room, and so on. Colored paper from the big rolls available in most schools works well. A wide marker will make the words easily visible. Use the same color paper and marker for all classrooms for any given week.

5. Teachers post vocabulary lists in the same places in all classrooms each week.

The lists are visual reminders of the words that will be key to understanding the concepts and skills emphasized during the week. All teachers should attempt to use every word on the list within the context of their classes. While "photosynthesis" rarely comes up in language arts, the word can still be examined because of its compound nature. The science teacher may not discuss this aspect of the word as the topic is explored. If "symmetry" is on the list as a math word, the art teacher may use the word to describe a painting rather than just mentioning the balance of elements. As you use a word, walk over to the list and point to it. Students are then hearing the word in different ent contexts and seeing the word on the list. Great reinforcement! Sharing vocabulary lets our students know we talk and plan together. Their view of the broad scope of our knowledge is enhanced as students learn vocabulary in deeper, more contextual ways. All this is accomplished through a painless process that takes very little time.

Shared vocabulary = Deciding on key words + Sharing words among teachers + Using words in a variety of contexts

Role-Play and Simulations

When students act out or dramatize a situation or idea in a class setting we call it *role-play*. Facilitating role-play in a middle grades classroom takes planning and thoughtful consideration. To be useful as an instructional strategy, role-play requires structure that includes a clear purpose and role descriptions. Expectations and incentives are needed both for those actively participating as well as those students not actively filling the roles but who need to pay attention. It is vital to debrief a role-play session to make sure students get the point(s). Once the students are accustomed to role-playing, we can be more spontaneous about initiating it.

Role play = Structuring scenario + Setting expectations + Imagining/ pretending + Debriefing

Simulations differ from role-play as they place students in models of real-life environments where they deal with possible consequences in more specific and guided ways than most role-play situations (Burden & Byrd, 1999). Lesson plans for using simulations, along with props and followup activities, can be purchased at teacher resource stores. Simulations are particularly useful in social studies classes to explore history and social/political dilemmas.

What Burden and Byrd (1999) tell us about role-play can be applied to simulations as well. They tell us that role-play helps students

- Understand perspectives and feelings of others
- Clarify and demonstrate attitudes and concepts
- Plan and test solutions to problems
- Prepare for real-life situations
- Deepen understanding of social situations
- Demonstrate creativity and imagination (p. 105)

We might add to their list such benefits as increased verbal and nonverbal learning, encouragement of divergent thinking, enhanced mental stimulation, and expansion of communication skills.

Projects

I have watched with great joy as middle school students suddenly "come alive" in the midst of a project experience that is carefully orchestrated and full of choices. Students who seldom show any semblance of interest in schoolwork often blossom when given the opportunity to choose a topic, a strategy, and/or a work product. I often ask college students to talk and write about what they remember about their middle school days. Invariably there are comments about the models of castles they built out of sugar cubes, the play they wrote and performed, the elaborate mobile of polyhedrons they concocted, or the nursing home visits they painfully began and then got hooked on. These are all projects. They allow our students to show initiative, take responsibility, be physically involved, make decisions, and create. In other words, students "bloom."

As you design units of study (more on units in Chapter 10), you'll find numerous opportunities to allow students to participate in projects. Some may be individually tackled, others accomplished in small groups, and still others may engage an entire class. The possibilities are practically unlimited. You have to be the guide and judge of how often, when, and why to use the project approach as an instructional strategy. It can be a much "messier" proposition than other alternatives.

The skills needed to facilitate project work may be different from the skills needed for many of the more traditional instructional strategies. We need to set expectations, ask questions that help students define their projects, assist them in sequencing tasks and organizing procedures (graphic organizers are ideal), remind them of problem-solving strategies for the big and small dilemmas that are inevitable, provide encouragement to stay on task, and celebrate with them as their work culminates into a product. In other words, we facilitate the acquisition and practice of life skills. Worthy effort!

> Projects = Setting expectations + Defining topics + Organizing procedures + Problem solving + Encouraging + Celebrating

Think–Pair–Share

Think–Pair–Share is a versatile and useful tool that can be employed almost any time, in almost any setting, and for any purpose. Here are the simple steps:

1. Ask a thought-provoking question or give a prompt.
2. Instruct students to think for a minute or two.
3. Have students turn to a neighbor and briefly discuss their thoughts.
4. Ask for volunteers to share with the class what they have discussed.

> Think-Pair-Share = Prompting/ questioning + Individual thought + Sharing thoughts with neighbor/whole class

I often have students write brief notes about their thinking before talking with a partner to lend some accountability to the process. You might want to establish a Think–Pair–Share journal where students date their thoughts and add their partner's opinions/answers to their own.

A variation of Think–Pair–Share, sometimes called Pyramid Think–Pair–Share, involves having pairs of students share with other pairs. In this way students go from individual opinions/answers, to hearing from another student and building on their own ideas or possibly being persuaded to change. They then have the benefit of two additional students' thought processes. This could be followed by whole-group sharing.

We've discussed the need for variety in format to accommodate sometimes limited attention spans. Think–Pair–Share is an easy and effective way to break up lectures, discussions, videos, and so on into brain-compatible chunks. I recommend that you put Think–Pair–Share on the top of your instructional toolbox and use it often!

Jigsaw

There is great power in students teaching students, and Jigsaw is an excellent technique that requires them to do so.

Here are the basic steps involved in using the Jigsaw model:

1. Choose a reading that can be logically divided into sections.
2. Divide your students into groups with the same number of students in each group as there are sections in the reading. For instance, if a chapter has four sections, your students should form "base" groups of four students each.
3. Within each group, have students number off one to four. Ask all the ones to get together, all the twos, all the threes, and all the fours. These groups become "expert" groups.
4. Assign each expert group a section of the reading to read and discuss. Their task is to formulate a plan to teach the material to members of their individual base groups. Encourage groups to develop graphics, written summaries, or other unique ways to make the material meaningful.
5. Reconvene base groups to teach each other the material they have mastered in their expert groups.

Jigsaw = Forming base groups + Assigning topics + Forming expert groups + Encouraging students teaching students

Figure 8.10 graphically shows how the model works. I have found that students enjoy Jigsaw. They like the idea of being experts and teachers. Naturally, your watchful facilitation will play a critical role in the success of this valuable instructional strategy.

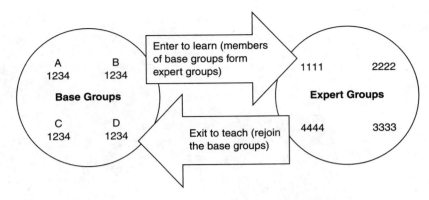

FIGURE 8.10 Jigsaw.

Learning Centers

Broadly speaking, *learning centers* are designated places in a classroom, or they consist of movable displays/activities, that provide students with opportunities to pursue interests and/or learn content and skills using a variety of modalities and in differing time frames. Learning centers are enjoying a resurgence of popularity due, in part, to a renewed emphasis on differentiating instruction (George & Alexander, 2003). Learning centers, or learning stations, were once thought of as instructional tools suitable for elementary classrooms only.

Learning centers = Planning + Durable materials + Procedures and expectations + Time to learn and enjoy

With the advent of longer class periods made possible through block scheduling, learning centers are gaining popularity in middle and high schools (Callahan, Clark, & Kellough, 2002). Requiring time and thoughtful effort to set up and maintain, learning centers provide enrichment and reinforce skills in ways that address different interests and ability levels.

There are as many kinds and levels of complexity of learning centers as there are topics and skills. Schurr (1995) provides us with some basic steps for creating learning centers in Figure 8.11. Once you have developed a center, don't be afraid to alter it as you observe changes that would improve its user friendliness. Learning centers can be maintained year after year if you plan carefully, use durable materials and packaging, and laminate written materials. Ideas and tips for success with learning centers are readily available at teacher resource stores.

REFLECTIONS ON STRATEGIES OF INSTRUCTION

Let's return to the nine categories of instructional strategies that positively affect student achievement. Although this chapter contains a limited number of strategies, all nine categories have been addressed, and some in multiple ways.

Identifying similarities and differences can be accomplished through direct and explicit teacher guidance or by asking students to do it independently. Through demonstrations and discussions we tell and/or guide students, while student discovery and inquiry

1. Determine the primary purpose and type of learning center to be developed.
2. Write a set of objectives that relate to the skill/concept to be taught.
3. Choose the best possible location, set-up, and design of the center.
4. Obtain and organize the necessary furniture, materials, and equipment for the center.
5. Create a set of learning alternatives or strategies.
6. Write a set of instructions for student use of the center.
7. Determine a feasible management system for the center.
8. Complete the physical set-up of the center.
9. Conduct an orientation to the center for all participating students, volunteers, parents, and support staff.

FIGURE 8.11   Checklist for creating and using learning centers.

Source: From *Prescriptions for Success in Heterogeneous Classrooms* (p. 47), by S. L. Schurr, 1995, Columbus, OH: National Middle School Association. Adapted with permission from National Middle School Association.

occur through brainstorming, questioning, and learning centers. Graphic organizers are ideal for recording similarities.

Summarizing and notetaking are possible in every subject. Summarizing can be accomplished as a followup to lectures and during the course of discussions. The Jigsaw model requires students to summarize material in order to teach it to others.

Project learning affords ample opportunity for reinforcing effort and providing recognition. This instructional category is wrapped up in attitudes and beliefs.

Practice is possible through most instructional strategies. The strategy discussed in this chapter as drill and practice most closely aligns with the traditional notion of practice. Homework will be discussed in Chapter 10 when we focus on planning.

Learning centers provide students with opportunities to work at their own pace in ways that address personal learning styles and multiple intelligences. Using graphic organizers gives students ways of making sense of concepts and content without verbalization. Projects often involve physical models that convey meaning without words.

Cooperative learning is a strategy that can be a vehicle for implementing many other strategies. We spent time in Chapter 7 examining the basics of cooperative learning. In this chapter we have specifically discussed group work in role-play and simulations, Think–Pair–Share, and the Jigsaw model.

Setting objectives and providing feedback are two categories at the heart of teaching. All the strategies in this chapter provide opportunities to either define learning (setting objectives) or determine what learning has occurred (feedback). Projects are fertile ground for both. Objectives for projects are set with the student and feedback provides guidance that is corrective (an explanation of what is correct and what is not correct) and timely.

Anytime we provide opportunities for our students to create, invent, discover, and inquire, we give them a structure in which to generate and test hypotheses. All of the strategies in this chapter, with the possible exception of lecture, can be used to encourage students to generate hypotheses. Through role-play and simulations, learning centers, and projects students have opportunities to test hypotheses.

Both teacher-generated and student-generated questions are powerful learning tools. When questions serve as advance organizers, they help to activate prior knowledge. Strategies in this chapter such as questioning, brainstorming, and discussion set the stage for new learning by prompting students to use their background knowledge and experiences.

Once again we return to the concept of balance, applying it in two ways. We should choose our instructional strategies based on the concepts and content to be taught/learned, student needs, and the classroom situation at hand. So we balance concepts, needs, and circumstances with strategies for instruction as illustrated in Figure 8.12. Our basis for creating balance rests in both the effectiveness of teaching/learning and the efficiency of delivery.

The second application of balance deals with instructional strategies themselves. Using only one or two consistently is not developmentally responsive. Through variety we address multiple intelligences, more learning styles and modalities, and all the differences in students we discussed in Chapters 2 and 3. Balancing a variety of both teacher-directed and student-driven strategies, as illustrated in Figure 8.13, will help create and maintain a positive learning environment and promote greater understanding.

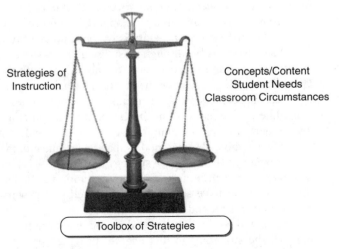

FIGURE 8.12   Achieving balance: Instruction and circumstances.

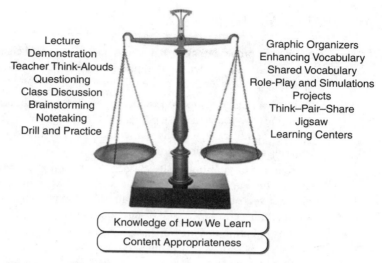

Lecture
Demonstration
Teacher Think-Alouds
Questioning
Class Discussion
Brainstorming
Notetaking
Drill and Practice

Graphic Organizers
Enhancing Vocabulary
Shared Vocabulary
Role-Play and Simulations
Projects
Think–Pair–Share
Jigsaw
Learning Centers

Knowledge of How We Learn

Content Appropriateness

FIGURE 8.13   Achieving balance: Instructional strategies.

Group Activities

1. There are 16 instructional strategies in this chapter. In pairs, choose one strategy and write three questions about it using the question stems provided in this chapter. Use the questions to teach another pair more about your chosen strategy.

2. In groups of three, plan 10-minute brainstorming sessions on one of the nine categories of effective instructional strategies in Figure 8.1. One person will elicit responses and manage the flow of ideas. Two people will be responsible for filling in a K–W–L chart with what we know and what we want to know. Add a category between the W and the L labeled H for "How will we find out?" Your chart will expand to a K–W–H–L chart allowing the brainstorming to suggest resources for learning the answers to "What do we want to know?"

3. Think–pair–share time. Individually think of how using procedures to share vocabulary within your team is developmentally responsive for young adolescents. Write your thoughts on a note card. Now pair with someone in your class and share what you have written. As a pair, connect with another pair and share responses. As a whole class, debrief the process.

4. In conjunction with your instructor, decide on sections of Chapter 9 that appear conducive to using the Jigsaw model. Determine base and expert groups. Use this model to teach each other about various aspects of assessment.

Individual Activities

1. Think of a process or skill that would be included in the subject you plan to teach that lends itself to a teacher think-aloud. Plan what you would say to help students understand the process or skill and be prepared to think-aloud for your classmates.

2. Using divergent questions to encourage higher-order thinking skills requires planning. Describe how you would use points 4 and 5 in Figure 8.2 to accomplish this goal. What are two additional questions you could ask students to encourage them to continue thinking and responding?

3. During one of your university classes, pay attention to the dynamics of a typical class discussion. Pay close attention to process while keeping up with the content. Take notes on what you observe. Write a critique of the experience and include ways the professor might have improved the discussion time.

4. By this point in your life you have no doubt developed notetaking techniques that you find effective for your learning style. Write a brief description of your technique to share with the class.

Personal Journal

1. What motivated you as a student? Can you remember teachers, projects, or other circumstances that prompted you to achieve?

2. Were you an eager participant in class discussion? Why or why not?

3. Can you recall any time as a student when having a choice in your academic work made a task more meaningful for you? When would options from which to choose have made an experience more productive?

4. What instructional strategies dominated your experience in middle grades? high school? university?

Professional Practice

(It would be helpful to reread the description of Mr. Jefferson in Chapter 4, as well as the description of Michael in Chapters 2 and 3. The Chapter 5 Professional Practice scenario is also about Mr. Jefferson, Michael, and Marrington Middle School.)

Lester Jefferson is planning for his sixth year at Marrington Middle School. He and his teammate, Sandra Henderson, taught seventh grade last year and will teach the same students as eighth graders in what they perceive as a successful looping plan. After years of teaching high school English, Mr. Jefferson has honed his skills in lecture, class discussion, and questioning to a fine art.

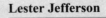

Lester Jefferson

When Marrington was created, Mr. Jefferson led the way in providing the school board, the community, and fellow teachers with information on middle school structures, teaming, and looping. He is proud of the school Marrington has become in his small rural community. However, since returning from his first National Middle School Association annual conference, he is no longer satisfied with his limited instructional approaches. He attended sessions on cooperative learning, graphic organizers, and the components of an inquiry-based approach to social studies. He also attended several sessions focusing on teaching reading in the middle grades and content area reading and writing. The conference was invigorating, but it left him feeling a bit overwhelmed. What could he do, or should he do, with all this fresh information? He could go back home and jump right into using new instructional strategies or he could go slowly, think some more, read some more, and find out what, if any, experience his fellow teachers have with the strategies. He opted to wait. Now it's July and school starts in 6 weeks.

A major benefit of looping is the possibility of strong positive bonds developing between teachers and students. Because Mr. Jefferson knows his 50 students so well after having taught them for a year, he feels prepared to go beyond his usual grouping techniques of "choose a partner," "three of you move your desks together," and "number off one to four." After reading more about purposefully putting students in groups, he's ready for this. He decides to go ahead and think through activities and create groups based on a variety of criteria. This is a good start. He's ready to plan more strategies.

1. As Mr. Jefferson increases his repertoire of instructional strategies, what would be the best explanation to give his students?

(a) "There's so much to learn in life. When I discovered some new ways of teaching I got so excited. So hang on. We're going to learn together!"

(b) "The National Middle School Association tells us we should use a variety of teaching strategies in middle school. So I've picked out some."

(c) "I've decided I was in a rut when it comes to teaching. So we're going to try some new things this year."

(d) "Our district has hired a new person to be in charge of middle and high school. We've been told to try some new teaching strategies."

2. Mr. Jefferson has decided to approach reading instruction and the writing process using materials that enhance his social studies content. Now he has the dilemma of finding appropriate text in a variety of genres. Which of the following would be the least useful approach?

(a) Asking the ninth grade teachers what books seem too easy for their students, ones that they are willing to let him use in eighth grade.

(b) Contacting the International Reading Association (IRA) and asking for a catalog of books with a suitable variety of themes for eighth graders.

(c) E-mailing two teachers who presented the NMSA workshop focusing on reading and writing in the content areas and asking for suggestions.

(d) Going online to see if the National Council for the Social Studies (NCSS) has reading lists, and possibly writing prompts, available for eighth grade.

3. Mr. Jefferson is fascinated with the seemingly endless possibilities for using graphic organizers in language arts and social studies. He bought a book about using visual tools and has decided to give it a try. What would be the best step to implement first?

(a) Copy some of the graphic organizer frames from his book and give them to his students along with an explanation of the uses of each.

(b) Give his students some sample items involving graphic organizers that are in his state standardized test practice materials.

(c) Write instructions for how to use a particular graphic organizer, give students the blank organizer structure, then ask them to fill in the organizer.

(d) Develop a graphic organizer to go with his prepared social studies lessons, think-aloud for his students about the thought process he used to develop it, and ask students to comment.

Michael, eighth grade

4. Michael is now an eighth grader. Mr. Jefferson has won his trust and Michael seems comfortable with school. Now it's time to try to spark Michael's academic interests. Which of the following would be least effective?

(a) Giving students some broad parameters and the expectations for a project and then allowing students to choose their specific topics.

(b) Telling Michael and others that high school is going to be much more difficult with more class changes and at least six different teachers a day. Now is the time to form the foundation of knowledge and skills.

(c) Allowing students to choose a partner as a "study buddy" to whom they are responsible for sharing notes, working on assignments, and studying for tests.

(d) Asking Michael to demonstrate his expertise in the outdoors during a unit on the American frontier and requiring him to relate what he knows to specific areas of study.

Constructed Response

What elements in the structure of Marrington Middle School make it a supportive environment for Mr. Jefferson and his new zeal for instructional strategies?

Internet Resources

Education World
http://educationworld.com

Middle Web
http://middleweb.com

Midlink Magazine
http://www.ncsu.edu/midlink

This site highlights creative work from classrooms around the world. It is maintained by a nonprofit organization and supported by North California State University and the University of Central Florida.

Teachers Network
http://teachnet.org

References

Burden, P. R., & Byrd, D. M. (1999). *Methods for effective teaching*. Boston: Allyn & Bacon.

Callahan, J. F., Clark, L. H., & Kellough, R. D. (2002). *Teaching in the middle and secondary schools*. Upper Saddle River, NJ: Merrill/Prentice Hall.

Ernst, J. (1996). *Middle school study skills*. Huntington Beach, CA: Teacher Created Materials.

George, P. S., & Alexander, W. M. (2003). *The exemplary middle school*. Belmont, CA: Wadsworth/Thomson Learning.

Marzano, R. J., Pickering, D. J., & Pollock, J. E. (2001). *Classroom instruction that works*. Alexandria, VA: Association for Supervision and Curriculum Development.

Moore, K. D. (1999). *Middle and secondary school instructional methods*. Boston: McGraw-Hill College.

National Middle School Association. (2003). *This we believe: Successful schools for young adolescents*. Westerville, OH: Author.

Powell, S. D. (2000). *Super strategies for succeeding on the standardized tests: Reading/language arts*. New York: Scholastic Professional Books.

Schurr, S. L. (1995). *Prescriptions for success in heterogeneous classrooms.* Columbus, OH: National Middle School Association.

Shalaway, L. (1998). *Learning to teach . . . not just for beginners.* New York: Scholastic Professional Books.

Stevenson, C. (1992). *Teaching ten to fourteen year olds.* White Plains, NY: Longman.

Tomlinson, C. A. (1999). *The differentiated classroom: Responding to the needs of all learners.* Alexandria, VA: Association for Supervision and Curriculum Development.

Wilhelm, J. D. (2001). Think alouds boost reading comprehension. *Instructor, 111*(4), 26–28.

Wormeli, R. (2001). *Meet me in the middle: Becoming an accomplished middle level teacher.* Portland, ME: Stenhouse.

Wright, S. P., Horn, S. P., & Sanders, W. L. (1997). Teacher and classroom context effects on student achievement: Implications for teacher evaluation. *Journal of Personal Evaluation in Education, 11,* 57–67.

9

Assessment in Middle School

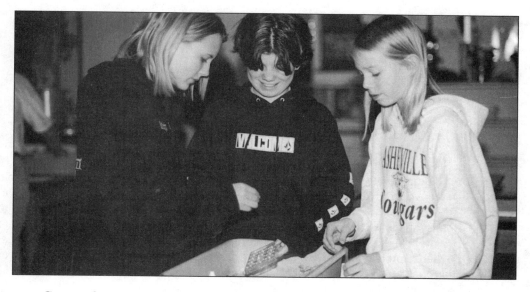

Curriculum, assessment, and instruction are intertwined, each inevitably affecting the other two. Any effort to change curriculum and assessment without changing instruction, or to change instruction without considering curriculum and assessment, will fail.

Jackson and Davis, 2000, p. 26

Use this diagram as an organizational tool. In the boxes beside the chapter headings, indicate the date by which the readings should be completed.

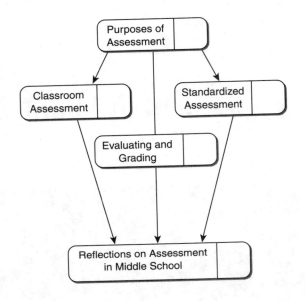

INTRODUCTION

In Chapter 6 we looked at the many faces of curriculum, from discipline-specific to integrative, and various options that seek to combine aspects of both of these ends of the curriculum spectrum. Chapters 7 and 8 explored the foundations, theory, and big ideas of instruction and instructional strategies from teacher-directed to student-initiated. In this chapter's opening quote, the authors of *Turning Points 2000* tell us that it is absolutely necessary to match the flexibility and variety of curriculum and instruction that we employ in middle school with a wide and developmentally responsive spectrum of assessment methods.

Standard 1

Performance 6: Middle level teacher candidates use multiple assessments that are developmentally appropriate for young adolescent learners.

Standard 5

Disposition 5: Middle level teacher candidates value the importance of ongoing and varied assessment strategies.

Returning to the concept of backward design, we are reminded that we should begin planning for teaching and learning in our classrooms with the end in mind. Wiggins and McTighe (1998) urge us to think like assessors. To do so requires us to continually ask two questions:

1. Where should we look to find "hallmarks of understanding?"
2. What should we look for in determining and distinguishing degrees of understanding? (p. 67)

Question number one calls for us to define which performances and behaviors will tell us that our students are meeting specified curricular goals. Wiggins and McTighe (1998) define *assessment* as "an umbrella term we use to mean the deliberate use of many methods to gather evidence to indicate that students are meeting standards" (p. 4). We'll explore broad categories of these methods in this chapter.

The second question involves evaluating, defined by Marzano (2000) as "the process of making judgments about the level of students' understanding or performance" (p. 13). *Evaluation* calls for measurement using scores that lead to grades. The journey from deciding about desired curricular outcomes to sending report cards home is a complex one that an entire chapter only begins to address.

Standard 3

Knowledge 7: Middle level teacher candidates understand multiple assessment strategies that effectively measure student mastery of the curriculum.

When we think of assessment, we generally classify it in two basic ways—classroom assessment and standardized assessment. For our purposes, classroom assessment is any form that occurs as a direct part of classroom teaching and learning. *Standardized assessment* may be in the form of commercially produced tests administered by local, state, or national mandate, or tests designed by individual states based on curriculum standards. As you probably realize, classroom assessment provides richer and broader options than standardized assessment and will be the focus of the majority of this chapter.

Two classifications of assessment = Classroom + Standardized

Before delving into either classroom or standardized assessment, we need to consider some of the purposes of assessment.

 ## PURPOSES OF ASSESSMENT

As a child and, I'm embarrassed to say, even into my first years of teaching, I considered assessment to be tests and quizzes given only for the purpose of assigning grades. As a student, I anticipated getting grades, and as a teacher I dreaded giving them. My hope is that you will begin your career with a more informed sense of assessment. The simplest but most comprehensive way to view the purposes of assessment comes to us from the National Council of Teachers of Mathematics (see Figure 9.1). NCTM includes evaluating student achievement (that is, grading) and thereby recognizing accomplishment—or lack of it—as one of the four purposes of assessment. Another purpose of assessment is to monitor student progress and, in doing so, promote student growth. The other two purposes are related to

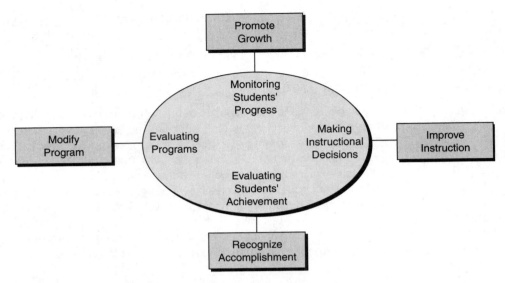

FIGURE 9.1   Four purposes of assessment and their results.

Source: From *Assessment Standards for School Mathematics* (p. 25), by National Council of Teachers of Mathematics, 1995, Reston, VA: Author. Reprinted with permission.

either instructional or program revisions and are recognized and acted upon less frequently than the first two. Assessment provides us with needed information to make instructional decisions that improve how we design the teaching and learning environment. Plainly stated, if the kids don't "get it," we find another way to provide learning opportunities. If they do "get it," we are free to move on, move up the Bloom's taxonomy hierarchy, and offer enrichment. Related to instructional decisions are program decisions. Deciding to modify, discontinue, or adopt new programs should be based on assessment results, generally results gathered over time or from larger samples than one classroom. Unfortunately, you may find that pro-

Standard 3

Performance 8: Middle level teacher candidates use multiple assessment strategies that effectively measure student mastery of the curriculum.

Standard 5

Knowledge 9: Middle level teacher candidates understand the multiple roles of assessment in the instructional process (e.g., monitoring learning, evaluating student progress, and modifying teaching strategies).

Disposition 8: Middle level teacher candidates are committed to using assessment to identify student strengths and enhance student growth rather than deny student access to learning.

gram decisions are too often based on criteria other than student assessment results. Be aware and watchful concerning programmatic decisions.

You can see that assessment can and should serve multiple purposes. With this realization comes the responsibility to assess purposefully, in multiple ways, and with an eye toward using the results to promote increased learning.

Regardless of the assessment used, there are three broad categories to consider—diagnostic, formative, and summative.

> Three categories of assessment =
> Diagnostic + Formative +
> Summative

Diagnostic Assessment

How can we plan curriculum and instruction if we don't have information about what our students know and don't know, what they can and can't do? Content area standards give us broad expectations by subject, topic, and grade level. Within each standard is the "stuff" of teaching and learning. Classroom time is too precious to use on content and skills that students have already mastered. Conversely, jumping right into standards and realizing days later that students lack the prior knowledge necessary to relate meaningfully to new content, or lack the skills necessary to progress to new skill levels, also wastes valuable instruction time. The solution is *diagnostic assessment,* sometimes called pretesting. Far from being a waste of time, this form of assessment is an important teaching and learning tool that is often neglected.

Standard 5

Disposition 6: Middle level teacher candidates realize the importance of basing instruction on assessment results.

Diagnostic assessment may indicate deficiency or mastery of whole groups of students, or it may help us in planning for differentiation if we discover wide variations in prior knowledge or achievement levels. Diagnostic assessment makes us more informed about our students and better able to develop a classroom perspective more closely matched to reality. This information is power when it comes to effectively planning for teaching and learning.

Formative Assessment

The purpose of *formative assessment* is "to monitor learning progress during instruction and to provide continuous feedback to students and parents" (Burden & Byrd, 1999, p. 333). Formative assessment methods vary according to content/skills and instruction and may be as informal as teacher observation. The purpose is to find out where our students are on the path toward mastery. The results of formative assessment should guide our instructional decisions. Later in the chapter, we'll discuss the pros and cons of using formative assessment in evaluation and grading.

The feedback provided by formative assessment helps students know where they are in relation to learning goals, as well as what they need to do to continue to improve. Feedback needs to be as timely as possible to allow us to take advantage of "teachable moments." Giving specific and instructional corrective feedback not only guides future efforts, but also tells our students loudly and clearly that what they do and learn is important to us, and therefore **they** are important to us. What we know about young adolescent development tells us that providing feedback promotes positive cognitive and emotional development.

> *Standard 3*
>
> *Disposition 4:* Middle level teacher candidates realize the importance of connecting curriculum and assessment to the needs, interests, and experiences of all young adolescents.

Summative Assessment

The purpose of *summative assessment* is to make judgments about the quality of a process or product. It typically occurs at the end of a unit of study, is more formal than diagnostic or formative assessment, and is used as a major factor in determining student grades. Summative assessments should be carefully thought out, implemented, scored, and reported (more on this later). Summative assessments should not be limited to paper-and-pencil exams, but should allow students to demonstrate what they can do with what they know.

Figure 9.2 compares formative and summative assessment in terms of purpose, timing, types, and uses of information.

Because formative assessment occurs all along the journey toward mastery, it guides our instruction. Figure 9.3 shows how this path proceeds. Although the graphic shows formative

	Formative	**Summative**
Purpose	To monitor and guide a process or product while it is still in progress	To judge the success of a process or product at the end (however defined)
Time of assessment	During the process or development of the product	At the end of the process or when the product is complete
Types of assessment techniques	Informal observation, quizzes, homework, teacher questions, worksheets	Formal observation, tests, projects, term papers, exhibitions
Uses of assessment information	To improve a process or product while it is still going on or being developed	To judge the quality of a process or product; grade, rank, promote

FIGURE 9.2   Comparison of formative and summative assessments.
Source: From *Classroom Assessment,* 2nd ed. (p. 136), by P. W. Airasian, 1994, New York: The McGraw-Hill Companies, Inc. Adapted with permission.

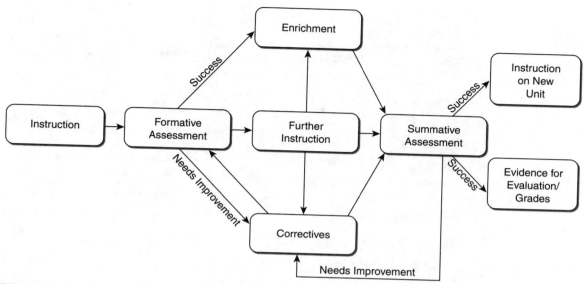

FIGURE 9.3   The role of formative and summative assessment.

Source: From *Developing Grading and Reporting Systems for Student Learning* (p. 98), by T. R. Guskey and J. M. Bailey, 2001, Beverly Hills, CA: Sage Publications, Inc. Copyright © 2001 by Corwin Press. Reprinted with permission.

assessment only in one cell, we should think of it happening over and over, creating multiple opportunities to provide enrichment and/or correctives in our instructional plan. At each juncture, we make decisions about reteaching and reassessing, using the many strategies in our instructional toolboxes.

As we approach our learning goals as evidenced by summative assessments, we see in Figure 9.3 that we have evidence for evaluation and grading as we move on to a new unit. In the next section, we will explore answers to the second question posed in the beginning of the chapter: how to determine and distinguish degrees of understanding.

 CLASSROOM ASSESSMENT

Three categories of knowledge and skills = Enduring understandings + Essential to mastery + Worthy of familiarity

---

Wiggins and McTighe (1998) have us consider that there are three basic categories of knowledge and skills that we include in learning goals. The first category is enduring understandings—the big ideas worthy of being retained. The second category is knowledge and skills that are essential to master, and the third, those things that are worthy of familiarity.

They tell us it is neither desirable nor feasible for students to get inside every element in a subject or curriculum standard. A major teaching responsibility involves knowing our subjects deeply and broadly enough to distinguish where, along the continuum from enduring understanding to familiarity, specific knowledge and skills belong. Experience, reflection, and collaboration among colleagues serve as our best sources for effectively fulfilling this responsibility.

Standard 3

Knowledge 4: Middle level teacher candidates are knowledgeable about local, state, and national middle level curriculum standards and of ways to assess the student knowledge reflected in those standards.

Knowledge 11: Middle level teacher candidates understand the key concepts within the critical knowledge base and know how to design assessments that target them.

Standard 4

Knowledge 3: Middle level teacher candidates are knowledgeable about teaching and assessment strategies that are especially effective in their teaching fields.

Performance 2: Middle level teacher candidates use effective content specific teaching and assessment strategies.

Standard 5

Disposition 5: Middle level teacher candidates value the importance of on-going and varied assessment strategies.

Depending on where knowledge and skills fall on the continuum, we set about determining if understanding, mastery, and/or familiarity have occurred, and to what degree. "Classroom assessments can actively promote access to learning. In fact, assessments might be the best way to connect more students to conversations and activities directly related to standards" (Cole, Coffey, & Goldman, 1999, p. 56). Assessment can take multiple forms, from informal to formal. Anytime we gather information about students' achievement and behavior we are assessing, and thus answering the first question in the introduction that asks where we should look to find hallmarks of understanding.

Seven Forms of Classroom Assessment

Marzano (2000) tells us that there are seven basic forms of classroom assessment. They are briefly stated in Figure 9.4. We will discuss each one—some in more detail than others. As we explore the seven forms, think about how each one might serve the function of being diagnostic, formative, and/or summative.

Forced-choice items.   The first form of assessment is very traditional and is the most common type of both classroom assessment and standardized assessment. Forced-choice items can be graded objectively, even by machines. Students simply choose a correct response from the choices provided. Examples of forced-choice assessments include matching, true/false, multiple-choice, and fill-in-the-blank. Although fill-in-the-blank typically doesn't provide answer choices, only one response is generally considered to be correct.

Of these forced-choice assessments, multiple choice is the most difficult to write. The hardest aspect of writing multiple-choice items is coming up with viable detractors. The incorrect detractors should be plausible enough to be considered, but inaccurate enough to be considered wrong by students who know the content. It is possible to write multiple-choice

1. Forced-Choice Items
2. Essay
3. Short Written Responses
4. Oral Reports
5. Teacher Observation
6. Student Self-Assessment
7. Performance Tasks

FIGURE 9.4   Seven forms of classroom assessment.

Source: From *Transforming Classroom Grading* (p. 87), by R. J. Marzano, 2000, Alexandria, VA: Association for Supervision and Curriculum Development. Reprinted with permission.

items that require higher-order thinking, but it's a very time-consuming proposition. True/false items are also difficult to write so that they are not strictly knowledge based or so blatantly true or false that they do not require careful consideration.

Something to consider when assessing with forced-choice items is the role of probability. With true/false, the students have a 50–50 chance of getting items right simply through guessing. When we consider this fact we have to wonder if true/false items discriminate between students who have mastered the content and those who have not. With multiple-choice items there's either a 20% or 25% likelihood that guessing will produce accurate answers. A student who is "test wise" (more on this later in the chapter) may have an advantage not related to understanding.

Essays.   Essay questions require students to write responses in narrative form, to answer questions in complete sentences and in an organized fashion. In that respect, essay questions can assess knowledge, comprehension, application, analysis, synthesis, and evaluation, as well as communication skills.

Short written responses.   These are mini-essays requiring brief answers/explanations. An example of a short written response item in math would be: "Briefly compare a triangular prism and a triangular pyramid by telling about their bases, faces, edges, and vertices." In language arts a short written response item might be: "Briefly describe the bicycle stolen in *Pee-Wee's Great Adventure.*" These items don't require synthesis or evaluation. The math item asks for knowledge and comprehension-level aspects of the two polyhedra. The language arts item merely requires recall, but has some variability possible since an exact number of bicycle attributes are not specified as they would be in a forced-choice item.

Oral reports.   Oral reports are similar to essays in that they require organizing multiple facts/concepts to express information. Generally students are given time to prepare answers. Students must not only be able to write their essays coherently (even if they do not have to be turned in), but they also are required to deliver them orally, using visual tools as appropriate. It is possible then to assess not only levels of Bloom's taxonomy but also organizational skills and oral communication ability.

Teacher observation.   Marzano (2000) tells us that teacher observation is "one of the most straight-forward ways to collect classroom assessment data" (p. 99). Observations are useful when assessing process-oriented skills such as reading fluency, spatial abilities as demonstrated through hands-on tools like tangram puzzles, dexterity skills used in the manipulation of science experiment materials, and so forth. While different students may have the same knowledge about how to do something, their process skills of efficiency and accuracy may vary.

Teacher observation may be the only way to assess nonachievement factors such as attitude, effort, behavior, time on task, and so on. Having definite aspects to observe and then creating a system for recording those observations are vital to lend consistency and a measure of objectivity (though admittedly small) when using teacher observation as a classroom assessment. Think about this—it's impossible not to observe in our classrooms. It will happen continually. The danger in using teacher observation in overt ways as a form of assessment is that the "squeaky wheel gets the grease." By this I mean that certain young adolescents may draw more attention than others, either positively or negatively. If we don't occasionally make teacher observation very purposeful, we are likely to miss key growth-enhancing or remediation opportunities.

One variation of teacher observation is the teacher-student informal interview. These sessions are time-consuming, but quite valuable when the right questions are asked and students are comfortable expressing themselves. Teacher-student interviews may be a luxury when you are on a five-person team and have more than 100 students. Finding the time needed could be one result of a block schedule and careful team planning.

Student self-assessment.   "Although the most underused form of classroom assessment, student self-assessment has the most flexibility and power as a combined assessment and learning tool" (Marzano, 2000, p. 102). Understanding the developmental aspects of young adolescents, this assertion makes sense. Noted middle school expert Gordon Vars (1997) speaks positively about efforts to engage students in self-evaluation and then asking them to share their insights with trusted and caring teachers. Self-assessment is definitely a skill that requires guidance to be both an assessment and a learning tool. Simply saying "Tell me how you think you did," or "Did you do a good job?" will not elicit thoughtful responses from most middle grades students. They need specific aspects to assess, an array of understood descriptors from which to choose, and a reporting process that assures them respect and confidentiality.

Teacher think-alouds can be valuable for teaching students to self-assess. Through teacher self-assessment we can demonstrate to students how to think about progress, accomplishment, quality factors, and indicators of understanding.

We can use self-assessment as a tool for setting goals and determining needs for remediation or augmentation. Marzano (2000) writes that teachers who use student self-assessment extensively report that students tend to assess their own work quite realistically, with honesty and candor. Their remarks and criticisms are often more severe than those of the teachers. Having students self-assess following corrective measures builds independence and proactive behavior.

A question to consider is whether student self-assessment, if recorded in some viable way, should have some bearing on a teacher's assessment or if it should be its own category added to many forms of assessment used within a unit of study. The answer to this question is dependent on circumstances such as how the self-assessments are gathered, how much guidance students have had in doing the self-assessment, and what the stated purpose of the self-assessment is.

Performance assessment.   Several descriptions of assessment are used interchangeably— alternative, authentic, and performance. *Alternative assessment* generally refers to any assessment that is not primarily a forced-choice, essay, or short written response. *Authentic assessment* tends to be real-life in nature. *Performance assessment,* according to Marzano, refers to "any task in which students are asked to apply knowledge, regardless of how contrived or real-life in nature it may be" (p. 97). He chooses to use **performance** as the umbrella term in that it includes real-life as well as contrived aspects. The Venn diagram in Figure 9.5 illustrates that both authentic and performance assessments are alternative in nature, that authentic assessment is performance-based, and that performance assessment is broader than authentic assessment.

Standard 5

Knowledge 3: Middle level teacher candidates know that teaching higher order thinking skills is an integral part of instruction and assessment.

NMSA.

Performance assessment methods are generally considered to be those outside the realm of traditional assessment. O'Connor (2002) broadly describes performance tasks as demonstrations of knowledge and skills. These demonstrations may be created and

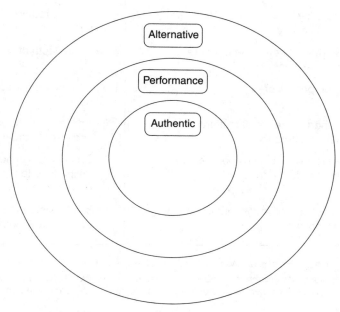

FIGURE 9.5   Alternative, performance, authentic assessment.

perceived within the domain of each of the four learning modalities discussed in Chapter 3—auditory, visual, kinesthetic, tactile—or in any combination of the four. Classifying an assessment as traditional or alternative, authentic and to what extent, depends on our experiences and viewpoint. Figure 9.6 gives us Schurr's (1999) viewpoint of some of the characteristics of what she considers traditional and authentic assessment.

Jackson and Davis (2000) tell us that authentic tasks that we have established as performance tasks do the following:

1. Concentrate on complex tasks
2. Allow students to demonstrate what they can do
3. Help students make connections between themselves and the world
4. Encourage students to reflect on their own understanding
5. Push students to apply and transfer knowledge and skills in different contexts (p. 56)

This is an impressive list. It emphasizes the value of developing performance opportunities for our students.

Characteristics of Traditional Assessment	Characteristics of Authentic Assessment
1. Sequence of simple, distinct tasks	1. General, complex task involving interrelated sub-tasks
2. Recall of limited amounts of knowledge, despite ever-increasing scope of knowledge	2. Internalization and application of knowledge and thinking processes generalizable to all sorts of knowledge
3. Quick and easy to score objectively, even if there is little validity	3. Scoring requires complex and more subjective considerations
4. Tests breadth of knowledge better (e.g., by numerous questions)	4. Tests depth of knowledge better
5. Easy to compare scores	5. Scores tend to be too contextual to compare easily
6. Easy to standardize for all students regardless of differences	6. Adapts more to strengths, needs, and choices of unique students
7. Encourages low-level thinking to arrive quickly at one right answer	7. Encourages critical and creative thinking, taking time to arrive at the best of many possible answers
8. Requires only reactive response, usually by student in isolation	8. Involves students very actively and cooperatively in productive process

FIGURE 9.6 Characteristics of traditional and authentic assessment.

Source: From *Authentic Assessment: Using Product, Performance, and Portfolio Measures from A to Z* (p. 4), by S. Schurr, 1999, Westerville, OH: National Middle School Association. Adapted with permission from National Middle School Association.

Standard 5

Knowledge 4: Middle level teacher candidates know how to select and develop formal, informal, and performance assessments based on their relative advantages and limitations.

NMSA

Matching Instruction and Assessment

Once again we return to the concept of balance as illustrated in Figure 9.7. We've looked at seven forms of classroom assessment, each fulfilling a need and serving a purpose depending on the content/skill and the methods of instruction.

With the large variety of assessments available, it is possible to match assessment methods to instructional methods. For instance, if a unit in social studies involves students studying the Bill of Rights and then discovering events in history to which they apply, assessing the unit by using fill-in-the-blank items that call for verbatim recitation of the amendments would be inappropriate. A performance that requires students to write or analyze a scenario and then apply the amendments would be an assessment that matches the instruction. There will be occasions when true/false and multiple-choice assessments are appropriate, particularly when the learning goal is retention of knowledge and comprehension of concepts.

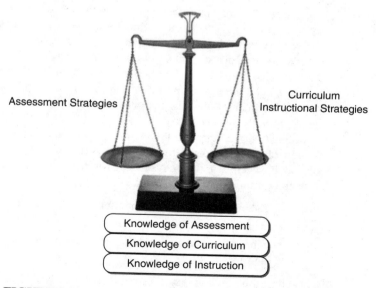

FIGURE 9.7   Achieving balance: Assessment/curriculum/instruction.

Portfolio Assessment

A *portfolio* is a collection of student work that may be selected to showcase best quality, show progress over time, or both. Portfolios are flexible vehicles for organizing and viewing all kinds of assessment tools, from traditional paper-and-pencil tests to performances that include teacher feedback and student self-assessments. A portfolio should emphasize both process and product and should serve as a short evolutionary record of progress toward learning goals.

As collections of work, portfolios allow individual differences to be seen as assets. Because students are given opportunities to make choices within guidelines as to what to include, they stand a good chance of being able to express their own multiple intelligences. For instance, they may have the opportunity to include artwork, video productions, photographs of sporting events, items from nature, Internet searches and results, annotated lists of books they've read, timelines, graphic organizers, poems . . . the list is endless. If a portfolio is to show what a student knows and can do in a discipline or multiple disciplines, then student choice leads to student self-expression. As with project learning discussed in Chapter 8, light bulbs go on in some young adolescents' heads when they see learning as a whole, rather than isolated assignments, and when they make decisions to shape a product they can proudly display.

In Shelbourne, Vermont, the middle school Alpha Team implemented the use of student portfolios as the cornerstone of their assessment program for their multiage team that loops sixth, seventh, and eighth grades. The reasons stated by two of the teachers, Carol Smith and Cynthia Myers (2001), include

- teachers should provide varied opportunities for students to make sense of their learning
- students need time to reflect on their work
- students need to make connections between and among tasks and note improvement along the way

They report that students learn to recognize quality and improve their decision-making skills as they look at other students' portfolios, as well as their own, over time. Their organizational skills improve, as do their self-assessment skills.

According to the Alpha Team, the portfolio provides "concrete evidence of learning and represents the perfect format for students to discuss progress with their teachers and parents" (p. 11). Jay McTighe (1997) reports that in Frederick, Maryland, a principal lists one of four major benefits of portfolio assessment as school-to-home communication with students presenting and explaining their work to their parents and other adults.

Many books and articles have been written about portfolios, detailing their development and benefits. I urge you to consider the portfolio as a viable assessment tool in your classroom. Teams that use portfolios can share advice and the lessons learned in implementing them. Whole middle schools that use portfolios reap the benefits of having students view them as a "way of life" and excellent evidence of the depth and breadth of their learning and maturing progress. The portfolio "creates a portrait of the student as a learner" (Burden & Byrd, 1999, p. 339).

 ## EVALUATING AND GRADING

We began this chapter with two basic questions. The first involved looking for performances and behaviors that tell us if our students are meeting specified learning goals. We examined broad categories of classroom assessment and discovered there are many ways to diagnose prior knowledge and skills, to monitor progress along the way through formative assessment, and to determine if goals are reached through summative assessment. We looked at single assignments as well as collections of performances in portfolio format.

Now we will address the second question—the issue of distinguishing degrees of understanding and clarifying the criteria for judging performance (Wiggins & McTighe, 1998). Let's agree on some definitions of terms before addressing the details of determining degrees of quality and understanding.

evaluation—the process of judging levels of quality of student work/performance/ understanding

score—the number given to student work to indicate evaluation

weight—the value given to specific student work relative to other assignments

grade—the number or letter representing scores of evaluation received over time and reported to students and adults

For decades, some educators have questioned the wisdom of assigning grades to students. They have argued that grades are meaningless, do not represent understanding and the application potential of knowledge, are harmful to student self-esteem, impede progress if either too low or too high—the list goes on and each flaw has a degree of validity. But as Marzano (2000) tells us, "Americans have a basic trust in the message that grades convey— so much so that grades have gone without challenge and are, in fact, highly resistant to challenge" (p. 1). We received grades, our parents received grades, and, as teachers, chances are we will assign grades because they are expected and desired in our society. Recently researchers like Marzano have taken up the challenge of looking at grades in new ways. With the advent of standards and acceptance of differentiating instruction and multiple intelligences, we may see meaningful change in grading practices in the future.

Standard 5

Performance 9: Middle level teacher candidates maintain useful records and create an effective plan for evaluation of student work and achievement.

Rubrics

To assess in ways that speak to "how good is good enough," we turn to rubrics, both as valuable instructional tools and as means of assessment. A *rubric* is a scoring guide that provides the criteria for assessing the quality of a piece of work and includes a gradation for each criterion, generally from excellent to poor, with quality often indicated by numbers. The use of rubrics in middle school, or most any school, is a recent phenomenon. Schmoker (1999) refers to the advent of the rubric as the "rubric revolution" and says rubrics are "one of the most promising developments in assessment . . . with their capacity to provide useful, quantitative data on clear, carefully selected, qualitative criteria" (p. 78). You have probably experienced rubrics as scoring tools and have discovered their benefits. Figure 9.8 shows a generic rubric that could be adapted for specific topics in most any subject area.

Some schools have joined the "rubric revolution" and use them frequently. Students and parents are accustomed to the valuable feedback they provide. Chances are that these schools had a few rubric zealots who attended a workshop or a session at a conference where rubrics were explained and the development process was clarified. Once teachers experience their benefits, they are willing to take the time to develop rubrics to assess the performances of their students.

Criteria	4	3	2	1	0
Choice of topic	Interesting and current	Interesting but not current	Generic and uninteresting	Not at all relevant	Not enough information for judgment
Depth of research	Evident and compelling	Evident but not compelling	Some research	Little evidence	Not enough information for judgment
Organization of ideas	Clear, easy to follow	Can be followed	Little organization evident	Ideas cannot be followed	Not enough information for judgment
Quality of information	Correct and detailed	Correct but without detail	Incomplete, some incorrect	Mostly incorrect or missing	Not enough information for judgment
Use of conventions	Correct usage of grammar and punctuation	Some errors but not distracting	Errors that interfere with content	Too many errors to be coherent	Not enough information for judgment

FIGURE 9.8   Generic rubric.

Developing rubrics.   It would be beneficial for you to find a rubrics mentor, someone who is willing to share rubrics and advice about using them. The basic steps for creating a rubric include the following:

1. Consider carefully what you will assess. If you have them, examine samples of the products or performances (remember how inclusive this term is) to determine the best, the unacceptable, and variations in between. If you don't have examples, spend time visualizing and making notes about what you should consider examples to be or to include.

2. List the criteria on which you would judge the work. For instance, if the performance is an essay you might consider the topic choice, the development of the main idea, the organization, sentence flow, mechanics, etc.

3. Decide on the attributes of an acceptable quality for each criterion. In other words, how good is good enough? From there, decide what attributes would make each criterion better than merely acceptable and what attributes would amount to less than acceptable for the criterion. While using descriptors such as excellent, good, fair, and poor may be appropriate, many teachers simply use numbers. Andrade (2000) tells us that finding satisfactory labels is difficult and that on a 0–4 scale, a 4 is obviously what students should try to achieve while avoiding a 0 or a 1. Figure 9.9 gives us possible descriptions of what the numbers mean.

4. Share the rubric with your students as part of the explanation of the assignment or project. Students who are familiar with rubrics will probably accept your rubric gratefully. Students who are unfamiliar with them will require a "walk through" of the criteria and the gradations. This is an excellent opportunity to use the teacher think-aloud technique.

5. Use the rubric to assess student work. As you do, make notes about how you might want to alter the rubric to better reflect the criteria and/or gradation descriptors. The next time you use the rubric it will be even more effective.

Rubrics as instructional tools.   When you share a rubric with your students, it becomes an excellent instructional tool. If detailed enough, a rubric lets students know what the expectations are for an assignment. Rubrics paint a clear picture, much better than

---

4—Students understand the important information accurately and with detail.

3—Students understand the important information, but the details are fuzzy or nonexistent.

2—Students have a basic understanding of the information mixed with some misconceptions and/or gaps.

1—Students have so many misconceptions that the basic information is not understood.

0—Students provide insufficient indicators on which to judge their understanding.

FIGURE 9.9   Number scale for rubrics.

Instructional rubrics . . .

- are easy to use and to explain

- make teachers' expectations very clear

- provide students with more informative feedback about their strengths and areas in need of improvement than traditional forms of assessment do

- support learning

- support the development of skills

- support the development of understanding

- support good thinking

FIGURE 9.10   Reasons to use instructional rubrics.

Source: From "Using Rubrics to Promote Thinking and Learning," by H. G. Andrade, 2000, *Educational Leadership, 57*(5), pp. 14–16. Adapted with permission.

simple directions. If you have examples of products, share them with students and discuss what each criteria looks like. Be sure to save products so you'll have some to show the next time you make similar assignments.

Using rubrics as instructional tools takes thought and effort. In fact, the first rubrics you create will take you deeply into the nuances of what you expect of your students. However, once you have written a rubric, using it will make your role as assessor more efficient and effective. Andrade (2000) gives a brief description of the benefits of rubrics as instructional tools in Figure 9.10.

Rubrics serve as valuable communication tools between teacher and student, teacher and parent, and student and parent. The clear expectations and level of feedback communicate thoughtful, purposeful assignments with rubrics providing the basis of conversation about teaching and learning.

Standard 5

Performance 10: Middle level teacher candidates communicate assessment information knowledgeably and responsibly to students, families, educators, community members, and other appropriate audiences.

Subjectivity

Grades are subjective. No matter how many numbers we add or how we apply percentages, a full grade book does not equal objectivity. Forced-choice items are often thought of as objective in nature. But someone wrote the items and, in doing so, made judgments about what is important to know. Essays and performances of all kinds are often considered more subjective, but with the use of rubrics we define what we are looking for in terms of quality. In this light, evaluating knowledge and our comprehension with a multiple-choice test may be just as subjective as evaluating a writing assignment or science project using a rubric. We will look at decision points that give us opportunities to use our content area expertise and our knowledge of student development and diversity to take advantage of subjectivity in ways that result in positive progress for your students.

Consistency

Your school and your team will have established grading procedures in terms of scales and reporting. Be sure you understand these procedures and what leeway you may have in determining student grades. Some schools will require a minimum number of grades per quarter or semester. Many principals will ask to see your record keeping system, and parents expect a clearly defined system. Work with your teammates to establish a grade book recording system that can be explained and justified. As a team, you will want the message that grades send to students and adults to have a measure of consistency and absolute fairness.

Purposes of Grades

Grades provide information. A grade assigned to a student serves multiple purposes depending on who views it.

• *As viewed by students.* An obvious purpose of grades is to inform students about their achievement. With ongoing formative assessment, summative grades should not surprise students. What they do is lend seriousness to the whole assessment process. The surprise is often perceived by the adults who receive grade reports without adequate communication about sources of grades and student progress.

Low letter grades without accompanying details and descriptions of deficits have never been shown to be motivators. The threat of even lower grades if study habits aren't changed will probably prove to have negative effects. However, descriptive narratives, even if they contain negative comments, can be motivational if approached as opportunities for improvement (Burden & Byrd, 1999). Receiving a high grade, especially if it shows progress, can be motivating with or without an explanation. As with so many aspects of middle grades education, perspective and teacher attitude determine in large measure the receptiveness and dispositions of students toward grades.

• *As viewed by parents.* Grades are expected features of school. Attempts at the middle level to convey progress, or lack of it, with narratives alone (replacing letter grades) have generally been met with disapproval and been considered unacceptable by families. Grades are traditional, and even though parents may realize they are subjective measures, they usually still want to know if Johnny's work is of A, B, C, D, or F quality. Praise and punishment are both doled out based on the grades received by students.

• *As viewed by teachers.* If grades and the process of grading do not guide instructional planning, then we are missing a major function of assessment and evaluation. We have already discussed the value of diagnostic assessment in decision-making. The same premise applies to grades. We look at the academic achievement of our students, or lack of it. We determine content depth, remediation, instructional strategies, sequencing, pacing, and so on. At the same time, individual student grades give us guidance for grouping/regrouping and differentiating instruction.

When considering placement in what are considered advanced courses in middle schools, such as Algebra I and foreign language, grades provide a guidance function. They also provide information used in determining summer school or after-school options often used for remediation.

• *As viewed by administrators.* Administrators at school and district levels use grades as indicators of academic success of groups of students—classes, grade levels, and whole schools. Individual student grades influence promotion and retention, and help determine placement of students in homogeneous or heterogeneous groups.

Establishing Scoring Criteria

Regardless of the assignment or assessment, scoring needs to be based on pre-established criteria. For forced-choice assessments, students need to know how many points each item is worth and then how those points translate to scores and figure into overall grades. For projects, students need scoring guides. Rubrics may be used to provide number scores when points are assigned to each descriptor of quality.

Clear and precise scoring criteria set targets for our students. With assignments that receive scores, and assessments that are evaluated, knowing what is expected in terms of standards to be met and the credit to be given adds clarity and definitive goals.

Having defined criteria helps us deal with the basic question of what grades mean. What, after all, is an A? How about a C? There are general notions, but consistency from state to state, school to school, and even classroom to classroom does not exist. As we look at the different percentages in Figure 9.11 commonly associated with letter grades, keep in mind that even with percentages established for a district, the assignments and assessments that are evaluated and scored to come up with the percentages are subjective. Even if there were ways to eliminate the subjectivity of scoring, you can see that districts and states have different ideas about the percentages comprising the traditional A through F grades.

Probably the best we can hope for in terms of consistency of scoring criteria and subsequent transfers to letter grades is that our own policies and procedures are understood by our students and their parents/guardians. Ideally you will have agreement and consistency among your teammates.

A	B	C	D	F
90–100%	80–89%	70–79%	60–69%	<60%
93–100%	85–92%	78–84%	70–77%	<70%
95–100%	85–94%	75–84%	65–74%	<65%
95–100%	88–94%	81–87%	75–80%	<75%

FIGURE 9.11   Varying grade scales.

What to Include

Even though academic achievement is the implied focus of grades, we know that other factors are often included. In some schools and on some teams, it is understood that dispositions such as effort, participation, attitude, and other behaviors receive weight in a grade. A noted researcher and author on the topic of grading, Ken O'Connor (2002), cautions us against including dispositions in academic scores to develop letter grades. He tells us that unless a nonacademic outcome or behavior process is part of a stated learning goal it should not be part of a content area grade. "Hard work (effort), frequent responses to teacher questions, intense involvement in class activities, and a positive . . . demeanor are all highly valued attributes. However, they should not be included directly in grades" (p. 99). He continues by stating that the attributes mentioned are difficult to define and even more difficult to measure.

Along with reporting academic grades, it is entirely appropriate to give feedback on dispositions and behavior. If your school or team doesn't have a mechanism in place for doing so, you may be instrumental in establishing one. A commonly used rating scale for nonacademic outcomes includes descriptors such as superior, excellent, above average, average, satisfactory, and so on. An alternative to these scales, which sometimes lack specificity, are checklists of specific behaviors such as uses time wisely, organizes work well, works effectively with others, or completes assignments on time.

Weighting Grades

Some assignments and assessments are more valuable than others because they demonstrate learning more accurately and require more knowledge and skills to complete. For this reason, we don't want a homework assignment to be scored on a 0–100 point scale and a major writing project to also be scored 0–100. There are a number of ways to remedy this dilemma. You may want to designate the compiled or averaged scores of major assignments and assessments as a larger percentage of the overall grade. You might reserve 0–100 points for the bigger assignments and assessments and relegate fewer points (0–5) for daily work. This is what weighting is all about—an admittedly subjective process.

When using a rubric, you could have three criteria with a 1–4 scale for each. This would give a score range of 3 to 12. If the rubric applied to a major assessment, you would want to multiply the achieved score by a factor that would show its relative importance.

An Alternative to Mean Average

When an idea required more than passive consideration, my mother would say "Put your thinking cap on." Here's a concept so simple, yet so radical, that it may require your thinking cap. For me it resulted in a response of "Wow! What a revelation!" My experience leads me to believe that the overwhelming majority of teachers use the mean average to compute grades. Recall that the mean is the total of scores divided by the number of values. The mean is a measure of central tendency, and so is the median. The median is the middle value when the scores are placed in numerical order.

When using the mean, all scores or possible scores are added, even the zeros. The mean "emphasizes quantity over quality and completing all work rather than doing some superbly and missing some" (O'Connor, 2002, p. 143). Few students realize what one zero will do to an average. If a student has four scores, three of which are 100% and one of which is zero, the mean average is 75%. According to Figure 9.11 that means a C, a D, or even an F. Do any of those three letters accurately indicate the student's achievement? Perhaps the median (100, 100, 100, 0) of 100 is not completely accurate either, especially if the zero resulted from a lack of understanding or skill. But chances are a zero indicates a behavior (nonacademic) outcome, and perhaps should not even be included in calculating a content-area letter grade.

Using the median as a measure of central tendency rather than the mean takes into consideration that we all stumble occasionally and have days when we are not at our best. If this philosophy applies at any age, it should apply in young adolescence. We expect variability. Being developmentally responsive calls for us to reward achievement and growth over time while diminishing the effects of social and emotional changes and traumas.

Take time to examine Figure 9.12, which illustrates issues with the mean from *How to Grade for Learning*. Note that the mean for each of the four students is 63%. Now look at the medians. Consider the 10 scores for each student. Which students appear to have a solid grasp of the knowledge and skills? Should they all receive Ds and Fs? Their point totals are the same, but their degrees of understanding are certainly different.

Consider the value of using the median, or perhaps a combination of the mean and median. Discuss this issue with your teammates.

Reporting Grades

Progress reports and report cards are standard fare in most middle schools. They should be considered the bare minimum in terms of efforts to communicate grades to students and parents/guardians. The traditional system calls for grade reporting every 4 to 5 weeks. Ideally your team will have a system to communicate progress, or the lack of it, more frequently in cases where outstanding progress is being made or a sudden or chronic lack of progress is noted.

Report cards vary in the amount and types of information included. This is often outside your control. You and your team will want to supplement communication in ways that keep parents informed and invite their participation.

Grading for Success

Tomlinson (2001) tells us "grading grows from a philosophy of teaching and learning. It reflects what a teacher believes about learning" (p. 12). She outlines five guidelines for grading.

1. Grade so that students' degrees of success "reflect the degree of their own growth." (p. 14)
2. Assign appropriate work and "grade the student's work on the basis of clearly delineated criteria for quality of work on that task." (p. 14)
3. As a part of grading, "give students consistent, meaningful feedback that clarifies for them—and for me—present successes and next learning steps." (p. 14)

Assessments in Order	Karen	Alex	Jennifer	Stephen
Assessment #1	0	63	0	0
Assessment #2	0	63	10	0
Assessment #3	0	63	10	62
Assessment #4	90	63	10	62
Assessment #5	90	63	100	63
Assessment #6	90	63	100	63
Assessment #7	90	63	100	90
Assessment #8	90	63	100	90
Assessment #9	90	63	100	100
Assessment #10	90	63	100	100
Total	630	630	630	630
Mean	63%	63%	63%	63%
Median	90%	63%	100%	63%

FIGURE 9.12   Issues with the mean.

Source: From *How to Grade for Learning* (p. 142), by K. O'Connor, 2002, Arlington Heights, IL: Skylight Professional Development. Copyright 2002 by Pearson Education, Inc. Reprinted with permission.

4. Look for growth patterns over time when assigning grades.
5. Show individual growth as well as relative standing among classmates.

To sum up Tomlinson's grading philosophy she writes, "Can grading be a part of efforts to help all students succeed? Absolutely, when it grows from a philosophy of teaching for maximum individual growth" (p. 15).

STANDARDIZED ASSESSMENT

Standardized tests are a fact of life in public education. The demand for accountability in our schools has never been higher. We hear it from parents, legislators, and citizen groups. Understanding, as defined by Wiggins and McTighe, and performance assessment, which is deemed the preferred measure of what students know and are able to do, are not easily or accurately measured by paper-and-pencil tests. Standards of learning established by subject area organizations and state departments of education provide goals. How to measure progress toward those goals, which include understanding and performance, is a dilemma.

While calls for accountability lead to standardized testing, the process itself and the results are often viewed critically.

Validity and reliability are two concepts important for all assessment, but of particular importance for standardized assessment. Validity refers to the degree to which an assessment measures what it is supposed to measure. For classroom assessment, validity is within our control. For standardized testing based on imposed standards, validity can be verified through comparisons of standards and test items. For nationally marketed standardized assessments, the scope of the content and skills assessed is extensive. If a test is to measure seventh grade knowledge and skills, determining what is included is the publisher's decision, making validity difficult to establish or dispute. Reliability refers to the consistency with which an assessment measures what it is meant to measure. Reliability can be complicated to establish, requiring field testing of sample populations. With classroom assessment, teacher judgment makes up for whatever an assessment lacks in terms of reliability. Before a standardized assessment is administered, schools, districts, and states should be very careful to make sure that reliability standards for the assessment are in place.

Vital components of standardized assessment = Validity + Reliability

---

Comparing Standardized and Classroom Assessment

As classroom teachers we can follow the adage of "Teach what you test and test what you teach." If classroom assessment is interwoven with curriculum and instruction, and standards are incorporated, then the package of learning and testing can be neatly and cohesively bundled. Classroom assessment in its many forms derives content and skills to be tested from the learning opportunities of the classroom.

State standardized assessments derive content and skills to be tested from state standards documents that are available to us. While we don't write the items, we have the standards they supposedly measure.

Most standardized tests derive content and skills from many sources including national subject area organizations and textbooks. They supposedly match grade level expectations, but generally contain items and/or complete sections that are unfamiliar to our students. We can use published preparation materials, but in doing so we may find that we actually end up presenting isolated facts out of context.

With classroom assessments, we are free to determine the value of items in the overall scheme of our planned assessment and measure student success against our learning goals. We then assign a score to the assessment and a weight to indicate its importance relative to other assessments. Assessing student success in meeting stated learning goals and expectations is referred to as *criterion-referenced assessment*. Student scores reflect what they know and the degree to which they know it. National tests provide what we refer to as raw data, or how many items a student answers correctly out of the number possible. While score reports are available, the overall results of national tests focus on normative reporting. They are norm-referenced, which means students are rated relative to other students within a segment or population. *Norm-referenced tests* are expressed in percentiles. On a classroom assessment, usually criterion-referenced, an "85%" means that 85% of the knowledge and skills assessed were correct. On a national standardized assessment, usually norm-referenced, an "85%" means that 85 of every 100 students tested lower than the student with 85% and 15 of 100 students tested higher. This simply compares student performance and provides little information about the level or mastery of learning goals. If most of the students actually did very poorly on the assessment, then a norm score of 85% would represent questionable success. If most of the students did exceptionally well on the assessment, then a norm score of 85% would represent outstanding success. Based on student success relative to learning goals, state standardized test results typically place students in one of four groups labeled "below basic," "basic," "proficient," and "advanced." This information is reported in ways that individuals can be compared with other students within the same class, school, district, or state. In the same way, schools and districts are compared with others within a state.

Benefits of Standardized Assessment

Standardized assessment is not going away in the foreseeable future. The capacity, debatable as it is, to provide comparisons and gauge annual progress makes standardized assessment a fixture in public education. I have often referred to it as a "rite of spring," since most standardized assessments are administered in March through May in traditional school calendars. Given their undeniable presence, our best stance is to be proactive. To be both proactive and positive, we must consider the possible benefits of standardized assessment. Figure 9.13 lists a sampling of those benefits.

Preparing for Standardized Assessment

There is a prevailing fear that preparing for standardized assessments, both nationally published and state developed, will lead to almost exclusive drill and practice, or as some call it, drill and kill, instruction. Obviously, that would be very inappropriate, particularly for middle grades students. Most researchers who study test preparation practices and their results tell us that we should avoid the temptation to drill isolated information not just because we know it's not developmentally responsive, but because it doesn't work. Classrooms that concentrate on the "big ideas," active student involvement, and a comprehensive curriculum have students who excel on standardized assessment. "Teachers who have seen scores go up

---

Standardized tests . . .

- provide data on how well students, and consequently teachers, schools, districts, and states, are performing.

- if directly tied to standards, promote a common instructional focus.

- show patterns of strengths and weaknesses to guide decision-making.

- when results indicate mastery and/or improvement, build public trust.

- provide a mode of comparison, although approximate, for schools, districts, and states.

- may prompt us to ask probing and important questions concerning instructional practice as we analyze results.

FIGURE 9.13   Benefits of standardized tests.

in proportion to concerted, optimistic instructional-improvement efforts know that teaching makes a difference" (Schmoker, 2000, p. 64). Here are some practices to keep in mind.

1. *Be positive concerning the necessity of standardized tests.* If we convey (even if we don't say out loud) the message, "We've got to put up with those stupid standardized tests in April," our students will sense our negativity and their preparation, and subsequently their scores, will suffer. If we approach standardized tests with an attitude of, "This is a great opportunity to show what we know and can do!" I guarantee you happier, more productive students along with the real possibility of higher scores.

2. *Focus on student reading ability,* regardless of the subject area tested. Remember that we are all teachers of reading. Help students improve their reading skills within the context of your subject area and continually assist them with vocabulary acquisition.

3. *Know your state curriculum standards intimately,* including the ones written for previous and subsequent grade levels, and include them in your lesson plans.

4. *Obtain and use previous standardized test results for your students.* Look for strengths, weaknesses, and both individual and team trends. Use these results diagnostically for instructional planning.

5. *Provide an abundance of authentic opportunities* that call for not only knowledge and comprehension, but also application, analysis, synthesis, and evaluation.

6. *Emphasize problem-solving* in all content areas. Math does not have a monopoly when it comes to problem-solving opportunities. After all, history is just one problem after another, with attempted resolutions along the way.

7. *Teach the skills of editing* and then give lots of opportunity for practice. Help students recognize errors and areas for improvement in their own and others' writing.

8. *Provide frequent opportunities for students to interpret and create representations* like tables, graphs, and maps. As with problem-solving, this is not the exclusive purview of math. Some estimates tell us that 25% of the standardized test items in social studies and science involve charts, tables, graphs, and maps.

9. *Use a variety of assessment methods* to help develop student flexibility. We know it is possible to assess the same content and skills in many ways.

10. *Locate and use appropriate test preparation and test-specific materials* from publishers and as provided by state departments of education. Using material that is written in the same format as the test to be administered is advisable. After all, we don't want the test to measure format familiarity more than content knowledge and skills.

Preparation for standardized testing should not be thought of as separate from daily instruction. Using a variety of instructional practices to present a broad and comprehensive curriculum will be the best possible preparation.

 ## REFLECTIONS ON ASSESSMENT IN MIDDLE SCHOOL

Curriculum, instruction, and assessment are interwoven. We have looked at each separately and examined components and issues. What we teach, how we teach it, and then how we gather evidence of learning must be developmentally appropriate and responsive, as well as interdependent. Diagnostic assessment informs our decisions concerning curriculum and instruction; formative assessment tells us if we need to move toward enrichment or correctives; and summative assessment provides information for grading and signals the timing for moving on to new curriculum.

Assessment can be accomplished through a rich variety of means, whether diagnostic, formative, or summative. Assessment allows us to evaluate student achievement and recognize accomplishment, make informed instructional decisions and improve instruction, monitor student progress and promote growth, and evaluate and modify programs.

Classroom assessment establishes hallmarks of understanding. To distinguish degrees of understanding, we develop ways of evaluating classroom assessment and answering the question of just how good is good enough. Using rubrics allows us to set criteria of quality in advance of assignments, use narratives and descriptions to give feedback, and be specific and open in what otherwise can be a very subjective and vague process.

Performance assessment involves any task in which students are required to demonstrate understanding and skills. Paper-and-pencil tests that require more than recitation of facts, complex tasks requiring extensive planning, and every level in between may be considered performance assessment.

Standardized assessment is a stable feature of public education. It's not going away. Understanding that standardized assessment has limitations and merits criticism, we also realize that there are benefits. Taking a proactive stance involves including strong instructional practices that strengthen learning and lead to improved standardized test scores.

Accountability is essential at all levels. Assessment allows our students to show what they know and what they are able to do. The results of assessment serve as accountability measures for us. Schools and districts are responsible for providing support for teaching and learning. Assessment results hold them accountable to us and to our students. The important role of classroom and standardized assessment cannot be overstated. *This We Believe* (National Middle School Association, 1995) tells us that "Continuous, authentic, and appropriate assessment and evaluation are essential components of the learning process" (p. 26).

Group Activities

1. In pairs, interview a middle school teacher to discuss assessment. Take a list of the seven basic forms of assessment covered in this chapter and ask the teacher to comment on if and when she uses each. Write a summary of this information to be shared with the class. Include summaries in your school file.

2. In subject area groups, choose a standard and develop an overview of a performance that would assess a hallmark of understanding. Be prepared to share your overview and assessment with the class.

3. In subject area groups, write lists of items that might be included in a student portfolio for a particular topic of study.

4. Respond to these and other questions/prompts appropriate for your area/state.

   - Does your state mandate a nationally produced standardized test? If so, find information on the administration of the test (timing, grade levels, frequency, use of results, etc.).

- What information is available concerning your state's standardized assessment? (grade levels, developers, Web site for preparation, uses of results, etc.)
- Locate state and district test results. Put in a form to share with the class.
- Locate state test results for the middle schools in your school file. Put in a form to share with the class.

Add information gathered to your class files.

Individual Activities

1. What type of assessment can you remember from your middle school years? High school? College? Which type did you find easiest? Most difficult? Most meaningful?
2. Write a paragraph that compares and contrasts alternative, performance, and authentic assessment.
3. Do you think a missing homework assignment should receive a grade of zero? Why or why not? What might you do to lessen the impact of an "off week" for a student?
4. Discuss the pros and cons of using the median rather than the mean to determine grades.
5. How are the concepts of performance assessment especially appropriate for middle grades?
6. Write a letter you might send home to parents to explain the value of rubrics. Assume they are unfamiliar with the concept and you plan to use a rubric to assess a student project.

Personal Journal

1. How do you typically react to assessment? Do your grades generally mirror your self-assessment of knowledge/skill level?
2. Do you remember taking standardized tests? Achievement type? SAT or ACT? Praxis? Write about your anxiety levels for these tests.

Professional Practice

(It would be helpful to reread the description of Maggie Chin in Chapter 4, as well as the descriptions of Barry in Chapters 2 and 3. This teacher and student were also featured in the Chapter 6 Professional Practice section.)

Accountability was not something the administration and faculty of Hoyt River Middle School of the Performing Arts (HRPA) ever considered avoiding. In fact, "excellence in education" are words in their mission statement and they pride themselves on achievement.

The student scores on the state standardized test were expected any day, and they would need to be analyzed and used for future planning. So when the district director for curriculum and instruction called the principal for a consultation in late July, Ms. Stadalis assumed the director wanted her to head up a committee or chair a task force. She was wrong.

The director closed the door and began explaining the political mood of the state and district. With a new governor and state superintendent of education and at least a 15% budget cut, the district was being forced to take a fresh look at magnet programs and their effectiveness as measured by state test scores. All programs were up for grabs as schools were asked to justify their existence based on evidence that they measured up.

Hoyt River state test scores were above average for the district. The only tests given in all the middle schools were language arts and math. Here's a chart that shows the data presented to Ms. Stadalis by the district director.

Score Report for Hoyt River Middle School
Language Arts

	Below Basic	Basic	Proficient	Advanced
HRPA	8%	42%	32%	18%
District	19%	55%	17%	9%

Math

	Below Basic	Basic	Proficient	Advanced
HRPA	20%	51%	15%	14%
District	21%	57%	14%	8%

For any other middle school, this data would have drawn praise for language arts and a satisfactory nod for math. However, Hoyt River is a magnet school with the inherently greater need for funding for transportation for students who qualify regardless of where they live in the district, a lower teacher-student ratio for performance classes, instruments, equipment, travel to special events, etc. It seems that in times of budget crunches, the arts— or anything other than core curriculum that is tested— are fair game for funding cuts. The bottom line is that HRPA had to come up with a plan by October to demonstrate academic accountability and progress, especially in math, or risk closure the following school year.

The academic accountability plan needed to be comprehensive. The district was asking for higher scores on the state test, revamping of the grade reporting system, evidence of the work accomplished in the arts classes, and letter grades based on quantifiable data for all classes.

The teachers at Hoyt River are there because they believe in their program and fully support the schools-within-a-school concept with emphasis on drama, vocal music, instrumental music, and dance. They see firsthand how practicing principles based on multiple intelligences is developmentally appropriate for young adolescents. They didn't want to jeopardize their school by not complying with district mandates. When Ms. Stadalis explained the situation, the teachers came together in support of keeping their school a vital choice for middle grades students across the district. They immediately formed study groups to address assessment and accountability issues.

1. As artists themselves, the teachers of the performing arts classes have always considered themselves competent judges of growth and quality in their fields. Now they needed to move from a high degree of subjectivity in assessing and reporting (which was done through narrative), to a paper-and-pencil justification using letter grades. Which of the following is the best way to approach this dilemma?

   (a) Contact local arts organizations and ask for volunteers to serve on panels of judges to give a wider spectrum of opinions of quality.

   (b) Work with students to construct rubrics for performances. Send letters to parents about the new approach along with an explanation of how grades would be assigned based on rubric scores.

   (c) Look at the narratives written the year before to serve as progress and quality indicators. Together decide on letter grades that match general categories of descriptors in the narratives. In the future, assign letter grades compared with past performances.

   (d) Survey parents to ask if they have been satisfied with the narratives received in the past. With the predictable positive response, go to the district personnel and attempt to justify the current system.

2. Hoyt River uses a very loosely constructed portfolio approach. Students plan with the teachers their goals and steps toward reaching those goals, along with a culminating performance. All of this is written and then documented as the steps are attempted. This system is used only in the arts classes, and folders that are kept in file drawers serve as the portfolios. Which of the following would have the least positive impact on district personnel?

   (a) Expand portfolios to include the core four subjects with student work in each subject, accompanied by arts goals and performance evidence.

(b) Assign letter grades to both the goal narratives and the performances. Record these grades on a checklist-style chart on the front of the folders and have folders available at all times for parents and district personnel to review.

(c) Have portfolios visible in the arts classrooms in student-designed packets complete with photographs and programs from practices and performances.

(d) Work together to design a uniform format for arts classes that includes the national organization standards and a way to indicate how and when the standards are met.

Maggie Chin

3. Maggie Chin recognizes the fact that many of her students excel in their arts areas of interest and giftedness and, more often than she would like, view mathematics as simply a necessity to be passed, but neither enjoyed nor worthy of extra effort. Barry, now an eighth grader, is a prime example. The district views magnet schools as places where all students should excel in the basics while nurturing their talents/interests. Ms. Chin and her fellow math/science teachers came up with four ideas/concepts to implement. Which should be the first and which should be the last of the four in terms of priority?

(a) Use the median rather than the mean to average scores since students sometimes miss whole or partial days of school due to arts-related performances and events.

(b) Spend time understanding more fully the relationship among state math standards and their planned curriculum.

(c) Develop ways to teach math concepts and skills within contexts that will interest and motivate students.

(d) Use a broader span of assessments to allow students to more accurately demonstrate what they know and are able to do.

A. B first, A last

B. B first, D last

C. C first, A last

D. C first, D last

Constructed Response

The HRPA staff appears willing to work together to develop a plan that they know they can implement to meet the demands of the district, increase test scores, and adapt to accountability measures. Through their work, the staff will reap other benefits. Describe a major benefit that may come of their efforts.

Internet Resources

Assessment Training Institute
http://www.assessmentinst.com

While this site primarily promotes a particular for-profit assessment training program, there are articles and information available on the site that make it useful for all teachers.

Education World
http://educationworld.com

Middle Web
http://www.middleweb.com

NCREL Pathways to Assessment

http://www.ncrel.org/sdrs/areas/as0cont.htm

This part of the North Central Regional Educational Laboratory Web site features articles on assessment that contain links to detailed explanations of key words and phrases relevant to understanding assessment.

References

Airasian, P. (1994). *Classroom assessment* (2nd ed.). New York: McGraw-Hill.

Andrade, H. G. (2000). Using rubrics to promote thinking and learning. *Educational Leadership, 57*(5), 13–18.

Burden, P. R., & Byrd, D. M. (1999). *Methods of effective teaching.* Boston: Allyn & Bacon.

Cole, K., Coffey, J., & Goldman, S. (1999). Using assessments to improve equity in mathematics. *Educational Leadership, 56*(6), 56–58.

Guskey, T. R., & Bailey, J. M. (2001). *Developing grading and reporting systems for student learning.* Beverly Hills, CA: Sage Publications.

Jackson, A. W., & Davis, G. A. (2000). *Turning points 2000: Educating adolescents in the 21st century.* New York: Teachers College Press.

Marzano, R. J. (2000). *Transforming classroom grading.* Alexandria, VA: Association for Supervision and Curriculum Development.

McTighe, J. (1997). What happens between assessments? *Educational Leadership, 54*(4), 6–12.

National Council of Teachers of Mathematics. (1995). *Assessment standards for school mathematics.* Reston, VA: Author.

National Middle School Association. (1995). *This we believe: Developmentally responsive middle schools.* Columbus, OH: Author.

O'Connor, K. (2002). *How to grade for learning.* Arlington Heights, IL: Skylight Professional Development.

Schmoker, M. (1999). *Results: The key to continuous school improvement.* Alexandria, VA: Association for Supervision and Curriculum Development.

Schmoker, M. (2000). The results we want. *Educational Leadership, 57*(5), 62–65.

Schurr, S. (1999). *Authentic assessment: Using product performance and portfolio measures from A to Z.* Westerville, OH: National Middle School Association.

Smith, C., & Myers, C. (2001). Students take center stage in classroom assessment. *Middle Ground, 5*(2), 10–16.

Tomlinson, C. A. (2001). Grading for success. *Educational Leadership, 58*(6), 12–15.

Vars, G. F. (1997). Assessment and evaluation that promote learning. *Middle School Journal, 28*(4), 44–49.

Wiggins, G., & McTighe, J. (1998). *Understanding by design.* Alexandria, VA: Association for Supervision and Curriculum Development.

10

Planning for Teaching and Learning

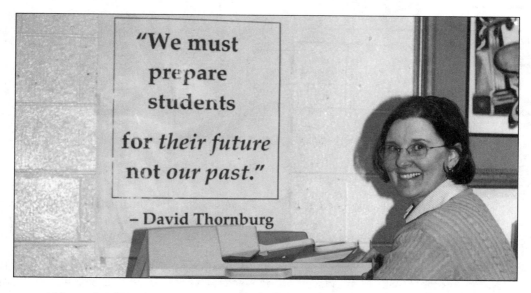

"We must prepare students for *their future* not *our past.*"

– David Thornburg

Although planning is a critical skill for a teacher, a well-developed plan will not guarantee the success of a lesson or unit or even the over-all effectiveness of a course. But lack of a well-developed plan will almost certainly result in poor teaching. Like a good map, a good plan helps you reach your destination with more confidence and with fewer wrong turns.

Callahan, Clark, and Kellough, 2002, p. 61

Use this diagram as an organizational tool. In the boxes beside the chapter headings, indicate the dates by which the reading should be completed.

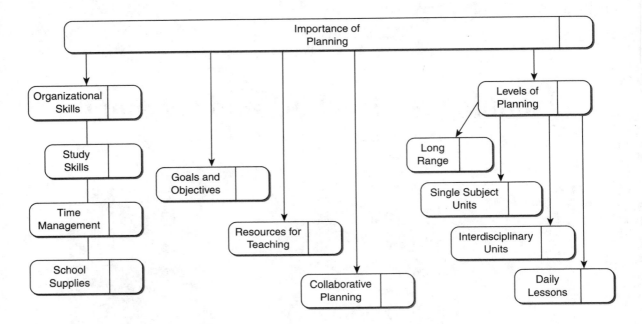

INTRODUCTION

In this chapter we will put it all together—curriculum, instruction, and assessment, tempered by what we know about our students' developmental characteristics and differences. This is a tall order, but it's the craft of teaching. Planning the days, the weeks, even the semesters and year is the task that will determine the level of success we, and our students, achieve in making the teaching and learning connection. It is serious business with tremendous consequences. Overwhelmed? Possibly—well, probably. But take heart. Like any other active endeavor that requires hard work and energy, planning for teaching and learning builds cognitive muscles that may seem overworked or incapable in the beginning but become stronger and more suited for the challenge as we gain momentum in the process. This isn't to say that it's ever easy, but with experience we become more comfortable with the planning process. Its importance should never be diminished regardless of how many years of experience we have.

 ## THE IMPORTANCE OF PLANNING

To understand how important planning is, simply consider some of the elements involved: content; sequence; strategies; who does what, when, where, and in what order; resources, materials; standards; learner needs; technology; homework; classroom climate; student assessment . . . the list could go on and on. The elements of planning involved on a daily, weekly, semester, and yearly basis must all be organized and coordinated. Decisions must be made that involve student needs and interests, curriculum requirements, and lesson delivery. Effective, comprehensive planning requires thoughtful and wise decision-making.

Planning for teaching and learning serves many purposes. Burden and Byrd (1999) tell us that among other things, planning can help do the following:

- Give a sense of direction, and through this, a feeling of confidence and security. Planning can help you stay on course and reduce your anxiety about instruction.
- Organize, sequence, and increase familiarity with course content.
- Prepare us to interact with students during instruction. This may include preparing a list of important questions or guidelines for a cooperative group activity.
- Incorporate techniques to motivate students to learn in each lesson.
- Take into account individual differences and the diversity of students when selecting objectives, content, strategies, materials, and requirements.
- Arrange for appropriate requirements and evaluation of student performance.
- Become a reflective decision-maker about curriculum and instruction.

And you thought a plan was whatever you could squeeze into a 2-inch by 2-inch box on a page with many other boxes to remind you which pages to cover in a textbook! Let's take an in-depth look at this extremely important function of a classroom teacher.

In this chapter we'll discuss four distinct levels of planning—long-range, single subject units, interdisciplinary units, and daily lessons. Before doing so we need to look at some topics that will be integral factors in the planning process.

Standard 5

Disposition 3: Middle level teacher candidates believe that instructional planning is important and must be developmentally responsive.

Standard 1

Performance 3: Middle level teacher candidates create positive, productive learning environments where developmental differences are respected and supported, and individual potential is encouraged.

Performance 10: Middle level teacher candidates respond positively to the diversity found in young adolescents and use that diversity in planning and implementing curriculum and instruction.

Standard 7

Disposition 6: Middle level teacher candidates are committed to refining classroom and school practices that address the needs of all young adolescents based on research, successful practice, and experience.

ORGANIZATIONAL SKILLS

Just as we are all teachers of reading, we are all teachers of the organizational skills required for effective study. Organizational skills involve forming habits. Our students are going to form habits with or without our guidance. Helping them to be "creatures of habit" in positive ways that promote learning and success is one of our greatest services to middle school students. Planning for organizational skill acquisition involving productive habits will enhance students' chances of success in future academic situations and will also serve them later in life.

Organizational skills = Forming productive habits

The acquisiton of organizational skills is not an innate or inevitable process. D. Robert Sylwester, an expert on brain-based learning, explains that between the ages of 10 and 14 the brain's frontal lobe, which is associated with problem-solving, critical thinking, and organizational skills, develops. He used the term **hovering** to describe how he believes we should walk students through this maturation process (Dyck, 2002). The implication here is that we need to plan to include direct instruction, consistent practice, and monitoring when it comes to study and organizational skills. He concludes that

> This means we must put detailed structure into place, share successful organizational strategies and tools, and use varied methods of explaining new concepts to students. Then we need to repeat all these steps until the process of learning and retaining information becomes second nature to them. (p. 19)

Study Skills

We have already discussed the necessity of directly teaching students how to read the material in specific subject areas—that reading a math text requires different emphases than reading a short story. Looking up vocabulary in a glossary and thinking about words in context, reading captions under pictures, understanding information in tables and graphs, knowing how to use a map legend, recognizing the importance of key names and time frames, taking time to dissect a formula and its applications, and reading a story carefully to determine characters, plot, setting, and voice—all of these skills require us to "hover" and guide. This should be part of our planning.

Standard 4

Disposition 3: Middle level teacher candidates are committed to using content specific teaching and assessment strategies.

Summarizing and notetaking, discussed in Chapter 8, are vitally important instructional strategies that correlate with student learning. As with reading in content areas, they must be explicitly taught and monitored. Outlining is a related skill that will prove invaluable.

The skills needed to study for a test often elude middle grades students. Some think simply sitting in class should be enough, even when they are unsuccessful over and over again. Others rely on last-minute cramming with possible short-term, but little long-term,

1. Visualize the information. Create a picture in your mind that portrays what you want to remember.

2. Divide the information you want to memorize into small chunks. In dividing the information, do so as logically as possible. The act of categorizing will make retention even easier.

3. Recite out loud the information you need to remember. Listen to your own voice. When trying to recall, it is easier when you can remember what your voice sounded like as you recited.

4. Make flash cards. No, they're not just for math facts. You can use them for words/definitions, events/people and dates, sequencing, random bits of information, etc.

5. Create acronyms for lists or groups. Did you know that radar stands for "radio detection and ranging?" It's an acronym that is so accepted that it has become a word in itself. To create an acronym, simply arrange the first letters of each item you want to memorize into a real or made-up word.

6. Write what you want to memorize in varying ink colors. The color will help you visualize the information you want to recall.

FIGURE 10.1   Techniques for memorizing.

success. Others don't have a clue. If we teach what we test, and test what we teach, then assessment in the form of quizzes and tests should not be a mystery. We need to help our students learn how to show what they know and can do. In doing so, they will more readily recognize when they don't know what they need to know and can't do what is expected.

Even with our emphasis on the big concepts and in-depth understanding, we ask our students to memorize numerous things in order to problem-solve, accurately complete a time line, perform an experiment, and so on. Most of us have tricks that work for our learning styles. Share them with your students. Try new ones yourself and then think aloud about them for your students as you model how they work. Figure 10.1 is a brief list of memorizing techniques.

Time Management

As adults we know how important time management is, not only to our productivity, but also to our comfort and enjoyment of both work and leisure. Middle grades students are moving from the dependency of childhood toward independence when their own personal decision-making concerning time will affect what they accomplish or fail to accomplish.

While in the classroom, with effective planning on our part, students work within a structure on various tasks. However, simply having the structure does not guarantee that young adolescents will use their classroom time productively. They may go from sitting alone in a desk with a book open during silent reading time, to sitting in a circle during group discussion time, and back to a desk for journal writing, and still accomplish absolutely nothing.

To an outside observer they appear to have cooperated with the teacher and followed directions. Well, physically yes, cognitively no. Our emphasis must be on using class time wisely to engage students mentally. Interesting lessons requiring individual and group accountability will help engage and elicit participation from the reticent, sometimes mentally lazy, occasionally daydreaming kids who inevitably inhabit our middle schools. We know that the potential for creative and intelligent alter egos are in those rapidly developing minds and bodies—just waiting to be tapped.

When given work/study time in school, and homework to do at home, our students need to understand that assignments take time and that the amount of time varies from student to student. If, for instance, we ask Noah to show the problem steps and find the answers to three math items, read the social studies text section on reconstruction, fill in a lab sheet with science experiment data from class, and write a paragraph summarizing the setting of *The Cay*—all this while preparing for a band presentation at Tuesday's PTA meeting—we need to provide time management guidelines that realistically portray his Monday afternoon and evening. He needs to understand approximately how much time he'll have to devote to academics and how much time he'll have for other activities like sports, video games, dinner, home chores, and, perhaps most importantly to him, hanging out.

Many middle schools require students to use assignment pads. Some even provide these valuable organizational tools and insist that they be maintained in consistent ways. I'm completely in agreement with this practice. My calendar (adult assignment pad) is invaluable. It is my ultimate time management tool. Figure 10.2 shows a sample assignment pad where Noah has written his Monday assignments. Of course this doesn't guarantee accomplishment, but when adequately filled in, and then consistently checked upon arrival home by a parent, Noah stands a greater chance of managing his time and completing his work. Assignment pads also serve as reminders of what materials need to be taken both to class and home.

Success using an assignment pad = Adequately filled in + Consistently checked at home

School Supplies

Providing a team-coordinated list of required school supplies is essential. For instance, if your teacher team prefers mechanical pencils and black ink, then specifically state that these are necessary. If three classes require pocket and brad folders, then they should be on the list. Binders for subject areas and spiral notebooks for journaling, protractors and rulers for math, colored pencils for social studies—whatever is needed must be listed explicitly.

Some teachers provide an extra service for students by having a dry-erase board outside their classroom doors to list what is required for the day. For instance, vocabulary notebooks, poetry anthology, and highlighters may be needed Wednesday, but not literature books or *The Cay*, with the opposite being true for Friday. Staples such as paper, pencils, and assignment pads are a given.

Depending on your particular situation, you may want to keep extra supplies in a drawer to be loaned to students who infrequently arrive without what they need. For students who perpetually forget or intentionally fail to have needed supplies, team action may be required to emphasize the importance of having necessary items.

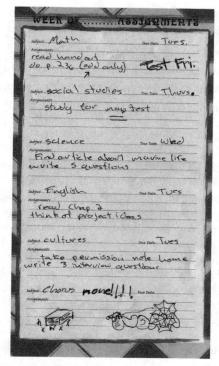

FIGURE 10.2   Sample assignment pad.

GOALS AND OBJECTIVES

To effectively plan instruction, we have to know where we're going and what the desired outcomes look like. In writing goals and objectives, we are practicing backward design as we state the learning to be done. Backward design asks us to strengthen our goals and objectives by envisioning the final product or performance as we design paths to get our students where we want them to go.

Goals

Goals are general statements of intent. They are broad and do not specify steps toward reaching them. An educational goal may be written at the national, state, district, or school level to provide a guide or direction for learning. We set personal goals for our students over and above those set by the education system and government. Goal-setting is an essential aspect of being a thoughtful, reflective teacher, and is a worthwhile endeavor that guides our instructional planning.

In writing goals there are three broad concepts to consider—needs of the learner, the subject matter, and needs of society (Gunter, Estes, & Schwab, 1999). With what we know about young adolescents, including all three of these components makes sense. Here are some examples of classroom goals:

- Students will understand how math is used in everyday life.
- Students will grasp the importance of conservation with regard to natural resources.
- Students will appreciate the musical contributions of major composers.
- Students will understand the influence of William Faulkner on the image of the South.

Objectives

"A learning objective is a statement of the measurable learning that is intended to take place as a result of instruction"(Gunter, Estes, & Schwab, 1999, p. 24). I like this definition for three reasons. First of all, the term **learning objectives** encompasses other terms you may hear like performance objectives, cognitive objectives, affective objectives, content objectives, and other modifications of the basic word *objectives*. We realize that regardless of what we want our students to know or do, and the source from which the knowing and doing emanate, the result we're going for is learning. The second thing I like about the definition is the emphasis on objectives as measurable. While goals may state ideals, even "pie in the sky" objectives use verbs to define specific learning and provide ways to determine if the learning occurs. The third reason is that the objective is accomplished as the result of instruction. For an objective to be meaningful, it must guide instruction and be the reason for doing what we do in the classroom.

While learning objectives include all the qualifiers in the previous paragraph, the difference between content objectives and performance objectives is worth noting. Content objectives focus on specific knowledge and skills. Performance objectives are tasks that demonstrate the ability to apply knowledge and skills. The distinction between content and performance objectives is often blurred. As long as we recognize that knowledge and skills are needed for performance, and plan instruction with ample opportunities to learn content and perform, we are providing balanced experiences.

Using active verbs to describe the learning we want to occur makes it possible to select instructional strategies to bring about the learning and to design assessments to verify the learning. Most learning objectives begin with the statement "Students will." Keeping a chart containing verbs associated with Bloom's taxonomy, similar to Figure 7.5 in Chapter 7, on your desk as you write objectives is a good way to check for inclusion of each of the six categories of learning while varying verb usage. Here are some examples of objectives and the category of Bloom they address:

- Students will recall the order of the major wars involving the United States. (knowledge)
- Students will match the authors to the titles of the books listed on the Great American Authors chart. (knowledge)
- Students will classify each polyhedron as a pyramid or a prism. (comprehension)
- Students will summarize a paragraph, preserving the main idea. (comprehension)
- Students will construct an equilateral triangle given their knowledge of angles and a compass. (application)

- Students will interview a community member on the topic of increasing voter participation given the recent study of communication techniques and the political process. (application)
- Students will compare and contrast the Dust Bowl era to the current drought situation. (analysis)
- Students will verify the relative accuracy of information from a variety of graphs. (analysis)
- Students will design an electrical circuit. (synthesis)
- Students will compose a short story with all the prescribed elements. (synthesis)
- Students will support one candidate for governor using recent newspaper reports. (evaluation)
- Students will defend their position on gun control. (evaluation)

Learning objectives are often included in textbooks and other instructional materials. If they express what you want your students to know and be able to do, then use them—if not verbatim, then as starting points. Many state standards are written in forms that are readily translatable into learning objectives. You will probably not have to write objectives from scratch, but you will be the decision-maker regarding both the depth of content and the order in which the desired learning will take place.

As a learner, you know how important it is for you to understand desired outcomes. The same is true for our students. Middle grades students are capable of hearing and/or seeing a well-written learning objective and understanding the desired outcome(s) of a lesson or an activity. Writing your learning objectives in a particular place on the board each day gives students a sense of organization and purpose. Refer to the objective at the beginning of a class period and then draw student attention to it again toward the end of the class and ask for opinions on whether or not the objective was reached. If so, ask how we know. If not, ask what needs to happen to bring about the learning. Young adolescents are capable of this kind of critical thought. Let's give them opportunities to practice.

 ## RESOURCES FOR TEACHING

There is an amazing array of resources for classroom teachers. Visit a teacher resource store and you'll find books, games, videos, CD-ROMs, manipulatives, and so on, for all subject areas and grade levels. To those outside our profession, a conclusion might be drawn that teaching is practically done for us through these materials. While the materials enhance what we do, they certainly don't do the teaching for us.

In addition to what's available in the public domain, there are many teaching resources available through national organizations. Throughout this book you'll find references to the National Middle School Association (NMSA) and the Association for Supervision and Curriculum Development (ASCD). These two organizations publish materials for teachers to use to increase their effectiveness in the classroom and resources that guide our professional practice. Subject area organizations such as the National Council of Teachers of Mathematics (NCTM) publish resources for teacher development as well as material that may be used in the classroom.

State departments of education and school districts provide resources for teachers and students. There are curriculum guides, benchmarks and standards documents, sample lesson plans on special Web sites, practice materials for standardized tests, and other resources deemed important by those who have oversight responsibilities.

Selection of Resources

With all the print and electronic resources produced continually, the dilemma of what to use and when to use it requires common sense decision-making. We can't use it all. We wouldn't want to use it all.

The resources published by companies not affiliated with school or national organizations should be chosen with care, with our choices guided by the curriculum content we teach and grade/developmental appropriateness.

Some districts and schools give teachers set amounts of money to spend each year on classroom resources. This is a luxury and we need to be good stewards of these funds. Principals have resource budgets that allow them to take teacher requests and buy resources as far as their budgeted dollars will allow. Most teachers have more resources at their disposal than they will ever use over the course of a school year. Because of this, new teachers should never feel handicapped by lack of "stuff." Don't be afraid to ask. Team leaders and principals should periodically ask teachers to open their storage closets, clean out their shelves and filing cabinets, go through the trunks of their cars and recesses of their attics, and bring together resources seldom/never used to share with other teachers. The adage "One person's junk is another person's treasure" certainly applies to classroom resources as we individualize our approaches to curriculum and instruction.

There are many things to consider when choosing resources, including

- relationship of resources to course objectives and curriculum standards
- educational value in terms of curricular and instructional goals
- absence of bias concerning gender, race, religion, etc.
- relative worthiness of the time necessary to implement or use the resource
- motivational attributes from a student perspective
- accuracy and timeliness of content

Just because a workbook or lesson or manipulative is attractive and potentially fun to use does not qualify it as appropriate for our classrooms. If it does not have the potential to increase student learning, then it is wasting precious minutes. Good instructional planning promotes the best possible use of classroom time.

Standard 5

Knowledge 7: Middle level teacher candidates understand how to motivate all young adolescents and facilitate their learning through the use of a wide variety of developmentally responsive materials and resources (e.g., technological resources, manipulative materials).

Textbooks

When we talk about adopting a textbook series at the state, district, or school level, we are talking about more than a solitary book. Publishers have responded to the call for accountability, subsequent testing, and ever-burgeoning technology by providing amazing tools for teachers. A few decades ago a textbook came with a teachers' guide and maybe an extra map or two or an accompanying spelling/vocabulary workbook. Things have changed.

Today, along with the basic textbook and teachers' edition, you may receive consumable workbooks (each student gets his own each year), CD-ROMs full of supplemental materials, booklets for student and parental interactive practice, special workbooks designed specifically for state standards test preparation, interactive software, supplemental literature books, packets of maps, boxes of math and science manipulatives, videos, black-line masters to reproduce, and overhead transparencies. . . . Can we use all of these resources over the course of a semester or a year? Absolutely not. The choice of a text series will probably not be yours, but how and when you use the book and assorted "goodies" that come with it will probably be within your control.

Let's consider what a textbook (and its ancillary components) is not. It is not the curriculum, it is not the shaper of all instruction, it is not necessarily the sequencer of content, and it is not the only source of information in your subject area. However, a well-chosen text that aligns closely with national and state subject area/grade level standards can form a basis for our instructional planning.

There are things we can do in the beginning of the school year to make students more comfortable with the basic textbook. For instance, we can prepare a text scavenger hunt that requires students to look at the title page, table of contents, illustrations, organization of chapters, purpose of boldface print, index, appendix, glossary, and more. Or we can create a series of questions, form pairs or small groups, provide a "game show" atmosphere, and begin. Middle grades students respond positively to creative activities of this kind. The time invested will pay dividends all year long.

 ## COLLABORATIVE PLANNING

While the ultimate responsibility for planning what occurs in your classroom is yours, some of the planning on any of the levels may be done collaboratively. In the following sections, we will discuss levels of planning and you will see the benefits of planning with others.

Standard 5

Disposition 4: Middle level teacher candidates value opportunities to plan instruction collaboratively with teammates and other colleagues.

Performance 3: Middle level teacher candidates plan effective instruction individually and with colleagues.

Team Planning

In Chapter 5, we discussed that one of the major benefits of teaming is the possibility of planning with other teachers. Planning objectives and activities in your content area with a teammate whose curriculum complements yours is not only a joy, but also a boon to student learning.

Teachers on a team should compare their long-range plans to find connections. This will be discussed in the next section, as will other aspects of interdisciplinary planning.

Same Subject Planning

If your school is large enough to have more than one team per grade level, then you will have one or more colleagues who teach the same subject at the same grade level. This is a great benefit. Chances are you have the same curriculum guide, standards, textbook, and basic materials. The adage "two heads (or three or four) are better than one" applies here. We each approach content and instruction in our own way. When we put more than one approach on the table and collaborate in planning, chances are the result will be richer and potentially better for our students.

Occasionally planning with same subject teachers on different grade levels is very helpful. Some refer to this as *vertical articulation*—vertical because it crosses grade levels and articulation because of the communication factor. It is extremely helpful to understand the standards and instructional methodology your students experienced before they came to you, as well as the expectations that await them when they leave your classroom. Regardless of the size of your school, vertical articulation is valuable for looking at student experiences over time to see the big picture and enhance continuity among grade levels.

Planning with Students

In Chapter 6 we discussed James Beane (1993) and his concept of an integrative curriculum. A major feature of Beane's concept of middle grades curriculum is that it be based on student interests and needs. To ascertain what the interests and needs are, teachers spend time talking with students to determine curricular direction.

Like every other aspect of education, there are degrees of implementation of teacher and student *collaborative planning*. Many middle grades classrooms encourage student input in the planning process. The concept of curriculum integration involves "a student-centered approach in which students are invited to join with their teachers to plan learning experiences that address both student concerns and major social issues" (Vars, 2001, p. 8). Student involvement in planning helps create a student-centered classroom regardless of the degree of curriculum integration.

Teachers are ultimately responsible for the curriculum and instruction in their classrooms. Involving students in the planning process does not diminish that responsibility. Determining when and how to bring students into the process may be based on many factors including a teacher's comfort level with the required standards and the planning process in general. Vars (2001) tells us that any collaboration with students has benefits in terms of making the curriculum personally relevant and meaningful.

LEVELS OF PLANNING

Too often when we think of planning we concentrate primarily on daily lesson plans. There are other levels that are significant to student learning that warrant careful consideration, and provide the context for daily planning. Figure 10.3 illustrates levels of planning and some of the factors that guide decision-making at each level. Long-range planning serves as a framework for unit planning. Unit planning provides a framework for both weekly and daily planning. By beginning with long-range planning, we are planning from whole to part.

Long-Range Planning

Long-range plans are comprehensive guides for facilitating learning involving student profiles,

> Long-range planning = Thinking ahead + Considering the big picture

content and sequencing, classroom management philosophy, instructional strategies, and overall organizational factors. Writing a long-range plan requires that we think ahead and consider the big picture.

Your district/school will probably require that you write a long-range plan for the school year. They may provide detailed guidelines for the plan and check to make sure certain elements are included. Even if you are not required to write a long-range plan, I strongly urge you to do so. Here are some key elements to include.

Student information—Develop a student profile by reading permanent files, looking at test scores, talking to teachers who have taught them, driving through the neighborhoods

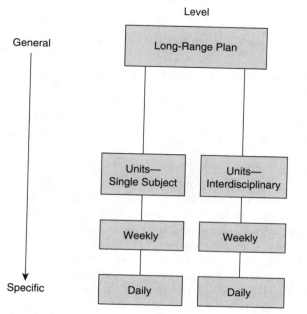

FIGURE 10.3   Levels of planning.

where your students live, considering socioeconomic factors such as free/reduced lunch status, and gauging student interests through some sort of survey in the first few days of school.

Content information—Identify the body of knowledge and skills that compose your course content.

Sequence—Determine the sequence of the content you will teach. Develop a time line.

Materials—List the instructional resources you will need to organize or order.

Assessment—Determine major forms of assessment for evaluating student progress.

Units of study—Determine large "chunks" of content that may be considered units of study.

Records—Select or design a system of record keeping for student progress and achievement.

Management—Develop rules, consequences, and procedures for classroom management, as well as noninstructional routines.

Communication—Determine ways to communicate with parents and the community.

Writing a long-range plan that includes all of these elements may seem like a daunting task, particularly if you don't have a mentor or teammates to emulate. Even if you do not produce a formal document to be reviewed, the process of thinking through the key elements and making notes concerning your plans will provide a structure for life in your classroom.

In her valuable book *Mapping the Big Picture,* Heidi Hayes Jacobs (1997) explains the concept of curriculum mapping and proposes teachers individually map, and then share their maps with teammates, grade levels, same subject area teachers, and others. Curriculum maps become a major part of long-range plans. Jacobs tells us that the major elements of a curriculum map are

- the process and skills emphasized;
- the content in terms of essential concepts and topics; and
- the products and performances that are the assessments of learning. (p. 8)

Curriculum maps are calendar based. They indicate what is taught and when it is taught, not in specific detail, but rather on a "macro level" (p. 8). Jacobs says to look for "repetitions, gaps, meaningful assessments, matches with standards, potential areas for integration, and timeliness" (p. 11).

We have considered what we know about student development and differences, simple curriculum mapping, and assessment and grading. The key elements of a long-range plan that we have not discussed deal with management and parent/community communication. These elements will be included in Chapters 11 and 12.

Developing and adjusting a long-range plan is part of being a reflective practitioner. Just as navigators rely on maps and charts to determine the track they want to follow from starting point to destination, teachers rely on plans and their decision-making abilities to effectively and efficiently orchestrate learning. Long-range plans should be thought of as working documents that are flexible enough to be altered to accommodate varied rates of learning or to respond to unforeseen events.

Single Subject Units

As you create your long-range plan, you will be sequencing major chunks of content and skills in your subject area. These chunks may be organized into manageable units of study through *single subject planning*. Simply going from topic to topic without organizing them into discrete units will likely seem disconnected and less meaningful than if topics are grouped together in a unit with a central theme. Moore (1999) tells us that a unit "links goals, objectives, content, activities and evaluations" (p. 119).

Most of the content and skills included in middle grades curriculum will fall neatly into units around themes. State standards and district curriculum guides are typically organized in ways that are "unit friendly" so that creating single subject units need not be forced or artificial. Because a theme is unifying, the whole, or unit, becomes more valuable than the sum of the parts, or individual lessons. A unit can provide context for learning by revolving around, and being based on, a big idea.

Basic steps.   Let's look at some basic steps that lead to the creation of a unit, followed by two specific views of unit design as found in books we have already visited in previous chapters, *Understanding by Design* (Wiggins & McTighe, 1998) and *Classroom Instruction That Works* (Marzano, Pickering, & Pollock, 2001). By considering three different approaches, we'll see common elements as well as variability in unit creation. There are no set rules. The premise is simple—connect learning and build on prior knowledge concerning a unifying big idea. Here are some basic steps:

1. *Select a suitable theme.* The theme may be obvious, such as westward settlement, the writings of Mark Twain, photosynthesis, or measurement, or it may be necessary to combine or divide topics as they occur in your long-range plan.

2. *Determine goals and specific objectives for the unit.* These may be spelled out for you in your state standards documents or district curriculum guides. As you examine goals and objectives you will likely see ways to incorporate standards that may not have been readily apparent. For instance, in a unit on measurement there will be many opportunities for students to practice, and even master, their knowledge and skills of working with fraction and decimal numbers. In a unit on photosynthesis there will be opportunities to discuss the earth's relationship to the sun and other concepts of astronomy.

3. *With your goals and objectives in mind, determine assessments that will gauge learning.* Keep in mind the broad array of assessments discussed in Chapter 9.

4. *Develop preassessments to determine prior knowledge.* This may be as simple as a K–W–L session (see Chapter 8) on the unit theme or as traditional as a paper-and-pencil test over the concepts of the unit.

5. *Involve students in unit planning.* Tell them the overall goals and give them a sense of where you are heading. Allow them to brainstorm projects and activities that relate to the theme. Incorporate as many of their ideas as possible.

6. *Develop an outline of the breadth of the unit and an approximate time line.* If you use a textbook as a primary source, determine how much of the text will be included. Be conscious

of the school calendar so that your timing makes sense and refer to your long-range plans to make sure your plans will allow for the other units you will teach during the year.

7. *Sequence learning objectives and make daily plans.* (More on daily planning in the next sections.)

8. *Gather resources and arrange for special events that will enhance the unit.* If books need to be reserved and videos ordered, see the media specialist. If guest speakers are desired, call them well in advance. If you want to use facilities other than your classroom, make the arrangements.

All of these steps may be taken independently or in collaboration with another teacher who teaches the same subject in the same grade level. Make sure your team knows about your unit planning. Hopefully you will discuss curriculum regularly so that each of you is aware of what's being taught and learned by teammates and students. The whole process of sharing long-range plans leads naturally into discussions of units of study.

Using WHERE.   Wiggins and McTighe (1998) detail design criteria or filters for developing quality units with the acronym WHERE. As you read the elements, compare them with the basic steps of unit planning.

1. W—"Where are we headed? Why are we headed there? What are the students' final performance obligations—the anchoring performance assessments?"

2. H—"Hook the students through engaging and provocative entry points: thought-provoking and focusing experiences, issues, oddities, problems and challenges that point toward essential and unit questions, core ideas, and final performance tasks."

3. E—"Explore and enable/equip. Engage students in learning experiences that allow them to explore the big ideas and essential questions. . . . Equip students for the final performances through guided instruction and coaching . . . "

4. R—"Reflect and rethink. . . .Guide students in self-assessment and self-adjustment, based on feedback from initial inquiry, results and discussion."

5. E—"Exhibit and evaluate. Reveal what has been understood through final performances and products. Involve students in a final self-assessment to identify remaining questions, set future goals, and point toward new units and lessons." (pp. 115–116)

Using the principles of WHERE makes the basic unit planning process richer and then takes us into the implementation phase.

Three Phases.   In *Classroom Instruction That Works* (Marzano, Pickering, & Pollock, 2001), we find a three-phase design for a unit that emphasizes the use of the nine categories of instructional strategies we discussed in Chapter 8. The design takes us from planning through implementation to post unit reflection.

Before looking at the phases of unit planning, let's refresh our memories concerning the nine categories of strategies that are proven to have a strong effect on student achievement. The letter designating each of the nine categories of strategies will be used to show how they relate to the three phases of unit planning.

A. Identifying similarities and differences.

B. Summarizing and notetaking.

C. Reinforcing effort and providing recognition.

D. Homework and practice.

E. Nonlinguistic representations.

F. Cooperative learning.

G. Setting objectives and providing feedback.

H. Generating and testing hypotheses.

I. Questions, cues, and advance organizers. (p. 146)

Marzano and colleagues (2001) incorporate these nine categories of strategies into beginning, during, and ending phases of unit planning. The letters in parentheses indicate when the nine strategies are directly addressed.

Phase One is the beginning of the unit: This is when teachers and students identify and record goals (G).

Phase Two is lengthy and involves the monitoring of learning goals: Students keep track of what they accomplish (C) and receive feedback to reinforce their efforts and self-assess (G). New knowledge is introduced, practiced, reviewed, and applied, prior knowledge is assessed (I), advance organizers are presented (I), and students compare prior knowledge with new knowledge (A). Students take notes (B) and find ways to represent their knowledge (E), both individually and in groups (F). Homework is assigned (D) and work is done on projects involving hypotheses (A).

Phase Three is the end of the unit: In this phase, the teacher's role is to provide clear assessments of student progress (C, G). Students are asked to self-assess and articulate and demonstrate what they have learned (B, E).

When planning your first single subject unit, follow the basic steps and consider what the authors of *Understanding by Design* and *Classroom Instruction That Works* tell us about enhancing student achievement.

Interdisciplinary Units

Think back to the discussion of levels of integration in Chapter 6. You will recall that not only are there a variety of philosophies concerning curriculum integration, there is also a semantics dilemma as various practitioners and authors use different words to describe basically the same practices. As stated in Chapter 6, anytime connections are made among concepts, within or among subject areas, our students benefit, whether the connections are labeled complementary, multidisciplinary, interdisciplinary, or integrative.

Gatewood (1998), a former president of NMSA and an advocate of realistic approaches to middle school practices, states that interdisciplinary connections "can be practical, realistic, and sound ways to integrate curriculum that can work in the real world of large, diverse schools and classrooms" (p. 40). Rather than revolving the entire curriculum around student-generated themes, Gatewood urges teachers to find and teach the natural links among subject areas. Developing and implementing an interdisciplinary unit once each semester can make the most of these natural links while preserving opportunities for students to be "thoroughly grounded and prepared with a strong and rigorous base of problem solving skills and knowledge within disciplines" (p. 40).

I use the term **interdisciplinary** because it expresses the cooperative nature of the unit we will discuss. A well-planned interdisciplinary unit can energize teachers and students and create meaningful learning opportunities for all involved. As you might imagine, there are numerous approaches for developing units and even more numerous possibilities for implementing them. I hope your interest will lead you to seek out, read, and use books and articles on the topic. What you are about to read is only the proverbial tip of the interdisciplinary unit (IDU) iceberg.

Creating an interdisciplinary unit.   Let's explore the basic steps necessary for the creation of an *interdisciplinary unit.* Each step is important, but the order of accomplishing the steps can vary depending on individual schools, team organization, or even the topic or theme chosen. Some teams might have units already written or previously implemented that may only need to be tweaked to make them more effective and engaging. A unit requires interest and communication among each of the teachers involved, along with ample time together to plan.

1. *Choose a theme.* The choice of a theme is crucial. By comparing long-range plans it is possible for teams to choose a theme that accommodates the standards of each subject area. Typically we think of themes as either content based or concept based. A content theme is something tangible or specific, such as airplanes, Native Americans, Middle Ages, or the environment. There is nothing wrong with a content theme as long as related concepts become the focus of lessons and activities. According to Tomlinson (1998), "Concepts . . . are building blocks of meaning of any area of study. A concept is a category or class of things with shared commonalities" (p. 5). A concept related to airplanes is flight. Flight is a richer theme than airplanes. In an IDU with a theme of airplanes we can certainly talk about flight. If the IDU theme is flight, however, we can deal with airplanes and much more. An IDU with a theme of Native Americans can deal with culture, heritage, and gentrification. An IDU with a theme of heritage can certainly deal with Native Americans plus much more.

   Creating an IDU with a concept theme increases the possibilities of subject area standards being included in authentic and meaningful ways. Examples of concepts include change, conflict, interdependence, patterns, and power. Tomlinson (1998) tells us that a concept will be an effective unit theme if it fulfills the conditions listed in Figure 10.4.

2. *Develop essential questions and big ideas.* Heidi Hayes Jacobs (1997) writes, "When composing a unit of study . . . creating meaningful and clear essential questions can serve as scope and sequence to the structure of the study" (p. 29). She compares essential questions to a table of contents as they guide students through the unit. She says that essential questions frame the essence of what your class can realistically examine in the amount of time you have to spend. Now is also the time for all subject area teachers involved to closely examine standards documents to ensure that relevant standards are included within the unit.

   The answers to essential questions, which may be many and varied, contribute to the big ideas of the unit. Think of the big ideas of a unit as the principles every student should take away from the unit. These are widely accepted ideas within our shared culture.

A concept will be an effective unit theme if it

- applies broadly and persuasively within and/or across subjects
- shows fundamental patterns essential to the areas studied and students' lives
- reveals similarities and differences
- is likely to connect with students' experiences and understandings
- fosters creative and critical thinking
- is valid for the disciplines in which it will be used
- will continue to evolve as the student grows in thinking and learning over years
- promotes in students a sense of what it means to be an effective, contributing human being in a complex world

FIGURE 10.4   Effectiveness of concepts as unit themes.

Source: From "For Integration and Differentiation Choose Concepts Over Topics," by C. A. Tomlinson, 1998, *Middle School Journal, 30*(2), pp. 3–8. Copyright 1998 by National Middle School Association. Adapted with permission from National Middle School Association.

Figure 10.5 includes additional concepts accompanying the theme of Celebrating Differences along with essential questions, big ideas, and a basic subject web.

3. *Web the theme.* Using a simple graphic organizer, the theme/subject web, the team members and related arts teachers should spend considerable time brainstorming ways to use standards, activities, research, readings, etc., to address the theme. This can be a very invigorating exercise for teachers as we consider our own subject area(s) as well as a wider view of all possible connections. As a math teacher, I may have a vague recollection of a song that relates to a particular theme. I hum a line or two and the music teacher recognizes the tune and proceeds to fill in the lyrics that directly relate to the theme. I have experienced brainstorming sessions like this and have found them to not only be productive, but great fun! It's a teacher/team activity that reveals teacher interests and talents that may otherwise lay dormant.

Now include students in this successful and enjoyable webbing experience. Hold on—they'll surprise you with their ideas and energy. Pick a time frame, perhaps advisory or a common time taken from a block of team time, for each team teacher to conduct a brainstorming session with a group of students. Put the theme in the middle of a web on the board or a transparency. Tell students that you want their help in planning a study of whatever the theme is and ask them for ideas. Because you have already had the benefit of thinking with others about the theme, you'll be able to prompt with suggestions if there is a lull. Remember that inviting and implementing student-generated curriculum infuses developmental responsiveness into our classrooms.

4. *Plan beginning, culminating, and schedule-changing events.* Let the brainstorming session(s) "gel" for a day or so and then plan the major events of the unit. Walking into class on a Monday morning and saying, "For the next few weeks we're going to study

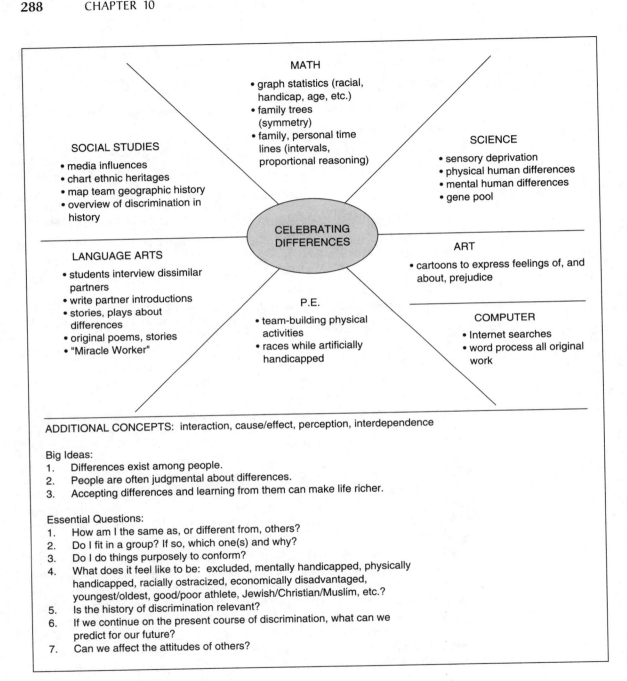

FIGURE 10.5 Celebrating differences.

flight as it relates to living things. Please get out your textbooks and turn to page 146 and begin reading about Orville and Wilbur Wright" effectively takes a great theme like flight and turns it into instant drudgery. Try this scenario instead:

Gather your team into a large dark room. Play a recording of bees buzzing, then bird wings flapping, then geese honking, then helicopter blades whirling, and then jets soaring. On a large screen show footage of a rocket launch and then the historic "One small step for man, one giant leap for mankind" sequence. Then turn up the lights and announce that for three weeks we will study flight in many forms and human's quest to soar. Now **that's** the way to begin a unit!

It takes planning—from an attention-garnering beginning through schedule-changing events to a meaningful and unforgettable culmination. Guest speakers, field trips, research projects, community involvement, permission forms, bus transportation, parent participation, supply gathering, and more all take time to arrange. Where imagination takes you, and practical/realistic constraints allow you to go, plan ahead and enjoy the process.

5. *Write daily plans.* In the next section of this chapter we'll discuss writing daily lesson plans. For the sake of this discussion of units, I'll simply say that this step will make or break the cohesiveness of any unit. A meaningful and well-written unit depends on the everyday classroom experiences to draw together the connections related to the theme within and among the subject areas. For instance, the study of aerodynamics, the examination of statistics of passenger airline service, analysis of the significance of President Kennedy's inaugural promise of a man on the moon within a decade, and the study of literature about man's quest to fly all require careful planning and coordination within the unit time frame.

As teachers begin planning what, when, and how to teach aspects of a unit, they need to talk frequently and share tentative plans. There will be overlaps and obvious connections on which to capitalize. Some topics and activities may be jointly approached because subject area boundaries are blurred. Combining classes, co-teaching, supporting activities, lengthening/shortening class time—so many educationally sound variations are possible within an interdisciplinary unit.

6. *Plan assessments.* In step two, the essential questions and big ideas are planned, fulfilling the concept of backward design. We know what we want to accomplish in the unit. Once teachers have talked through the parameters of the unit (what, when, how), it's time to view the unit as a whole. In this step we create ways of determining what students know and are able to do as a result of the unit.

This is not a time for "assessment as usual." Units present wonderful opportunities for combining subject standards in projects and group activities. Students could develop portfolios of their unit work, present a simulation of an event that demonstrates understanding, conduct a research project individually or in groups that incorporates big ideas and new vocabulary, and perform in many other authentic ways.

You might want to approach the students and ask, "How will I know you know this stuff?" They will undoubtedly surprise you with unusual assessment ideas. For instance, when asked this question in connection with a unit based on the theme of flight, one 12-year-old suggested that he make a set of wings for our principal using what he would learn about flight. The principal would then jump off the second-story roof. If he could fly, then learning had taken place. If not, oh well. We all had a good laugh (and, fortunately, so did the principal as the story was told during a faculty meeting).

The suggestion broke the ice and students brainstormed other ways that actually became part of the unit assessment plan. All of the student suggestions were experiential in nature. This is an example, along with the discussion in step 3, of what Erlandson and McVittie (2001) reported in the *Middle School Journal* when they wrote: "Collaborating with our students in planning . . . which included experiential, hands-on activities they had a voice in designating or selecting, would demonstrate our commitment to ensuring that the curriculum is both personally relevant and meaningful to our students" (p. 35).

7. *View unit as a whole.* Several weeks before implementation, teams need to reexamine the big picture of the unit and focus on support issues. Here are some examples of questions to address:

   - Are all the planned activities meaningful with opportunities for higher-order thinking?
   - Have all arrangements been made? Facilities reserved, permission forms written, phone calls made, materials ordered, transportation confirmed?
   - Have we been realistic in our planning, or overly ambitious?
   - Are the media specialist and others aware of our plans and prepared for the increase in activity resulting from the unit?
   - Has everyone who would be affected by schedule changes been informed?
   - Have responsibilities been equitably delegated?

   As with most anything we undertake in middle grades education, flexibility should rule. We pay attention to our students' needs and follow their lead when possible. When planning a unit, always have mechanisms for monitoring and adjusting. As with any planning and implementation, if something isn't working, change it and move forward.

8. *Enjoy the unit.*

9. *Evaluate the unit.* Allow everyone involved to give feedback. Team teachers and related arts teachers all need to give detailed feedback in a meeting and/or in writing. Debriefing is vital to future success. Figure 10.6 provides sample topics to consider.

   Provide comment/suggestion forms for guest speakers, administrators, personnel at field trip locations, administrators, even parents. If you call a parent and say, "We'd like your feedback on the unit we just finished" and the parent replies "What unit?" there's a good chance that the impact on your students was not what you had hoped. Along with unit-related questions, give parents and community participants an opportunity to comment on their interactions with students. In the middle grades, we understand our responsibility to teach the whole child, including the maturing process, attitudes, and behaviors.

   Asking students to evaluate a unit, or anything else for that matter, requires that our adult egos be intact for young adolescent honesty to be considered rationally. Most students will respond to our surveys thoughtfully and with candor, but be aware that there are boyfriend/girlfriend breakups, "I can't say anything positive" attitudes, and "Hey, it will be fun to write nasty stuff" mindsets that may enter

Unit _____   Team _____   Date _____

1. Did the plans address the big ideas?

2. Did the plans address essential questions?

3. Were all subject area standards adequately addressed?

4. Did all students have the opportunity to succeed?

5. Were all students challenged in some way?

6. Were higher-order thinking skills promoted?

7. Were all levels of Bloom's taxonomy addressed?

8. Was the pace of the unit satisfactory?

9. Are there other resources that may have enhanced the unit?

10. Were the student assessments appropriate?

11. Was there a balance of independent work and group work?

12. Have we asked the students to evaluate the unit?

13. Have we involved the appropriate people in debriefing the unit?

14. Was there school-wide or community involvement/interest in the unit?

15. Was the unit successful enough to justify the time and effort it took to plan and implement?

FIGURE 10.6   Unit evaluation for teachers.

the picture. So hold on to your hat when you try a student evaluation similar to Figure 10.7.

10. *Make a detailed log of the unit.* It's very important to keep a comprehensive summary of the planning, implementation, and feedback for each unit. I suggest a three-ring binder to organize plans, lessons, notes, resources, phone numbers, Web sites, evaluations, pictures— all the artifacts you can gather. While you may think the unit will remain fresh in your memory, there are details and reminders that will slip your consciousness by the time you want to implement the unit again. A review/critique session and a comprehensive log actually serve to make the next implementation less work. Why reinvent the wheel each time?

Name _____ Unit _____ Date _____

1. Three of the most important or interesting things I learned:

_____

_____

2. One question I still have is:

_____

_____

3. The thing(s) I liked best about this unit:

_____

_____

_____

4. The thing(s) I liked least about this unit:

_____

_____

_____

5. If my teachers do this unit again, I would recommend that they:

_____

_____

6. Here are some unit themes I would enjoy:

_____

_____

7. Comments and suggestions:

FIGURE 10.7 Unit evaluation for students.

In their book *Integrated Studies in the Middle Grades* (subtitled appropriately "Dancing Through Walls"), Stevenson and Carr (1993) provide excellent guidelines and advice for connecting the curriculum through units. They tell us to "think expansively but start small" (p. 194). They suggest replicating units that have been successfully implemented before. Along these same lines, it's fine to get ideas and actual lessons from teacher resource books and Internet sites. There's a wealth of resources available.

Standard 3

Knowledge 1: Middle level teacher candidates understand that middle level curriculum should be relevant, challenging, integrative, and exploratory.

Disposition 4: Middle level teacher candidates realize the importance of connecting curriculum and assessment to the needs, interests, and experiences of all young adolescents.

Disposition 5: Middle level teacher candidates are committed to implementing an integrated curriculum that accommodates and supports the learning of all young adolescents.

Performance 2: Middle level teacher candidates use current knowledge and standards from multiple subject areas in planning, integrating, and implementing curriculum.

Performance 3: Middle level teacher candidates incorporate the ideas, interests, and experiences of all young adolescents in curriculum.

Performance 4: Middle level teacher candidates develop and teach an integrated curriculum.

Performance 6: Middle level teacher candidates provide all young adolescents with multiple opportunities to learn in integrated ways.

Standard 4

Knowledge 2: Middle level teacher candidates know how to use content knowledge to make interdisciplinary connections.

Disposition 2: Middle level teacher candidates are committed to the importance of integrating content.

Performance 4: Middle level teacher candidates teach in ways that help all young adolescents understand the integrated nature of knowledge.

Daily Lesson Planning

The quality of day-to-day classroom experiences depends in large measure on the quality of teacher-designed lesson plans. You have probably been exposed to several philosophies of, and

---
Quality of planning = Quality of classroom experiences
---

formats for, lesson planning. There is no one right way to plan a lesson. The variability of our students and our subject areas determine appropriate approaches.

Very few teachers can "wing it" successfully, at least not for long or all the time. Certainly experience helps, but the process of writing a lesson plan in an organized way is beneficial to 30-year veterans as well as first-year teachers.

The mere act of putting in writing what we envision for our time with students will lead to more ideas, changes that will enhance, material/resource reminders, and structuring that will alert us to gaps. Thoughtful planning will

- clarify instructional objectives
- give confidence and security
- determine instructional strategies
- clarify appropriate assessments of learning
- guide material and resource selection (Burden & Byrd, 1999)

You have probably seen lesson plan books in resource stores or in classrooms during field experiences. Could all the information needed to do the things mentioned in the previous paragraph possibly fit in a 2-inch by 2-inch square? Absolutely not! What plan books do is provide overviews, usually a week at a time. They serve a valuable purpose in that they give us a bird's-eye view of our weeks. They help organize and sequence days and structure whole weeks. Many administrators require teachers to submit copies of a week's worth of plans on Friday or Monday. This accountability check is necessary, unfortunately, as an impetus for some teachers to structure their content and delivery practices. Teachers who thoughtfully plan with or without periodic accountability checks shouldn't mind administrative oversight. The weekly plan book is actually a great way to map out 5 days at a time within a single subject or interdisciplinary unit. For instance, if you know from unit planning that you will spend 4 weeks on Egypt and Egyptian history in sixth grade social studies, dividing the unit into four major chunks will help organize and give direction to your unit.

Keeping a three-ring binder of daily plans is a positive habit you will value more and more with time. When you have thorough, written plans, it is simple to transfer the main points to a weekly planner. The binder provides a complete picture of classroom activities that will aid in future planning.

Components of lessons.   Regardless of the lesson planning format you choose, there are basic components to consider when structuring a class period. Not every component will be present in every class period. Many times your basic plan will extend into a second, or even a third, day. The components of a lesson have been described by many authors and delineated in school and school district guidelines. One of the most well-known experts on lesson planning is the late Madeline Hunter. While she is credited with putting understandable structure into direct instruction, the components advocated by Hunter (1984) are basic and valuable in most any lesson planning. Here is an overview of the components, based loosely on Hunter.

1. *Anticipatory Set.* This is the beginning of the lesson that helps learners focus on what's ahead. Focus can be established in many ways. You might want to try . . .
   - reading a current events article
   - telling a brief story or joke
   - placing an object in the room to garner attention
   - projecting a picture on the ceiling

- demonstrating something interesting
- asking a provocative question

Just as the beginning of a unit is important to its success, the beginning of a lesson makes the difference between our students anticipating what's ahead and simply following along when and where they are led.

2. *Objective Clarification.* Thoughtful planning will include a clear view of the lesson's objectives, often established through state content standards. Just as rubrics let students know expectations for products, objectives tell students what they are expected to learn and be able to do as a result of the lessons. A clear objective communicated to students, along with an attention-getting anticipatory set, will "kick start" a lesson.

3. *Presentation of New Knowledge and Skills.* This step is wide open in terms of instructional strategies. All of the strategies discussed in Chapters 7 and 8 may be used in this step of lesson planning. The decisions we make about the appropriateness of strategies based on the content, and student interests and needs, must be made during the planning process, as well as decisions about individual and/or group work.

4. *Guided Practice with Feedback.* Practice can take many forms, depending on the content, skills, and classroom circumstances. If what has been taught/learned can be practiced in a traditional paper-and-pencil way, then it is entirely appropriate. If, however, practice involves a more authentic approach, then students may attempt to replicate a demonstration, perform a skill, respond to questioning, and so forth. Guided practice typically occurs during class and is brief enough to allow time for feedback. Teachers may choose to post answers or results and ask students to determine their own success. Students working in pairs or small groups may check each other's work as feedback. Teachers may "spot check" or simply ask students if there are problems or questions. Whatever the method, it's important to gauge student understanding of reasonable chunks of content and skills before moving on to independent practice or new knowledge and skills.

Further student inquiry or reteaching may be necessary. The results of the guided practice will tell us. This part of the planning step cannot be bypassed. As you give feedback or receive information about student understanding, you will need to make decisions about continuing whatever strategies you used in step 3 or changing gears to other instructional strategies. Flexibility is a must throughout the planning process, and nowhere more than in the Guided Practice with Feedback phase. Experience helps, but we are all occasionally surprised by the levels of understanding, as well as the pace of understanding, whether rapid or halting.

5. *Assignment of Independent Practice.* While guided practice generally takes place in class, independent practice usually amounts to homework. A discussion of homework comes later. Holding students accountable for completing independent practice is important and worthy of careful consideration. Not everything students do requires a grade, but students need their work acknowledged and, when not complete, they need a consequence. Finding a balance where independent practice is valuable to student learning and valued by them as a means to greater understanding and proficiency is one of our planning challenges.

6. *Closure.* A lesson should not end because the bell rings. Flexibility dictates that we not insist on completing all we have planned in a class period just because we wrote it as a class period "package." Closure may come about as planned in the form of summarizing the lesson, asking students to do a brief reflection exercise, or discussing how the lesson relates to what's ahead. Then again, you may glance at the clock and discover you have 4 minutes left and your lesson is still in the Guided Practice with Feedback phase. Regardless of the phase, you need to focus the students' attention on a closure that helps them see what has been accomplished during the class period and a brief comment about what's to come.

Formats for lesson planning.   The basic components of a lesson can be formatted in many ways. Figure 10.8 shows a commonly used planning form that includes aspects of standards and student variability. Forms such as this one work well because they remind us to include important components. I often need much more space than a single sheet of paper provides. Some lessons need to be "scripted" to a greater extent than others. For instance, if my lesson involves the examination of characters in a short story, I know that appropriate questions to direct student thinking need to be planned and organized. I would want to write the questions I plan to use to elicit thoughtful responses. On the lesson form I may write "Lead class discussion of characters by asking questions." Then I would attach a sheet of the questions.

Middle grades students are wonderfully creative and imaginative. If part of the planned lesson brings out these traits and learning is taking place that perhaps wasn't part of what you anticipated, allow yourself enough flexibility to go with the momentum. On the other hand, if a concept or skill you assumed to be either already mastered or easily grasped turns out to be surprisingly difficult or time-consuming, be ready to slow down, change strategies, reteach, or simply allow time for processing. Madeline Hunter is perhaps most famous for the phrase "monitor and adjust." Effective teachers are sensitive to levels and pace of student understanding and are willing and able to direct classroom activities to accommodate needs.

Varying class lengths.   Chapter 5 helped us understand that class lengths vary greatly in middle schools. Some may be as brief as 45 minutes and others as long as 100 minutes. Teams that use the flexible blocks may occasionally have classes that are 2 to 3 hours long. The strategies discussed in Chapters 7 and 8 may be more or less appropriate depending on the length of the class period. The value of knowing about, and having experienced, a wide variety of strategies is that we can pick and choose what will be best, given the circumstances of the day.

As you plan for a class, keep in mind that there are few activities or assignments that will engage young adolescents for more than 20 minutes or so at a time. A lab experiment, an active group project, or an invigorating class discussion may be exceptions, but planning for variety is the best policy. A brief class period may require only two distinct changes of pace, while a longer block of time may require five or six different activities/strategies to motivate and engage students.

Planning for a longer block of time is not as simple as putting two short plans together back to back. The need to check for understanding will be different, the pacing of activities

Teacher _____ Class _____ Date _____

Standards to be addressed:

Lesson objective(s):

Opening:

Procedures:

Whole group—

Small group—

Individual—

Plan for differentiation—

Guided practice:

Feedback:

Independent practice:

Assessment:

Closure:

Materials and resources:

FIGURE 10.8 Sample lesson plan format.

will vary, assessments may change in both nature and scope, and independent practice will certainly be different from the simple combination of two separate assignments. As discussed in Chapter 5, longer blocks of time with our students have many benefits, and the thorough nature of the planning process that is needed to effectively use the gift of more time is worth the effort.

Practical advice.   Here are some tips to consider when planning lessons:

1. Overplan rather than underplan to avoid wasting valuable class time. It's much easier to eliminate plan elements than it is to improvise in meaningful ways.
2. Check for levels of Bloom's taxonomy, use of multiple intelligences theory, differentiation to meet student needs—all the aspects that help ensure effective instruction.
3. Regardless of where you are in your plan, allow time for closure that wraps up the lesson.
4. Never leave school without a written plan for the following day.
5. Gather materials and arrange for resources at least a day ahead. The copier seems to know when we wait until the last minute and breaks down to teach us to plan ahead!
6. Be flexible. This is possible when we know the content, practice a variety of instructional strategies, and plan thoughtfully. Interruptions happen. They are inevitable. Altering our plans may be necessary for academic reasons as well as any number of other occurrences totally outside our control.
7. Spend time reflecting on lessons. Consider what worked well, what could have been better, and how to alter/adapt plans to be used in the future. Remember, there's always tomorrow. We can fill in gaps and make adjustments in the following day's plans if we take the time to reflect on our lessons.
8. Keep notes about the things you might change or add as resources for future planning.

Homework.   For every ardent supporter of homework you may find a naysayer. Harris Cooper (2001), a noted expert on the topic, tells us that the homework controversy is not new and will likely never be resolved. His research shows that every 15 years or so there's an outcry alternately for more or less homework. The call for increased homework coincided with the launch of *Sputnik* in the 1950s, while in the late 1960s homework was viewed as undue pressure on students. Following the publishing of *A Nation at Risk* in 1983, homework gained favor. In the late 1990s concern grew over stressed-out students and overworked parents.

Opinions aside, Cooper conducted a meta-analysis of the relationship of homework to academic achievement. He found that for elementary students assigning homework has little, if any, effect on achievement. For high school students, the benefits of being assigned and completing homework are substantial. For middle school students, the benefits are more evident than for elementary students, but no more than half as effective as for high school students. Cooper says that for young adolescents, improvement in achievement appears to continue through about an hour or so of homework and with more than an hour, achievement does not improve.

There are so many variables when it comes to why students complete, or do not complete, homework. Home circumstances play a role. Some students have quiet study areas and adults who check assignment pads and encourage students to do their homework. Then there are the rest of the students. While many believe that education is the "great equalizer," homework definitely is not. We can provide equal working conditions in our classrooms, but the home is basically outside our realm of control. A principal I know recently posed a question to a large gathering of teachers. He asked, "At what point do students stop doing homework?" Most teachers answered with grade level guesses. The principal then said, "No, it's when their parents no longer understand the material." Thought provoking, isn't it?

Homework—to assign or not, how much, what kind, what percentage of the grade it will be worth—should be a matter of team concern. One of the beauties of middle grades teaming is the possibility of coordinating the whole school experience for our students. The answers to the questions about homework should be guided by the needs and characteristics of our students.

If homework is assigned, then students should be held accountable for turning it in and given some sort of credit. To assign it and never require that it be completed is unfair to students and to the process. If it's important enough for students to use their out-of-school time to complete, then it's important enough to warrant checking, at least for completion or attempted completion. I view homework (and tests, papers, any assignment) as so important that I feel a strong obligation to provide as rapid feedback to students as possible. At the college level, I aim for returning student work with comments by the next class period and view the "midnight oil" it sometimes requires as well worth it. My students are demonstratively appreciative of the extra effort. Middle school students need immediate (or close to it) feedback to enhance their knowledge and skill building. Homework can be used to build responsibility in our students as it reinforces learning. We can model responsibility with our respect and acknowledgment of their efforts.

Not every student will turn in homework on time. As in every other area there is a great deal of variability. One way to attempt to instill personal responsibility in students is to not only require work, even if late, to be completed, but to also require documentation as to why the work was not completed on time. A form similar to Figure 10.9 may work for your classroom, and perhaps for your whole team.

When assigning homework, here are some ideas to consider:

- Arrange with your team/school to provide an after-school setting for students who want to stay to complete assignments.
- Check homework every time it is assigned to provide feedback, but only record grades for homework periodically.
- Give assignments in advance if appropriate, especially if they will be due following a holiday or on a Monday.
- Make homework only a small percentage of the total grade.
- Allow students to take "open homework" quizzes and tests occasionally as an extra motivation to complete assignments.

We need to think about **designing** homework, as well as **assigning** homework. Instead of asking students to answer questions about a section, we might ask them to write questions about what they read using question stems associated with Bloom's taxonomy. Or maybe we could ask students to talk to three others about a current events issue and take notes on their responses. When math practice is needed, 10 problems will often do as much good as 40.

Name _____ Class _____

Today's date _____ Date assignment was due _____

Assignment _____

I did not turn in this assignment on time because
(check all that apply)

_____ I was absent on _____ .

_____ I forgot to do it.

_____ I did not understand how to do it.

_____ I had extra home duties including _____ .

_____ I did not take the right materials home.

_____ I did not have the assignment written down.

_____ I did it, but left it at home.

_____ I did it, but could not find it when it was time to turn it in.

Here is what I plan to do to make sure my assignments are completed and turned in
on time.

_____

_____

_____

_____ (signature)

FIGURE 10.9   Student responsibility form.

Cooper (2001) proposes the "ten minute rule" which says the optimum time homework should require is 10 minutes per grade level. So, sixth graders should have 60 minutes maximum (total for all subjects), seventh graders 70 minutes, and eighth graders 80 minutes. Making homework reasonable, as interesting as possible, and doable without parental assistance will encourage students to complete it.

REFLECTIONS ON PLANNING

In the introduction to this chapter I stated that with experience we become more comfortable with the planning process. Exactly what will experience do for us in this process? Now that you have a glimpse at what's involved in long-range, unit, and daily planning, consider some benefits experience will bring.

- Your understanding of the content you teach will be deeper and broader allowing for more within-discipline and among-discipline connections to be made naturally as you plan.
- You will have a larger toolbox of instructional strategies to use in your planning.
- You will become more confident in your knowledge of student development leading to the ability to be more responsive to the needs of young adolescents.
- Your peripheral vision in the classroom will grow wider to allow for more effective observation of students.
- You will know more about available materials and resources to use in lesson planning.
- Your lesson planning will become more sophisticated as you understand how to use student prior knowledge to build on the potential of your class.

Most of us find ourselves in charge of a middle grades classroom and 70 to 120 students with only part of a semester of student teaching under our belts. All the benefits of experience lie out ahead of us as we mature in the teaching profession.

Planning is a series of decisions, each building on other decisions. Thorough, thoughtful, written plans determine to a large extent the learning that happens in your classroom.

Group Activities

1. In pairs, interview a teacher in one of the local schools in your school files. Ask the teachers for information concerning:

   homework policy

   long-range planning

   frequency of interdisciplinary units

   lesson planning formats

   If possible, obtain copies of long-range plans, formats for planning, and IDU plans to share with the class.

2. In groups of three or four, brainstorm ways to involve students in the planning process.
3. Form groups composed of different subject area concentrations. Agree on an interdisciplinary theme and create a web of possible topics/ideas similar to Figure 10.6. Include relevant concepts. Be prepared to explain your web to the whole class.

Individual Activities

1. Briefly describe the memory enhancing devices that work for you. Be prepared to share with the class.

2. Choose a subject area and find at least three Web sites that provide subject-specific resources that are user friendly and free.

3. Did you experience an interdisciplinary unit when you were in middle school? If so, briefly describe its impact. If more than one, list the themes you can remember. If not, describe other ways you may have experienced subject connection.

Personal Journal

1. Write about your memories of homework in the middle grades. Did you have a place at home conducive to completing academic work? Were your parents or siblings encouraging and helpful? Were you conscientious about completing independent practice assignments?

2. Do you have the organizational and time management skills to regularly develop thoughtful, written lesson plans? List reasons for an affirmative answer. Think of habits to create or break that may help you develop necessary skills if you feel this is a weak area for you.

Professional Practice

(It would be helpful to reread the descriptions of Marcus Hughes and Jennifer Blakely in Chapter 4, as well as the descriptions of Allison, Jeanetta, Darlene, and Lee in Chapters 2 and 3. These teachers and students are also featured in the Chapters 3 and 4 Professional Practice sections.)

Marcus Hughes and Jennifer Blakely both did their student teaching at Harvest Middle School. Mr. Jenkins, the principal, was quite pleased with their abilities and potential and offered them positions in eighth grade science and eighth grade language arts, respectively. They both accepted the positions as they joined the Stars team with two veteran teachers, Ms. Langley in social studies and Mr. White in math. They completed their first year as a team and are pleased with their camaraderie and effectiveness with students.

Marcus Hughes and Jennifer Blakely

Following a conference in June that focused on instructional leadership, Mr. Jenkins returned to his duties as principal fired up about the possibilities offered through well-planned interdisciplinary units. At the conference he learned about research on, and resources for, the creation and implementation of units. Fully aware that the teachers at Harvest occasionally made purposeful efforts to connect the subject areas, and that several teams had conducted versions of interdisciplinary units, Mr. Jenkins determined to encourage widespread use of the principles of connecting the curriculum.

Impressed with the Stars, Mr. Jenkins decided to make a pitch to them for the development of a comprehensive unit. He called each of the four teachers and asked them to join him for lunch. He offered to pay them a stipend to work together for a week or so during July to develop a unit. He pledged resources and support. The four teachers caught their principal's enthusiasm and agreed to accept the challenge. They left the luncheon, having set their meeting dates and pledging to give thought to possible themes.

They met in July and began discussing themes. Not surprisingly, Mr. Hughes and Ms. Blakely had the same idea. When they student taught, they shared Darlene as a student. When she was in elementary school her cousin who was a firefighter died in the World Trade Center tragedy. As a sixth grader Darlene had shared mementos from the event and poems she had written to express her family's grief and pride. Both Mr. Hughes and Ms. Blakely had been moved by Darlene's response to what occurred on September 11, 2001. Ms. Langley and Mr. White agreed that a unit revolving around 9/11 would be appropriate for their eighth graders, so they began the task of planning an interdisciplinary unit.

Darlene and Lee, eighth grade

Allison and Jeanetta, eighth grade

1. The team decides that the following tasks must be done. How should the tasks be sequenced to allow for the most efficient planning?

(A) Develop essential questions relating to the theme.

(B) Arrange to obtain selected videos of news coverage.

(C) Write parent letter explaining the unit, and specifically the group projects.

(D) Brainstorm subject area web prior to planning activities.

   a. A, B, C, D

   b. C, A, D, B

   c. A, D, B, C

   d. A, C, D, B

2. The team wants their students to work in small groups to develop a project that deals with either the cause of the tragedy and events leading to it, or the aftermath marked by renewed patriotism and national pride. As eighth graders, Darlene, Lee, Allison, and Jeanetta will be a group. Knowing what we know about these students from Chapters 2, 3, and 4, which is the least likely scenario?

(a) Allison will shy away from the subject of renewed patriotism because of her general lack of enthusiasm.

(b) Darlene will contribute in sensitive and thoughtful ways.

(c) Jeanetta will cooperate and do her part with the project.

(d) Lee will have considerable information to contribute because of his penchant for reading.

3. As the teachers work together it becomes obvious that language arts and social studies standards are more naturally addressed in the unit. As a math teacher, Mr. White

(a) should agree to spend several days during the 3-week unit showing videos related to the unit to free up more time in language arts and social studies.

(b) is justified in feeling compelled to help with the unit planning and assist with whole team activities, but elects to proceed with his math curriculum without alteration.

(c) would best support the needs of his students by compacting the planned 3-week math curriculum before and after the unit in order to support the unit fully, as well as mathematically, when possible.

(d) should incorporate as much unit-related mathematics in accordance with state standards as he feels is reasonable and otherwise carry on with his planned curriculum.

Constructed Response

The Stars team feels strongly that student involvement in planning is important. They consistently solicit and use student ideas. Because this interdisciplinary unit will culminate on September 11 and school begins August 18, most of the plans for the unit will need to be finalized before the students arrive. In what ways might the Stars teachers allow students to have input in the direction of the unit, or portions of the unit? Support your ideas with components of middle level philosophy.

Internet Resources

AskERIC Lesson Plan Collection
http://ericir.syr.edu/Virtual/Lessons

This site is part of the Educational Resources Information Center (ERIC), a service funded by the U.S. Department of Education. It provides more than 2,000 unique teacher-written lesson plans organized by subject area and grade level.

Education World
http://www.educationworld.com

This large site is loaded with practical information and strategies to assist teachers with lesson planning. There's a section titled "Tips for New Teachers," as well as information on the use of technology in classroom instruction.

Teachers Network
http://teachnet.org

References

Beane, J. A. (1993). *A middle school curriculum: From rhetoric to reality* (2nd ed.). Columbus, OH: National Middle School Association.

Burden, P. R., & Byrd, D. M. (1999). *Methods for effective teaching.* Boston: Allyn & Bacon.

Callahan, J. F., Clark, L. H., & Kellough, R. D. (2002). *Teaching in the middle and secondary schools.* Upper Saddle River, NJ: Merrill/Prentice Hall.

Cooper, H. (2001). Homework for all—in moderation. *Educational Leadership, 58*(7), 34–38.

Dyck, B. A. (2002). Hovering: Teaching the adolescent brain how to think. *Middle Ground, 5*(5), 18–22.

Erlandson, C., & McVittie, J. (2001). Student voices on integrative curriculum. *Middle School Journal, 33*(2), 28 & 36.

Gatewood, T. (1998). How valid is integrated curriculum in today's middle schools? *Middle School Journal, 29*(4), 38–41.

Gunter, M. A., Estes, T. H., & Schwab, J. (1999). *Instruction: A models approach* (3rd ed.). Boston: Allyn & Bacon.

Hunter, M. (1984). Knowing, teaching, and supervising. In P. L. Hosford (Ed.), *Using what we know about teaching* (pp. 169–192). Alexandria, VA: Association for Supervision and Curriculum Development.

Jacobs, H. H. (1997). *Mapping the big picture: Integrating curriculum and assessment K–12.* Alexandria, VA: Association for Supervision and Curriculum Development.

Marzano, R. J., Pickering, D. J., & Pollock, J. E. (2001). *Classroom instruction that works: Research-based strategies for increasing student achievement.* Alexandria, VA: Association for Supervision and Curriculum Development.

Moore, K. D. (1999). *Middle and secondary school instructional methods* (2nd ed.). Boston: McGraw-Hill.

Stevenson, C., & Carr, J. F. (1993). *Integrated studies in the middle grades: "Dancing through walls."* New York: Teachers College Press.

Tomlinson, C. A. (1998). For integration and differentiation choose concepts over topics. *Middle School Journal, 30*(2), 3–8.

Vars, G. F. (2001). Can curriculum integration survive in an era of high-stakes testing? *Middle School Journal, 33*(2), 7–16.

Wiggins, G., & McTighe, J. (1998). *Understanding by design.* Alexandria, VA: Association for Supervision and Curriculum Development.

11

Managing the Learning Environment

A nurturing and supportive classroom environment is essential for the intellectual as well as the emotional and social development of young adolescents. . . . The critical link between attitude and academic performance is especially evident with middle school students, whose psychological and emotional states are so fragile. . . . The environment that helps young adolescents develop emotionally and socially also enhances learning.

Vatterott, 1999, p. 23

Use this diagram as an organizational tool. In the boxes beside the chapter headings, indicate the dates by which the readings should be completed.

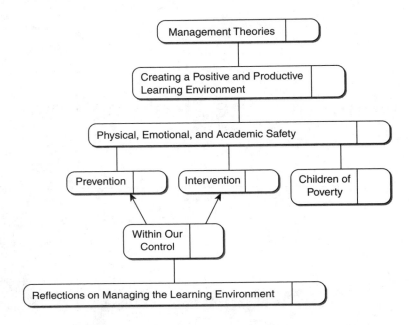

INTRODUCTION

We often hear that there are few absolutes in life, and I suppose that's true. But there is one certainty when it comes to teaching that is irrefutable—without effective classroom management, learning will be adversely affected and you will not enjoy your job. Years of experience teaching in the classroom, observing new and veteran teachers, and serving as a cooperating teacher in the field and as a college supervisor of student teachers have all confirmed this absolute for me.

Classroom management has many connotations. It is the terminology I choose to portray the proactive management of the learning environment by the teacher. Classroom management is a complicated task that involves creating a positive climate, ensuring that curriculum and instruction are engaging, and applying discipline measures when appropriate. Some may object to the use of the word *management* because to them it implies a cold set of controls over students. I am using management in this context to indicate a type of orchestrated oversight. Oversight is an appropriate way to think about classroom management because literally everything we do and everything that occurs in the classroom enhances or detracts from both student learning and our personal satisfaction with the profession of teaching. As with other aspects of teaching, approaches to classroom management vary. Keep in mind that nowhere is developmental appropriateness more critical.

Standard 5

Performance 7: Middle level teacher candidates employ fair, effective, developmentally responsive classroom management techniques.

People who wince at the thought of teaching middle school don't do so because we study ancient civilizations in sixth grade or learn about the Pythagorean theorem in seventh grade or read *The Outsiders* in eighth grade. They wince at the thought of being the lone adult in a room full of young adolescents. Memories of themselves and classmates, perhaps visions of their own 10- to 15-year-olds, and the general portrayal of middle grades kids as disturbed links between sweet childhood and maturing adolescence all contribute to the maligning of this wonderful age group. Sure, some of it is justified. There's no denying the element of challenge in middle school classrooms, but there's also no denying that teaching middle grades kids is an extraordinary adventure that can be "managed" to the benefit of students and adults alike. Young adolescents want parameters. They want their teachers to manage the environment so they can safely learn and grow.

Shalaway (1998) reminds us that our classrooms should reflect conditions that promote teaching and learning. She says that in the right environment students are more apt to

- dare to take risks.
- share their talents and encourage each other.
- know they are important.
- respect themselves, each other, and their communities.
- care for and trust each other. (p. 195)

In this chapter, we'll explore the creation and maintenance of a positive and productive learning environment as well as the perpetuation of academic, emotional/social, and physical safety. We'll discuss both prevention of problems and the when and how of intervention when prevention just isn't enough. Then we'll explore what our students expect of us and how we should respond to their expectations.

MANAGEMENT THEORIES

You have probably had courses in human development and classroom management. There's no need to dwell here on the major theories/programs such as behavior management (Skinner, 1971), assertive discipline (Canter & Canter, 1976), and Teacher Effectiveness Training (Gordon, 1974). I don't believe in adhering to any one of the prevailing theories or programs of effective classroom management to the exclusion of valuable principles and practices contained in other approaches. In order to be developmentally responsive to middle grades students we must pick and choose from a wide variety of approaches.

Chris Stevenson (1992, p. 219) recommends guidelines we may use to create and maintain a positive learning environment. He tells us that considering these four components will accomplish the order needed for learning while helping middle grades students to use their energies to work toward independent authority. This authority allows them to make choices about how to behave. Here is a brief description of the four components:

1. "Interpersonal climate"—Teachers are approachable as they promote good relationships with students. Where there is mutual respect, students are cooperative in the teaching-learning process.

2. "Worth and dignity assured"—Students are encouraged to believe in themselves and to develop positive self-esteem. No one in the classroom is allowed to belittle, tease, embarrass, or humiliate another.

3. "Approximating democracy"—Whenever possible, students are allowed to have a say in choices affecting individuals, classes, and teams. An open forum for discussion and solution seeking fills the student need for self-determination. This process in middle school contributes to more enlightened citizenship as adults.

4. "Redemption is always close, not closed"—Remembering that human growth and development occur in spurts, and are highly individual, leads teachers to address undesirable behaviors and offer fresh beginnings. It is vital to separate the offense from the student identity. Some students make many mistakes and require teacher maturity to forgive and move on.

Positive learning environment = Creating an interpersonal climate + Ensuring worth and dignity + Approximating democracy + Making redemption available

Knowing what we do about middle grades student characteristics and development, Stevenson's four provisos make sense. Embedding these components both in our classroom environments and within our team procedures is advisable.

CREATING A POSITIVE AND PRODUCTIVE LEARNING ENVIRONMENT

In Chapter 4 we discussed what it means for a classroom to be a community of learners. If it has been several weeks, or even months, since you read that section, it would be helpful to reread it now. Both *Turning Points* (Carnegie, 1989) and *This We Believe* (NMSA, 2003) exhort us to pay special attention to the creation and maintenance of a learning environment that has the earmarks of a caring community. Shalaway (1998) tells us that "In the right atmosphere and environment, students (and teachers) grow and flourish; problems and misbehavior do not" (p. 195). The learning environment affects how teachers teach and students learn. "Climate probably has as much to do with learning, productive work, and self-concept as does anything else in the educational program" (Burden & Byrd, 1999, p. 228).

Standard 5

Performance 6: Middle level teacher candidates establish equitable, caring, and productive learning environments for all young adolescents.

Membership

A positive and productive learning environment is characterized by a sense of community where each person (student and teacher) feels connected to both the group and the subject matter. In middle school the whole notion of teaming, with its lengthy list of benefits, is based on the value of membership. In a school where each teacher plans for and implements strategies that lead to classrooms as caring communities, the teams, the grade levels, and the entire school become productive learning environments.

> Productive learning environment = Connection to group + Connection to subject

In *Academic Success Through Empowering Students,* Vatterott (1999) helps us understand that membership entails being accepted by a group. Figure 11.1 lists student attitudes and beliefs that foster acceptance and membership along with school practices that lead to these important aspects of a positive and productive learning environment. An environment where acceptance and membership are the norm is especially important for at-risk students whose backgrounds of failure at school, indifference at home, and little support from communities outside the school all threaten their success. Vatterott contends that just as membership in a learning community affects academic success, academic success brings a sense of membership. Conversely, students who fail academically seldom feel accepted in a learning environment and often seek membership in antisocial settings.

Connecting with Students

To maintain a positive and productive learning environment where all feel like accepted members, we need to continually find ways to identify with our students. "Taking time to connect with our students, to win them over, is the first step in classroom management" (Cummings, 2000, p. 14). Just as young adolescents display a wide array of qualities, our

Need: Acceptance

Student Attitudes and Beliefs	School Practices
Students believe teachers like them.	Students have opportunities to "show off" special talents and skills.
Students believe the school is for "people like me."	Students are encouraged to share their opinions.
Students believe mistakes will be forgiven.	Teachers do not allow students to ridicule others.
Students believe their opinions are valued.	At-risk students are assigned to advisers for one-on-one help.
Students feel comfortable expressing feelings.	Teachers accommodate different learning styles.
Students believe they are some teacher's "favorite kid."	Teachers treat all students with equal respect.

Need: Membership

Student Attitudes and Beliefs	School Practices
Students can name friends in the school setting.	Opportunities are given for teachers and students to socialize outside class.
Students socialize with other students outside of school.	Multiple types of non-academic activities are available for students (games, contests, etc.).
Students identify themselves as members of a school-sponsored group (team, club, etc.).	A large number of students participate in co-curricular activities.
Students can name someone they could discuss confidential problems with at school.	Teachers and students proudly display "badges of membership."
Students believe they are missed when absent.	Teachers are knowledgeable about individual students' interests.

FIGURE 11.1 Fostering acceptance and membership.

Source: From *Academic Success Through Empowering Students* (p. 41), by C. Vatterott, 1999, Columbus, OH: National Middle School Association. Adapted with permission from National Middle School Association.

approaches to connecting with them—to "winning them over"—will vary. Here are some suggestions:

- Before school starts write a personal postcard welcoming the students who will enter your class. Yes, it's time-consuming and the cards and postage will cost (ask your principal to finance it), but the short- and long-term benefits are invaluable. I did this as a middle school teacher and continue the practice at the university level. I consider it a "must." (Parents love it, too!)

- Greet your students at the door the first day, and every day, of class.

- Learn student names very quickly, using whatever mnemonic device (memory aid) that works for you. Use names often in and out of the classroom. Even if you see 120 students on a team, you should know every name by the end of the second week of classes. It can be done.

- Use "getting to know you" surveys. Kids, like all of us, enjoy talking and writing about themselves. Give them an opportunity to do so and then use the information throughout the year to connect more personally with them. A simple survey is shown in Figure 11.2. Let students know that you understand their need to connect with each other. Experience shows us that if we don't provide socializing opportunities for young adolescents, they will use our instructional time to talk to each other. A policy of no talking in the halls or the cafeteria is deadly. Not only is it unenforceable, it's developmentally wrong. I am comfortable allowing socializing time in my classroom. Five minutes of free talking time helps ensure attention during the rest of the class period.

Self-Discipline

Helping middle grades students develop self-discipline is one of our highest callings. Young adolescents are in the midst of the transition from dependence to independence. Most have been accustomed to being told what to do, how to do it, and when to do it in elementary school. In middle school it should be to a lesser degree. We want our students to develop self-discipline as members of a community that exists in a positive and productive learning environment.

Teaching students how to monitor their own behavior is an important task. We need to remind them to be aware of their actions and attitudes and to adjust them when needed. Self-monitoring is the ultimate form of classroom management. Burden and Byrd (1999) suggest that we teach self-monitoring as a means of achieving self-discipline by prompting students to ask themselves questions when they are tempted to violate a rule or feel like they are about to lose self-control. The questions include, "Is this worth the trouble it will cause me?" and "Is this what I want to happen?" The authors write, "By pausing to question themselves, students will have the opportunity to assess the situation as well as calm down" (p. 237). As with other traits we want our students to acquire, teaching through the modeling of self-discipline techniques is very meaningful.

Traits	Agree	Somewhat Agree	Disagree
I like being alone.			
I prefer to study by myself.			
I am intuitive.			
I like team sports and activities.			
I enjoy working in a small group.			
I have many friends.			
I learn by doing, using my hands.			
I get fidgety if I have to sit and listen.			
I would rather build a circuit than read about it.			
I listen to music while studying.			
I'm aware of sounds in the environment.			
I would enjoy playing a musical instrument.			
Math is easy for me.			
I enjoy strategy games on the computer.			
I enjoy logic puzzles and brain teasers.			
I think with pictures and visual images.			
I like art and viewing movies.			
I doodle and daydream.			
I like to read.			
I enjoy listening to the spoken word (stories, tapes, radio commentary).			
I have a good memory for names, places, dates.			
I enjoy nature and being outdoors.			
I like to categorize plants and animals.			
I notice everyday changes in the environment.			

FIGURE 11.2 Who am I?

Source: From *Winning Strategies for Classroom Management* (p. 18), by C. Cummings, 2000, Alexandria, VA: Association for Supervision and Curriculum Development. Adapted with permission.

PHYSICAL, EMOTIONAL, AND ACADEMIC SAFETY

A positive and productive learning environment will include physical, emotional, and academic safety. In recent years we have become increasingly aware of the need for physical safety. From the shocking events at Columbine High School in 1999 to the daily reality of violence toward and among school age children and youth, our heightened focus on physical safety is justified. As important as physical safety is, it is imperative for educators to recognize the need for emotional and academic safety as well. "We must create a learning space in which children—their bodies, hearts, and minds—are protected" (Belair & Freeman, 2000, p. 3). This protection includes minimizing and, when possible, eliminating threatening events that may be physical, emotional, or academic in nature.

Safety in school = Physical + Emotional + Academic

Physical Safety

Physical safety requires the elimination of threatening and/or real scenarios including

- Fear of pushing, shoving, tripping in the hall
- Fear of having personal items stolen
- Worries about plans to escalate a disagreement after school
- Verbal threats about impending violence
- Fear of being caught up in a fight
- Fear of weapons being used in school
- Being tired or not feeling well (Cummings, 2000, p. 121)

In an interview printed in *Middle School Journal* (Erb, 2000), Gerald Bourgeois, a respected educator for more than four decades, talks in detail about school safety. Bourgeois says we must examine what is happening both in school and out of school. The cause of violence in schools is usually not what he terms "school stuff" (p. 5). The roots of the violence may be family-oriented and related to child abuse, domestic abuse, alcohol/drug abuse, viewing of violence in the media, availability of weapons, and other family or social problems happening outside of school. For this reason he tells us that school safety should be addressed from many perspectives. He suggests a community audit to recognize problems and begin addressing them. Concurrently, a school audit should include situations like vandalism, harassment, and bullying. Both audits can identify needs and match resources to address them.

Bourgeois recommends thorough consideration of school security both in daylight and at night, assessing access to the grounds, dark/hidden places, windows, lighting, door closures, and safety hazards. This assessment should lead to security precautions and changes. Next he recommends the writing of a building-specific contingency plan that goes beyond district safety policies and answers such questions as what do we do if

- an intruder enters the building?
- a bomb threat occurs?
- a suicide is attempted or occurs?

- •   a natural disaster threatens or occurs?
- •   a shooting is imminent or occurs?
- •   a gasoline tanker overturns in front of the school?
- •   a fire occurs or is nearby, releasing toxic fumes? (p. 7)

In addition, Bourgeois urges principals to establish procedures for teachers in the event of fights, sudden health problems, a classroom intruder, students with weapons, and so on.

Many middle schools employ resource officers who serve to prevent safety crises and maintain order. These officers are most useful when they do more than respond to rule infractions and act as police officers. Some coach sports, develop personal relationships with students, act as positive role models, and lend support when needed. Resource officers are typically members of the local police force assigned to school safety.

Other schools employ student concern specialists. These valuable individuals can serve as a second pair of eyes for a principal, concentrating on the physical well-being of the students. They can prevent acts of violence, intercept threats to student safety, and handle discipline problems. An effective student concern specialist listens carefully and watches constantly, interacting and intervening when appropriate.

Physical safety concerns in middle schools should also include health issues unrelated to the violence or safety issues already addressed. Most states require some form of health education in the middle school, but I've never heard a health educator state that the time devoted to health issues and related student decision-making is adequate. Standards for health education were discussed in Chapter 6. Health education programs in compliance with these standards serve middle school students well. Inadequately addressing the standards can have far reaching and unfortunate consequences.

Emotional Safety

We have spent considerable time discussing the emotional development of young adolescents and how the sensitivity and vulnerability of their emotions should be acknowledged and addressed in middle school. Educators who understand and care about middle grades students know the impact of an environment that provides *emotional safety*. Young adolescents need to be able to count on the school environment to provide a stable atmosphere where expressed emotions receive consistently caring responses. Their homes and communities may not provide emotional safety.

Some critics of the middle school emphasis on affective issues and growth are quick to say that we should concentrate on academics and leave the "touchy-feely" aspects of young adolescence to chance. In *What Every Middle School Teacher Should Know,* Knowles and Brown (2000) report on a number of research studies that have linked a caring environment (emotional safety) to cognitive growth. They make a case for positive student-teacher interpersonal relationships as vehicles for the improvement of the quality of learning. Joan Lipsitz, an influential proponent of middle level education, writes of her findings concerning the relationship of caring to academic success when she states that "caring did not substitute for learning; caring established an effective culture for learning" (1995, p. 666).

Emotional safety entails minimizing stress for students. Knowles and Brown (2000) tell us that many situations initiated by teachers may cause needless stress for young adolescents. They include

- frequently yelling at one student or an entire class
- applying punishment inappropriately
- threatening students
- making fun of students
- establishing unrealistic academic demands or expectations
- requiring students to open their lockers, get the appropriate books and notebooks, and get to their next class on time—all in less than 4 minutes
- pushing students to learn abstract principles that are beyond their cognitive capabilities
- assigning extensive homework that requires at least an hour or more of work each evening for each subject
- embarrassing students in front of their most significant audience—their peers (p. 55)

Knowles and Brown (2000) also say that we may disrupt the emotional stability needed for optimal student learning in subtle, and often unwitting, ways by

- refusing to lend a pencil, protractor, or paper to students
- caring more about completing the textbook than meeting each student's needs
- treating each student the same regardless of differences in learning abilities or learning styles
- preventing students from interacting socially during class time
- assessing student learning in only one way

- designing lessons that are primarily teacher directed without hands-on opportunities for student learning
- refusing to be flexible in curriculum design, instructional processes, or scheduling
- using quizzes to "catch" students who may not understand material
- ignoring young adolescents' stages of cognitive, social, and emotional growth (p. 56)

We see that making our classrooms less than emotionally safe can be quite inadvertent. It's pretty scary to know how much power a word, a look, a policy never intended to do harm, a withholding of support, and so on, may have in the life of a young adolescent. We must be very aware of our influence.

Bluestein (2001) tells us there are practices that characterize a school with an emotionally safe climate. Figure 11.3 contains some of these practices from *Creating Emotionally Safe Schools*.

---

1. We attempt to recognize positive behavior with statements that emphasize a positive outcome or meaningful benefit to the students, rather than using statements that emphasize the students' worth ("goodness"), our happiness or pleasure, or the students' ability to please us.

2. We attempt to reinforce positive behavior by allowing positive outcomes to occur, continue or become available, contingent, for example, on work completion or non-disruptive behavior.

3. We attempt to meet students' needs for attention in positive, constructive and proactive ways in order to diminish the tendency for them to act out to get these needs met.

4. We strive to stay aware of changes in patterns in students' behavior and to maintain a sense of how students are doing (that is, not just focusing on their academic performance).

5. We attempt to create emotional safety by noticing and supporting students in crisis.

6. We provide appropriate outlets for students in crisis.

7. Our students know that if they need to talk, we are willing to listen (or set a time when we can listen, or refer them to someone who can listen).

8. We respect students' needs for confidentiality to the degree that doing so will not put that student or anyone else in danger.

9. We strive to maintain awareness to how students treat one another.

10. We immediately respond to incidents we witness that involve any form of bullying, harassment or threat to a student's safety.

FIGURE 11.3 Creating emotionally safe schools.

Source: From *Creating Emotionally Safe Schools* (pp. 385–386), by J. Bluestein, 2001, Deerfield Beach, FL: Health Communications, Inc. Copyright 2001 by Jane Bluestein, Ph.D. Reprinted with permission.

Perhaps one of the most proactive things we can do to promote emotional safety is to listen to our students without condemning or even offering solutions. If they know we care about them, respect their absolutely natural fluctuations in mood, and are willing to allow them to grow, make mistakes, and begin again (and again!), they will tend to perceive emotional safety in our classrooms.

Academic Safety

Academic safety is a concept rarely discussed, and yet it is addressed regularly by teachers intent on creating a positive and productive learning environment. What exactly does academic safety mean? It means, in the words of *Turning Points* (1989), "Ensuring success for all students: All young adolescents should have the opportunity to succeed in every aspect of the middle grade program, regardless of previous achievement or the pace at which they learn" (p. 49). Success begets success. The corollary, unfortunately, is also true—lack of success begets lack of success.

"No adult would be foolish enough to participate in a losing effort for 180 days a year for thirteen consecutive years; yet we expect struggling students to return to school year after year despite their inability to succeed" (Knowles & Brown, 2000, p. 63). When we succeed, we are willing to exert effort and take risks to attempt new and more challenging feats. Unfortunately, academic risk-taking is buried in many students before they even reach middle school. For some it is a casualty of middle school. Our task as teachers is to minimize feelings of inadequacy by ensuring that every student succeeds at something.

One way to ensure some measure of success for each student is to internalize and act on our understanding of adolescent development by operationalizing the concept of differentiation as discussed in Chapters 6 through 9. Using what we know about multiple intelligences theory, learning styles and modalities, varying motivational levels, and maintenance of high expectations, we create a learning environment that at once validates cognitive progress and raises the bar to preserve momentum.

Standard 1

Disposition 3: Middle level teacher candidates hold high, realistic expectations for the learning and behavior of all young adolescents.

The negative effect peers can have on the academic success of members of their social groups always surprises and dismays me when I witness it. In middle school awards assemblies, I have heard kids jeer as one of their own is called to the front to be recognized for an accomplishment. As adults we understand that underlying the jeers is a tender jealousy that hasn't matured enough to recognize it for what it is, much less lead to a comment of "Good job, my friend." The student being jeered could not care less about the psychological origins of "Geek," "Teacher's pet," "Smarty pants," or other taunts I have heard but am reluctant to put in print. This same kind of thing happens daily on a smaller scale in most middle grades settings.

The opposite kind of embarrassment is even more prevalent. Our students are afraid of failing in front of their peers. After feeling stupid in the eyes of their classmates, many will simply clam up and not participate. To them, no notice is better than negative notice. A sudden headache or need to go to the bathroom may occasionally work to get them out of the academic spotlight of perhaps reading aloud, going to the board to work a problem, or answering questions about an assignment. When headaches and bathroom breaks are exhausted, many turn to misbehavior as a refuge from the academic arena. We need to recognize these avoidance tactics as we find ways to move each student toward some measure of success.

Once again we call on Knowles and Brown (2000) to focus us on concrete ways to promote academic safety. They ask us to consider how we would entice young adolescents to return to our classrooms day after day if school was not mandatory. A sobering thought to ponder, isn't it? Here are some comments on what academic safety means for kids.

- No one laughs at them when they attempt to ask or answer a question.
- Teachers establish realistic academic expectations and outcomes for each student.
- Students' efforts are recognized, as well as the products of those efforts.
- Teachers eliminate competitive situations that create inequity among students.
- Teachers develop cooperative grouping strategies that encourage students to collaborate in their learning and share their knowledge and expertise with one another.
- Teachers play the role of facilitator to encourage student independence.
- Teachers choose alternative instructional strategies to meet each student's learning style.
- Teachers recognize and appreciate talents other than academic skills.

Standard 5

Disposition 2: Middle level teacher candidates value the need for providing and maintaining environments that maximize student learning.

Healthy to Be Safe

Physical, emotional, and academic safety are imperative for a positive and productive learning environment. When all three are attended to, our classrooms are healthy places for our students. In *Discipline with Dignity*, Curwin and Mendler (1999) provide a list of nine characteristics of a healthy classroom. Consider each carefully.

1. Trust is established.
2. The learner perceives the benefits of changing his behavior.
3. The learner is aware of different options and is able to make a growth choice.
4. The evaluation of learning actively engages the learner.
5. Learning facts and concepts are important, but incomplete, goals for the learner. Personal meanings, uses, and understandings are the ends for which learning facts and concepts are means.
6. Learning is conceived as meaningful.
7. Learning is growth producing, actualizing, and therefore enjoyable.

8. Learning is process- and people-oriented, rather than product- and subject-oriented.
9. Learning includes more than just the cognitive or affective domain. (pp. 162–163)

Standard 1

Performance 8: Middle level teacher candidates create and maintain supportive learning environments that promote the healthy development of all young adolescents.

 # PREVENTION

The old saying goes, "An ounce of prevention is worth a pound of cure." The more proactively we address classroom management, the less reactive we will have to be. Everything we do in our classrooms might be characterized as either preventing the bad by promoting the good, or reacting to the bad and attempting to turn it into the good. I'd much rather spend time on the former than the latter.

Curwin and Mendler (1999) tell us there are three broad categories of students in a typical classroom and suggest the "80–15–5 principle" that goes like this:

- Eighty percent of students rarely break rules. They are reasonably motivated to learn and accept the parameters of the classroom. They have experienced enough success to expect to be successful in the future. For them, rules and consequences are realistically unnecessary.

- Fifteen percent of students break rules regularly. They can be completely on or completely off, depending on numerous factors. Their achievement range is vast and unpredictable. They need rules and consequences with a good measure of structure to keep them from disturbing the whole class.

- Five percent of students are chronic rule breakers and tend to be out of control much of the time. They typically have experienced failure over and over, either academically or behaviorally (or both), and see no hope of success.

"The trick of a good discipline plan is to control the fifteen percent without alienating or overly regulating the eighty percent and without backing the five percent into a corner" (p. 28). Given the 80–15–5 principle we might expect a middle school class of 30 to have 24 or so students who pose no discipline problems, 4 or 5 who are behaviorally volatile, and 1 or 2 who consistently challenge both our patience and resourcefulness.

> Typical classroom behavior = 80% rarely break rules + 15% regularly break rules + 5% often out of control

Jacob Kounin (1970) found when studying classroom management that teachers differ little in how they handle problems once they arise. The differences were dramatic, however, when observing what successful classroom managers do to prevent classroom problems. Kounin concluded that the skills demonstrated by successful classroom managers could be categorized in three areas—their "withitness," their ability to overlap activities, and their management of movement. As you observe classrooms or reflect on scenarios, think about what you would do in Kounin's three categories to be a proactive successful classroom manager.

> *Standard 5*
>
> *Knowledge 8*: Middle level teacher candidates know effective, developmentally responsive classroom management techniques.
>
> NMSA

Prevention Through Good Instruction

Principal Edna Varner (1999) recalls, "When I was a teacher, I tried to deal with discipline problems in ways that did not consume learning time. I believed then, and still do, that engaging and challenging instruction is the best deterrent to misbehavior" (p. 27). Varner's experience validates the 80–15–5 principle. She tells us that most discipline problems in middle schools involve a small number of students and contends that focusing on instruction will dramatically decrease chronic misbehavior. "Discipline is deceptive. It is not what ails chaotic classrooms; it is merely a symptom of problems teachers are having with instruction" (p. 27). Planning for instruction, implementing developmentally appropriate practices, and maintaining vigilant and responsive peripheral vision in the classroom are key elements of effective management that result in learning and enjoyment for students and teachers. Instructional planning and classroom management are inseparable.

Students are less likely to misbehave when the work is interesting and challenging, when there are routines, when resources are sufficient, and when they know their teachers will grade their papers and give feedback. These are all aspects of good instruction.

Planning for instruction as discussed in Chapter 10 and using a variety of appropriate strategies such as those in Chapters 7, 8, and 9 with a challenging and integrative curriculum as discussed in Chapter 6 will go a long way toward preventing classroom management problems. On the flip side, teachers who do not plan well are distracted by unrelated matters, don't have a clear notion of where the lesson is going, and communicate disorder to their students. "Too often, such a message of disorder leads to disrespect toward the teacher and a dislike of the subject" (Moore, 1999, p. 426).

Motivating students through good instruction is the best preventive medicine. Doing so requires our full attention.

> Motivated students cause fewer discipline problems because they care about what they are learning. Enthusiastic teachers who present their material in stimulating, meaningful ways motivate students. When students are actively learning content that has personal meaning for them, they have neither the time nor the energy to create discipline problems. Conversely, when students feel that they are passive receptacles for irrelevant knowledge, they become bored, turned off, and find satisfaction in acting out. (Curwin & Mendler, 1999, p. 159)

Routines

Students occasionally get thirsty, need to use the bathroom, forget supplies, are tardy or absent, need to see a counselor, or experience emotional crises. Each individual occurrence of this nature may have only a minor impact on the classroom. Collectively, these interruptions can significantly detract from the learning environment. Team and classroom routines are essential in minimizing the impact of relatively minor interruptions. Routines are rules organized around a particular time, concept, or place that help guide students and teachers to accomplish tasks in the quickest and most efficient manner possible. Speaking of the benefits of well-established routines, Borich (2003) says "they allow the teacher more time to teach and learners more time to become engaged in the learning process" (p. 105).

Established routines are not meant to be restrictive. Rather, they free us to concentrate on curriculum, instruction, and assessment more fully with fewer distractions. We may want to establish routines to address taking/reporting attendance, changing seating arrangements, turning in late work, distributing and gathering materials, beginning and dismissing class, seeing the nurse, and going to lockers. Anticipating times, concepts, and places that may be better addressed through routines, as opposed to repeating instructions over and over, will waste less time and help our classrooms run more smoothly.

Before establishing classroom routines it is important to consider the full range of school policies that might relate to the areas to be addressed. For instance, the guidance counselor will likely have a procedure for students to follow who feel the need for counseling; the office will have mandatory ways for reporting attendance, although the method of taking attendance is usually up to individual teachers; there will be a general policy for time allowed to make up work following an absence; and students will likely need some sort of identification when in the hallways. Many routines can be established as a team. If all of a student's teachers do something in the same way, the likelihood of the student following the routine is heightened.

Perhaps the most useful of all routines is one that allows us to get the attention of a group of students—the 30 or so in our classrooms, or the 100 or more in the cafeteria or on the field. The routine I have used for years is the hand-raising technique. Here's how it works. When you raise your hand, students raise theirs. During cooperative group work when many students are not facing you and most are actively engaged and not keeping their eyes on you, the few who may see your raised hand will raise theirs and other students will see them and follow suit. The key here is that when hands are raised, mouths are closed. When all hands are raised, all mouths are closed. You lower your hand and students do the same. Then you can speak, but the students can't. This technique works for 20 and for 200 if it is practiced from day one of school. It's most effective if whole teams consistently use it.

Getting attention of group = All raise hands + Student mouths close

One routine that builds responsibility in students and saves needless repetition for teachers is the use of a "What did I miss?" notebook. This is a binder with a page designated for each school day. At the end of each day the teacher writes a description of what happened in class. You may have only one preparation per day as part of an interdisciplinary team, or two or three different preparations if you cross disciplines or teach on a two-person team. Regardless, keeping an updated "What did I miss?" notebook on the chalk rail in your classroom is worth the time and effort.

A large calendar with important dates clearly indicated will help students stay organized. Insisting that students check the "What did I miss?" book and the calendar before asking about events/assignments is a routine that will save precious instructional time.

Designating baskets for each class period is a good idea. Students know they can turn in assignments or leave notes for you, and that they can pick up worksheets/handouts they may have missed from folders that are kept in their class basket.

Organizing materials/resources in a specific area and having a system for designated students to gather what's needed for themselves and others is an "antichaos" routine. Maybe one person per cooperative group is the material gatherer or the first person on each row in a more traditional classroom arrangement. Habits of picking up and putting away materials must be taught and practiced.

Classroom interruptions are inevitable. Late students, announcements, teachers and support staff at your door—the list could go on and on. Wise administrators do their best to protect instructional time, but schools, their occupants, and the public are unpredictable and you can count on being interrupted on a regular basis. Teaching your students how to react to interruptions is a valuable lesson. For instance, when the public address (PA) system comes on, teach your students to instantly be silent. This doesn't mean the announcement is in any way more important than what's happening in class, but listening and dealing with the request or information quickly will get you back on track sooner. When someone appears at your door, teach your students to freeze if you're in a whole group activity, or to lower their voices if they are doing group work to free you to respond to the visitor.

Time spent actually teaching and practicing routines in the beginning of the school year will pay dividends throughout the year. Our students are going to form habits with or without us. How much better it is for all of us if the habits they form coincide with the efficient management of our classrooms. Don't overlook or minimize the role of well-established routines as part of your classroom management plan.

Rules and Consequences

Rules define what is and what is not acceptable in the classroom. *Consequences* define what will happen when rules are broken. In addition to providing the structure for acceptable behavior, rules communicate expectations and help maintain a positive and productive learning environment.

Some rules are dictated by school and/or district policies. Some middle schools have a prescriptive plan of very specific rules that directly affect your classroom. If so, the plan may have a sequence of consequences that all teachers are to follow for specific infractions. I have seen whole school plans successfully administered, but I've also witnessed problems when school discipline policies conflict with what teams of teachers feel is best for their students. As a new teacher, you may sense that your hands are tied, and indeed they may be. Remember, however, that policies, agreeable or not, do not dictate your relationships with students.

As with routines, it's a good idea for teams to develop rules and consequences together when possible. The team is a unit that should function smoothly in logical and consistent ways. Rules help us govern how we work together and interact. It is my experience that teachers rarely agree on all the routines and rules needed for middle grades students. Part of being a good team member is understanding the value of compromise and being willing to enforce some rules that may seem relatively minor to you, but are viewed by teammates to be of greater importance. We all have our "pet" procedures, likes, and dislikes when it comes to students and classroom management. Keep a sense of perspective in this area. For instance, if there is no school policy concerning gum chewing but your teammates are opposed, allowing students to chew gum in your classroom, even if you think it's fine, would undermine the other teachers. The gum would not always be spit out as they left your class and students might unjustly label other teachers as "mean" for enforcing the "no gum" rule in their classes. If you think it's less than a big deal for shirts not to be tucked in but your teammates feel the rule is important, it's not going to hurt you to notice and ask students to comply. I have found that abiding by team rules vigilantly is best for everyone, even when I am not personally convinced of their worth.

Guidelines for establishing rules.

Borich (2003) contends there is no one single best set of rules for classrooms. "Rules make a statement about the type of climate desired in a behavioral setting. They are a message system whereby the teacher's beliefs and philosophy about academic and conduct-related behavior are communicated to students" (p. 101). Many educators have thought about and invested research time in establishing guidelines for classroom rules. Most are common sense and worthy of consideration.

Burden and Byrd (1999) provide guidelines for establishing rules that are straightforward and comprehensive. Their guidelines include:

1. Make classroom rules consistent with school rules.
2. Involve students in making the rules to the degree that you are comfortable and to the degree that the students' age level and sophistication permit.
3. Identify appropriate behaviors and translate them into positively stated classroom rules.
4. Focus on important behavior.
5. Keep the number of rules to a minimum (4–6).
6. Keep the wording of each rule simple and short.
7. Have rules address behaviors that can be observed.
8. Identify rewards for when students follow the rules and consequences for when they break the rules. (p. 183)

Taking a positive approach.

It is important to state rules in positive terms. Our goal is to promote appropriate behavior and, in doing so, curb inappropriate behavior. We want rules to state what our students should do, not what they shouldn't do. For example, a positively written rule would state "Be in your seats when the bell rings" as opposed to "Don't be out of your seat when the bell rings." Small differences in wording can have a real impact on how students respond. Positively stated rules are clear to students and provide observable behaviors for teachers to praise. Negatively written rules focus on what's wrong and put our classrooms in punishment mode (Bicard, 2000).

Using positive reinforcement simply means recognizing appropriate behavior, acknowledging it privately and/or publicly, and possibly rewarding it beyond acknowledgment. When rules are stated in positive terms, we can simply say "Thank you for being in your seat when the bell rang." The acknowledgment carries with it a reinforcement because students hear the rule repeated. For the 80% of our students who rarely break rules, positive reinforcement is generally enough to ensure appropriate behavior. For the 15% whose behavior vacillates between rule compliance and rule defiance, positive reinforcement stands a good chance of upsetting the balance between compliance and defiance in favor of appropriate behavior. For the 5% of our students who are chronic rule breakers, positive reinforcement (typically awarded the other 95%) allows them to hear and see what happens when rules are followed. Although not a common cure, finding occasions to positively reinforce this needy 5% will likely have an effect. It can't hurt. All of us seek attention. Disapproval is attention and so is approval. We want our chronic misbehavers to experience the difference between positive attention and negative attention. Our goal is to make the positive attention more enjoyable than the negative so "attention getting" might be redirected by the student. Our chronic misbehavers have so much room for improvement that we should have many opportunities to catch them doing better. Our responses to these students have much to do with their escalation or de-escalation.

George and Alexander (2003) give us an example of a positive set of simple, straightforward rules. Here they are:

1. Be prompt.
2. Be prepared.
3. Raise your hand when you wish to speak.
4. Follow directions.
5. Treat others with respect.

Teaching responsibility.   In *Discipline with Dignity* (Curwin & Mendler, 1999) we are told that "Teaching students responsibility requires more work than teaching for obedience" (p. 25). Although we may be tempted to simply say "Just do what I say" to our students, Pavlov's experiments with food, bells, and salivating dogs is hardly an appropriate model to use when considering rules and young adolescents. With our emphasis on developmental appropriateness and our quest to foster critical thinking, asking students to simply "obey or else" is incongruous. The work and time required to teach responsibility for actions is part of our jobs as middle school teachers and should be taken seriously.

Teaching responsibility when it comes to compliance with rules should be approached like any subject. We can use a variety of strategies and Bloom's guidance to promote knowledge (rules posted), comprehension (rules discussed), application (rules practiced), analysis (reasons for rules acknowledged), synthesis (rules applied in new situations), and evaluation (rules perceived as classroom governance). Stopping at the knowledge level or simply posting the rules and expecting compliance will be very disappointing. We know learning that leads to any kind of action requires more of the taxonomy than the first level.

Teaching responsibility entails the promotion of decision-making skills. Making decisions about rule compliance happens on a conscious level. Teaching students that they have choices and how to make the choices that will be best for them and everyone else involved is teaching responsibility.

For the first week of school it's a good idea to spend 5 minutes or so each day discussing, modeling, and having students role-play rules. We may ask them to write what

---
Reinforcing rules = Discussion + Modeling + Role play

---

compliance to a certain rule might "look like," or perhaps what the classroom would be like without a particular rule. For some classes, it may be helpful to do some rule-related activity each Monday. After long holidays it's very appropriate to emphasize rules again.

Developing consequences.   Curwin and Mendler (1999) explain the main differences between consequences and punishments:

> Consequences are simple, directly related to the rule, logical (that is, they are natural outcomes of the rule violation), and instructive. Punishments are not related to the rule, are not natural extensions of the rule, and tend to generate anxiety, hostility, and resentment in the student. (p. 71)

Even when we understand the differences, developing effective consequences can be difficult. According to Curwin and Mendler, consequences work best when they

1. Are clear and specific

   Knowing a rule and the consequence(s) of breaking the rule gives classroom management an important sense of predictability. Students know what will happen. Making up consequences (or rules, for that matter) on the spot conveys a sense of arbitrariness and can appear (and be) unfair.

2. Have a range of alternatives

   For each broken rule we can't have one consequence for the eighty percent, a more severe one for the fifteen percent, and a still more severe one for the five percent. A solution is a set of escalating consequences for each broken rule. For rules that, if broken, don't impose safety risks, the escalation could begin with a reminder and then a warning. This way, for the student who makes an occasional mistake, or does something wrong infrequently, there is a way to be consistent and yet not assign a consequence that is probably not needed.

3. Are related to the rule

   Punishments often work on a short term basis to stop an inappropriate behavior, but are generally ineffective for long-term change. The main thing we learn from punishment is how bad it is to get caught. When consequences are directly related to the rule they are both natural and logical. They are instructive rather than punitive (pp. 66–70).

Consequences that work = Understandable + Alternatives + Related to rule + Consistently applied

---

Consequences must be implemented consistently. Ignoring a rule infraction or threatening a consequence and not following through will render the rule-consequence relationship invalid.

Uniforms

I am a believer in uniforms for middle grades students. After some initial resistance, most schools that adopted uniforms in the 1980s and 1990s have stayed with the practice of requiring students to wear one of several variations on a clothing theme. While the practice is started for different school-specific reasons, all relate to middle school philosophy and student well-being.

In an article in *Middle School Journal,* David Kommer (1999), a former principal in Los Angeles, lists benefits of middle school uniforms:

- Schools become a place of more serious business and respect.
- Uniforms eliminate a source of contention among adolescents.
- Students [do not have] to keep up with current fashion to remain "in."
- Students [are not] left out of groups based upon clothing styles.
- Students can enjoy the connection to school—a sense of belonging. (p. 26)

According to Kommer (1999) and others, the key to successful development of a uniform policy is parental support. Parent-teacher committees generally select a variety of shirts/pants/skirts from an easily accessible vendor. Because instituting a mandatory uniform policy is risky, in the beginning at least, when it comes to student morale, having a

uniform fashion show with student models and then allowing students to vote for colors and styles within the adult committee's parameters is a great idea. Given the choice, students would probably never initially say "yes" to uniforms. However, it is typical to hear comments such as "I don't have to decide what to wear" or "Everybody dresses alike so we can think about other stuff" or "Now it's more fun to put on other clothes when I go places." If students are required to wear uniforms in elementary school, the requirement in middle school is a smoother transition. Many look forward to high school where uniform programs are not as widespread.

For uniform policies to "stick," they must be mandatory. Dress codes are a matter of school policy and can be difficult to enforce because of the generally subjective nature of the rules and the time/attention required of teachers to be vigilant when there are so many other instructionally important tasks to tend to. Uniform violations are easy to spot. To avoid any legal questions that would be time-consuming and costly to address, an "opt out" policy for parents who feel strongly about their students not wearing uniforms is advisable. In my experience, this option is exercised very rarely.

Prevention of misbehavior = Engaging instruction + Routines + Rules and consequences

---

 ## INTERVENTION

"Despite all your efforts (and those of your students) to prevent discipline problems from happening, conflicts will inevitably occur in any setting in which 20 to 30 people are expected to be together over an extended period of time" (Curwin & Mendler, 1999, p. 42). We must use prevention as our first line of defense—effective instruction that engages learners, well-established routines, and appropriate rules and consequences. While the prevention of misbehavior is our goal, there are times when intervention is necessary. It may be unobtrusive and involve implementation of consequences, or it may require aggressive action on our part.

Unobtrusive Intervention

Effective classroom management involves the ever-vigilant peripheral vision discussed earlier along with rational, calm decision-making. We have to determine when to do what, as well as when to do nothing. This may sound contradictory to consistently applying predetermined consequences to broken rules, but it isn't. I'm not implying that we should "do nothing" when clearly there is an infraction. However, classrooms are plagued most days not with major rule infractions, but by small disruptions that require a dose of plain old common sense to know when and how to intervene. Purkey and Strahan (2002) give us some questions to ask ourselves when deciding whether or not a situation is a matter of concern:

1. Will this situation resolve itself without intervention?
2. Can this situation be safely and wisely overlooked?
3. Does this situation involve a matter of ethics, legality, morality, or safety?
4. Is this the proper time to be concerned about this situation? (p. 102)

Small disruptions include a student asking another for a pencil during individual work time; a normally on-time, ready-to-work student slipping into class just as the bell stops ringing; and two students suddenly laughing loudly while gathering materials. To stop class momentum to address these small things would waste more time than they're worth. If you're conducting a class discussion of a reading passage and a student is just sitting with his book closed, publicly saying "Sean, open your book and sit up straight" will only alienate Sean and interrupt the thought processes of others. Casually walking toward Sean and opening his book, accompanied by a knowing look, may do the trick. This is an unobtrusive intervention.

Unobtrusive intervention serves in many ways as a form of prevention. It is intervention because students do something that requires a response. It is prevention because it will likely prevent escalation that would result in the need to implement consequences. Here are some unobtrusive things you might try doing to curb inattentiveness, annoying behavior, lack of participation, off-track distractions, and so on.

- Give "the look"—one your students recognize as disapproving.
- Move toward the student(s) in question.
- Pause and silently stare for a moment.
- Walk to the student's desk and put your hand on it.
- Use the student's name in an example.
- Ask the student to sum up what has been said or to repeat directions just given.

If necessary (and it often will be), you can be more assertive and still relatively unobtrusive by doing one of the following:

- Say "Sean, how should we be participating right now?"
- Ask the student to move to another part of the classroom.
- Ask the student to see you privately after class.

Cummings (2000) calls what has just been described "The Law of Least Intervention" (p. 137). When preventive measures are in place, simple unobtrusive intervention will keep most class periods running smoothly. Not using unobtrusive measures quickly and confidently will allow minor disruptions to escalate.

Implementing Consequences

When disruptions and rule violations interfere with your teaching and/or student learning, they require more than unobtrusive intervention. If appropriate, the consequence may be a reminder. When the misbehavior occurs again, a warning might be given. If it occurs one more time, the next step is taken. Some misbehaviors don't begin benignly. They may burst into being and be blatant enough to require implementation of predetermined consequences. A behavior may require instant action to curb the behavior or to remove the student from a situation.

Curwin and Mendler (1999) explain that how a consequence is implemented is as important as the consequence itself. "Tone of voice, physical distance from the student, body posture, use of eye contact, and other nonverbal gestures determine the effectiveness of a consequence as much or more than the actual content of the consequence itself" (p. 43). Rule violations actually provide opportunities for us to interact with students in ways that demonstrate maturity, restraint, concern for the overall good of the class, care for the misbehaver's well-being and growth, and wisdom. When we view instances of misbehavior as opportunities, we will address them in more positive ways.

Parents.   One of my favorite interventions, and one I included as often as possible in classroom consequences, was parental contact. Some teachers report that there is an increasing number of situations when contacting a parent or guardian is less than effective. There are many students who, sadly, experience little support and/or guidance outside school. Unfortunately, these are often the very students who require the most intervention. They need and deserve our best efforts. There are many students, however, who respond with panic to the thought of a call home saying there is a behavior problem. For these kids, parental contact is an excellent motivator.

Administrative assistance.   When consequences are dictated by you or your team, implementing them without the assistance of administrators is preferable. The more office referrals you write, the more diminished your power will be as a classroom manager. However, there are times when it is very appropriate to ask for administrative assistance. If a student reaches a consequence level that dictates an office referral, not giving one will send the message that you do not believe in the rule-consequence package that governs the classroom/team/school. There are violent misbehaviors that call for immediate administrative assistance. Verbal outrage, throwing objects in anger, instigating a fight, verbal abuse of teacher or another student, physical abuse (or the threat of), possession of contraband of any kind—these situations and others warrant calls for help. While we hope these scenarios occur rarely, we know that in some settings they are frequent. Students who repeatedly cause major disruptions are sometimes referred to as being out of control.

Out of control students.   Let's discuss approaches to students who repeatedly challenge your classroom management skills. We all have them. I can still name the students who, over the years, have presented me with more challenge than I could handle with prevention techniques or the occasional implementation of consequences. These are students who don't willingly become constructive members of our classrooms and who appear to enjoy disrupting the learning process. They often actually become legends in the school. Sixth grade teachers will have heard about them before they hit the middle school. If interventions have not had long-term positive effects, eighth grade teachers will have had years of warning.

The first step should be to seriously look at the student's history. Has she been referred for diagnostic testing? Are there home/family concerns? What interventions have been tried? Chances are the student has intellectual potential that isn't obvious from her grades. Helping her break out of the "I'm trouble" mode should be a group effort—the whole team plus the guidance counselor, school psychologist, administrator, and so forth. All may need to be involved to seek in-school solutions.

There are students who need more help than we are equipped to give. Chronic misbehavior, after interventions have failed to modify it, is a sign that alternative placement may be needed. The public school classroom is not the place for all students. The education of the vast majority of students should not be jeopardized by students who need more than we can give. Districts that provide a variety of school settings for students with special needs and special interests are doing a real service for all students.

Curwin and Mendler (1999) recommend three strategies to try with students who are, or have signs of becoming, out of control. One is Positive Student Confrontation involving a third party who briefly explains the problem and then asks the teacher and student to answer questions similar to these.

1. What do you dislike about how he/she behaves?
2. What do you like or appreciate about him/her?
3. What would you like him/her to do differently from what he/she is doing right now?

With the help of the mediator, the teacher and student reach an agreement. Responsibilities are established, the agreement is written and signed, and a follow-up session is scheduled.

The second strategy involves meeting with as many family members who have regular contact with the student as possible. Concrete measurable goals are established. These can be as short-term as class period to class period. Positive and negative consequences are designated. A contract is written and regular school-home communication is maintained.

The third strategy is the use of a daily student rating card to monitor agreed-upon behavior. The areas of concern are noted and a chart is made that allows each teacher during the day to rate progress. A number system is recommended that allows teachers to use a 1 for excellent, 2 for good, 3 for fair, 4 for poor, and 5 for terrible or did not work. The results are tallied with consequences, both positive and negative, applied at school and at home if the family is involved in the process.

More than one student.   No doubt there will be occasions when two or three students misbehave at the same time. When this happens you will be very glad you followed middle school philosophy that emphasizes the importance of understanding developmental processes and knowing your students well. Spending time analyzing the social dynamics of your classes pays off when faced with multiple behavior problems at once. If two or three students are involved, choose the one considered to be more of a leader. This could be the one who is most respected or considered funniest, or who, for whatever reason, wields the most influence. Concentrate on correcting or controlling this student's behavior. This may take care of the behavior of the others. If not, continue intervention down the "influence chain."

Dealing with misbehavior that appears to involve half or more of your class is cause for concern. The first step is to get their attention. Yelling is never the solution. If you use the hand-raising technique regularly, it will work in the majority of cases when there is more misbehavior than normal. Try turning off the lights . If you've never used this attention getter it may work. If you do it often it will not be effective in getting the students quiet enough to hear your directions. Standing silently in the front of the room with your arms folded may get their attention once you are noticed. On a few occasions when students were excessively agitated, I closed my classroom door loudly to get attention. It worked, but I would use it only as a last resort. Once you have students' attention, you can proceed. At this point you must address the causes of the disruption. A class meeting is called for, as well as appropriate consequences. You are responsible for figuring out, with the help of your students, how to make changes to prevent similar behavior problems in the future. Displaying calm reasonableness will help ensure resolution and prevent a repeat performance.

Avoiding power struggles.   When a teacher implements a consequence and the student refuses to comply, a power struggle is in the making. Power struggles, especially in a classroom, hallway, or cafeteria full of students, should be avoided. Quietly say to the student, "I feel a power struggle coming on and that's not the way I operate. Let's talk about this privately (or later or after class or . . .)." Some students have experienced "winning" a power struggle and have been viewed as tough by peers after succeeding in making the teacher angry, or exhausting the teacher to the point of getting out of the consequence. These are students who take pride in initiating verbal struggles.

It's good to find a way to acknowledge a student's feelings by paraphrasing what the student expresses. For instance, you might respond to "It wasn't my fault and I'm not serving detention for it," with "I understand you feel it's not your fault and that you don't believe you deserve a detention. So we have a problem. Let's talk about it after class." Then go on with the lesson in the same calm manner with which you began it. "By accepting that the problem was theirs and not only the student's, . . . the teacher . . . prevented what might have escalated into a classic power struggle" (Curwin & Mendler, 1999, p. 106).

Stopping a power struggle before it starts is important, and so is the procedure we use to follow up. If a rule has been broken, then a resolution must occur. Ideally it will be the prescribed consequence, if one exists. If the student attempts to engage in a power struggle publicly, we can't expect an easy private conversation, but it will give us the opportunity to actively listen, acknowledge feelings, show understanding, and say things like, "I sure don't like our relationship to be like this. Work with me here." Most young adolescents want to be heard. Listening and being willing to engage in conversation goes a long way toward not only peacefully resolving a current behavior problem, but also paving the way for future communication.

Many middle grades students find themselves on the verge of, or in the midst of, a power struggle before they realize what's happening. The whole situation may be defused by a sense of humor on our part. Often students are secretly hoping we will have a way to lighten up the mood and clear the air when they're not quite sure how to back off.

Will you always be able to calmly resolve potential power struggles? Unfortunately, no. There will be times when administrative assistance will be called for. Students will be suspended, in and/or out of school. Consequences will be imposed that none of us particularly like, or even think best for individual kids who have complicated personal circumstances. In these situations it is extremely important for the teacher to show public support for the administration, even if we privately want to take issue with the consequence imposed.

We are responsible for doing the best we can, even in uncomfortable and difficult situations. Our students depend on us to be adults and to remain in control and keep them from crossing the line, going too far, and getting into deeper trouble that causes consequences to become more and more severe.

 ## CHILDREN OF POVERTY

It is estimated that as many as 25% of middle grades students are living in poverty. In her book *A Framework for Understanding Poverty,* Ruby Payne (1998) lists behaviors often associated with poverty. Yes, this is a generalization and, of course, no student living in poverty will exhibit all of these behaviors. Some will not exhibit any of them, and students who do not live in poverty may exhibit any or all of them. We should be aware, however, that the condition of poverty may contribute to students

- laughing when disciplined
- showing disrespect to teachers
- arguing loudly with teachers
- responding angrily
- making inappropriate or vulgar comments
- fighting to survive
- verbally abusing other students

- having difficulty following directions
- being extremely disorganized
- talking incessantly
- cheating or stealing

Our awareness of the likelihood of these behaviors occurring more frequently with children of poverty will help increase our understanding and level of preparation.

PEER MEDIATION

As a supplement to teacher/administration classroom management procedures, some schools implement *peer mediation*. It may take many different forms, but basically peer mediation provides opportunities for students to problem-solve concerning their disputes in the presence, and with the help, of a student acting as a mediator. If successful, peer mediation can lead to students taking increased responsibility for their actions as they learn socially acceptable ways of solving conflicts. It can lead to greater self-control and an understanding of alternatives to aggression, which almost always results in emotional and/or physical harm.

A study reported by Robinson, Smith, and Daunic (2000) reveals five major areas of conflict often dealt with in peer mediation sessions:

1. minor issues such as arguments over inconsequential topics or "having a bad day"
2. personal attacks (e.g, picking on or insulting another student, spreading rumors)
3. social skills deficits (e.g., failure to see another's viewpoint, inability to communicate, inability to control one's temper)
4. typical teen issues (e.g., disputes with parents about staying out late or chores, boyfriend/girlfriend issues)
5. status (e.g., attempting to boost one's reputation through self-aggrandizement or exaggeration) (p. 25)

To successfully help students settle disputes and acquire skills for handling future problems, a peer mediation program needs enthusiastic and dedicated teachers, counselors, and administrators to sustain the program's momentum. Resources include adult trainers who understand young adolescent development; curriculum that is developmentally appropriate and relevant to how kids process information; a plan that allows sessions to take place during the school day on an as-needed basis; a private, comfortable space to meet; and a system of deciding who will benefit and how they may access the program.

The only way a peer mediation program can hope to have an impact on the school environment is for it to be considered a valid alternative for conflict resolution by the kids themselves. This kind of validity does not come easily in middle grades. The program must be presented to the whole student body as an attractive plan that may provide a way not only to peacefully coexist, but also to avoid consequences imposed by adults. Peer mediation will not be used if it is perceived as a "nerdy" or "wimpy" thing to do. The choice of peer mediators is crucial. They should be representative in terms of grade level, peer group identification, socioeconomic status, special program involvement, race, and gender. Recruitment and training of the right students in the school population is vital.

The Robinson, et al. (2000) study revealed a benefit of peer mediation that should be noted. Their research shows that the mediators reported that the training involved helped prepare them to solve their own conflicts. So regardless of their efficacy with their peers' disputes, a small contingency of the student body gains life skills because of the training. This implies that perhaps the whole school could benefit from peer mediator training. A valuable use of advisory time!

 ## WITHIN OUR CONTROL

We influence, but cannot always control, students, colleagues, parents, and resources. However, we can control the key variable in effectively managing the classroom learning environment—ourselves. The Haim Ginott (1993) quote in Chapter 4 bears repeating here. In fact, it bears repeating on a daily basis.

> I've come to the frightening conclusion that I am the decisive element in the classroom. It's my personal approach that makes the climate. It's my mood that makes the weather. As a teacher I possess the tremendous power to make a child's life miserable or joyous. I can be a tool of torture or an instrument of inspiration. I can humiliate or humor, hurt or heal. In all situations, it is my response that decides whether a crisis will be escalated or de-escalated, a child humanized or dehumanized. (p. 15)

Effective classroom management requires self-assured, competent adults to be effective. Whatever combination of strategies we choose, and in whatever set of circumstances we find ourselves, we are key to the management of the learning environment.

Understanding Our Role

"The challenge is to be with them without being like them; that distinction preserves generational distinctions while at the same time building important bridges of communication and trust" (Stevenson, 1992, p. 25). Understanding our students—their development, interests, concerns, and habits—is vital. Our ongoing purpose is to be with our students as they grow. We have already grown, at least out of adolescence. We are not, and shouldn't attempt to be, like our students. Joining the student culture in an attempt to win their acceptance or popularity is a mistake.

 Standard 7

Knowledge 3: Middle level teacher candidates are knowledgeable about their responsibility for upholding high professional standards.

As a teacher, you are both the instructional leader and the classroom manager. Middle grades students don't need or want an adult who at one moment is 13 and, in an instant, becomes the adult trying to control the classroom. The consistent message needs to be "I am the adult, you are the students. We will respect one another and learn from each other." Curwin and Mendler (1999) warn us that "mixed signals often lead to agitation and anxiety in

students. . . . Mixed signals often culminate in conflict, confusion, and classroom management problems" (p. 35).

As adults we have a wide spectrum of personalities and life experiences. It's good to let students get to know us. Believe me, what we don't reveal, they'll make up! So be yourself—your adult self. An adult has emotions, hopes, problems, a sense of humor. Our students should see how thoughtful, mature people handle life. Remember, even if young adolescents appear to learn little else, they "learn us."

Getting Off to a Good Start

"Effective classroom management is a daily and essential challenge to teachers. Managing a class basically involves getting off to a good start, then keeping the class moving smoothly toward established goals" (Moore, 1999, p. 433). Students, as well as teachers, are often nervous about the first days and weeks of school. We can reassure our students and ourselves that the school year will bring positive experiences by doing some basic things such as

- making the classroom organized and inviting
- greeting students warmly and sincerely
- establishing and explaining classroom routines
- establishing and clarifying rules and consequences
- conducting a survey of students' interests and concerns

- creating ways for students to get to know us and each other
- forming cooperative groups and conducting an activity in which students will experience success
- clarifying the major learning goals for the class
- explaining grading criteria

It takes lots of preparation to begin a school year in a proactive and engaging style. It's serious business. Wong & Wong (1991) write, "What you do on the first days of school will determine your success or failure for the rest of the school year. You will either win or lose your class on the first days of school" (p. 3). I strongly recommend that you read Harry and Rosemary Wong's book *The First Days of School*. It is filled with practical advice on starting and keeping the momentum of a positive learning environment.

Easier to Love than to Like

I can honestly say that I have loved my students—all of them. I have cared deeply for them and always wanted the best for their lives. However, I have to tell you there have been individual students I have had difficulty liking. Teachers are human. We are capable of loving the unlovable. However, liking the unlikable is much harder. Shalaway (1998) tells us, "Sometimes, despite our best intentions, we find ourselves actively disliking one of the children in our charge. The child may be rude, disrespectful, disruptive, obnoxious, or otherwise annoying. It's human nature; some personalities clash" (p. 183).

How can we make the most of a situation where we feel the responsibility to address the needs of every student, even the one or two we like the least? The first step is to view the student as a "work in progress." Indeed, she is! Understanding both the developmental certainties and the possibilities of young adolescents will help us conjure up an attitude of excitement to see what a school year of maturing might do to make her more likable. Another tactic that helps is to purposefully spend time talking to the student you find hard to like about topics other than school. Finding a common interest will do wonders for a relationship. Try complimenting the student on a daily basis. Even the most unlikable middle grades student will have some trait that can be viewed as positive. Finally, realize that if you find it this difficult to like a student, there's a chance you may be the only adult who is even trying to like her. It is within our control to at least treat each and every student with kindness and respect, regardless of the level of our personal affinity, and to do our best to appreciate them.

Being prepared for each new day, having common sense rules, possessing confidence that shows through in our relationships with colleagues and students—these actions are within our control. Managing the learning environment will become second nature to us when we recognize the personal power we possess to make a positive difference.

We will conclude this section about how much of the learning environment is within our control by considering some of the 12 processes that form the foundation of an effective discipline program according to Curwin and Mendler (1999) in *Discipline with Dignity*. Each process has been touched on in the chapter. There is value in this kind of summary, found in Figure 11.4, as we consider how we can make these guidelines realities in our classrooms.

1. "Let students know what you need" (p. 13). Establishing rules and consequences for students and then dealing with students in consistent ways fulfills this process.

2. "Provide instruction at levels that match the students' ability" (p. 13). Assessing the academic levels of students and adjusting instruction to meet them where they are and take them forward are vital in providing both success and appropriate challenge. This will help prevent behavior problems.

3. "Listen to what students are thinking and feeling" (p. 14). Listening actively, identifying with student feelings, and conveying understanding and empathy can help prevent behavior problems.

4. "Use humor" (p. 14). Humor can set a friendly mood and diffuse small problems. Using a sense of humor in a middle school classroom, even if there are times when the kids don't get it, makes the atmosphere comfortable. Never, ever make students the butt of jokes or use sarcasm toward them.

5. "Vary your style of presentation" (p. 15). Disruptions often accompany inattentiveness and restlessness that result from using the same instructional approach over and over. Keep in mind that middle grades students need a change in activity every 15 minutes or so.

6. "Be responsible for yourself and allow kids to take responsibility for themselves" (p. 16). This is part of allowing, and even prompting, students to move from dependence to independence that requires them to be responsible for their actions.

7. "Realize and accept that you will not reach every kid" (p. 16). When a student continually chooses misbehavior despite all our preventive measures and interventions, she needs more than we can give. This will happen occasionally. We need to ask for help, move on, and be at our best for all the other students we positively influence.

8. "Start fresh every day. What happened yesterday is finished. Today is a new day. Act accordingly." (p. 16)

FIGURE 11.4   Foundations of an effective discipline program.
Source: From *Discipline with Dignity* (pp. 13–16), by R. L. Curwin and A. N. Mendler, 1999. Reprinted by permission of Pearson Education, Inc., Upper Saddle River, NJ.

REFLECTIONS ON MANAGING THE LEARNING ENVIRONMENT

Let's return to the opening quote of the chapter. Vatterott (1999) tells us, "A nurturing and supportive classroom environment is essential for the intellectual as well as the emotional and social development of young adolescents. . . . The environment that helps young adolescents develop emotionally and socially also enhances learning" (p. 23). Every concept and practice we have discussed in this chapter has as its ultimate goal the creation and maintenance of a classroom environment that supports learning.

Managing the learning environment is a complex and comprehensive task. The part of the task that often receives the most attention is classroom management focusing on student behavior. We need to realize that student behavior is dependent on numerous variables, many of which are strongly influenced by our actions as teachers. Creating a positive and productive learning environment involves ensuring physical, emotional, and academic safety. Preventive measures include providing consistently engaging instruction; well-established and efficient routines; and appropriate and enforceable rules and consequences. When preventive measures are not sufficient, intervention becomes necessary. Deciding when and how to implement consequences, as well as wisely using resources such as parents, peer mediators, and other school personnel, are key to effective intervention.

As we have added to the description of effective classroom teachers discussed in Chapter 4, we see that many of the factors contributing to managing the learning environment are within our control. Knowing ourselves, addressing our personal maturity, and thoroughly planning our initial encounters with our students will lead us to "create the climate" and "make the weather" in our classrooms with the students for whom we are responsible.

Group Activities

1. In pairs, arrange to visit with a team of middle school teachers to find out how they

   - begin the school year in welcoming ways
   - establish and maintain routines
   - develop rules and enforce consequences

   Add findings to your school files.

2. In groups of three or four, write a set of classroom rules you consider appropriate to post in a middle school classroom. Make a poster of the rules and be prepared to justify them.

3. As a class, brainstorm consequences for the rules posted in activity 2. Spend time discussing whether each item on the brainstormed list is a logical, related-to-the-rule consequence or if it more resembles punishment.

Individual Activities

1. In addition to the suggestions given for connecting with students, describe another way you might "win them over."

2. Did you ever feel physically threatened in school? If so, describe the circumstances. If not, tell about the factors that helped you perceive safety in your middle school.

3. Why is sarcasm an inappropriate form of humor to use in middle grades classrooms? Will you have trouble controlling your use of it?

Personal Journal

1. Did you feel accepted as a member of a caring community in your middle school? If so, what did being accepted feel like? If not, what made you feel like you were not accepted?

2. Do you recall your emotional safety being jeopardized by something a teacher may have said or done? Write about the memory.

3. Do you anticipate having difficulty knowing where and when to draw the teacher-student line because you want to identify with your students? Will your desire to be liked by them sometimes cloud your judgment? If you had a teacher for whom this was a dilemma, write a description of the circumstances.

Professional Practice

(It would be helpful to reread the descriptions of Rita Lopez-Mitchell and Ashley Anderson in Chapter 4, as well as the descriptions of Hector, Anthony, Marvin, and Mia in Chapters 2 and 3. These teachers and students are also featured in the Professional Practice sections of Chapters 2 and 7.)

Central Middle School made the 11:00 p.m. news. A 17-year-old was arrested on the school field for possession of a gun. He was identified as a former student with a grudge against the Central principal. Student rumors were rampant about what might have happened if the perpetrator had not been spotted by a teacher who knew the former student should not have been on the Central campus. The 17-year-old was immature enough to have shown the gun to a group of boys as the teacher approached him. The teacher saw it and used his duty radio to call the office. Police were there within a minute and made the arrest.

The incident was cause for alarm both at school and in the community. Such things had happened at the high school, but not the middle school. The principal, Mr. Lewis, called an emergency faculty meeting. He gave the teachers all the information he had about the incident and expressed his desire to revamp emergency procedures. Shaken by the knowledge that a young man had a gun on campus and that he was supposedly the target, Mr. Lewis asked the teachers to think with him about how to really get to know each student and to meet individual needs in every way possible. The teachers agreed to renew their efforts to personalize in-struction and work on writing and/or rewriting emergency policies.

Rita Lopez-Mitchell and Ashley Anderson

Because of her experience with students in the Behavior Improvement Room (BIR), Rita Lopez-Mitchell was asked to chair the committee to review discipline procedures. Ms. Lopez-Mitchell was reluctant to accept the chair position, but she knew she had insight that other teachers might not have. Her frustration level was high over the gun incident and active involvement in making changes appealed to her as a way of dealing with the realities of some of her students' lives. In his explanation of the incident, Mr. Lewis told teachers the names of the boys with whom the perpetrator felt comfortable enough to show them his gun. Among them was Anthony, in whom Ms. Lopez-Mitchell saw tremendous potential.

She also learned that Hector was a cousin of the older teen with the gun.

To top it off, the perpetrator had been in her social studies class 4 years earlier and she was having a hard time picturing his face.

Among the committee members was Ashley Anderson. She had been concerned for some time that the school-wide discipline policy was too impersonal and did not include an element of counseling.

Anthony and Hector, eighth grade

Marvin and Mia, eighth grade

1. Given what we know about Anthony, Hector, Marvin, and Mia, which assessment based on the 80–15–5 principle do you think is most accurate?

   (a) Anthony 80%, Hector 80%, Marvin 80%, Mia 80%

   (b) Anthony 5%, Hector 80%, Marvin 15%, Mia 80%

   (c) Anthony 15%, Hector 80%, Marvin 5%, Mia 80%

   (d) Anthony 15%, Hector 80%, Marvin 15%, Mia 80%

2. Ms. Lopez-Mitchell, Ms. Anderson, and the majority of the other committee members believe that whatever plan they design should have room to accommodate individual differences, in some respects at least. Given Anthony's "leadership" qualities plus his record of being on the receiving end of every discipline measure short of permanent expulsion, what might the committee consider in their efforts to be developmentally responsive?

   (a) Invite Anthony to be part of a student contingency on the committee to consider a new school-wide discipline program.

   (b) In their consideration of discipline "rungs" on a ladder toward suspension, place students on various rungs according to their histories.

   (c) Develop a new discipline plan and then ask Anthony to help get the word out among those students who follow his example and/or revere him.

   (d) Tell Anthony he starts with a "clean slate" provided he is willing to meet with them periodically to inform them of possible problems brewing.

3. Hector was absent for a week after the incident. Because the perpetrator was a family member, Ms. Lopez-Mitchell was both understanding and alarmed. She knew all about close family ties—the positive side, as well as the sometimes "blind" side. Which of the following would be the least appropriate action for a developmentally responsive teacher?

   (a) Make a home visit to check on Hector and show her support for him.

   (b) Because his absences were unexcused, hold fast to the "no make-up" rule of her team to show Hector and the rest of the students that consistency is important.

   (c) Call Hector's mom and express concern over his absences.

   (d) Call Hector and tell him about the work he is missing so he can begin to catch up, as well as urge him to return to school.

4. By this time in her eighth grade year, Mia has found her niche. Her floral notebook of poems expanded to include short stories. At the urging of her language arts teacher, Mia shared her writing with her. The teacher entered a story in a contest and Mia was awarded first prize. She has a small group of friends now and her confidence is growing. Following the gun-on-campus incident, the language arts teacher asked students to express their concerns in writing. When she read the poem

Mia wrote about the incident, she was struck by its meaningfulness. She should do which of the following:

(a) Ask Mia to read it to the class.
(b) Read the poem in an assembly on violence prevention as a surprise to honor Mia's talent.
(c) Both a and b.
(d) Definitely a, but reconsider b.

5. In Ms. Anderson's zeal to incorporate counseling into the Behavior Improvement Room, which of the following suggestions seems most appropriate for middle grades students?

(a) Make a 15-minute session with the guidance counselor a mandatory part of being assigned to BIR.
(b) As a requirement for getting out of the BIR, a student must write an apology letter for her offense.

(c) While in the BIR, a student must write a description of the behavior that landed him there and fill out an appointment form asking to meet with an adult of his choice in the building to discuss his behavior.
(d) Students in BIR participate in a group counseling session each day regardless of their offenses and/or grade level.

Constructed Response

The gun-on-campus incident has had an effect on Marvin. After it happened, he made jokes about it, especially when a teacher or student expressed concern. When his behavior begins to surface, how might a teacher curb it using unobtrusive measures? If his misguided attempts at humor continue, what kind of consequence might be appropriate?

Internet Resources

Education World
http://educationworld.com

Middle Web Ideas for New Teachers
http://www.middleweb.com

This part of the Middle Web site features tips on management routines and procedures, as well as classroom discipline strategies.

Middle Web Middle School Diaries
http://www.middleweb.com

This part of the Middle Web site features first hand accounts from new and experienced teachers on a variety of topics that change regularly.

Northwest Regional Educational Laboratory
http://www.nwrel.org/national/

The U.S. Department of Education Office of Educational Research and Improvement supports this large site. It contains a link to the National Resource Center for Safe Schools that provides information to help schools create safe school environments.

References

Belair, J. R., & Freeman, P. (2000). Protecting bodies, hearts, and minds in schools. *Middle School Journal, 31*(5), 3–4.

Bicard, D. F. (2000). Using classroom rules to construct behavior. *Middle School Journal, 31*(5), 37–45.

Bluestein, J. (2001). *Creating emotionally safe schools.* Deerfield Beach, FL: Health Communications, Inc.

Borich, G. D. (2003). *Observation skills for effective teaching*. Upper Saddle River, NJ: Merrill/ Prentice Hall.

Burden, P. R., & Byrd, D. M. (1999). *Methods for effective teaching*. Boston: Allyn & Bacon.

Canter, L., & Canter, M. (1976). *Assertive discipline: A take-charge approach for today's educator*. Los Angeles: Canter and Associates.

Carnegie Council on Adolescent Development. (1989). *Turning points: Preparing American youth for the 21st century*. New York: Carnegie Corporation.

Cummings, C. (2000). *Winning strategies for classroom management*. Alexandria, VA: Association for Supervision and Curriculum Development.

Curwin, R. L., & Mendler, A. N. (1999). *Discipline with dignity*. Upper Saddle River, NJ: Merrill/ Prentice Hall.

Erb, T. (2000). Interview with Gerald Bourgeois: Voice of experience on school safety. *Middle School Journal, 31*(5), 5–11

George, P. S., & Alexander, W. M. (2003). *The exemplary middle school*. Belmont, CA: Wadsworth/Thomson Learning.

Ginott, H. G. (1993). *Teacher and child*. New York: Collier Books, Macmillan.

Gordon, T. (1974). *Teacher effectiveness training*. New York: David McKay.

Jackson, A. W., & Davis, G. A. (2000). *Turning points 2000: Educating adolescents in the 21st century*. New York: Teachers College Press.

Knowles, T., & Brown, D. F. (2000). *What every middle school teacher should know*. Westerville, OH: National Middle School Association.

Kommer, D. (1999). Beyond fashion patrol: School uniforms for the middle grades. *Middle School Journal, 30*(5), 23–26.

Kounin, J. (1970). *Discipline and group management in classrooms*. New York: Holt, Rinehart and Winston.

Lipsitz, J. (1995). Prologue: Why we should care about caring. *Phi Delta Kappan, 76*(9), 665–666.

Moore, K. D. (1999). *Middle and secondary instructional methods*. Boston: McGraw-Hill.

National Middle School Association. (2003). *This we believe: Successful schools for young adolescents*. Westerville, OH: Author.

Payne, R. (1998). *A framework for understanding poverty*. Highlands, TX: RFT Publishing.

Purkey, W. W., & Strahan, D. B. (2002). *Inviting positive classroom discipline*. Westerville, OH: National Middle School Association.

Robinson, T. W., Smith, S. W., & Daunic, A. P. (2000). Middle school students' views on the social validity of peer mediation. *Middle School Journal, 31*(5), 23–29.

Shalaway, L. (1998). *Learning to teach . . . not just for beginners*. New York: Scholastic Professional Books.

Skinner, B. F. (1971). *Beyond freedom and dignity*. New York: Knopf.

Stevenson, C. (1992). *Teaching ten to fourteen year olds*. New York: Longman.

Varner, E. (1999). Turn discipline problems into opportunities to improve instruction. *Middle Ground, 2*(4), 27–28.

Vatterott, C. (1999). *Academic success through empowering students*. Columbus, OH: National Middle School Association.

Wong, H. K., & Wong, R. T. (1991). *The first days of school*. Sunnyvale, CA: Harry K. Wong Publications.

12

They Are All Our Children

Making these several school years momentous in ways that can lead kids to continue developing their minds, bodies, and souls in directions that are compatible with the educational values that our schools are charged with accomplishing is a formidable but critical mission. But it is also a possible one. Whether this mission is accomplished in any particular classroom or school, however, depends more on the teacher's vision and commitments than on any other factor.

Stevenson and Carr, 1993, p. 184

Use this diagram as an organizational tool. In the boxes beside the chapter headings, indicate the date by which the readings should be completed.

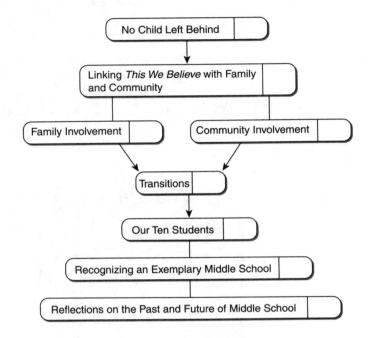

INTRODUCTION

This chapter is all about sharing—and ownership. Not until we consider all middle school students as our own will we understand our part in the shared responsibility for their growth. Only then will we understand and view each unique child as a significant individual around whom our efforts center. "Research shows that where there is shared responsibility for student learning, student achievement—for every subgroup—improves" (Conzemius & O'Neill, 2001, p. 3). Since we know that shared responsibility is the key, our mandate as teachers is not only to do our part as best we can, but also to draw others into the process for every subgroup, every child.

Standard 6

Performance 2: Middle level teacher candidates act as advocates for all young adolescents in the school and in the larger community.

Schools where shared responsibility is a reality most often exhibit the following evidence of success:

- rising standardized test scores
- classroom-, school-, district-developed assessments that show steady improvement for every individual and every group of students
- increasing rates of student, parent, teacher, and community satisfaction on a variety of indicators important to these constituents
- improved efficiencies in the use of resources such as staff development dollars, curriculum choices, staff development decisions, and time
- evidence of renewed energy for teaching, learning, and leading
- students actively engaged and taking responsibility for their learning
- deeper, more enduring connections among students, teachers, parents, administrators, and the community (Conzemius & O'Neill, 2001, p. 4)

The last measure of success is echoed by NMSA in *This We Believe* (2003).

> Schools do not presume to educate children alone. In today's society, genuine family and community involvement are fundamental components of successful schools for young adolescents. . . . Research studies clearly link the involvement of both family and other adults in the community with higher levels of student achievement, improved student behavior, and greater overall support for schools. (pp. 17–18)

Sharing responsibility with family and community is considered so vital by the National Middle School Association that one of the seven Performance-Based Standards for Initial Middle Level Teacher Preparation is devoted to the concept. Standard Six, titled Family and Community Involvement, states, "Middle level teacher candidates understand the major concepts, principles, theories, and research related to working collaboratively with family and community members, and they use that knowledge to maximize the learning of all young adolescents."

Throughout this chapter I will refer you to the knowledge, dispositions, and performances that flesh out this standard. We will explore the No Child Left Behind Act, family involvement, community involvement, transitioning of students into and out of middle school, and recognizing an exemplary middle school. Finally, we will reflect on the past and future of middle grades education.

 ## NO CHILD LEFT BEHIND

The title of this chapter—They Are All Our Children—echoes the intent of the federal legislation passed in January 2002—the *No Child Left Behind Act (NCLB)*. Sue Swain, Executive Director of the National Middle School Association, assures us that the objectives of the act are right in line with NMSA's beliefs that every child, regardless of circumstances, should receive a quality education (George, 2002).

While we will not argue with the impetus behind the legislation to provide quality education for all children, the challenges presented to middle schools by the mandates and deadlines of the act are daunting. The success of a school, according to NCLB, rests solely in student achievement as measured by standardized tests. The mandates of NCLB are accompanied by a time line for accomplishment. The act proposes financial support for schools that need it most to facilitate changes necessary for meeting the deadlines. This is a positive step, as long as the funds are a reality and the human and material resources are available.

NCLB calls for all students to score at proficient levels or above by 2014. States must present their definitions of proficiency in math, reading, and science and their assessments for measuring student achievement to the U.S. Department of Education for approval. Schools whose students are not making adequate yearly progress toward proficiency must provide options to parents including transfers to other schools and Title I funding for tutoring. Provisions are made for replacing a school staff after 4 years of failure to make adequate progress and a state takeover of a school with 5 years of failure.

Particularly problematic for middle schools, again not in intent but in feasibility, is the provision for a "highly qualified" teacher in every classroom. NCLB defines "highly qualified" as having a degree in the content area taught or passing a Praxis content area exam. Being a content specialist is very important and we should all be working toward that goal. However, many middle school teachers have degrees in elementary education and few universities offer middle level degrees requiring coursework in a subject area equivalent to a major in that area. Filling all our classrooms with what our government defines as "highly qualified" teachers by 2006 is, therefore, totally unrealistic. NMSA continues to set the standard for middle level teachers being content certified in two subject areas. To comply with both NMSA and NCLB would take more than a 4-year college degree.

NCLB emphasizes the importance of family/community involvement with schools. If schools attempt to meet the standards outlined in the legislation alone, the likelihood of success is doubtful. However, with family and community support the standards are more within reach.

This is a very cursory discussion of No Child Left Behind. As states struggle to fulfill the mandates and middle level educators attempt to reconcile the demands of the act with the balance of developmental responsiveness and academic rigor, no doubt there will be adjustments and compromises along the way.

We'll now turn our attention to families and communities as we attempt to involve them as our partners in educating young adolescents in excellent and equitable ways.

 ## LINKING *THIS WE BELIEVE* WITH FAMILY AND COMMUNITY

In 2001, the National Middle School Association published *This We Believe. . . and Now We Must Act,* a compilation of relevant articles addressing the 12 tenets of the 1995 version of *This We Believe: Developmentally Responsive Middle Level Schools.* One of the articles by Joyce Epstein (2001), noted specialist in the area of home-school connections, is titled "School, Family, and Community Partnerships." In the article, Epstein states that the 12 characteristics of responsive middle level schools are interrelated. She tells us that it is "particularly important for middle level educators to understand how school-family-community partnerships are linked to other recommended elements so that parent involvement is not something extra, separate, or different from the 'real work' of a school" (p. 50). What follows are excerpts in Epstein's own words relating partnerships with the 12 tenets of *This We Believe* (National Middle School Association, 1995).

Educators committed to young adolescents: To understand young adolescents, educators need to understand their students' families—their cultures, hopes and dreams. In a good partnership program, families are helped to understand young adolescents, middle level schools, peer pressure, and other topics of importance, and educators are helped to understand students' families.

A shared vision: Along with educators and students, families and community members must contribute to the shared vision of a responsive middle level school. . . . Vision and mission statements should be presented and discussed each year as new families and students enter or transfer to the middle level school.

High expectations for all: National and local surveys of middle grades students and their families indicate that they have very high expectations of success in school and in life. . . . Responsive middle level schools must incorporate students' and families' high aspirations into the school's high expectations for all . . .

An adult advocate for every student: School-based advocates and teacher advisors need to know each student's family. . . . The advocate can serve as a key contact for the family should questions or concerns arise, facilitating two-way channels of communication before problems become too serious to solve.

Positive school climate: A safe, welcoming, stimulating, and caring environment describes a good school for students, educators, families, and the community. In a school with strong partnerships, family and community members are more likely to volunteer to help ensure the safety of the playground, hallways, and lunchroom; to share their talents in classroom discussions; and to lead or coach programs after school to create a true school community.

Curriculum that is challenging, integrative, and exploratory: Families and communities need to know about all of the courses, special programs, and services that are offered to increase student learning in the middle grades. . . . Families also need good information about how their students are progressing in each subject, how to help students set and meet learning goals, how to monitor and discuss homework, and how to work with students to solve major problems that threaten course or grade level failure . . .

Varied teaching and learning approaches: Families need to know more about the varied instructional approaches that middle grades teachers use in all subjects, including group activities, problem-solving strategies, prewriting strategies, students as historians, hands-on science, and other challenging innovations that promote learning.

Assessments and evaluations that promote learning: Families and community members need to know about the major tests, new or traditional assessments, report card criteria, and other standards that schools use to determine children's progress and paths . . . There are many ways to include students and families in important assessments and evaluations in order to make those measures more meaningful.

Flexible organizational structures: Families need to understand "interdisciplinary teams" and "houses," schedules, electives or exploratories, and other arrangements that define middle level school organizations (MacIver & Epstein, 1991). Every middle level school should have annual group meetings and individual meetings of parents, teachers, and advisors to ensure that families understand how classes are organized and to gather family input for the decisions that affect their children's experiences and education.

Comprehensive guidance and support services: Families need to know about formal and informal guidance programs at the school. . . . In some middle level schools, guidance counselors are members of interdisciplinary teams and meet with teachers, parents, and students on a regular schedule and in other meetings as needed. (pp. 49–53)

 ## FAMILY INVOLVEMENT

As discussed in Chapter 3, the definition of family has changed and expanded. Rubenstein (1994) says, "The family today is often a conundrum: Who's related to whom and who's responsible for the child?" (p. 97). While most books and articles discuss parent involvement, I choose to use the word **family** to encompass biological parents, stepparents, grandparents, aunts/uncles, older siblings, and others who either live in the home or share guardianship of our students. So while the word family in this chapter is still synonymous with the word **parent** for the majority of our students, the implications should be stretched to more realistically encompass all our students and their individual circumstances. The principles are the same, even if the players are changing.

Families = Traditional + Nontraditional

Standard 6

Knowledge 1: Middle level teacher candidates understand the variety of family structures.

No matter how we define family, involving those closest to our students in the life of the school, and specifically in their students' schoolwork and relationships at school, has a positive impact on learning. "Positive family dynamics have been deemed a vital ingredient in the academic success of middle level students. The benefits of parental involvement on student achievement and attitude toward school have been documented" (VanHoose & Legrand, 2000, p. 32).

Standard 6

Knowledge 9: Middle level teacher candidates understand the roles of family and community members in improving the education of all young adolescents.

Performance 1: Middle level teacher candidates establish respectful and productive relationships with family and community members that maximize student learning and well-being.

Involvement Decreases

A discouraging fact of life in most middle schools is decreasing family involvement compared with elementary schools (Downs, 2001). Most middle schools experience sharp decreases in family involvement between grades 6 and 8. Let's face it. How often do you hear someone say,

"Gee, I wish I were 13 again." Few of us have fond memories of our own self-image and we would probably not wish to be back in a junior high/middle school setting as students.

Jackson and Davis, the authors of *Turning Points 2000,* report that families "check out" as their children progress to and through middle school. They tell us that many families genuinely believe that their involvement should decrease to promote independence. Another reason for withdrawal of involvement stems from many young adolescents' negative view of their families being part of their school experiences, even their lives in general. Families and teachers can tell humorous, and not so humorous, stories of students ignoring family members who attempt involvement. After a couple of "funny" instances, families decide to back off and give their students the space they appear to want.

A very real reason many families decrease involvement is academic intimidation (L'Esperance & Gabbard, 2001). When schoolwork becomes too difficult for family members, they shy away from school. Perhaps they dropped out before high school graduation or were never successful academically. Immigrant families often experience intimidation due to language barriers. Language minority students are increasing in numbers, and finding ways to involve their families is becoming a dilemma of growing magnitude. Along with language barriers, cultural differences can create misunderstandings and reluctance. Some immigrant families don't realize that direct contact with schools and teachers is desirable, and that asking questions and giving input with regard to teaching and learning are sure to improve the process. Understanding reticent families and approaching them in appropriate ways about a variety of opportunities for their involvement will benefit all of us.

Getting to Know Families

A commitment to involving families means making efforts to get to know them. Inviting families to get involved needs to be guided not only by what schools have to offer them, but what they have to offer schools. Matching potential family contributions to school needs, and then being sensitive to what families expect of schools will make for positive and productive relationships. A healthy balance will be established as illustrated in Figure 12.1.

Standard 6

Disposition 1: Middle level teacher candidates respect all young adolescents and their families.

NMSA.

There are many questions we can ask families to ascertain what they want and expect from us, as well as what they have to offer the home-school partnership. A questionnaire might be used in a before-school contact. This is an ideal initiative for teams. Each teacher takes responsibility for a homeroom or advisory group. The questionnaire can be sent with a letter of welcome. If possible, a stamped, self-addressed envelope is a good idea to increase the probability of a high rate of return. As an alternative, send the questionnaire home with students in a packet of materials to be signed and returned. A contest to see which homeroom or advisory group has the highest return rate may help get

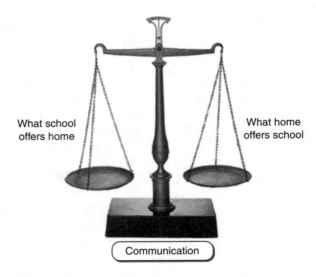

What school
offers home

What home
offers school

Communication

FIGURE 12.1   Achieving balance: School and home.

information back from a large percentage of students. Figure 12.2 shows a sample form to send home.

Familiarizing Families with Middle School

Every August we can count on talk shows and morning news programs to address issues relevant to the beginning of the new school year. Inevitably among the topics and within the discussions we hear nervous parents voice concern over sending their children to middle school after 6 or 7 years in what they considered the safe haven of an elementary setting. The eager interviewer chimes in with, "It's so frightening to send children to middle school these days." They may have a psychologist on camera giving advice for distraught parents and supposedly terrified children.

If families understand middle grades philosophy with its student-centered focus on developmental appropriateness, their concerns may be at least partially allayed. A study reported in 2001 found that "Parents reporting high familiarity with middle level practices were more likely to report positive attitudes and engagement at their child's school . . ." (Mulhall, Mertens, & Flowers, 2001, p. 60). The study also showed that middle level practices are a mystery to the majority of parents. Figure 12.3 shows the results of a survey of 20,584 parents with students in 131 Arkansas, Louisiana, and Mississippi schools at various stages of middle school implementation. From the chart you can see that none of the practices reached the "very familiar" status with even one quarter of the parents. In fact, only cooperative learning made the "somewhat familiar" or "very familiar" status with half, and cooperative learning is a strategy used in elementary schools as well as middle schools.

We are aware of how important each of the six survey practices are to middle level philosophy. If families are unfamiliar with what we do all day with their children, then their concerns are understandable. As we will discuss later in the chapter, we are our own best

1. Who lives in your household?
   Name   Age   Relationship to Student

2. What do you think your student's greatest strengths are?

3. What is your goal for your student during this school year?

4. Are there certain concerns, home situations, or medical problems we should be aware of in order to work more effectively with your student?

5. What activities does your student enjoy?

6. What one subject area do you think your student will struggle most with this year?

7. What does your student do after-school? Is someone home when he/she arrives? Does he/she have regular activities?

8. Would your student benefit from regular after school sessions designed to help with homework? Would transportation be needed to take him/her home?

9. One of our team goals is to expand opportunities for our students to explore many interests. What special interest do you have that you would share with us this year (e.g., occupation, hobby, talent, etc.).

10. Because we believe that education is a home-school partnership, we ask that you participate in ways in which you are comfortable. Here are some possibilities.

    Please check ways you would like to be involved occasionally.

    bake for events _____   field trip chaperone _____
    collect project supplies _____ homeroom parent _____
    tutor after school _____   big brother/sister program _____
    organize fundraisers _____   field day volunteer _____
    assist in classroom _____   materials preparation _____
    "phone tree" leader _____   career day speaker _____

    How would you prefer we communicate with you?
    mail _____   address: _____
    e-mail _____   address: _____
    phone _____   number: _____ best times: _____
    notes sent with student_____   addressed to: _____

FIGURE 12.2   Sample questions for getting to know families.

public relations specialists. If familiarity with middle level practices equates to more positive attitudes and increased family participation, and if, according to meta-analyses like the one reported by Henderson and Berla (1994), family participation in early adolescent schooling results in increased learning and student success, then public relations specialists we need to be!

Middle Level Practices	Familiarity with Middle Level Practices (% responding)			
	Not at all familiar	A little familiar	Somewhat familiar	Very familiar
Interdisciplinary teaming	42	17	20	20
Advisory programs	52	18	17	13
Integrated lessons	43	22	21	14
Heterogeneous grouping	41	20	21	18
Exploratory	29	24	27	20
Cooperative learning	24	24	28	24

FIGURE 12.3   Parents' familiarity with middle grades practices.

Source: From "How Familiar Are Parents with Middle Level Practices?" by P. F. Mulhall, S. B. Mertens, and N. Flowers, 2001, *Middle School Journal, 33*(2), p. 58. Copyright 2001 by National Middle School Association. Reprinted with permission from National Middle School Association.

Communicating the value of interdisciplinary teaming, advisory, integrated lessons, heterogeneous grouping, exploratory, and cooperative learning is an ongoing process. These practices, after all, permeate what we do. It's important to show how the practices are interrelated and, to a great extent, interdependent.

Communication

Getting to know families and familiarizing them with middle school philosophy and practices happens through effective communication. Ongoing communication with families enlists them as partners as long as the communication includes listening as well as giving information by both families and teachers. "The key to building critical communication with parents is being an effective listener, . . . realizing the possibilities of a partnership with parents depends upon success in establishing effective dialogue between home and school" (Stevenson, 1992, p. 319).

Standard 6

Knowledge 4: Middle level teacher candidates know how to communicate effectively with family and community members.

Disposition 7: Middle level teacher candidates realize and value the importance of communicating effectively with family and community members.

School and home communication = Face-to-face + Telephone + Written + Electronic

Some communication vehicles are school-wide such as open house and report cards. Others are initiated by teams and individual teachers. Most communication between home and school is either face-to-face, by telephone, in writing, or accomplished electronically.

Face-to-face.   Most middle schools have an open house at the beginning of the school year that many call *back-to-school night*. Typically, a family is given their student's schedule. They follow the schedule through each of the periods, which are shortened to 10 to 15 minutes. This allows them to meet all of their student's teachers and get a feel for the paths the student walks each day. Back-to-school night provides a wonderful opportunity to make a positive first impression on families. Here are some guidelines for a successful back-to-school experience:

- Make your room as neat and attractive as possible. Even though it's the beginning of the year, be sure you already have some student work displayed.
- Greet families at the door with a smile and firm handshake.
- Give families a handout that may include your background, a brief statement about the importance of your subject area, a list of needed materials/supplies, classroom management policies, grading policies, etc.
- Pass around a sign-in sheet asking for student name and family member name(s).
- Prepare to speak for about 5 minutes and then welcome questions. It is preferable that this brief speech be planned. Experienced teachers can give you ideas about questions your students' families will typically ask.
- Offer a clipboard on which families can request individual conferences. Back-to-school night is not the time to discuss individual students.
- Thank families for attending and express the need and desire for their participation throughout the year.

Family-teacher (parent-teacher) conference.   A critically important face-to-face communication opportunity that seldom receives more than a mention in preservice education is the *family-teacher (parent-teacher) conference.* Often the skills and tactics for these potentially stressful "little talks" are learned on the job through trial and error. Most schools have organized times when families are invited to sign up for 15- to 30-minute conference times with either individual teachers or teams of teachers. Some schools have half days or evenings when teachers are available to talk with families. These conferences may be for exchange of information with mostly positive, affirming dialogue, or they may entail the necessity of corrective plans dealing with academics or behavior. Some schools designate a day following report card distribution when families are invited to the school. Three to four opportunities may be scheduled for conferences of this nature each school year.

Preparing for a drop-in conference is different than preparing for a called conference. For drop-ins, it is helpful to have a general information sheet available for families to read, perhaps while they wait for a turn to speak with you. Up-to-date student folders with sample work and any notes about the student should be readily available along with an accurate and complete list of assignments and grades. One secret to success for drop-in conferences is the ability to tactfully end each one so you can visit with all the families that show up at your door. This isn't easy. If there are individual concerns that can't be adequately addressed in 10 minutes or so, ask the family to make an appointment for another time.

Called conferences, or ones that are initiated for specific reasons, require another level of preparation. If you are conferencing as an individual teacher you will want to have the same resources listed in the previous paragraph. You will also want to make some notes to

Standard 6

Performance 7: Middle level teacher candidates demonstrate the ability to participate in parent conferences.

organize the information you want to convey as well as the questions you want to ask. Some tentative action plan ideas are helpful. If you are conferencing as a team, each teacher needs to be ready and you will need to spend a few minutes deciding who will lead the conference. This person is responsible for stating the main purpose of the conference, keeping the discussion focused, and summarizing the agreed-upon strategies to be implemented. Another teacher needs to take notes during the conference and complete a form similar to the one in Figure 12.4. Make sure at least one teacher can open the conference on a positive note to help put the family more at ease. You can see how efficient a team conference can be. As an individual teacher conferencing with a family, the whole responsibility falls on you. You still must document the conference fully and file your conference form.

Family conferences may be initiated either by teachers or by families because of specific concerns. These may occur anytime during the year. I strongly recommend that teams of teachers meet with families together. I have seen the positive dynamics, the cohesive solutions, and the growth of empathy that is possible when a group of adults share information and formulate proactive strategies and agreements to benefit an individual student. Here's a fairly common scenario.

Maurice's grades are slipping and it's only the sixth week of school. He has been referred to the office several times for behavior problems. He became very angry in fourth block yesterday and called an eighth grade girl a bitch very loudly during social studies. He was sent to the BIR for the rest of the day and his mom was called. She agreed to meet with Maurice's team of teachers at 7:30 the next day. The team got together after school the day before the conference to talk about

Student name _____ Date _____

Family attending _____

Teachers attending _____

Others _____

Notes: (continue on back as needed)

Summary of concerns:

Plan of action:

Follow-up communication plan:

FIGURE 12.4 Sample family conference form.

Maurice. They discovered, as almost always happens, that one or more teachers have not seen the dramatic grade drop, nor do they regularly see any misbehavior.

When the conference begins, the teachers who are having relatively more success with Maurice speak first and give the positive side. Then a designated teacher explains the problems the other teachers are observing as well as the office referrals and BIR incidents. Teachers express their desire for Maurice to succeed and ask his mom to talk about anything she has observed, to ask questions, to give insights, etc. The conversation then becomes one about planning ways to help Maurice find both academic and behavioral success.

The resulting value of the whole team and the family meeting together depends in large measure on the attitude and demeanor of the teachers. There is a very real chance that Maurice's mom could have been intimidated and overwhelmed by four or five teachers sitting in desks where they are very comfortable and confident. Friendliness and the offer of coffee or a soft drink go a long way toward making the conference one of honest, sincere communication. Bottom line is that we all have the same goal—Maurice's success. Say it often, and mean it.

Room arrangement is important for conferences. A circle of chairs works best. Using all student desks will prove embarrassing. Provide at least two sturdy, armless chairs so that all sizes of family members and teachers can be seated comfortably. Teachers should never sit behind a teacher desk with family members on the other side.

Another consideration is our choice of words. We are the experts in education, but most families are the experts on their students. We would not expect them to spout adolescent development theory, but rather to use straightforward language to convey their concerns and descriptions of circumstances. So should we. The education jargon should be eliminated as much as possible. For instance, saying "Jennifer sometimes doesn't respond to the pedagogy research tells us is most aligned to the content" is journal talk, not family talk. Instead try, "Jennifer doesn't seem to understand what we're talking about in class. I need your help to find ways of teaching that will help her 'get it.'"

"Sandwich" conference = Positive comments + Negative concerns + Positive comments
---

Always have at least two positive things to say about a student with whose family you are meeting. This allows you to employ what teachers sometimes call the "sandwich formula." You place negative slices between layers of positive comments at the beginning and end of the conference. The "sandwich" will be much more palatable than a steady diet of negative information!

There is an ongoing debate about the value of a team policy that calls for students to, almost without exception, be present for conferences. I've been on teams where the majority insisted that students attend with their families, and I've been on teams with the opposite philosophy. I see the benefit of both positions and have concluded over the years that it's a good idea to make student attendance dependent on individual circumstances. It's true that we want students to learn and practice responsibility, and participating in a family conference allows all parties to hear the same things at the same time while actively involving the student in the specified improvement plan. However, there are times when families may have information to share with teachers that they prefer not to discuss in front of their students. There are also cultural considerations. Some families may abide by the "seen but not heard" philosophy of childhood. I recommend that families be asked their preference and that teams abide by that preference. During the adult-only conference a time can be set for the group to meet with the student to convey specific concerns and/or praise or to talk about the improvement plan.

Student-led conferences.   Growing in popularity for a wide array of reasons, *student-led conferences* have the potential to bring more families into the teaching-learning process. In *Classroom Connections,* an NMSA publication, student-led conferences are defined as events "in which parents and students sit down and talk about one of the most important aspects in their life—school. The student is not only the focal point of the conversation, they are the leader of the conference" (Berckemeyer, 2001, p. 1). Schools implementing this innovative way of informing families of student progress and goals report very favorable results.

As with traditional family conferences, student-led conferences vary logistically. They may be:

- one teacher, one student, one family with teacher staying the whole time—or popping in and out
- team of teachers, one student, one family with teachers staying the whole time—or rotating in and out
- two to four family-student conferences in the same room with one teacher rotating among conferences
- two to four family-student conferences in same room with team of teachers rotating among conferences

It is clear that the most vital elements of a student-led conference are the student and the family. The teacher's role is one of consultation and encouragement.

The reasons for having student-led conferences are the same as the benefits. They include:

- student ownership of the quality of academic work
- provision for student-family interactions based on student effort and accomplishment
- focal point that is academic rather than behavioral
- process of organizing portfolio that gives student a sense of "wholeness" and connectedness of work
- student acquisition and practice of communication skills
- student goal-setting for academic progress
- greater family participation (families always show up in larger numbers when their students are involved)

In order to make these reasons/benefits reality, preparation is very important.

When student and family meet, the student tells about the team classrooms—the curriculum, the activities, the projects and assignments, the learning. Typically, the conference includes the presentation of a portfolio of projects and assignments from each class followed by explanation of evaluations agreed upon by student and teacher, and then a joint process of setting goals for the months ahead (Farber, 1999).

The portfolio should contain not only the best student work, but it should also reflect a range of efforts including tests, essays, problem-solving scenarios, creative endeavors, and other student and/or teacher chosen items. When reflecting on the overall package, students should analyze reasons for their successes as well as their less than successful efforts. This is one of the best results of developing portfolios and then figuring out what to say about each element. Students come to view themselves as learners.

Students need guidance as they begin to prepare for student-led conferences. Students should be asked to outline, if not script, what they will say to their families. If time permits, they benefit from practicing with peers. It's a great idea to choose a student to work with privately on his presentation. Then role-play as the family member of the student to demonstrate what a conference might look and sound like. Few strategies teach more efficiently and effectively than modeling. This is also an ideal time for students to learn communication skills, as well as basic manners. Dressing appropriately, opening doors for families, and introducing families to teachers are appropriate life skills for conferences. Speaking clearly, asking for and answering questions, and communicating organized points are skills that can benefit students for a lifetime.

Families also need to be prepared for the student-led conference. Sending a letter home informing parents about what to expect in a student-led conference is advisable.

We know how important it is to evaluate new or different efforts from several perspectives. Figure 12.5 contains samples of evaluations that can be completed by families and students.

In *Turning Points 2000* (Jackson & Davis, 2000) David Linzey, principal of Southridge Middle School in Fontana, California, is reported to contend that student-led conferences are "the most powerful delivery of information that schools have today" (p. 201). They are powerful because students analyze and present themselves as learners in conversations with their families.

Student-led conferences = Student responsibility + Student analysis of achievement + Student/parent communication

---

Telephone communication.   After a face-to-face conversation, the next most personal communication is a telephone call. That dreaded "call from the teacher" has given this form of communication a bad rap. However, calls can and should be made for positive reasons as well as for problem situations.

Reaching families by phone during the day can be difficult and the proliferation of answering machines makes our machine phone etiquette important. If you are suddenly faced with a recorded message, never just hang up. With caller ID, the family will know someone from school called. If you are calling with a student compliment, you may want to cheerfully deliver the positive message and say that if the family would like to hear more good things they can feel free to reach you during your planning period and leave a convenient number. Be sure you are readily available if the family member returns the call during the times you specify. If the subject is less than positive, always let them know that the student is fine, but that there is a matter you'd like to discuss at their convenience. Ask the family to call you the following day during your planning period or to leave a message in the office giving a time and number where they can be reached later in the day. If the situation warrants a more immediate response or definitely requires a conference, your message should indicate the appropriate sense of urgency and let the family know you will keep trying to reach them in the evening if you or the office hasn't heard back by the end of the school day.

If you call a family and discover that the phone number has changed or the phone has been disconnected, let your administrators know immediately. They will follow up to get the most recent information.

Student Evaluation

1. What was the best thing about your family conference?

_____

_____

2. What would you change about the conference?

_____

_____

3. Were your family's reactions what you expected? Explain.

_____

_____

4. How will you prepare for the next conference?

_____

_____

Family Evaluation

Thank you for joining us today for your student-led conference. Please take a minute to give us some feedback about your experience by circling the response closest to your opinion.

1. The student-led conference was

    very worthwhile

    worthwhile

    not worthwhile

2. The time we spent in conferencing was

    too short

    the right amount

    too long

3. The amount and nature of what our student presented was

    revealing and informative

    adequate, but still leaves questions

    inadequate

4. Access to team teachers before, during, and after our conference was

    satisfactory

    unsatisfactory

If you have comments you would like to share with us, please write them below or call us. Thank you for participating in this important event with us!

FIGURE 12.5 Student-led conference evaluations.

Always begin a family phone conversation by clearly identifying who you are and the subject you teach. If at all possible, say something positive, even if it's "My, my, what energy Barry has! It's one of the benefits of being 12." This kind of statement usually puts the family member at ease. Chances are Barry's "energy" is experienced by them as well. Before calling about a problem, whether academic or behavioral, have several possible solution paths to discuss and welcome family input and suggestions. Express confidence that together progress can be made.

Written communication.   Probably the most frequently used form of communication between school and family is the written word. Often it's one-way communication and, if we rely on students to deliver the message, it's likely to be "no way" communication. Written communication is by far the easiest way to relay information. Because it seems easy, it often has a tendency to become sloppy. I can't overemphasize the need to proofread everything that is sent to families, or to the public in general. We are educators and are expected to be educated. Our communication should show it. Educational jargon and obscure vocabulary are neither necessary nor desirable. Plain, to the point, informative writing is called for—with no grammatical or spelling errors.

Written communication can take many forms: progress reports, report card comments, general school information typically sent in the beginning of the year, announcements of meetings/events, letters about school picture day, fund raising information—the list is long. Your team will send a welcome letter with multiple bits of information; you'll send your own letter about your subject area, expectations, grading, and behavior policies; and your team may opt to send home periodic newsletters featuring student activities, outlining projects, recognizing accomplishments, and announcing future events.

Sending individual notes that are less than positive home with students and expecting them to be promptly delivered is unrealistic. If you have problem-oriented subjects to convey, better use the telephone or the post office. On the other hand, positive and complimentary notes almost always end up under a refrigerator magnet. The yearlong benefits of occasional "happy notes" cannot be overstated. Family appreciation and support will likely be yours for just a few minutes of your time in recognizing a positive trait or action. All students have them. It may not be for outstanding academic progress, but all young adolescents have something to their credit that can be praised. Find that something and be proactive about developing family relationships.

Electronic communication.   In *Meet Me in the Middle,* Rick Wormeli (2001) discusses the use of online postings to communicate with families. He posts class/team announcements, assignments, and due dates. He reports that close to 100% of his students do their homework because everyone knows the expectations. Using free sites such as schoolnotes.com and blackboard.com to electronically communicate with home may prove very successful in some communities. In others, where families either do not have Internet access or don't have enough time or concern to use it, only a small percentage of your students may benefit. It's worth exploring.

With the proliferation of e-mail, this is another option to investigate. For families who work in places with computer access and those who habitually check their e-mail, this is a time efficient, and usually "kid proof," way to communicate.

Why we hesitate to communicate.   It's one thing to say school-home communication is important, or hear it said in a teacher workshop, and quite another to regularly practice communication in varied formats. Why? Let's take a minute to consider this.

New teachers often say that the thought of talking to families is terrifying. And why shouldn't it be? Many of the parents of middle grades students are old enough to be the parents of some new teachers. Talking with them with confidence and authority takes practice and time. Listening in as experienced teachers do it is a great way to pick up tips and phrases, and a sense of composure. However, actually talking with parents is the only way to acquire the skill. It gets easier with time, but the butterflies in the stomach will probably never stop fluttering entirely. It's one of those challenges of teaching that we had better not avoid, because avoidance will come back to haunt us sooner rather than later.

Time constraints often pose problems. There are only so many hours in a day and, yes, we do have lives—hopefully rich, full ones—outside the classroom. In terms of positive communication, set some goals. I found it very reasonable to make five "happy calls" a week along with sending at least five "happy notes" home. These are nonconfrontational, even fun, communications that take surprisingly little time, but often go undone solely for lack of resolve.

Letting problems fester because we are either too nervous or too short on time to communicate with families is detrimental to the student involved and the learning environment in our classrooms. Lack of academic progress needs to be addressed early in order to be remediated, or at least improved, with family help. Although families should keep a close watch on student progress, and many do try, weaker students rapidly become experts in communicating only good news about school while concealing the less positive aspects of their actual performance. Calling home the week before the end of a grading period is not using communication effectively. It's very frustrating for families to realize that it's almost too late to have any real effect. When behavioral problems are the issue and are allowed to fester because of our reluctance to communicate, not only will the student's behavior problem escalate, but chances are other students will be affected and our efficacy will be diminished.

In some cases, families may be seen as part of the problem rather than partners in seeking solutions. This view may or may not always be justified. Jumping to the conclusion that families contribute to whatever the problem may be to the extent that they would not be positive allies is dangerous. Every option of involving families in solution paths should be explored and utilized.

I have heard some teachers state that their job is 8 hours a day with students. They say their training and expertise is directed toward children, not adults. This attitude is contrary to all of NMSA's Standard Six (see p. 347). We are responsible for attempting to affect every possible aspect of our students' lives. Families are, by and large, within our scope of responsibility and influence. Bill Bradley, athlete and statesman, likened trying to educate children without involving the family to trying to play a basketball game without having all the players on the court (McLaughlin, 1993).

There are experienced teachers who, in some situations, have become jaded when it comes to encouraging family involvement. They live with a history of unsuccessful attempts to positively involve families in the education of young adolescents. A succession of ignored attempts, and even blatant refusals to work toward solutions, have colored their view of the value, or even the feasibility, of families being part of the process. They may be justified in their skepticism, but you may hold the key to reaching families by merit of tenacity, untried strategies, or the strength of your personality. While I generally hesitate to advise new teachers to pay little heed to experienced teachers, in this case my hope is that you will consistently communicate with families, even those with reputations of reticence, and extend multiple invitations to participate in their students' education.

Opportunities for Involvement

So far we've explored face-to-face, telephone, written, and electronic avenues of communication that involve families in the school life of our students. The involvement already discussed centers on individual student progress. Beyond this focus is a whole world of possibilities for families to volunteer time and energy. Rarely do families of middle schoolers eagerly approach the school and ask to be part of the activities. It is usually up to us to initiate and organize opportunities. The form in Figure 12.2 asks families to volunteer for a number of service needs. If a family member checks an area, by all means find a way to invite him to participate in that area at some point during the year.

Families have a wealth of knowledge, experiences, talents, hobbies, and special skills that can be used to enrich the lives of the students on your team. You'll probably never know the extent of the possibilities until you ask. A simple survey question such as the one in Figure 12.6 may be used.

If the note in Figure 12.6 is given to students at 3:15 with a "Please take this home," the response rate will be minimal. I suggest that this be part of the beginning of the year

---

Because we strongly believe that middle school is an ideal time for students to explore and discover their own interests and talents, we'd like to invite you to share yours with us. From time to time we organize opportunities for family members to tell about and/or demonstrate what they do professionally or how they enjoy their leisure/hobby time. Your special skills and training may fit perfectly into an area of study or be appropriate for a "Buffet of Exploration" involving many adults and their areas of expertise. Sound like fun? You bet! We'd love to hear from you.

Name _____

Student _____

I would like to share my interest in

_____

_____

You may contact me at (phone or e-mail)

_____

Thanks for your time. You are our partners in learning at Belmont Middle School!

FIGURE 12.6 Family interests survey.

packet along with emergency cards and federal forms that carry penalties for nonreturn. If the note is attached to progress reports or report cards that must be signed and returned, your response will improve. Again, I'm not above bribery. Promising homeroom or advisory groups some special privilege when there's an 80% return rate boosts participation.

It's helpful to compile and organize responses as a team. There will be "natural fits" that can be easily incorporated into the planned curriculum. If the topic of driving an 18-wheeler doesn't leap out as a curricular bright spot, it may fit nicely into an afternoon "Buffet of Exploration" where students sign up to attend four 20-minute sessions according to their interests. Clogging, fly tying, kite building, a day in the life of a CPA, baseball card collecting—what an interesting assortment you're likely to find. I've found that families greatly appreciate an acknowledgment when they are open enough to say "Here's what I do and I'm willing to share it with the kids." A postcard, telephone call, or e-mail note will complete the communication loop and let you express your appreciation.

Here are some more volunteer opportunities to offer families. Those who are not comfortable in the spotlight of a career day or an afternoon of interest sharing may, if asked, be willing and often pleased to help out in other ways.

- participating in school "spruce up" days including grounds work, cleanup, painting, fixing, etc.
- translating to help language minority families communicate with teachers and school
- participating in service learning ventures
- sponsoring clubs and special events
- performing clerical duties related to a special event
- providing child care for younger siblings during family conferences or other school events
- setting up and monitoring "phone tree" communication
- assisting in the school office or library

Family volunteers should be treated with respect and courtesy. They should not have to wonder what to do or how to do it. Specific directions and time frames provide the structure to keep everyone in a comfort zone. Always acknowledge the value of volunteerism in whatever ways you can. A handshake with a sincere thank you is the minimum. A note, a call, or a listing of volunteers in a newsletter will help ensure repeaters.

COMMUNITY INVOLVEMENT

The word **community** to this point has been used to describe the goal for our classroom, team, grade level, and even our entire school. In Chapter 4 we discussed the creation of a community of learners, building on Sergiovanni's (1996) definition that says communities share ideas and ideals to the point of going "from a collection of 'I's to a collective 'we'" (p. 48). However, some clarification is necessary for this section. When I speak of community here I simply mean people who live in the same geographical area, "a collection of 'I's."

Standard 6

Knowledge 5: Middle level teacher candidates understand that middle level schools are organizations within a larger community context.

Our schools function within communities of people of all ages who inevitably have different lifestyles. Finding ways to draw them into the teaching-learning cycle of our middle schools is a challenge worth pursuing, as we will soon discuss. The community is involved with public education in one way, like it or not, and that is financial. The federal government funds about 6% of public education costs, while state and local taxes share close to equally, in most cases, the remaining 94%. With or without children of school age, and whether they approve or disapprove of school board decisions, are bothered by the noise of P.E. classes on the field, or comforted by the enthusiasm of youth, the public still funds the overwhelming portion of public education financial requirements. Our schools run the gamut from sources of pride for the community to sources of embarrassment. Pride and embarrassment, and everything in between, stem from perceptions of what we do and the results of our efforts. Sometimes the perceptions are based on accurate information, but many times they are not. Remember that a person's perceptions are realities to him. If a school is perceived negatively, getting the positive word out when things are going well is difficult, but doable.

Communities Matter

I have known many young adolescents over whom I wish only our school teams had influence. These are the kids who have to grow up way too early in an attempt to cope with the cards of life they have been dealt. They're the ones for whom we may say, "If I only had the money to run a great big happy home for dozens of kids, this one would be one I could help." No matter how physically, emotionally, and academically safe we make our learning environment, when the school is locked up for the evening our kids go out into the community and away from our protection and influence. Jackson and Davis (2000) put it this way:

> It doesn't take a rocket scientist to realize that the middle grades school experience is only one of a myriad of influences on the trajectory of an adolescent's development. What happens to young people within their families, neighborhoods, peer groups, religious institutions, out-of-school programs and a wide range of formal and informal relationships and settings can easily have as much or more impact on how young people "turn out" as the middle grades school. (p. 209)

Some communities have qualities that enhance, or at least don't appear to hinder, our teaching-learning efforts. They offer physical comfort and relative safety, family participation, and recreational and cultural options, and at least give lip service to the value of education. What generally distinguishes these communities from those in the previous paragraph? You guessed it—socioeconomic status. Statistics will bear this out, but just because it seems to be so doesn't mean it can't be changed. A growing number of communities are refusing to rest on excuses for failure and are committing to what the title of this chapter states—They Are All Our Children. The school, the children, and the community are, for better or worse, inextricably linked. We can't expect 10- to 15- year-olds to lead the way and, without passionate leadership, communities by themselves seldom bring about school (and thereby student) reform. The school is in a position to make a difference for 7 to 10 hours a day. In partnership, the community and the school can grow together in claiming all the children as their own.

Two Successes

Prince George's County, Maryland.   Superintendent Jerome Clark challenged his diverse community to place children first. Faced with a decade of poor test scores, high dropout rates, low local funding for education, and high teacher turnover, Clark dared the community to take a stand. The plan called for partnerships with businesses, churches, and civic organizations along with 8 hours of volunteerism asked of individuals. The "Children First" document's seven goals helped inspire the people of Prince George's County to give time, energy, and funding (White-Hood, 1998). The goals included the following:

1. Student achievement will meet or exceed state and national standards in all curricular areas and reflect higher order thinking skills.
2. Achievement for all students will increase.
3. Curricula will reflect a multicultural perspective.
4. School climate and facilities will be safe, orderly, and supportive of teaching and learning.
5. Parents and the community will be meaningfully and consistently involved in the educational process and the decisions that shape it.
6. The school system will be fully accountable for all its programs, practices, and results.
7. Programs and functions supporting instruction will provide effective and efficient results. (p. 41)

The "Children First" campaign got things moving in Prince George's County. To accomplish the seven goals volunteers were asked, among other things, to

- provide computer training
- manage fitness programs
- offer music and art experiences
- tutor students
- assist with homework
- read to students
- share real-life stories
- provide practical problem-solving
- listen (p. 41)

The volunteer program helped, among other things, to

- enhance the self-esteem of students and volunteers
- improve deficiencies in reading and math
- teach social skills
- expose students to careers, organizations, and community work
- increase dialogue between communities and schools

- enhance skill levels of volunteers
- show students the community cares (p. 41)

Reports show that thousands of individuals have volunteered in excess of 8 hours each. They have mentored, tutored, and, in general, become allies of the school system.

Marion White-Hood (1998), principal of Kettering Middle School in Upper Marlboro, Maryland, tells us programs like the one in Prince George's County "can have a major impact on students, teachers, and communities. As volunteers face the challenge, they will help create a future for everyone. Students will grow to become volunteers too" (p. 42).

Greensboro, North Carolina.   The staff of Guilford Middle School determined to involve a particular segment of their attendance population, those in a low-income housing project. They chose to capitalize on an existing program called TOPS, "Teaching Our Pupils Success," that provided extra academic support to all students who were having difficulty with schoolwork. The staff reported, "The lack of close ties, particularly with caretakers of our at-risk students, was judged to be a major barrier . . . to the continuous improvement of some students" (VanHoose & Legrand, 2000, p. 33). A comprehensive program called "Expanding Horizons" was initiated. Families and others interested in the well-being of the middle school students at Guilford Middle School formed a resident association. Community participants, with the support and guidance of the school staff, established the following goals:

1. Promoting academic success and greater interest in school by students through afternoon assistance and tutoring.
2. Providing materials and programs to promote positive decision-making.
3. Providing opportunities for success that would contribute to personal growth, increased self-esteem, and a positive self-concept.
4. Providing positive role models in the program through local organizations and colleges.
5. Coordinating information between the middle school, community, and agencies involved in the outreach program.
6. Initiating fund-raising activities to establish an ongoing media resource center in the community center to be used for tutoring, homework, and self-improvement.
7. Using community resources to foster the development of a safe and orderly environment for the resident families.
8. Increasing cultural awareness among young people by facilitating attendance at activities in the larger community and beyond. (p. 34)

Expanding Horizons has experienced success in reaching its comprehensive goals due in part to the willingness of educators to spend the time and energy needed to reach out to their community. At the same time, it took courage for families and community members to join and sustain the efforts (VanHoose & Legrand, 2000).

Successful community involvement = Inform + Invite + Coordinate + Appreciate

These two stories of success speak of ownership and a realization that they are all our children. The communities and schools acknowledge a shared responsibility for all children. Both instances clearly demonstrate the value, and the necessity, of collaboration among schools, families, and communities.

After-School Programs

"The mere fact of being without supervision seems to have malignant effects on young adolescents, and all too many children find themselves home alone after school every day" (Jackson & Davis, 2000, p. 213). In *Turning Points 2000,* a research project is reported to have found significant differences in levels of self-esteem, behavior problems, depression, and academic success of "latchkey" young adolescents compared with students who were with or around adults after school in a home setting or organized program. After-school programs not only enhance students socially and cognitively, but they also prevent unhealthy encounters and behaviors.

Some after-school programs are exclusively established and staffed by school personnel. However, the majority are the result of coalitions among community groups and schools. Sponsors of these programs may include Boys and Girls Clubs, 4-H, YMCA, YWCA, churches, youth service organizations, chambers of commerce, and parent organizations. Effective programs aim to provide three components: positive relationships between adults and young adolescents, enriching activities, and a safe place. Often the most successful programs have found a way to link and balance recreational and academic content. "After-school programs should not primarily be 'more school, after school,' but rather an opportunity to learn for the sheer joy of learning" (Jackson & Davis, 2000, p. 215).

Business Partners

Some schools have formed partnerships with local businesses. *Business partners* support the school in whatever fashion suits their expertise. For instance, a pizza restaurant may occasionally donate pizzas for some special student recognition or event. An industry may offer field trip tours to explain how a business operates. A dry cleaning business might clean school curtains or band uniforms. A catering business might contribute goodies to a back-to-school gathering. And of course cash donations are seldom refused! Besides tangible contributions, employees may volunteer their time to tutor or mentor individuals and/or be part of an after-school program. Recognition is vitally important. The school should publicize the fact that a particular business has agreed to be a partner in education through newsletters and signs in and around the school. Teachers and staff should always welcome volunteers and be overtly appreciative of those willing to partner with us.

What We Can Do

To accomplish widespread community initiatives, the involvement of entire schools or school districts is required. However, there are ways that we, as individual teachers and teams, can promote positive perceptions and relationships within the community. Here are 10 categories to consider.

1. *Be informed.* Information is power. There's a lot to understand about public education. As the adults closest to the "action," we should not only know what's going on, but also be aware of the influences that determine the who, what, when, and where of education locally, statewide, and nationally.

2. *Be positive public relations agents.* To people who do not have students in school or are not at all involved in schooling, we **are** the school. We may provide the only portrayal of education some people see, aside from an occasional news story, and these are often negative. The overriding image of what we do in schools should be positively portrayed.

3. *Acknowledge problems, suggest solutions.* If we are informed, and if we determine to be positive public relations agents, we can and should acknowledge problems in a forum that allows for more than cursory discussion. It is also our responsibility to seek solutions and offer them publicly. If there are glaring achievement gaps at your school, you should admit to it and be able to facilitate discussions within the community about solution paths.

4. *Don't overemphasize the need for funding.* You probably have heard community members make a blanket statement similar to "Throwing money at schools won't fix anything." No, blindly throwing money won't do much for us. However, additional funding could make huge differences in upgraded facilities, salaries to attract the best and the brightest to our profession, ongoing professional development opportunities, fully funded after-school programs available to all students, appropriate technology for all schools, and more. An adequately funded and well-managed budget **will** make a difference. When we propose greater funding, let's be able to back up the request with how it will make a difference.

5. *Use the media proactively.* The influence of television and newspapers is tremendous. Part of being informed involves watching news reports and reading articles about education. If you are infuriated by negative publicity to the exclusion of what's happening that's positive, do something about it. Call the media about positive events and write intelligent letters to the editor while encouraging students to do the same.

6. *Spotlight students.* Search for ways to get student work in front of the community. From artwork in galleries to ideas on public issues, our students are so very capable of contributing to the community good.

7. *Invite the community in.* When the community feels welcome and has positive reasons to walk through the school doors, they are likely to feel a sense of identification and ownership.

8. *Actively participate in the community.* We can be positive for our schools in the community by being actively involved in things that interest us, including civic, religious, service, and social groups. The wider our sphere of influence, the more opportunities we have to promote community awareness and involvement in our schools.

9. *Promote community service.* We have discussed the impact service learning has on our students. Let's not underestimate the impact of service learning on the community. Not only do the deeds involved make a difference, but the community perception of our students can be greatly enhanced when they know about or see firsthand the services our students perform.

10. *Know about community resources.* There are times when it is beneficial to extend our classrooms into the community to take advantage of the wealth of knowledge and facilities available. In addition, community resources provide family counseling, medical assistance, legal advocacy, and a tremendous number of services to assist students and their families. We may not know the extent of these services, but we should be able to point those who trust us in the right direction so that they can take advantage of community resources.

Standard 6

Knowledge 6: Middle level teacher candidates understand the relationships between schools and community organizations.

Knowledge 7: Middle level teacher candidates know about the resources available within communities that can support students, teachers, and schools.

Disposition 3: Middle level teacher candidates value the variety of resources available in communities.

Disposition 4: Middle level teacher candidates are committed to helping family members become aware of how and where to receive assistance when needed.

Disposition 8: Middle level teacher candidates accept the responsibility of working with family and community members to increase student welfare and learning.

Performance 4: Middle level teacher candidates identify and use community resources to foster student learning.

Performance 5: Middle level teacher candidates participate in activities designed to enhance educational experiences that transcend the school campus.

TRANSITIONS

When considering shared responsibility for all our children, we realize that the responsibility extends to the *transitions* of students who are about to enter middle school and those who are completing their middle school years. "The transitions from elementary to middle school and from middle to high school have the elements of many adolescents' worst social nightmares—not knowing anyone, being ignored by peers, getting lost, and confronting demanding classes and teachers" (Allen, 2001, p. 1). Understanding young adolescent development issues prompts us to want to do everything we can to make the "into and out of" middle school transitions as smooth and painless as possible.

Entering Middle School

The fear of the unknown can be daunting for 10- and 11-year-olds. They have been in an elementary setting for years and are typically comfortable with how things work. In fact, they are the "big kids." Now it's time to go to middle school—usually a larger, more adultlike facility; as many as seven teachers and classes a day; multiple books and supplies to be put in and taken out of lockers; much older and more mature eighth graders to both fear and avoid; new kids in classes from other elementary schools—so many unknowns.

Articulation between the upper grade elementary teachers, typically fifth grade, and the lower grade middle school teachers, typically sixth grade, is important. To ease the transition to middle school, a coalition of these key people makes sense. "Recognizing the need and choosing to make a difference in easing the transition is the first step. This conscious choice on the part of principals, teachers, counselors, and parents, coupled with commitment, precedes the formation of a plan" (Powell, 2000, p. 24).

Here are some strategies to help ease the transition into middle school:

1. Sixth grade teachers, counselors, and the middle school principal visit elementary schools to talk with fifth graders to inform them and answer their questions.

2. Sixth grade students visit elementary schools to talk about "kid stuff," including the things they may remember worrying about a year earlier. It's very encouraging to hear survival stories.

3. Make a video of the middle school to be shown to fifth graders. I have organized several of these, with students carrying the camera and narrating the tour. It's great fun for the kids who make the video and equally so for the ones who watch. The middle schooler's sense of humor shines through, putting the rising sixth graders more at ease.

4. Offer tours of the middle school for fifth graders to take as a group. They have the security of their buddies with them as they walk around the new environment, listen in on classes, meet teachers and students, and see where they will enjoy the next 3 years. Include a "walk through" of a typical schedule and a demonstration of how to open and secure lockers. If possible, let the fifth graders try opening a locker, preferably with success. As silly as it may seem to us, there is an inordinate amount of fear linked to lockers, both how to use them appropriately and how to avoid being stuffed into one.

5. Send information to families and students about class scheduling, team assignments, books and supplies, school hours, transportation, and dates of special open houses only for rising sixth graders and families. This information might also be published in the local newspaper.

Moving On

The first year is pivotal to many adolescents who enter high school wracked by feelings of abandonment and isolation. There is an abundance of research and literature that points to ninth grade as the year of unprecedented absenteeism and high academic failure (DaGiau, 1997). Figures for ninth grade dropout rates are as high as 52% in some schools (McAdoo, 1999). Communities and high schools are recognizing the dire need to better care for our students as they move from middle school to high school. Some high schools have ninth grade academies where ninth graders are set apart from the rest of the high school. They have their own administrators and elements that help them create their own identity, like separate facilities for classes and lunch. Continuing middle school practices such as teaming to whatever degree possible is advisable. If eighth graders know they will be eased into high school, their fears can be at least partially allayed. Hertzog and Morgan (2000) caution us to remember that transition is a process, not an event.

OUR TEN STUDENTS

There is one overriding theme in this book that by now should be second nature in your thoughts about teaching. The message is that the diversity of background, ability, motivation, and life circumstances of our students must be considered in everything we do in and out of our classrooms. Middle school may be the last, best hope of incorporating enough differentiation to reach our students in ways that will bring out their potential and give them hope and confidence for the future.

We have met 10 individuals and followed them from sixth grade to eighth grade. If you have 100 students on your team you can multiply the diversity of these 10 by 10. To consider each one's needs and talents is a daunting task and one at which we are never quite fully successful. There's always more that might be done.

Take a last look at our 10 students as they approach high school where the complexity of the program, the size of the institution, and the potential for "slipping through the cracks" may make a strong middle school foundation even more important.

Michael, eighth grade

Michael's transition into high school should present few problems. Because he is 2 years older than most of his classmates and was relieved to leave elementary school, he will probably sense that same relief as he enters the ninth grade. He will be in a small high school on the same campus as his middle school. What Michael will miss is the strong relationship he has developed with Mr. Jefferson in seventh and eighth grade. Because of the personal touch of looping and a caring role model, Michael is confident he will graduate. Planning his coursework will be crucial. His love of the outdoors and physical skills, and his hope of attending a community college should guide his choices.

Allison, *eighth grade*

Allison, while always younger than her classmates in years, made up for it in enthusiasm and spunk. By eighth grade she matured to the point of knowing when and how to exercise self-control. Rather than spending the next 4 years in her local high school, she is considering going to France for her junior and senior years. She has no doubt that she will go on to college and then do graduate work, but she doesn't yet know what she wants to become. The local high school offers a wide array of elective courses from which she can choose. Allison's dilemma is that she wants to experience more than her schedule will allow. She would be wise to discuss the options with her parents and look carefully at what will be available to her at the high school in France.

Marvin, *eighth grade*

Marvin spent much of his time in middle school on shaky ground when it came to discipline. His attention-getting antics wore thin on teachers and students alike. By eighth grade, however, he had channeled at least some of his energy into the mixed chorus at Central Middle School where he was recognized for his talent. His grades are acceptable and signs of maturity are encouraging. The local high school boasts several vocal music groups that perform at civic events. Ms. Lopez-Mitchell has given Marvin information about the groups and has arranged for Marvin to audition in July before his ninth grade year begins. Marvin is excited. This is likely to be a key element in Marvin's success in high school. As his need to pull outlandish stunts gives way to maturity, Marvin should have a successful high school experience.

Hector, *eighth grade*

Hector quietly went through middle school and shied away from the attention his teachers often gave him for his steady work habits and academic success. While his grades remained excellent, the only real "spark" they saw in him in terms of interest was his ability to play baseball. He was a sought-after player on the community recreational teams. The high school baseball coach is aware of Hector and approached him as an eighth grader about playing on the high school team. Hector agreed and is excited about the prospects. No one in Hector's family has gone to college, but Hector wants to. The coach has hopes for a baseball scholarship. He knows Hector would not only be a fine college athlete, but that he has the potential to be very successful academically. The future is bright for Hector, but his success will require close mentoring to keep his sights set on what he can do and be, and not on some of the outside influences he may face.

Jeanetta, eighth grade

Jeanetta made it through middle school with quiet grace. By eighth grade she was on the A-B honor roll and participated in girls chorus and basketball. She looks forward to high school because socially she fits in with older students. The one thing she is not looking forward to is being compared with her two older sisters who seemed to do it all, and do it well. Her middle school teachers were sensitive to the situation and treated her as an individual, separate from her well-known principal dad and teacher mom and two successful sisters. Jeanetta just doesn't seem to have the same drive that her other family members have. In high school, it will be important for her to choose courses and activities that suit her as she thinks about her future. One of the most positive actions for Jeanetta would be to find a female high school teacher who understands her and can provide a listening ear and some wise counsel.

Barry, eighth grade

Barry has thrived at Hoyt River Performing Arts Middle School. He struggled a bit with math and science, but excelled in language arts and was a star in drama class and in school productions. His district does not have a performing arts high school, so Barry may experience some difficulty adjusting to a new setting. What will help his comfort level is the fact that many of his friends from HRPA will transition with him. He will need to complete 24 high school credits, including 7 in math and science. His mom recognizes the dual challenge of steering Barry into courses that will allow him to express his creativity and of communicating regularly with teachers in the courses where he may struggle.

Mia, eighth grade

Mia is a gifted writer, a fact that became clear as early as seventh grade. Growing up an only child with a quiet disposition, spending most of her time with her parents, and wearing a hearing aid since third grade all contributed to the way she appeared to turn inward emotionally and socially. Rather than expressing herself to other kids, she wrote about her feelings and made up stories from her fantasies. By eighth grade, her talents were recognized. The confidence that accompanied this recognition led to better grades and more courage to involve herself with a group of girls. The prospects of high school frighten her a bit, but she knows she will have her new friends with her in ninth grade. Mia's eighth grade language arts teacher made a point of calling the English department chair to tell her about Mia's talent and to ask that a ninth grade language arts teacher pay special attention to her and nurture her academically as well as socially.

Anthony, eighth grade

Anthony surprised many adults at Central Middle School by completing the eighth grade. Many had predicted he would involve himself in some illegal activity and either be placed in a state facility or simply disappear from school. His involvement in the writing of a new discipline plan seemed to bring out his "leadership" skills in a positive way. His eighth grade teachers took it upon themselves to meet with a high school guidance counselor to talk about Anthony. The counselor pledged to personally write Anthony's schedule and to place him with teachers who have an affinity for at-risk students. The influences in Anthony's life outside school along with his moody, intense personality will make it a challenge for him to successfully complete high school. It will take charismatic teachers who purposefully look for, and cultivate, his interests to help him succeed. The guidance counselor will need to watch for attendance problems and attempt to involve Anthony in positive ways.

Darlene, eighth grade

Darlene has kept her sweet spirit through middle school. She was deeply affected, as was her whole family, by the World Trade Center tragedy. Her contributions, and those of her family, to the Stars team interdisciplinary unit were meaningful and appreciated. The experience gave her more confidence in her academic potential that will serve her well as she transitions to high school. She is determined to succeed because she now has dreams of becoming a nurse. She knows she will likely struggle with some of her math and science courses and should confide in a high school counselor who will hopefully put Darlene in touch with a community-run after-school tutoring program.

Lee, eighth grade

Lee has used his love of reading, and the ability he has developed by virtue of reading a lot, to help him in all his subject areas. He often expresses his gratitude to his neighbor who has faithfully supported him. She asked that he "repay" her by teaching and nurturing his younger brothers and sister. The neighbor has been delighted to see this happen and amazed at how much English Lee's parents now speak because of his determination. Lee's transition to ninth grade will be smooth because he is, and will continue to be, a reserved young man who finds adventure in books. Career and college counseling will be an important part of Lee's high school experience. It is unlikely that his family will be able to afford his college education, so staying on track for state-funded scholarships will be important. A counselor should create a scenario of courses and required grades with Lee as he looks toward a sure graduation.

RECOGNIZING AN EXEMPLARY MIDDLE SCHOOL

I wish I could say that recognizing an exemplary middle school is as easy as compiling a master list of characteristics from *This We Believe, Turning Points*, the comparison of junior high and middle school traits, and the many other sources available, and then checking off say, 75%, and **Voila**, you've found an exemplary school! That would certainly simplify our task as educators. However, defining a successful or "true" middle school is, like most things in life, a complex issue. There are few, if any, black and white areas. Most have abundant shades of gray with occasional contradictions thrown in. There are middle schools I would term exemplary that exhibit only some of the tenets that have been discussed. There are combinations of characteristics that "work" for different reasons in different settings.

There is no one best prescription for success. Yes, there are some basics without which it is more difficult to create and maintain a developmentally responsive middle grades school. For instance, teaming carries with it so many possibilities for success that it is considered by most educators to be an absolute for middle schools. Heterogeneous grouping is another structure that has been shown over and over to be best for all students—the motivated and the unmotivated, and the high-achievers as well as the low-achievers. Connecting elements of the curriculum using active learning strategies, and measuring knowledge and skills with authentic and varied assessments leads to a more cohesive bonding of teaching and learning. Decisions about what to do and when, where, and how to do it should be based on the needs, strengths, and diversity of our students and our community.

The concept of balance needs to be applied when we examine individual tenets of middle school practice. Every one of them has the potential to lose effectiveness, and perhaps even be detrimental, if carried to extremes. These "extremes" may distort the intended positive qualities of a tenet or may prevent other tenets from fulfilling their promise. For instance, if we emphasize "flexible organizational structures" from *This We Believe* to an extreme and lose the basic concepts of consistency and routine (valuable elements in the education of young adolescents) we are not providing the best environment for our students. From the *Turning Points* (Carnegie Council on Adolescent Development, 1989) tenet "Empowering Teachers and Administrators" we read, "Creative control of young peoples' educational experiences should clearly be the responsibility of teaching teams" (p. 18). If we as teachers fail to include parents' and students' views in our decisions about educational experiences, then we risk losing valuable insights. Forte and Schurr (1993, p. 31) state that middle school "focuses on creative exploration and experimentation of subject matter" versus junior high that "focuses on mastery of concepts and skills in separate disciplines." The key word here is **focus**. If we lose sight of this word and abandon our efforts to help students master concepts, then we have shortchanged them.

The key to creating balance in our middle schools as illustrated in Figure 12.7 is equipping ourselves with options and the judgment to know when and how to implement and adjust. This has everything to do with recognizing (and creating!) exemplary middle schools. The better we know our students and the broader our grasp of practices that reflect middle level philosophy, the more likely it is that who we are and what we do will bring us closer to a school environment that works for young adolescents.

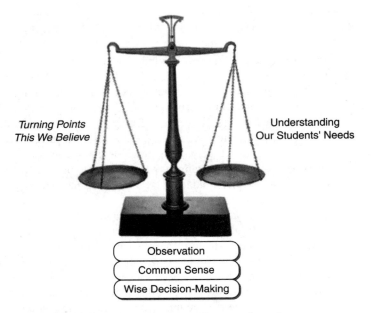

Turning Points
This We Believe

Understanding
Our Students' Needs

Observation
Common Sense
Wise Decision-Making

FIGURE 12.7   Achieving balance: Theory and practice.

 ## REFLECTIONS ON THE PAST AND FUTURE OF MIDDLE SCHOOL

It has been more than 40 years since the words **middle school** were proposed as an alternative structure within which to educate young adolescent students. Middle schools grew out of both dissatisfaction with the junior high philosophy and a realization that the middle years, typically 10 to 15, are unique and require a developmentally responsive philosophy to effectively bridge the gap between childhood and full-blown adolescence/young adulthood. Recognition of the legitimacy of early adolescence as a life stage needing and deserving its own special educational experience has garnered the attention of more and more educators and researchers. What has evolved over more than four decades is a middle grades teaching and learning philosophy that is coherent in its unswerving dedication to developmental responsiveness and academic rigor. Perpetuation of these two basic tenets depends in large measure on you, the future generation of middle level leaders.

"If middle school leaders expect to soon cross the finish line now that the 21st century has dawned, maybe they have not set their goals as high as they should" (George & Alexander, 2003, p. 584). These are Paul George's final words in the new edition of *The Exemplary Middle School*. He reminds us that when we see our goals almost fulfilled it's time to raise the bar. Some middle schools have implemented all the tenets of *Turning Points* and embraced the philosophy of *This We Believe*. For these schools, and the teachers who are the backbone, heart, and head of the organization, the challenge is to continue serving young adolescents in developmentally responsive ways that promote even greater academic rigor and achievement. They should look toward modifying and/or adding tenets to our guiding documents as students, society, subject matter, and political realities evolve.

For many schools and teachers, George's "finish line" is so far away on the cluttered landscape of their circumstances that the danger lies in losing sight of the ideals needed to guide their efforts. If in your first years of teaching you find yourself in such a situation, perhaps your greatest gifts to the school and students will be your optimism and recent indoctrination into the possibilities of middle level education.

It's difficult for me to end this book. My head and heart are in the contents. I love my career in education, and specifically middle school education. I can think of no better profession. One of my mantras is "Teachers make all other professions possible." What a privilege and what a joy. I congratulate you on your choice to teach middle school. You will never be bored. You will always be challenged. And you will have fun along the way. Welcome to the adventure!

Group Activities

1. Visit a school in your class file and ask the following questions:

   a. How is back-to-school night orchestrated in your school or by your team?

   b. Do you send an individual and/or team "welcome to school" letter? (Ask for a copy.)

   c. How do you/your team use community resources such as business partners, service organizations, mentors, etc.?

   d. How do you/your team conduct family conferences? Have you tried student-led conferences? (Be ready to explain how they work.)

2. Divide the 10 students among your class members. Each of you will write a paragraph describing what you might have done as one of the students' teachers to make his/her middle school experience more successful than indicated in the Professional Practice sections. Be prepared to share your ideas.

Individual Activities

1. Write a brief narrative that you might use on back-to-school night to introduce yourself and your philosophy of teaching middle school.

2. While in the mall you run into a parent who is quite angry about a decision her student's teacher team made. The team is on your grade level. You are well aware of the situation and disagree with the decision that was made. Write a narrative of how you would handle the situation.

3. How has No Child Left Behind affected your plans to teach middle school? Does your coursework provide enough hours in a subject area to allow you the status of "highly qualified"?

Personal Journal

1. Do you remember when you entered middle school/junior high? Write about how you felt and your first impressions.

2. Was your family involved in your school while you were in middle school? If so, in what ways? If not, did you want them to be?

3. When it was time for you to go to high school, what were your main concerns? Was it a difficult or pleasant transition?

Internet Resources

National Parent Teacher Association (PTA)
http://www.pta.org

This site supports the traditional school PTA and provides information for families and communities.

NCREL—After-School Programs
http://www.ncrel.org/after/beyond/linkage

This site offers information on how to establish and maintain quality after-school programs.

Schools to Watch
http://www.schoolstowatch.org

This site provides a visual tour of four high-performing middle schools selected by the National Forum to Accelerate Middle Grades Education.

Turning Points
http://www.turningpts.org

Turning Points is a comprehensive education reform model that focuses on improving student learning. The organization assists member schools in strengthening the academic core of middle school while establishing a caring, supportive environment that values young adolescents. Information about schools at various stages in the reform process is available.

References

Allen, R. (2001). Passages to learning: Schools find ways to help students make transitions. *Education Update, 43*(9), 1–7.

Berckemeyer, J. C. (2001). Student-led conferences. *Classroom Connections, 3*(3), 1.

Carnegie Council on Adolescent Development. (1989). *Turning points: Preparing American youth for the 21st century.* New York: Carnegie Corporation.

Conzemius, A., & O'Neill, J. (2001). *Building shared responsibility for student learning.* Alexandria, VA: Association for Supervision and Curriculum Development.

DaGiau, B. (1997). *A program for counseling and guidance to facilitate the transition from middle school to high school.* Upper Montclair, NJ: Montclair State University. (ERIC Document Reproduction Service No. ED413562).

Downs, A. (2001). It's all in the family: Middle schools share the secrets of parent engagement. *Middle Ground, 4*(3), 10–15.

Epstein, J. L. (2001). School, family, and community partnerships. In T. O. Erb (Ed.), *This we believe. . . and now we must act (pp. 42–55).* Westerville, OH: National Middle School Association.

Erb, T. O. (Ed.). (2001). *This we believe . . . and now we must act.* Westerville, OH: National Middle School Association.

Farber, P. (1999). Speak up: Student-led conference is a real conversation piece. *Middle Ground, 2*(4), 21–24.

Forte, I., & Schurr, S. (1993). *The definitive middle school guide: A handbook for success.* Nashville, TN: Incentive Publications.

George, P. (2002). *No child left behind: Implications for middle level leaders.* Westerville, OH: National Middle School Association.

George, P. S., & Alexander, W. M. (2003). *The exemplary middle school.* Belmont, CA: Wadsworth/Thomson Learning.

Henderson, A. T., & Berla, N. (Eds.). (1994). *A new generation of evidence: The family is critical to student achievement.* Washington, DC: Center for Law and Entertainment.

Hertzog, J., & Morgan, L. (2000, November). *Helping students in transition: Transition practices that work.* Paper presented at National Middle School Association Annual Conference, St. Louis, MO.

Jackson, A. W., & Davis, G.A. (2000). *Turning points 2000: Educating adolescents in the 21st century.* New York: Teachers College Press.

L' Esperance, M. E., & Gabbard, D. (2001). Empowering all parents. *Middle Ground, 4*(3), 10–15.

MacIver, D. J., & Epstein, J. L. (1991). Responsive practice in the middle grades: Teacher teams, advisory groups, remedial instruction, and school transition programs. *American Journal of Education, 99*, 587–622.

McAdoo, M. (1999). Studies in transition: How to help adolescents navigate the path to and from middle school. *Middle Ground, 2*(3), 21–23.

McLaughlin, C. K. (1993). *The do's and don'ts of parent involvement: How to build a positive school-home partnership.* Torrance, CA: Innerchoice Publishing.

Mulhall, P. F., Mertens, S. B., & Flowers, N. (2001). How familiar are parents with middle level practices? *Middle School Journal, 33*(2), 57–61.

National Middle School Association. (1995). *This we believe: Developmentally responsive middle level schools.* Columbus, OH: Author.

National Middle School Association. (2003). *This we believe: Successful schools for young adolescents.* Westerville, OH: Author.

Powell, S. D. (2000). Forming middle and high school partnerships: Easing the transition. *Voices from the Field, 2*(2), 24–28.

Rubenstein, R. E. (1994). *Hints for teaching success in middle school.* Englewood, CO: Teacher Ideas Press.

Sergiovanni, T. J. (1996). *Leadership for the schoolhouse.* San Francisco: Jossey-Bass.

Stevenson, C. (1992). *Teaching ten to fourteen year olds.* New York: Longman`.

Stevenson, C., & Carr, J. F. (1993). *Integrated studies in the middle grades: "Dancing through walls."* New York: Teachers College Press.

VanHoose, J., & Legrand, P. (2000). It takes parents, the whole village, and school to raise the children. *Middle School Journal, 31*(3), 32–37.

White-Hood, M. (1998). Community challenges: How many hours have you volunteered in your school? *Schools in the Middle, 8*(1), 39–42.

Wormeli, R. (2001). *Meet me in the middle: Becoming an accomplished middle level teacher.* Portland, ME: Stenhouse.

Glossary

ability grouping: assigning a student to classes based on academic ability and achievement

academic safety: an environment that ensures opportunities for success for all students regardless of previous achievement or pace of learning

academic self-esteem: a personal perception of a student's level of ability and academic accomplishment

accountability: being held responsible for student progress and efficient/effective use of resources

ADD: attention deficit disorder; often characterized by an inability to focus for a sufficient length of time

ADHD: attention deficit hyperactivity disorder; ADD often accompanied by a lack of impulse control

advance organizer: a way of focusing attention on, and generating interest in, the beginning of a lesson; in Hunter, also referred to as anticipatory set

advisory: a special time regularly set aside for a small group of students to meet with a specific school staff member

affective learning: learning that is connected to, and/or dependent on, attitudes, feelings, interests, and values

alternative assessment: generally any assessment that is not a traditional pencil-and-paper test

ASCD: Association for Supervision and Curriculum Development

assessment: methods to gather evidence of student learning

at-risk factors: conditions/behaviors that endanger student success

auditory modality: learning through hearing

authentic assessment: assessment that involves, and occurs within, a meaningful and/or real-life context

back-to-school night: an event designed to introduce families to the middle school environment

backward design: planning for curriculum and instruction by first making decisions about the desired learning results and methods of assessment

block schedule: any schedule that allows for more time to be spent in a given class than the traditional 50 minutes

brain-based learning: using what we know about how the brain functions to guide decisions concerning curriculum content and instructional strategies

business partners: businesses that agree to support schools in a variety of ways, depending on their expertise and/or interest levels

classroom management: maintaining an ordered environment in which learning may be accomplished

cognitive type theory: provides ways of determining and categorizing learning preferences and styles

collaboration: working together to accomplish a task or goal

collaborative planning: planning for instruction with other teachers, typically team members (interdisciplinary) or those who teach the same subject

community of learners: close, trusting school-based relationships that encourage both personal and intellectual growth

complementary content and skills: content and skills that relate to one another in ways that enhance meaning and relevance

conflict resolution: the settling of student disputes

consequences: define what will happen if rules are broken

constructivism: students using higher order thinking skills to construct or discover their own learning

cooperative learning: students working together in small groups to accomplish a learning task or a learning objective

core curriculum: subject areas generally considered basic for middle school—language arts, math, science, and social studies

creative thinking: thinking "outside the box," using imagination and ingenuity

criterion-referenced assessment: assessing what students know and are able to do according to stated learning goals

critical thinking: higher-order thinking requiring purposeful objectivity and consistency

culture: specific shared values, beliefs, and attitudes

curriculum: planned and unplanned aspects of what students experience in school; typically thought of as the "what" of teaching

curriculum map: calendar-based plans of the sequence of what is taught; a tool for recognizing repetitions and gaps, comparing plans within a team in order to find potential areas for integration

developmental responsiveness: actions and attitudes attuned to developmental needs and interests of students

diagnostic assessment: assessment that determines existence and level of mastery for purposes of planning curriculum and instruction

differentiation of instruction: providing differing learning opportunities in terms of content, process, and product based on students' levels of readiness, interests, and learning profiles

dispositional theory: characterizes multiple intelligences in terms of sensitivities, inclinations, and abilities

diversity: differences among students that may include, but are not limited to, gender, learning style, interest, family structure, race, culture, socioeconomics, and multiple intelligences

early adolescence: typically considered the period of life between the ages of 10 and 15

emotional safety: an environment that provides a stable atmosphere where expressed emotions receive consistently caring responses

ESL: English as a Second Language

ethnicity: sense of group identification, political and economic interests, and behavioral patterns

ETS: Educational Testing Service

evaluation: making judgments about the quality of work or products of work

exploratory class: course that encourages students to take a broad, overview-oriented look at a subject or interest area; typically 6 to 9 weeks in length but may last an entire school year

family/parent-teacher conference: an opportunity for family members to meet with teacher(s) to discuss student progress in work/performance/understanding/behavior

flexible block: schedule that allows teachers to divide class time in a variety of ways as appropriate to best address specific academic plans

formative assessment: ways of monitoring learning and providing feedback to students and teachers on progress toward mastery

goals: broad statements of intent without specific steps to fulfillment and often lacking in means of measuring success

grade: number or letter representation; score of evaluation received over time and reported to students and adults

graphic organizers: visual representation of knowledge that emphasizes relationships

guidance counselor: professional who addresses students' affective needs and concerns that impact personal and academic growth

heterogeneous grouping: grouping of students without consideration of academic abilities or achievements

homogeneous grouping: see *ability grouping*

house: a word that designates a "school-within-a-school"

hovering: in Sylwester, a term describing a philosophy of closely monitoring young adolescents as they mature

IDEA: Individuals with Disabilities Education Act

IEP: Individualized Education Plan

inclusion: assignment of students with special needs to regular classrooms; sometimes referred to as mainstreaming

inquiry-based learning: learning by questioning and investigating

integrative curriculum: subject areas are interwoven around a conceptual theme chosen as a result of student needs and interests

interdisciplinary instruction: subject areas are related and blended, often blurring subject boundaries

interdisciplinary planning: planning for instruction with teachers of different subject areas, typically in a team setting

interdisciplinary teaming: see *teaming;* interdisciplinary because different subjects, or disciplines, are represented

interdisciplinary unit: a unit of study addressing a theme with individual subject areas contributing and sometimes blending, and with subject boundaries often blurring

IRA: International Reading Association

junior high: a precursor to middle school, with departmentalized organization much like a high school, typically encompassing grades 7 through 9

kinesthetic modality: learning through movement

LD: Learning Disabled, a designated special needs category

learning centers: designated places in a classroom with information and activities to promote independent or small group learning using a variety of modalities. Sometimes called learning stations

learning style: how students perceive and internalize knowledge and skills

long-range plan: comprehensive guide for facilitating learning involving student profiles, content and sequencing, classroom management philosophy, instructional strategies, and overall organizational factors

looping: a team of teachers and students who stay together for more than one academic year

LRE: Least Restrictive Environment, an environment in which students with special needs function that incorporates the fewest possible restrictions; for many of these students, the LRE is the regular classroom setting

magnet school: public school that offers a different focus involving curriculum, instruction, or both

membership: in middle school, a sense of community where each person feels connected to both the group and the subject matter

middle school: a school specifically structured to meet the developmental needs of young adolescents, typically 10- to 15-year-olds

MSBA: a fictitious degree that stands for Middle School By Accident

MSBD: a fictitious degree that stands for Middle School By Design

multiage grouping: students of two or more grade levels intentionally placed together as ability and/or interests dictate

multicultural education: purposeful process of incorporating opportunities for students to gain insights about cultural differences locally and globally with the goal of increased acceptance and appreciation

multidisciplinary instruction: instruction in which subjects remain distinct, but are linked together by a common theme

multiple intelligences: theory that expands the narrow notion of intelligence beyond the traditional view to include verbal-linguistic, logical-mathematical, visual-spatial, bodily-kinesthetic, musical, interpersonal, intrapersonal, and naturalist; individuals may have varying combinations of the intelligences in a wide spectrum of degrees

NAEP: National Assessment of Educational Progress

NBPTS: National Board of Professional Teaching Standards

NCATE: National Council for the Accreditation of Teacher Educators

NCLB: No Child Left Behind federal legislation

NCSS: National Council for the Social Studies

NCTE: National Council of Teachers of English

NCTM: National Council of Teachers of Mathematics

NMSA: National Middle School Association

NSTA: National Science Teachers Association

nonlinguistic representations: graphic or physical models that elaborate on a basic concept

norm-referenced test: compares individual student performances relative to the overall performance of a group of students using percentile rankings

objectives: statements of measurable learning that results from instruction; more specific than goals

peer mediation: opportunity for students to problem-solve concerning their disputes in the presence, and with the help, of a student acting as mediator

performance assessment: involves tasks that require students to apply knowledge

physical safety: the elimination of threatening and/or real scenarios such as theft, verbal abuse, weapons, and unwanted horseplay

portfolio: collection of student work that may show progress over time or may be limited to the students' best quality products

Praxis: series of tests developed by the Educational Testing Service to assess the knowledge and skills of preservice and practicing teachers

puberty: biological transition between childhood and young adulthood

race: categorizes individuals based on certain outward physical characteristics

reflection: purposeful analysis of actions and/or experiences with the goal of altering and improving future actions and/or experiences

reliability: refers to the consistency with which assessment measures what it is meant to measure

role-play: assuming another person's perspective and mimicking circumstances when given specific parameters

rubric: scoring guide that provides the criteria for assessing the quality of a performance or product and includes a gradation for each criterion, generally from poor to excellent, with quality often indicated by numbers

rules: define what is and what is not acceptable in the classroom

school-within-a-school: a segment of teachers and students of a large school population who function as a unit with regard to organization, use of space, and scheduling

score: number given to student work to indicate evaluation

service learning: students providing services to individuals and groups with volunteerism accompanied by academic learning

single subject planning: planning lessons within one specific subject

socioeconomic integration: blending of students of differing social and economic backgrounds

standard: a benchmark against which progress is measured; what a student should know and be able to do

standardized assessment: assessment with content typically representing a broad base of knowledge and administered to many segments of a general population, usually either nationwide or statewide

student-focused instruction: creating opportunities that empower students to be self-directed learners

student-led conference: event during which families and teachers focus on, and are led by, the student in discussions and displays of classroom accomplishments

student-oriented: developed explicitly for student benefits and dependent on high levels of student participation

students with special needs: students who require special services due to differences in physical and/or mental characteristics, and sensory and/or processing patterns

summative assessment: means of making judgments about the quality of a process or product; typically administered at the end of a unit of study and used as a basis for assigning grades

synergy: created by individual actions working together to result in greater good; the whole is greater than the sum of the parts

tactile modality: learning through touch

teacher think-aloud: teacher verbally models the thinking process involved in problem-solving, approaching a task, or processing new information

teaming: a specific group of teachers (usually two to five) representing different subject areas and responsible for collaboratively facilitating the academic and social growth of a designated group of students

team planning: see *interdisciplinary planning*

thematic instruction: subjects are linked by a common theme

This We Believe: position statement of the National Middle School Association

TIMSS: Third International Math and Science Study

tracking: placing and keeping students in specific ability groups (see *ability grouping*)

transescence: term for developmental life phase used interchangeably with young adolescence

transitions: moving from grade to grade for middle school, and the time when students leave elementary school and the passage into high school; in the classroom, the process of going from activity to activity

***Turning Points*:** 1989 publication by the Carnegie Council on Adolescent Development that outlines middle level education philosophy

***Turning Points 2000*:** written in 2000 by Jackson and Davis, it serves as an update of the 1989 *Turning Points* document, with strategies for implementation of middle level philosophy based in part on the experiences of schools that have attempted to implement the original *Turning Points* tenets

underachievement: occurs when ability exceeds accomplishment

undersocialization: absence of healthy socialization resulting in missed learning and developmental opportunities

validity: refers to the degree to which an assessment measures what it is designed to measure

vertical articulation: communication with teachers in other grade levels

visual modality: learning through sight

wayside teaching: extracurricular opportunities to teach for which there are no official lesson plans, such as encounters with students in the hallway or cafeteria, or at the bus stop

webbing: a graphic way of connecting subject areas to a common theme

weight: value given to specific student work relative to other assignments

whole language: learning to read and write within an authentic context as opposed to learning skills in isolation

"withitness": in Kounin, a teacher's ability to overlap activities; the competent and confident management of classroom movement

Name Index

Subject Index